T0323464

Principles of Sustainable Finance

Principles of Sustainable Finance is also supported by teaching materials and cases available at https://www.rsm.nl/erasmus-platform-for-sustainable-value-creation/our-work/book/

PRAISES FOR THE BOOK

'Sustainable finance has emerged as a major new field for practitioners, but has largely bypassed the classroom for lack of a good textbook. *Principles of Sustainable Finance* is an impressive textbook that fills this important gap. It lucidly explains the fundamental challenge climate change poses for financial markets. It is extremely well-informed about the latest developments and weaves together a coherent account of widely dispersed approaches, including research that is otherwise inaccessible to the layman. It is essential reading for any student seeking to understand the main ideas and trends in sustainable finance.'

Patrick Bolton, Professor of Business at Columbia University

'The financial system is integral to achieving a smooth transition to a low carbon economy. Based on their extensive careers in finance and academia, Schoenmaker and Schramade set out an insightful vision for a sustainable financial sector, one where social and environmental dimensions are integrated within financial decisions. At a time when the need for a sustainable financial system becomes ever more pressing, this book furthers the debate on how to get there and what role each financial market participant has to play.'

Mark Carney, Governor of the Bank of England

'The UN Sustainable Development Goals 2030 are predicated on the idea that current and future generations have the resources needed to ensure access to clean water, food, shelter, health, education and energy, irrespective of the place of birth, while caring and preserving our common home: the Earth. In *Principles of Sustainable Finance*, Dirk Schoenmaker and Willem Schramade discuss the importance of sustainable finance and how it can help allocate resources to individual and social needs, over time, while respecting our planet's boundaries. It is an indispensable read for students, professionals and policy-makers.'

Vitor Gaspar, Director Fiscal Affairs Department
at the International Monetary Fund

'I am sometimes asked what a biologist is doing at the Ministry of Finance. The answer is simple: there is no better place for a biologist than working with finance. With the monumental challenges we are facing, such as climate change and the loss of biodiversity, mainstream finance needs to become truly sustainable. This implies that a larger skillset is needed for those dealing with economics. This textbook contributes to the change needed.'

Per Bolund, Minister for Financial Markets in Sweden

'The investment decisions of today shape our future. We have a choice. Do we maximise short-term returns, or create long-term sustainable value? It is becoming increasingly clear that society is reaching ecological and social boundaries, and that we can only prosper if we respect these boundaries. *Principles of Sustainable Finance* provides investors and financiers with the tools to make the right decisions, now and in the future.'

Eloy Lindeijer, Chief Investment Officer at PGGM

'With this work, Schoenmaker and Schramade make an invaluable contribution to the role of finance in the transition of the global economy to a low carbon growth path. It should be required reading in the C-suite of any bank grappling with what climate change means for its lending strategy.'

Stewart James, Managing Director Public Affairs at HSBC

'*Principles of Sustainable Finance* comes with a perfect timing: all around the planet a new, long-term and responsible capitalism is emerging. It requires combining a new academic perspective and attention to its concrete implementation. This is exactly what this important book achieves and makes it so valuable for both students, researchers and practitioners.'

Frédéric Samama, Co-Head of Institutional Clients at Amundi

Principles of Sustainable Finance

Dirk Schoenmaker and

Willem Schramade

OXFORD
UNIVERSITY PRESS

Great Clarendon Street, Oxford, OX2 6DP,
United Kingdom

Oxford University Press is a department of the University of Oxford.
It furthers the University's objective of excellence in research, scholarship,
and education by publishing worldwide. Oxford is a registered trade mark of
Oxford University Press in the UK and in certain other countries

First Edition published in 2019

Impression: 10

Published in the United States of America by Oxford University Press
198 Madison Avenue, New York, NY 10016, United States of America

British Library Cataloguing in Publication Data
Data available

Library of Congress Control Number: 2018948514

ISBN 978–0–19–882660–6

Printed and bound in Great Britain by
CPI Group (UK) Ltd, Croydon, CR0 4YY

If your plan is for 1 year, plant rice.
If your plan is for 10 years, plant trees.
If your plan is for 100 years, educate people.

Confucius

PREFACE

As a team of authors we have followed the emergence of sustainable finance (SF) from different angles. We have been teaching a course on finance and sustainability, from which this book has emerged, and we have contributed to the academic literature on this topic. On the policy side, we have advised the government on the role of large shareholders in long-term value creation. Moving to the practices of SF, we have been directly involved in impact investing at leading sustainable asset managers and have advised banks and pension funds on sustainability practices.

How does this textbook compare with other books?

Principles of Sustainable Finance differs from other textbooks in its wide coverage, as it deals with the various elements of SF, supported by examples. This coverage implies that we not only discuss sustainability challenges but also apply them to the corporate and financial sector. We cover the full range of financial intermediaries, from institutional investors to banks and insurance companies. Based on new data, we document the gradual shift from finance as usual to SF.

While there are several sustainability books in the field of business (e.g. *Business Sustainability*, by Rezaee, 2017) and economics (e.g. *Ecological Economics*, by Daly and Farley, 2011), the field of finance is only partly covered. There are titles in sustainable investing (e.g. *Evolutions in Sustainable Investing: Strategies, Funds and Thought Leadership*, by Krosinsky, 2012; *Sustainable Investing: Revolutions in Theory and Practice*, edited by Krosinsky and Purdom, 2017) and sustainable banking (e.g. *Sustainability in Finance: Banking on the Planet*, by Jeucken, 2004; *Sustainable Banking: Managing the Social and Environmental Impact of Financial Institutions*, by Weber and Feltmate, 2016). However, many books are edited volumes comprising a collection of papers (e.g. *Designing a Sustainable Financial System*, edited by Walker, Kibsey, and Crichton, 2018). These books are not primarily meant for pedagogical purposes.

Principles of Sustainable Finance is different in five respects:

1) it first deals with thematic issues (sustainability, externalities, governance, strategy, and integrated reporting) before moving on to SF;

2) it covers the full scope of SF: investing (both equities and bonds), banking, and insurance;
3) it adopts an interdisciplinary approach;
4) each chapter starts with an overview and learning objectives; at the end of each are suggestions for further reading and a list of key concepts used;
5) there is extensive use of figures, boxes, and tables to clarify concepts and provide examples.

How to use this book?

Principles of Sustainable Finance is an accessible textbook for undergraduate, graduate, and executive students of finance, economics, business administration, and sustainability. Each chapter initially provides an overview and identifies learning objectives. Throughout the book we use boxes in which certain issues are explained in more detail, by referring to theory or practical examples. Furthermore, we make abundant use of graphs and tables to give students a comprehensive overview of the sustainability challenges and their application to finance. At the end of each chapter we provide suggestions for further reading. Oxford University Press provides a supporting website for this book. This website contains exercises (and their solutions) for each chapter.

A very basic understanding of finance is needed to use this textbook, as we assume that students are familiar with well-known finance tools, such as the discounted cash flow model and the capital asset pricing model. The book can be used for third-year undergraduate, graduate, and executive courses.

Dirk Schoenmaker
Willem Schramade

Rotterdam,
April 2018

ACKNOWLEDGEMENTS

We would like to thank our colleagues at the Rotterdam School of Management, Erasmus University, for their very generous support and guidance in shaping this book, which draws on different disciplines. Special thanks to Dion Bongaerts, Mathijs Cosemans, Mathijs van Dijk, Gianfranco Gianfrate, Abe de Jong, and Marno Verbeek (finance), Steve Kennedy and Eva Rood (business sustainability), Paolo Perego (accounting), Derk Loorbach (transition management), and our students, who commented on draft chapters and provided valuable feedback. We are grateful to Peter Roosenboom, chair of the Finance Department, who provided an excellent teaching and research environment for writing this book.

At NN Investment Partners we would like to thank in particular Hendrik-Jan Boer, Bram Bos, Jeroen Bos, Jeroen Brand, Adrie Heinsbroek, Faryda Lindeman, Johan Vanderlugt, Huub van der Riet, and Alex Zuiderwijk for their feedback and support—and for being great colleagues who help shape the practice of sustainable investing.

We would also like to thank Andrew Coburn, Jaap van Dam, Adrian de Groot Ruiz, Han van der Hoorn, Marcel Jeucken, Jan van der Kolk, David Korslund, Rob Lake, Karen Maas, Roland Mees, Simon Moolenaar, Andrew Newton, Ilan Noy, Paul de Ruijter, Frédéric Samama, Hans Stegeman, Thomas Steiner, and Rens van Tilburg for valuable advice and comments on draft chapters.

Dirk Schoenmaker
Willem Schramade

Rotterdam,
April 2018

CONTENTS

LIST OF FIGURES

LIST OF TABLES

LIST OF BOXES

LIST OF ABBREVIATIONS

ABS	Asset-Backed Securities
AMH	Adaptive Markets Hypothesis
AUM	Assets Under Management
BII	Biodiversity Intactness Index
BRI	Bank Rakyat Indonesia
CAPEX	Capital Expenditures
CAPM	Capital Asset Pricing Model
CDP	Carbon Disclosure Project
CDS	Credit Default Swap
CEO	Chief Executive Officer
CF	Cash Flow
CFCs	Chlorofluorocarbons
CIO	Chief Investment Officer
COP	Conference of the Parties (governed by the UN)
CSR	Corporate Social Responsibility
DCF	Discounted Cash Flow
DU	Dobson Unit
EBIT	Earnings Before Interest and Taxes
ECCE	European Centre for Corporate Engagement
EES	Economic, Environmental, and Social (Factors)
EMH	Efficient Markets Hypothesis
EMS	Environmental Management System
EPS	Earnings Per Share
ESG	Environmental, Social, and Governance (Factors)
ETFs	Exchange Traded Funds
ETS	Emissions Trading System
EV	Environmental Value
FCF	Free Cash Flow
FCLTGlobal	Focus Capital on the Long-Term Global
FV	Financial Value
G20	Group of Twenty
GAAP	Generally Accepted Accounting Principles

GABV	Global Alliance for Banking on Values
GDP	Gross Domestic Product
GHG	Greenhouse Gas
GIIN	Global Impact Investing Network
GRI	Global Reporting Initiative
G-SIBs	Global Systemically Important Banks
GVA	Gross Value Added
IASB	International Accounting Standards Board
ICMA	International Capital Markets Association
IEA	International Energy Agency
IFC	International Finance Corporation
IFRS	International Financial Reporting Standards
IIRC	International Integrated Reporting Council
IOSCO	International Organization of Securities Commissions
IP&L	Integrated Profit and Loss (Account)
IPCC	Intergovernmental Panel on Climate Change
IPO	Initial Public Offering
IR	Integrated Reporting
IV	Integrated Value
KPIs	Key Performance Indicators
LTIFR	Lost Time Injury Frequency Rate
LTVC	Long-Term Value Creation
M&As	Mergers and Acquisitions
MDGs	Millennium Development Goals
NGO	Non-Governmental Organization
NOPLAT	Net Operation Profit Less Adjusted Taxes
NPS	Net Promoter Score
NPV	Net Present Value
OCF	Operating Cash Flow
P&C	Property and Casualty (Insurance)
P&L	Profit and Loss (Account)
PE	Price–Earnings Ratio
PPE	Property, Plant, and Equipment
PRI	Principles for Responsible Investment
PV	Photovoltaic
R&D	Research and Development
RCP	Representative Concentration Pathway

REDD+	Reducing Emissions from Deforestation and forest Degradation
ROA	Return on Assets
ROE	Return on Equity
ROI	Return on Investment
ROIC	Return on Invested Capital
S&P	Standard & Poor's
SASB	Sustainability Accounting Standards Board
SDGs	Sustainable Development Goals
SEV	Social and Environmental Value
SF	Sustainable Finance
SIB	Social Impact Bond
SME	Small- and Medium-Sized Enterprise
SPO	Seasoned Public Offering
SPV	Special Purpose Vehicle
SRI	Socially Responsible Investing
SV	Social Value
TCFD	Task Force on Climate-related Financial Disclosures
TE	Tracking Error
TP	Technical Provisions
TV	Total Value or True Value
UN	United Nations
UNEP	United Nations Environment Programme
UNFCCC	United Nations Framework Convention on Climate Change
VaR	Value at Risk
VBBs	Values-Based Banks
VDA	Value Driver Adjustments
WACC	Weighted Average Cost of Capital
WBCSD	World Business Council for Sustainable Development
WEF	World Economic Forum
WEO	World Energy Outlook
WTC	World Trade Center
WWF	World Wildlife Fund
YTM	Yield to Maturity

Part I

What is sustainability and why does it matter?

1 Sustainability and the transition challenge

Overview

Our economic models were developed in the age of *resources abundance*, when natural resources were plentiful and carbon emissions were limited. No environmental concerns were factored into these models, only labour and capital. Likewise, financial theory does not account value to natural resources beyond their near-term cash flows (CFs). Possibly fatal depletion of resources is ignored. These models are still widely used, but no longer tenable. We are now in a transition to a low-carbon and more circular economy to overcome environmental challenges. While an early transition allows for a gradual adjustment of our production and consumption patterns, a late transition will cause sudden shocks and lead to stranded assets, which will have lost their productive value. Many natural resources companies are still in denial, irrationally counting on a late and gradual transition.

Mass production in a competitive economic system has led to long working hours, underpayment, and child labour, first in the developed world and later relocated to the developing world. Social regulations have been increasingly introduced to counter these practices and to promote decent work and access to education and health care. To guide the transition towards a sustainable and inclusive economy, the United Nations (UN) have developed the 2030 Agenda for Sustainable Development, which will require behavioural change.

Sustainable development is an integrated concept with three aspects: economic, social, and environmental. This chapter starts by explaining the sustainability challenges that society is facing. On the environmental front, climate change, land-use change, biodiversity loss, and depletion of natural resources are destabilizing the Earth system. Next, poverty, hunger, and lack of health care show that many people live below minimum social standards. *Sustainable development* means that current and future generations have the resources needed, such as food, water, health care, and energy, without stressing the Earth system processes.

Why should finance contribute to sustainable development? The main task of the financial system is to allocate funding to its most productive use. Finance can play a leading role in allocating investment to sustainable corporates and projects and thus accelerate the transition to a low-carbon and more circular economy. *Sustainable finance* (SF) looks at how finance (investing and lending) interacts with economic, social, and environmental issues. In the allocation role finance can assist in making strategic decisions on the trade-offs between sustainable goals. Moreover, investors can exert influence on the corporates in which they invest. In this way, long-term investors can steer corporates towards sustainable business practices. Finally, finance is good at pricing risk for valuation purposes and can thus help dealing with the inherent uncertainty about environmental issues, such as the impact of carbon emissions on climate change. Finance and sustainability both look at the future.

The thinking about SF has gone through different stages over the last decades, whereby the focus is gradually shifting from short-term profit towards long-term value creation (LTVC). This chapter analyses these stages and provides a framework for SF. In addressing social and environmental challenges, a key development is the move from risk to opportunity. While financial firms started to avoid unsustainable companies from a risk perspective, the front-runners are now increasingly investing in sustainable companies and projects.

Learning objectives

After you have studied this chapter, you should be able to:

- explain the planet's social and environmental challenges;
- list and understand the UN Sustainable Development Goals (SDGs);
- understand the transition of the economic system;
- explain the main functions of the financial system and how to apply them to sustainability;
- explain the various stages of SF.

1.1 Why does sustainability matter?

Our economic models were developed in an empty world with an abundance of goods and services produced by nature (Daly and Farley, 2011). That was at the onset of the Industrial Revolution in the 19th century. Labour and capital were the scarce production factors to optimize in economic production, while nature and its services were freely available. But the Industrial Revolution had profound impacts on the economy, society, and the global ecosystem. Human society became largely dependent on fossil fuels and other non-renewable resources, partly in response to the depletion of forests as fuel. This increased energy use provided access to other raw materials. Technological advances dependent on fossil fuel (starting with the steam engine) allowed unprecedented production of consumer goods, spurring economic and population growth. Urbanization led to a reduction of arable land, driving further deforestation.

Back in the early 1970s, the Club of Rome was the first to highlight that the Earth system could not support these rates of economic and population growth much beyond the year 2100, even with advanced technology. In their aptly titled report *Limits to Growth*, the Club of Rome examined five basic factors that determine and, in their interactions, limit growth on this planet: (i) population increase; (ii) food production; (iii) non-renewable resource depletion; (iv) industrial output; and (v) pollution generation. They also suggested that humankind can create a society in which it can live indefinitely on Earth if it imposes limits on itself and its production of material goods to achieve a state of global equilibrium, with population and production in carefully selected balance (Meadows et al. 1972).

To illustrate the limits to growth, the Club of Rome developed a world model that analyses the carrying capacity of the planet and population growth. Population growing in a limited environment can approach the ultimate carrying capacity of that environment in several possible ways. It can adjust smoothly to an equilibrium below the environmental limit by means of a gradual decrease in growth rate, as shown in the left panel of Figure 1.1. It can also overshoot capacity by consuming some necessary non-renewable resource or causing pollution, as shown in the right panel. This behaviour has occurred in many natural systems. A major purpose in constructing the world model has been to determine which, if any, of the behaviour modes will be most characteristic of the world system as it reaches the limits to growth.

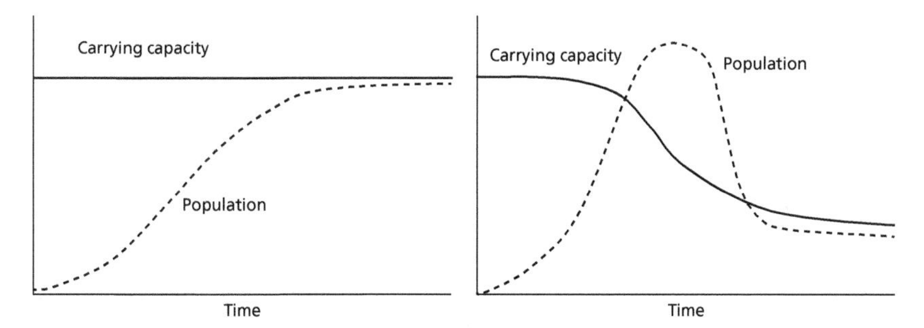

Figure 1.1 The world model

Source: Meadows et al. (1972).

While the Club of Rome was a private initiative, the UN installed the Brundtland Commission, formally known as the World Commission on Environment and Development, to unite countries to pursue sustainable development together. Gro Harlem Brundtland, former Prime Minister of Norway, was chosen as chair due to her strong background in the sciences and public health. The Brundtland Report (1987) argues that 'the "environment" is where we live; and "development" is what we all do in attempting to improve our lot within that environment. The two are inseparable.' The report defines *sustainable development* as 'development that meets the needs of the present without compromising the ability of future generations to meet their own needs'. The Brundtland Report thus reinforces the fact that sustainability is about the future.

Climate change is one of the largest environmental risks affecting society. Starting at the Earth Summit in Rio de Janeiro in 1992, the United Nations Framework Convention on Climate Change (UNFCCC) is an international environmental treaty to 'stabilise greenhouse gas concentrations in the atmosphere at a level that would prevent dangerous anthropogenic interference with the climate system'. The parties to the convention have met annually from 1995 in Conferences of the Parties (COP) to assess progress in dealing with climate change. In the 2015 Paris Agreement on climate change (COP21), countries reconfirmed the target of limiting the rise in global average temperatures relative to those in the pre-industrial world to 2°C (two degrees Celsius), and to pursue efforts to limit the temperature increase to 1.5°C (UNFCCC, 2015). Doing this would ensure that the stock of carbon dioxide and other greenhouse gases (GHGs) in the atmosphere does not exceed a certain limit. The Intergovernmental Panel on Climate Change (IPCC, 2014) estimates that the remaining carbon budget amounts to 900 gigatons (Gt) of CO_2 from 2015 onwards. The speed with which the limit is reached depends on the emissions pathway. If current global carbon emissions at about 40 Gt a year are not drastically cut, the 2°C limit would be reached in two decades.

Section 1.2 discusses the fact that climate risk, land-system change, biodiversity loss, nitrogen and phosphorus flows, poverty, food, fresh water, and health form the most pressing environmental and social challenges. Our economic system, organized through business firms, has these environmental and social impacts on society; these externalities are thus not separable from production decisions. To highlight the tension between unbridled economic growth and sustainable development, we provide two examples. Box 1.1 describes the Deepwater Horizon oil spill in the Gulf of Mexico. Box 1.2 shows the impact of the collapse of a factory building in Bangladesh. These examples have an underinvestment in safety to increase short-term profits in common.

BOX 1.1 THE DEEPWATER HORIZON OIL SPILL

Oil began to spill from the Deepwater Horizon drilling platform on 20 April 2010, in the British Petroleum-operated Macondo Prospect in the Gulf of Mexico. An explosion on the drilling rig killed 11 workers and led to the largest accidental marine oil spill in the history of the petroleum industry. The US government estimated the total discharge at 4.9 million barrels. After several failed efforts to contain the flow, the well was declared sealed on 19 September 2010.

A massive response ensued to protect beaches, wetlands, and estuaries from the spreading oil, using skimmer ships, floating booms, controlled burns, and oil dispersant. Oil clean-up crews worked on 55 miles of the Louisiana shoreline until 2013. Oil was found as far from the Deepwater Horizon site as the waters off the Florida Panhandle and Tampa Bay, where the oil and dispersant mixture was embedded in the sand. The months-long spill, along with adverse effects from the response and clean-up activities, caused extensive damage to marine and wildlife habitats and the fishing and tourism industries.

Numerous investigations explored the causes of the explosion and record-breaking spill. Notably, the US government's September 2011 report pointed to defective cement on the well, laying the fault mostly with BP, but also rig operator Transocean and contractor Halliburton. Earlier in 2011, a National Commission (2011) likewise blamed BP and its partners for a series of cost-cutting decisions and an inadequate safety system, but also concluded that the spill resulted from 'systemic' root causes and that without 'significant reform in both industry practices and government policies, might well recur'.

BOX 1.2 RANA PLAZA FACTORY COLLAPSE

The Rana Plaza collapse was a disastrous structural failure of an eight-storey commercial building on 24 April 2013 in Bangladesh. The collapse of the building caused 1,129 deaths, while approximately 2,500 injured people were rescued alive from the building. It is considered the deadliest garment factory accident in history and the deadliest accidental structural failure in modern human history.

The building contained clothing factories, a bank, apartments, and several shops. The shops and the bank on the lower floors were immediately closed after cracks were discovered in the building the day before the collapse. However, the building's owners ignored warnings to evacuate. Garment workers, earning €38 a month, were ordered to return the following day, and the building collapsed during the morning rush hour.

The factories manufactured clothing for brands including Benetton, Bonmarché, the Children's Place, El Corte Inglés, Joe Fresh, Monsoon Accessorize, Mango, Matalan, Primark, and Walmart.

1.2 **Sustainability challenges**

> There can be no Plan B, because there is no Planet B.
>
> Former United Nations Secretary-General, Ban Ki-moon

1.2.1 ENVIRONMENTAL CHALLENGES

The aim is to keep the planet liveable for current and future generations. There is increasing evidence that human activities are affecting the Earth system, threatening the planet's future liveability. The planetary boundaries framework of Steffen and colleagues (2015) defines a safe operating space for humanity within the boundaries of nine productive ecological capacities of the planet. The framework is based on the intrinsic biophysical processes that regulate the stability of the Earth system on a planetary scale. The medium dark zone in Figure 1.2 is the safe operating space, light grey represents the zone of uncertainty (increasing risk), and dark indicates the zone of high risk. Table 1.1 specifies the control variables and quantifies the ecological ceilings.

Applying the *precautionary principle*, the *planetary boundary* itself lies at the intersection of the medium dark and light grey zones. To illustrate how the framework works, we look at the control variable for climate change, the atmospheric concentration of GHGs. The zone of uncertainty ranges from 350 to 450 parts per million (ppm) of carbon dioxide. We crossed the planetary boundary of 350 ppm in 1995, with a level of 399 ppm in 2015, and are adding at a rate of around 3 ppm every year. The upper limit of 450 ppm is consistent with the goal (at a fair chance of 66 per cent) to limit global

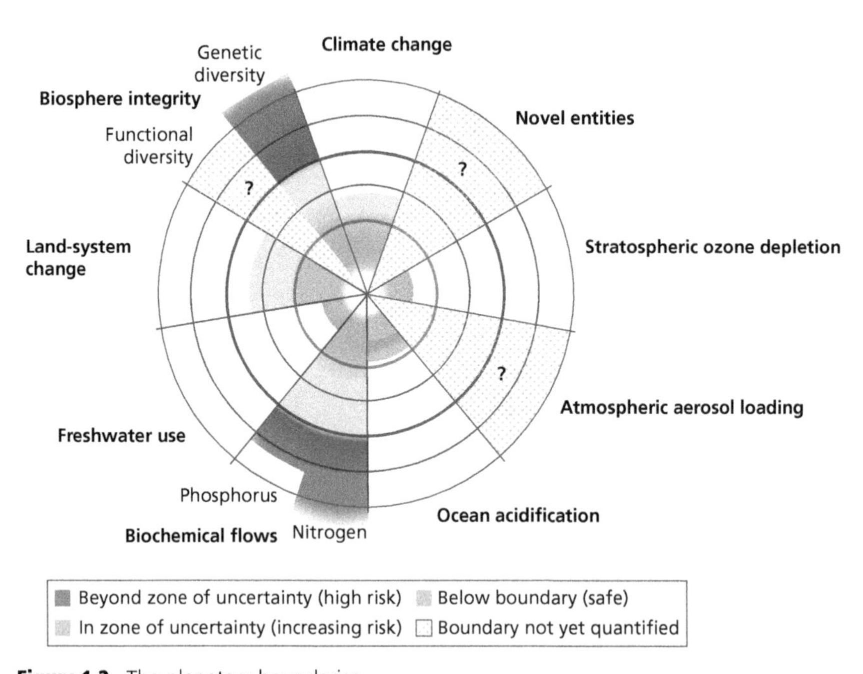

Figure 1.2 The planetary boundaries

Source: Steffen et al. (2015).

Table 1.1 The ecological ceiling and its indicators of overshoot

Earth system pressure	Control variable	Planetary boundary	Current value and trend
Climate change	Atmospheric carbon dioxide concentration; ppm	At most 350 ppm	399 ppm and rising (worsening)
Biosphere loss	Genetic diversity: rate of species extinction per million species per year	At most 10	Around 100–1,000 and rising (worsening)
	Functional diversity: Biodiversity Intactness Index (BII)	Maintain BII at 90%	84% applied to Southern Africa only
Land-system change	Area of forested land as a proportion of forest-covered land prior to human alteration	At least 75%	62% and falling (worsening)
Freshwater use	Blue water consumption; cubic kilometres per year	At most 4,000 km^3	Around 2,600 km^3 and rising (intensifying)
Biochemical flows	Phosphorus applied to land as fertilizer; millions of tons per year	At most 6.2 million tons	Around 14 million tons and rising (worsening)
	Reactive nitrogen applied to land as fertilizer; millions of tons per year	At most 62 million tons	Around 150 million tons and rising (worsening)
Ocean acidification	Average saturation of aragonite (calcium carbonate) at the ocean surface, as a percentage of pre-industrial levels	At least 80%	Around 84% and falling (intensifying)
Air pollution	Aerosol optical depth; much regional variation, no global level yet defined	–	–
Ozone layer depletion	Concentration of ozone in the stratosphere; in Dobson Units (DU)	At least 275 DU	283 DU and rising (improving)
Novel entities (e.g. chemical pollution)	No global control variable yet defined	–	–

Source: Steffen et al. (2015).

warming to 2°C above the pre-industrial level and lies at the intersection of the light grey and dark zones.

Another example of increasing risk in the light grey zone is land-system change. The control variable is the area of forested land as a proportion of forest-covered land prior to human alteration. The planetary boundary is at 75 per cent, while we are currently at 62 per cent and the percentage is falling.

The current *linear production and consumption system* is based on extraction of raw materials (take), processing into products (make), consumption (use), and disposal (waste). Traditional business models centred on a linear system assume the ongoing availability of unlimited and cheap natural resources. This is increasingly risky because non-renewable resources, such as fossil fuels, minerals, and metals, are increasingly under pressure, while potentially renewable resources, such as forests, rivers, and prairies, are declining in their extent and regenerative capacity.

Moreover, the use of fossil fuels in the linear production and consumption system overburdens the Earth system as natural sink (absorbing pollution). Baseline scenarios (i.e. those without mitigation) for climate change result in global warming in 2100 from 3.7° to 4.8° Celsius compared to the pre-industrial level (IPCC, 2014). Figure 11.6 in Chapter 11 depicts this high emission scenario.

With this linear economic system we are crossing planetary boundaries beyond which human activities might destabilize the Earth system. In particular, the planetary boundaries of climate change, land-system change (deforestation and land erosion), biodiversity loss (terrestrial and marine), and biochemical flows (nitrogen and phosphorus, mainly because of intensive agricultural practices) have been crossed (see Figure 1.2). A timely transition towards an economy based on sustainable production and consumption, including use of renewable energy, reuse of materials, and land restoration, can mitigate these risks.

1.2.2 SOCIAL FOUNDATIONS

Mass production in a competitive economic system has led to long working hours, underpayment, and child labour, first in the developed world and later relocated to the developing world. Human rights provide the essential social foundation for all people to lead lives of dignity and opportunity. Human rights norms assert the fundamental moral claim each person has to life's essentials, such as food, water, health care, education, freedom of expression, political participation, and personal security. Raworth (2017) defines *social foundations* as the 12 top social priorities, grouped into three clusters, focused on enabling people to be: (i) well: through food security, adequate income, improved water and sanitation, housing, and health care; (ii) productive: through education, decent work, and modern energy services; and (iii) empowered: through networks, gender equality, social equity, having a political voice, and peace and justice.

While these social foundations only set out the minimum of every human's claims, sustainable development envisions people and communities prospering beyond this, leading lives of creativity and fulfilment. Sustainable development combines the concept of planetary boundaries with the complementary concept of social foundations or boundaries. It means that current and future generations have the resources needed, such as food, water, health care, and energy, without stressing processes within the Earth system (Raworth, 2017).

But many people are still living below the social foundations of no hunger, no poverty (a minimum income of $3.10 a day), access to education, and access to clean cooking facilities (see Table 1.2). More broadly, political participation, which is the right of people to be involved in decisions that affect them, is a basic value of society. The UN's Universal Declaration of Human Rights states that 'recognition of the inherent dignity and of the equal and inalienable rights of all members of the human family is the foundation of freedom, justice and peace in the world'. Human rights are an important social foundation. Next, decent work can lift communities out of poverty and underpins human security and social peace. The 2030 Agenda for Sustainable Development (see Section 1.2.3) places decent work for all people at the heart of policies for sustainable and inclusive growth and development. Decent work has several dimensions: a basic living wage (which depends on a country's basic living basket), no discrimination (e.g. on gender, race, or religion), no child labour, health and safety, and freedom of association.

From a societal perspective, it is important for business to respect these social foundations and to ban underpayment, child labour, and human right violations. Social regulations forbidding these practices have been introduced in developed (high- and medium-income) countries, but these practices are still happening in developing (low-income) countries. A case in point is the use of child labour in factories in low-income countries producing consumer goods, like clothes and shoes, to be sold by multinational companies in high- and medium-income countries. These factories often lack basic worker safety features (Box 1.2). Another example is the violation of the human rights of indigenous people, often in combination with land degradation and pollution, by extractive companies in the exploration and exploitation of fossil fuels, minerals, and other raw materials.

Kate Raworth (2017) has summarized the social foundations and planetary boundaries in the Doughnut, which shows how the safe and just space for humanity lies between the social foundation of human well-being and the ecological ceiling of planetary pressure (see Figure 1.3). Table 1.1 specifies the ecological ceiling and Table 1.2 the social foundation.

1.2.3 SUSTAINABLE DEVELOPMENT

To guide the transition towards a sustainable and inclusive economy, the UN has developed the 2030 Agenda for Sustainable Development (UN, 2015). The 17 UN SDGs stimulate action over the 2015–30 period in areas of critical importance for humanity and the planet. To facilitate implementation, the 17 high-level goals are specified in 169 targets (see https://sustainabledevelopment.un.org/topics/sustainabledevelopmentgoals).

Following Rockström and Sukhdev (2016), we classify the SDGs according to the levels of the economy, the society, and the environment. Nevertheless, we stress that the SDGs are interrelated. A case in point is the move to

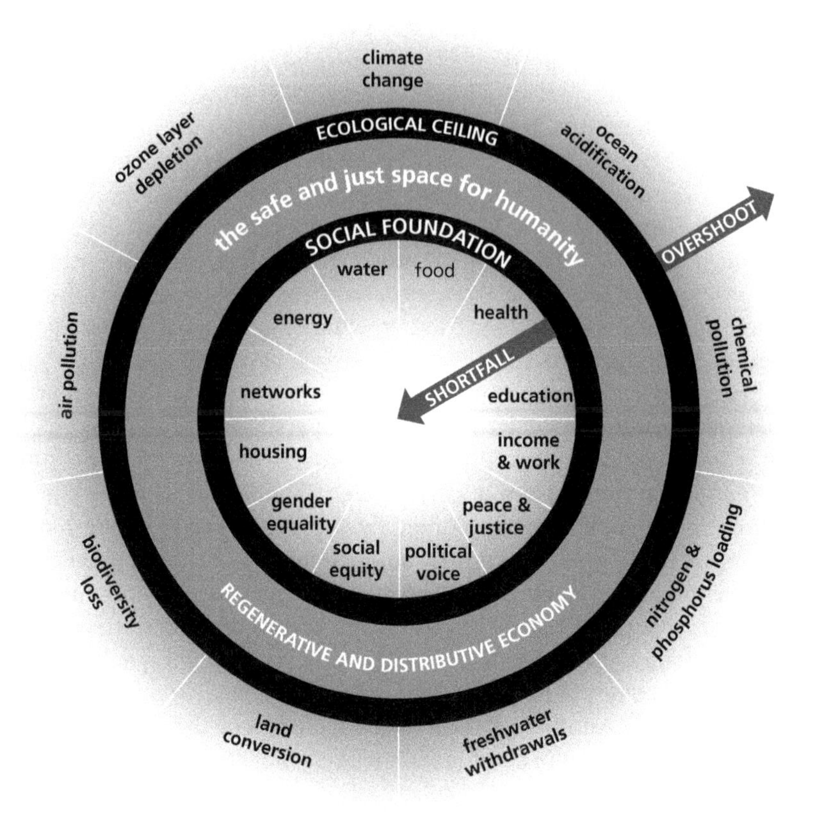

Figure 1.3 The doughnut: the safe and just space for humanity

Source: Raworth (2017).

sustainable consumption and production (economic goal 12) and sustainable cities (societal goal 11), which are instrumental to combat climate change (environmental goal 13). Another example is an appropriate income and decent work for all (economic goal 8), which is instrumental in attaining societal goals 1 to 4. Through a living wage, households can afford food, health care, and education for their family.

The 17 UN SDGs are as follows (UN, 2015):

Economic goals

- Goal 8. Promote sustained, inclusive, and sustainable economic growth, full and productive employment and decent work for all.
- Goal 9. Build resilient infrastructure, promote inclusive, and sustainable industrialization and foster innovation.
- Goal 10. Reduce inequality within and among countries.
- Goal 12. Ensure sustainable consumption and production patterns.

Table 1.2 The social foundation and its indicators of shortfall

Dimension	Illustrative indicator (% of global population unless otherwise stated)	%	Year
Food	Population undernourished	11%	2014–16
Health	Population living in countries with under-five mortality rate exceeding 25 per 1,000 live births	46%	2015
	Population living in countries with life expectancy at birth of less than 70 years	39%	2013
Education	Adult population (aged 15+) who are illiterate	15%	2013
	Children aged 12–15 out of school	17%	2013
Income and work	Population living on less than the international poverty limit of $3.10 a day	29%	2012
	Proportion of young people (aged 15–24) seeking but not able to find work	13%	2014
Water and sanitation	Population without access to improved drinking water	9%	2015
	Population without access to improved sanitation	32%	2015
Energy	Population lacking access to electricity	17%	2013
	Population lacking access to clean cooking facilities	38%	2013
Networks	Population stating that they are without someone to count on for help in times of trouble	24%	2015
	Population without access to the Internet	57%	2015
Housing	Global urban population living in slum housing in developing countries	24%	2012
Gender equality	Representation gap between women and men in national parliaments	56%	2014
	Worldwide earnings gap between women and men	23%	2009
Social equity	Population living in countries with a Palma ratio of 2 or more (the ratio of the income share of the top 10% of people to that of the bottom 40%)	39%	1995–2012
Political voice	Population living in countries scoring 0.5 or less out of the 1.0 in the Voice and Accountability Index	52%	2013
Peace and justice	Population living in countries scoring 50 or less out of 100 in the Corruption Perceptions Index	85%	2014
	Population living in countries with a homicide rate of 10 or more per 10,000	13%	2008–13

Source: Raworth (2017).

Societal goals

- Goal 1. End poverty in all its forms everywhere.
- Goal 2. End hunger, achieve food security and improved nutrition, and promote sustainable agriculture.
- Goal 3. Ensure healthy lives and promote well-being for all at all ages.
- Goal 4. Ensure inclusive and equitable quality education and promote lifelong learning opportunities for all.

- Goal 5. Achieve gender equality and empower all women and girls.
- Goal 7. Ensure access to affordable, reliable, sustainable, and modern energy for all.
- Goal 11. Make cities and human settlements inclusive, safe, resilient, and sustainable.
- Goal 16. Promote peaceful and inclusive societies for sustainable development, provide access to justice for all, and build effective, accountable, and inclusive institutions at all levels.

Environmental goals

- Goal 6. Ensure availability and sustainable management of water and sanitation for all.
- Goal 13. Take urgent action to combat climate change and its impacts.
- Goal 14. Conserve and sustainably use the oceans, seas, and marine resources for sustainable development.
- Goal 15. Protect, restore, and promote sustainable use of terrestrial ecosystems, sustainably manage forests, combat desertification, halt and reverse land degradation, and halt biodiversity loss.

Overall goal

- Goal 17. Strengthen the means of implementation and revitalize the Global Partnership for Sustainable Development.

1.2.3.1 **Global strategy**

The UN SDGs are the global strategy of governments under the auspices of the UN and provide direction towards (future) government policies, such as regulation and taxation of environmental and social challenges. The global strategy is boosted by technological change (e.g. the development of solar and wind energy and electric cars at decreasing cost), which supplements government policies (e.g. carbon pricing). Some companies are preparing for this transition (future makers) and are part of the solution (Mercer, 2015). Other companies are waiting for the transition to unfold before acting (future takers). A final category of companies is unaware of this transition and continues business as usual. They are part of the problem.

We, as authors, attach a positive probability to the scenario that the SDGs are largely met. Our observation is based on the success of the earlier Millennium Development Goals in reducing poverty, hunger, and child death rates in Southeast Asia and Latin America, and even to a large extent in Africa (Rosling, 2018). Of course, opinions can and do differ about the probability that the transition towards a sustainable economy will largely succeed. But the status quo scenario, which assumes no transition, is highly implausible. While the pathway and the speed of the transition are uncertain and may even

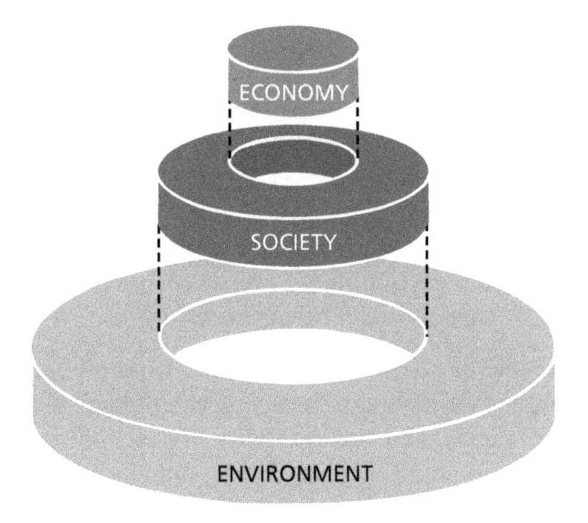

Figure 1.4 Sustainable development challenges at different levels

Source: Adapted from Rockström and Sukhdev (2016).

be erratic, with failures along the way, the sustainable development agenda gives direction to thinking about the future. This book is about the role finance (investors and lenders) can play in shaping this future and making production and consumption more sustainable.

The UN SDGs address challenges at the level of the economy, society, and the environment (or biosphere). Figure 1.4 illustrates the three levels and the ranking between them. A liveable planet is a precondition or foundation for humankind to thrive. Next, we need a cohesive and inclusive society to organize production and consumption in order to ensure enduring prosperity for all. In their seminal book *Why Nations Fail*, Acemoglu and Robinson (2012) show that political institutions which promote inclusiveness generate prosperity. Inclusiveness allows everyone to participate in economic opportunities. Reducing social inequalities is thus an important goal (goal 10). Next, there can be resource conflicts: unequal communities may disagree over how to share and finance public goods. These conflicts, in turn, break social ties and undermine the formation of trust and social cohesion (Barone and Mocetti, 2016).

Gladwin, Kennelly, and Krause (1995) define five principles of sustainable development:

1. **Comprehensiveness**: the concept of sustainable development is holistic or all-embracing in terms of space, time, and component parts. Sustainability embraces both environmental and human systems, both nearby and far-away, in both the present and the future.

2. **Connectivity**: sustainability demands an understanding of the world's challenges as systemically interconnected and interdependent.
3. **Equity**: a fair distribution of resources and property rights, both within and between current and future generations.
4. **Prudence**: keeping life-supporting ecosystems and interrelated socioeconomic systems resilient, avoiding irreversible actions, and keeping the scale and impact of human activities within regenerative and carrying capacities.
5. **Security**: sustainable development aims at ensuring a safe, healthy, high quality of life for current and future generations.

Although sustainable development is a holistic concept, Norström and colleagues (2014) argue that trade-offs between the ambition of economic, social, and environmental goals and the feasibility of reaching them, recognizing biophysical, social, and political constraints, should be addressed.

1.2.4 SYSTEM PERSPECTIVE

While it is tempting to start working on partial solutions at each level, environmental, societal, and economic challenges are interlinked. It is important to embrace an integrated social-ecological system perspective (Norström et al. 2014). Such a perspective highlights the dynamics that such systems entail, including the role of ecosystems in sustaining human well-being, cross-system interactions, and uncertain thresholds.

Holling (2001) describes the process of sustainable development as embedded cycles with adaptive capacity. A key element of adaptive capacity is the *resilience* of the system to deal with unpredictable shocks (which is the opposite of the vulnerability of the system). An adaptive cycle that aggregates resources and periodically restructures to create opportunities for innovation is a fundamental unit for understanding complex systems, from cells to ecosystems. But some systems are maladaptive and trigger, for example, a poverty trap or land degradation (i.e. the undermining of the quality of soil as a result of human behaviour or severe weather conditions). Holling (2001) concludes that ecosystem management via incremental increases in efficiency does not work. For transformation, ecosystem system management must build and maintain ecological resilience as well as social flexibility to cope, innovate, and adapt.

1.2.4.1 Examples of cross-system interactions and uncertain thresholds

As we have argued, economic, social, and environmental systems interact. A well-known example of cross-system interaction is the linear production of consumption goods at the lowest cost, which contributes to 'economic growth' while depleting natural resources, using child labour, and producing carbon emissions and other waste. In this book, we use carbon emissions as shorthand for all GHG emissions, which include carbon dioxide CO_2, methane CH_4, and nitrous oxide N_2O.

Another example of cross-system interaction is climate change, leading to more and more intense weather-related disasters, such as storms, flooding, and droughts. The low- and middle-income countries around the equator are especially vulnerable to these extreme weather events, which could damage a large part of their production capacity. The temporary loss of tax revenues, and increase in expenditure to reconstruct factories and infrastructure, might put vulnerable countries into a downward fiscal and macro-economic spiral with an analogous increase in poverty. Social and environmental issues are thus interconnected, whereby the poor in society are more dependent on ecological services and are less well protected against ecological hazards.

A related example is land degradation in the form of soil erosion, salinization (exacerbation of natural soil salinity level), peatland and wetland drainage, and forest degradation. The resulting damage is estimated at $6.3 trillion a year (8.3 per cent of global GDP) in lost ecosystem service value, which includes agricultural products, clean air, fresh water, climate regulation, recreational opportunities, and fertile soils (Sutton et al. 2016). Land degradation also exacerbates losses in biodiversity and jeopardizes the livelihoods of half a billion mostly poor people who depend on forests and agricultural land. Declining land productivity undermines sustainable development, threatens food and water security, and leads to involuntary human migration and even civil conflict.

An example of an uncertain threshold combined with feedback dynamics is the melting threshold for the Greenland ice sheet. New research has found that it is more vulnerable to global warming than previously thought. Robinson, Calov, and Ganopolski (2012) calculate that a 0.9°C of global temperature rise from today's levels could lead the Greenland ice sheet to melt completely. Such melting would create further climate feedback in the Earth's ecosystem, because melting the polar icecaps could increase the pace of global warming (by reducing the refraction of solar radiation, which is 80 per cent from ice, compared with 30 per cent from bare earth and 7 per cent from the sea) as well as rising sea levels. These feedback mechanisms are examples of tipping points and shocks, which might happen.

An important conclusion from this section is that we cannot understand sustainability of organizations in isolation from the socioecological system in which they are embedded: What are the thresholds, sustainability priorities, and feedback loops? Moreover, as well as the socio-environmental impact of individual organizations, we should also consider the aggregate impact of organizations at the system level (see Section 4.2 in Chapter 4). The latter is relevant for sustainable development.

1.3 The role of the financial system

How can the financial system facilitate decision-making on the trade-offs between economic, social, and environmental goals? Levine (2005) lists the following functions of the financial system:

- Produce information ex ante about possible investments and allocate capital.
- Monitor investments and exert corporate governance after providing finance.
- Facilitate the trading, diversification, and management of risk.
- Mobilize and pool savings.
- Ease the exchange of goods and services.

The first three functions are particularly relevant for SF. The allocation of funding to its most productive use is a key role of finance. Finance is therefore well positioned to assist in making strategic decisions on the trade-offs between sustainable goals. While broader considerations guide an organization's strategy on sustainability, funding is a requirement for reaching sustainable goals.

Finance plays this role at different levels. In the financial sector, banks, for example, define their lending strategy regarding which sectors and projects are eligible for lending and which are not. Similarly, investment funds set their investment strategy, which directs in which assets the fund invests and in which assets they do not. The financial sector can thus play a leading role in the transition to a low-carbon and more circular economy. If the financial sector chooses to finance sustainable companies and projects, they can accelerate the transition.

In terms of monitoring their investments, investors can also influence the companies in which they invest. Investors thus have a powerful role in controlling and directing corporate boards. The governance role also involves balancing the many interests of a corporation's stakeholders. In Section 1.4, we review the progressive thinking about how interests should be balanced, including the interests of the environment and society. A rising trend in sustainable investment is engagement with companies in the hope of reducing the risk of adverse events occurring in those companies.

Finance is good at pricing the risk of future CFs for valuation purposes. As there is inherent uncertainty about environmental issues (e.g. exactly how rising carbon emissions will affect the climate, and the timing and shape of climate mitigation policies), risk management can help to deal with these uncertainties. *Scenario analysis* is increasingly used to assess the risk and valuation under different scenarios (e.g. climate scenarios; see Chapter 2). When the potential price of carbon emissions in the future becomes clearer, investors and companies have an incentive to reduce these emissions. The key challenge is to take a sufficiently long horizon, because sustainability is about the future. Chapter 3 discusses the appropriate horizon for SF and ways to overcome the bias towards short-termism.

1.4 **Three stages of SF**

How can finance support sustainable development? Figure 1.5 shows our framework for managing sustainable development. At the level of the economy, the financial return and risk trade-off is optimized. This financial orientation supports the idea of profit maximization by organizations and the economic growth of countries. Next, at the level of society, the impact of business and financial decisions on society is optimized. And finally at the level of the environment, the environmental impact is optimized. As we have argued, there are interactions between the levels. It is thus important to choose an appropriate combination of financial, social, and environmental aspects.

The concept of SF has evolved as part of the broader notion of business sustainability since the 1990s (see Chapter 5). Table 1.3 shows the typology for SF on four aspects: (i) the value created; (ii) the ranking of the three factors; (iii) the optimization method; and (iv) the horizon. The evolution highlights the broadening from *shareholder value* to *stakeholder value* or triple bottom line: people, planet, profit. The final stage looks at the creation of common

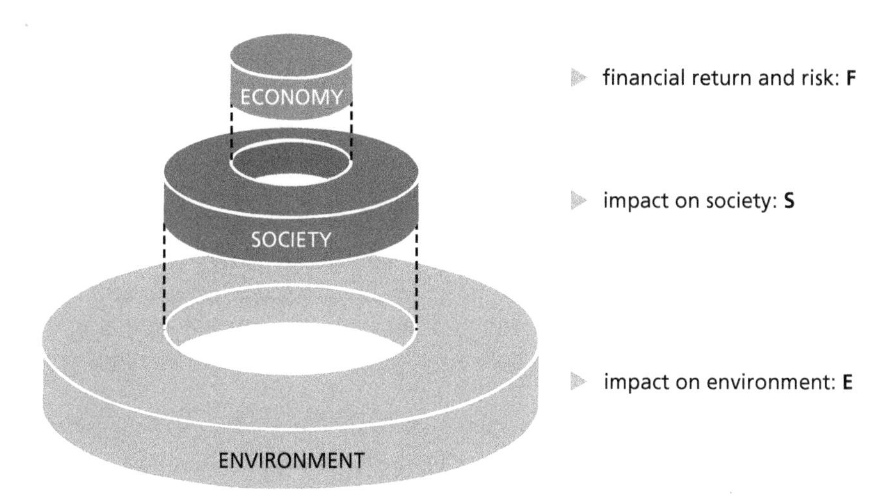

Figure 1.5 Managing sustainable development

Source: Schoenmaker (2017).

Table 1.3 Framework for SF

SF Typology	Value created	Ranking of factors	Optimization	Horizon
Finance as usual	Shareholder value	F	Max F	Short term
SF 1.0	Refined shareholder value	F » S and E	Max F subject to S and E	Short term
SF 2.0	Stakeholder value (triple bottom line)	I = F + S + E	Optimize I	Medium term
SF 3.0	Common good value	S and E > F	Optimize S and E subject to F	Long term

Note: F = financial value; S = social impact; E = environmental impact; I = integrated value. At SF 1.0, the maximization of F is subject to minor S and E constraints.

Source: Schoenmaker (2017).

good value (see also Tirole, 2017). To avoid the dichotomy of private versus public goods, we use the term *common good* to refer to what is shared and beneficial for all or most members of a given community. Next, the ranking indicates a shift from economic goals first to societal and environmental challenges (the common good) first. Importantly, the horizon is broadened from short term to long term along the stages.

In traditional finance, shareholder value is maximized by looking for the optimal financial return and risk combination. Table 1.3 labels this the finance-as-usual approach. Although shareholder value should also look at the medium to long term, there are built-in incentives for short-termism, such as quarterly financial reporting and monthly/quarterly benchmarking of investment performance (see Chapter 3). Finance as usual is consistent with the argument of Friedman (1970) that 'the business of business is business'. The only social responsibility of business is to use its resources and engage in activities designed to increase its profits so long as it stays within the rules of the game. Friedman (1970) argues that it is the task of the government to take care of social and environmental goals and set the rules of the game for sustainability. However, product demand ultimately derives from societal needs. Moreover, externalities are not perfectly separable from production decisions (Hart and Zingales, 2017). While there is a good case against corporate philanthropy, there is not a case against integration of sustainability into strategy and finance.

The three stages of our SF typology in Table 1.3 are discussed one after another. The stages move from finance first, to all aspects equal, and finally to social-environmental impact first (the ranking of factors in the third column of Table 1.3).

1.4.1 SF 1.0 PROFIT MAXIMIZATION, WHILE AVOIDING 'SIN' STOCKS

A first step in SF is that financial institutions avoid investing in, or lending to, so-called 'sin' companies. These are companies with very negative impacts. In the social domain, they include, for example, companies that sell tobacco, anti-personnel mines and cluster bombs, or that exploit child labour. In the environmental field, classic examples of very negative impacts are waste dumping and whale hunting. More recently, some financial institutions have started to put coal and even the broader category of fossil fuels on the exclusion list because of carbon emissions. These exclusion lists are often triggered under pressure from non-governmental organizations (NGOs), which use traditional and social media for their messages (Dyllick and Muff, 2016).

But the initial effects of exclusion and divestment are limited (Skancke, 2016). From an equilibrium perspective, fewer investors hold the excluded companies, leading to lower stock prices and a higher cost of capital. In an empirically calibrated model, Heinkel, Kraus, and Zechner (2001) indicate that over 20 per cent of green investors are required to induce any polluting companies to reform. Existing empirical evidence indicates that at most 10 per cent of funds is invested by green investors. Divestment by a growing number of investors might turn the balance. Another effect is that divestment may stigmatize a sector or companies to the point where they lose their social licence to operate (see Section 1.4.3). This might lead to less investment in that sector. An exclusion criterion targeted at a sector or the worst performers within a sector could have an effect by setting a norm for acceptable standards.

A slightly more positive variant of the refined shareholder value approach is if financial institutions and companies put systems in place for energy and emissions management, sustainable purchasing, IT, building and infrastructure to enhanced environmental standards, and all kinds of diversity in employment. The underlying objective of these activities remains economic. Though introducing sustainability into business might generate positive side-effects for some sustainability aspects, the main purpose is to reduce costs and business risks, to improve reputation and attractiveness for new or existing human talent, to respond to new customer demands and segments, and thereby to increase profits, market positions, competitiveness, and shareholder value in the short term. Business success is still evaluated from a purely economic point of view and remains focused on serving the business itself and its economic goals (Dyllick and Muff, 2016). Shareholder value or profit maximization is still the guiding principle for the organization, though with some refinements. Box 1.3 contains the formal objective function for the refined profit maximization approach of investors.

BOX 1.3 REFINED PROFIT MAXIMIZATION

Investors optimize the financial value *FV* of their portfolio by increasing profits and decreasing their risk (i.e. the variability of profits), while avoiding excessive negative social and environmental impact by setting a minimum level SEV^{min}. The objective function is given by:

$$max\ FV = F\ (\text{profits, risk})\ subject\ to\ F'_{\text{profits}} > 0, F'_{\text{risk}} < 0, SEV \geq SEV^{min} \quad (1.1)$$

Where *FV* = financial value = expected current and discounted future profits, and *SEV* = social and environmental value. $F'_{profits}$ is the partial derivative of *F* with respect to the first term, and F'_{risk} with respect to the second term. This optimization can be used by investors in a mean-variance framework to optimize their portfolio and by banks and corporates in a net present value framework to decide on financing new projects.

1.4.2 SF 2.0 INTERNALIZATION OF EXTERNALITIES TO AVOID RISK

In SF 2.0, financial institutions explicitly incorporate negative social and environmental *externalities* into their decision-making. Over the medium to long-term horizon, these externalities might become priced (e.g. a carbon tax) and/or might impact negatively on an institution's reputation. Incorporating the externalities thus reduces the risk that financial investments become unviable. This risk is related to the maturity of the financial instrument and is thus greater for equity (stocks) than for debt (bonds and loans). On the positive side, internalization of externalities helps financial institutions and companies to restore trust, which is the mirror image of reputation risk.

Attaching a financial value to social and environmental impacts facilitates the optimization process among the different aspects (F, S, E). Innovations in technology (measurement, information technology, data management) and science (life-cycle analyses, social life-cycle analyses, environmentally extended input–output analysis, environmental economics) make the monetization of social and environmental impacts possible (True Price, 2014). In this way, the integrated value I can be established by summing the financial, social, and environmental values in an integrated way. Financial institutions and companies use a private discount rate (which is higher than the public discount rate because of uncertainties) to discount future CFs. As social and, in particular, environmental impacts become manifest over a longer horizon and are also more uncertain than financial impacts, private discounting leads to a lower weighting of social and environmental value than financial value. Chapter 2 sets out the methodology for calculating and optimizing the integrated value (which is also labelled total or true value).

However, integrated value optimization can lead to perverse outcomes: the negative environmental impact of deforestation, for example, can be offset by large economic gains; in other words legitimizing destruction. To avoid

BOX 1.4 INTERNALIZATION OF EXTERNALITIES

To internalize the social and environmental externalities, investors optimize the integrated value IV of their portfolio. The integrated value is the sum of the financial value, the social value, and the environmental value: $IV = FV + SV^p + EV^p$. The superscript p stands for the privately discounted value of the social and environmental impacts.

Investors thus optimize the integrated value IV of their portfolio by increasing their integrated profits and decreasing their risk (i.e. the variability of integrated profits), while not worsening their social and environmental impact SEV^p. The objective function is given by:

$$max\ IV = F(\text{integrated profits, integrated risk})\ s.t.\ F'_{\text{integr. profits}} > 0, F'_{\text{integr.risk}} < 0,$$

$$SEV^p_{t+1} \geq SEV^p_t \tag{1.2}$$

See Box 1.3 for the explanation of the variables. SEV^p_{t+1} = next period social and environmental impact. In line with the integrated value methodology, not only profits but also risk is assessed in an integrated way (i.e. integrated across the three values), which includes the covariance between the profits.

these outcomes, we incorporate in equation 1.2 the constraint that the social-environmental value cannot be worsened compared to its initial value. Another caveat is the inherent uncertainty (e.g. underlying climate scenarios) that makes pricing difficult. A final issue is participation (Coulson, 2016). Producers could involve stakeholders in the application of the integrated value methodology to form a more inclusive and pluralist conception of risk and values for social and environmental impacts. Box 1.4 provides the formal objective function of investors for optimizing the integrated value of their portfolio.

SF 2.0 comes in different shapes. Examples are triple bottom line (people, planet, profit) and integrated profit and loss accounting. Within corporate governance, we can speak of an extended stakeholder approach, whereby not only direct stakeholders, such as shareholders, suppliers, employees, and customers, but also society and environment, as indirect stakeholders, are included. Nevertheless, Dyllick and Muff (2016) claim that corporates still adopt an *inside-out perspective* by asking how they can reduce their social and environmental impact. While this is helpful, it also restricts their potential to address social and environmental challenges.

1.4.3 SF 3.0 CONTRIBUTING TO SUSTAINABLE DEVELOPMENT WHILE OBSERVING FINANCIAL VIABILITY

SF 3.0 moves from risk to opportunity. Rather than avoiding unsustainable companies from a risk perspective, financial institutions invest only in sustainable companies and projects. In this approach, finance is a means to foster sustainable development, for example by funding health care, green buildings, wind farms, electric car manufacturers, and land-reuse projects. The starting point of SF 3.0 is a positive selection of investment projects on their potential to generate social and environmental impact; creating an inclusion list instead of an exclusion list as in SF 1.0. In this way, the financial system serves the sustainable development agenda in the medium to long term.

The question that then arises is how the financial part of the decision is taken. An important component of sustainable development is economic and financial viability. Financial viability, in the form of a fair financial return (which at the minimum preserves capital), is a condition for sustainable investment and lending; otherwise projects might need to be aborted prematurely because of financial shortfalls. Box 1.5 derives the formal objective function for this approach. The key change is that the role of finance turns from primacy (profit maximization) to serving (a means to optimize sustainable development). It moves from the front row in equation 1.1 to the back row in equation 1.3.

What is a *fair financial return*? Of the respondents to the Annual Impact Investment Survey (GIIN, 2016), 59 per cent primarily target risk-adjusted, market-rate returns. Of the remainder, 25 per cent primarily target returns below market rate that are closer to market-rate returns, while 16 per cent target returns that are closer to capital preservation. So the great majority pursue returns at market rate or close to it, while a small group accepts lower returns for sustainability reasons.

More broadly, the question is whether investors, including the ultimate beneficiaries, such as current and future pensioners, are prepared to potentially forego some financial return in exchange for social and environmental returns (e.g. enjoying their pension in a liveable world). Social preferences play an important role for investors in socially responsible investment (SRI) funds,

---

BOX 1.5 CONTRIBUTING TO SUSTAINABLE DEVELOPMENT

To foster sustainable development, investors optimize the social-environmental impact or value SEV of their portfolio, which is the sum of the social and environmental value $SEV = SV + EV$, by increasing their impact, and decreasing their risk (i.e. the variability of impact), subject to a minimum financial value FV^{min}. The objective function is given by:

$$max\ SEV = F(\text{impact}, \text{risk})\ s.t.\ F'_{\text{impact}} > 0, F'_{\text{risk}} < 0, FV_{t+1} \geq FV^{min}_{t+1} \quad (1.3)$$

See Boxes 1.3 and 1.4 for the explanation of the variables. The financial viability or minimum financial value can be presented as follows: $FV^{min}_{t+1} = (1 + r^{fair})FV^{min}_{t}$, where $r^{fair} \geq 0$ is a fair financial return for one period.

---

while financial motives appear to be of limited importance (Riedl and Smeets, 2017). SRI investors expect to earn lower returns from SRI funds than from conventional funds, suggesting that they are willing to forego financial performance in order to invest according to their social preferences. However, ex ante it is not clear what the ultimate effect of impact investing is on financial return. If investor coalitions, for example, could accelerate the transition towards sustainable development, there would be less chance of negative financial returns because of extreme weather events or stranded assets. This argument depends on sufficiently large amounts of investment moving to SF (see Chapter 4).

On investment performance, there is a mixed picture on the relationship between corporate social-environmental performance and financial performance. Reviewing several studies, Busch, Bauer, and Orlitzky (2016) conclude that, at the very least, there is no clear indication of a negative relationship, or trade-off, between corporate social-environmental performance and corporate financial performance.

In banking, the Global Alliance for Banking on Values (GABV 2016) compares a group of 25 sustainable banks with the group of 30 global systemically important banks (selected and published by the Financial Stability Board). The sustainable banks maintained their financial return through the global financial crisis with a return on equity (ROE) fluctuating between 4 and 10 per cent over the 2006–15 period. At the same time, the median ROE for the global banks fluctuated between 0 and 15 per cent over the same period (see ECB (2015) for a similar result for the euro-area banks). While the average ROE for the group of sustainable banks is slightly lower at 8.3 per cent compared to 8.7 per cent for the global banks over the 2006–15 period, the variance of the ROE is lower for the sustainable banks at a standard deviation of 4.9 per cent compared to 7.7 per cent for the global banks. This smaller variance can be explained by two factors: stable return on assets (around 0.5 to 0.7 per cent for sustainable banks versus 0.2 to 0.8 per cent for the global banks over the 2006–15 period) and a higher capital ratio (1 to 1.5 per cent higher for sustainable banks).[1] High leverage with more debt and less equity—which is equivalent to a lower capital ratio—contributes to variability in banks' ROE and thus increases bank risk, as found in the case of the global banks.

Ortiz-de-Mandojana and Bansal (2016) investigate the short and long-term benefits of *organizational resilience* through sustainable business practices. In the long run, a higher survival rate of sustainable organizations is expected, as resilience helps companies to avoid crises and bounce back from shocks. They show that companies that adopt responsible social and environmental

[1] We refer here to the unweighted capital ratio, also known as the Basel leverage ratio, which is defined as Tier 1 equity divided by total assets.

practices, relative to a carefully matched control group, have lower financial volatility, higher sales growth, and higher chances of survival over a 15-year period. Yet they do not find any differences in short-term profits. This suggests that there is no short-term cost to adopting sustainability practices.

However, the evidence on SRI, which incorporates environmental, social, and governance (ESG) issues in investment decisions, is mixed. In a meta-study on the performance of SRI funds, Renneboog, Ter Horst, and Zhang (2008) report that existing studies at the portfolio level hint but do not univocally demonstrate that SRI investment funds perform worse than conventional funds. But Bauer, Koedijk, and Otten (2005) find little evidence that the average performance of SRI in the United States and the United Kingdom is different from that of conventional funds. More recently, Ferrell, Liang, and Renneboog (2016) find a positive relation between corporate social responsibility (CSR) and value (measured by Tobin's Q, which stands for the market value divided by the book value). CSR can thus generate more returns for investors through enhanced firm value. Although results have been mixed, the majority of the research suggests a positive relationship between corporate environmental performance and corporate financial performance (Dixon-Fowler et al. 2013).

Moving to corporate governance, *legitimacy theory* underpins SF 3.0, which targets LTVC for the common good. Legitimacy theory indicates that companies aim to legitimize their corporate actions in order to obtain approval from society and thus ensure their continuing existence (Omran and Ramdhony, 2015). This social licence to operate represents a myriad of expectations that society has about how an organization should conduct its operations. The corporation thus acts within the bounds and norms of what society identifies as socially responsible behaviour, including meeting social and environmental standards.

Finally, Dyllick and Muff (2016) argue that corporates need to develop an *outside-in perspective* by asking how they can contribute effectively to solving social and environmental challenges (instead of looking inside out by asking how they can reduce their social and environmental impact). This outside-in perspective allows corporates to take a system approach towards sustainability at the macro level. As indicated in Section 1.2, an integrated social-ecological system perspective is needed to address the discrepancy between emerging practices in sustainable investments and business at the micro level and outcomes or impacts at the macro level. On the environmental aspect, this system approach starts with the planetary boundaries or ecological limits. So, natural resources are not depleted, waste is reused, and carbon emissions stay within the available carbon budget to limit global warming. In short, the available or sustainable 'budgets' respect the closed cycles of the natural environment and thus point to a circular or closed-loop economy (Busch, Bauer, and Orlitzky, 2016). Chapter 4 discusses ways to achieve a system approach.

1.4.4 COMPARING THE STAGES: WHERE ARE WE?

The three stages of SF lead to different levels of realized social-environmental value. SF 1.0 introduces a minimum level, SEV^{min}, below which investors cannot go. Corporates or investment projects that do not meet this minimum level are on an exclusion list. The next stage, SF 2.0, balances the privately discounted financial, social, and environmental value in an overall approach optimizing the integrated value. We label this $SEV^{private}$. For illustration purposes we incorporate this privately discounted social-environmental value halfway between the minimum and optimal level on our social-environmental value scale in Figure 1.6. Finally, SF 3.0 optimizes the social-environmental value, $SEV^{optimal}$. Companies and projects that deliver this optimized social-environmental value are eligible for investment or lending and are on an inclusion list.

The first two stages aim to avoid reputation risk, because the public demands a minimum level of CSR and externalities are expected to be priced-in at some stage. The third stage aims to grasp the opportunities of realizing social-environmental impact through investment and lending.

Where are we currently on the social-environmental axis? The majority of firms are at the SF 1.0 level, putting financial value first. About 30 to 40 per cent of financial institutions and 20 to 30 per cent of corporates adopt sustainable principles in their investment and business practices (see Table 4.3 in Chapter 4). But these firms are only partly (fraction α) maximizing IV. They are somewhere between SF 1.0 and 2.0, which can be expressed as $maxV = (1 - \alpha)FV + \alpha IV = FV + \alpha(SV + EV)$, in which V stands for the overall value maximized by the firm, FV for financial value, IV for integrated value ($IV = FV + SV + EV$), SV for social value, and EV for environmental value.

A fair approximation is that financial value is dominant and social-environmental value is incorporated for about 10 per cent (α = 0.1). This implies that we are just above, but still quite close to, SEV^{min}. To increase the social-environmental value, the real challenge is to switch from SF 1.0 to SF 2.0. This is similar to the dichotomy of Hart and Zingales (2017), who distinguish between shareholder value (SF 1.0) and shareholder welfare (SF 2.0). Box 3.2 in Chapter 3 reports on a recent battle between the shareholder

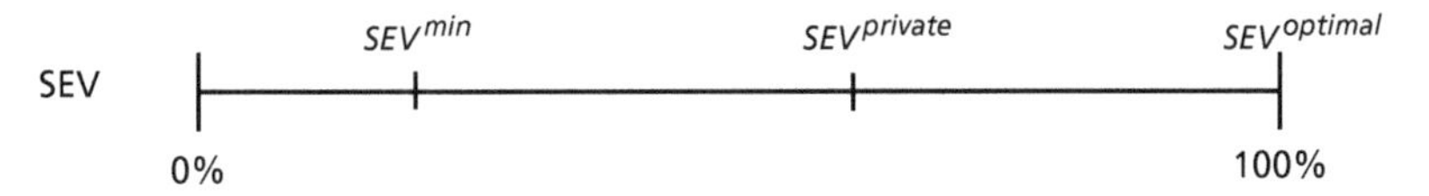

Figure 1.6 Levels of SEV

Note: SEV^{min} = minimum level of social and environmental value; $SEV^{private}$ = optimized integrated value (= privately discounted financial, social, and environmental value); and $SEV^{optimal}$ = optimized social and environmental value.

Source: Schoenmaker (2017).

model (SF 1.0) and the stakeholder model (SF 2.0). Finally, the group of financial institutions adopting SF 3.0 is tiny at less than 1 per cent (Table 4.3).

The framework is dynamic. NGOs put pressure on investors to raise the minimum level by expanding the number of exclusions. The introduction of government regulation or taxation on social and environmental externalities can cause an upward shift of the social-environmental component in the integrated value calculation.

1.5 Challenges to integration of sustainability into finance

The obvious answer to deal with social and environmental issues is to simply put them in our economic models. However, these models are still confined to capital and labour, without the services and goods of nature. The famous Cobb–Douglas production function, using labour input (the total number of person-hours working in a year) and capital input (the value of machinery, equipment, and buildings) for the production of goods (Cobb and Douglas, 1928), is still being taught to first-year economy and business students. The problem is that many of the social and environmental issues are externalities or external effects, which affect other parties without these effects being reflected in market prices. Neoclassical models employ market prices as relevant signals for decision-making (e.g. investment, production, or consumption decisions) and thus do not incorporate social and environmental externalities. Governments can use regulation or taxation to price or internalize externalities. Moreover, there are societal forces at work, which put pressure on investors and businesses to internalize social and environmental externalities. Chapter 2 discusses the concept of externalities and the rate of internalization.

Figure 1.7 illustrates the inputs (in the form of capitals) and players in the economy (governments, corporates, and households) for value creation. Panel A shows the traditional finance regime that is aimed at financial value creation and builds on linear production and consumption processes and locked-in government budgets for incumbent sectors (e.g. agricultural production and fossil-fuel-based energy infrastructure). Panel B illustrates the SF regime aimed at LTVC. This chapter stresses the need to have an integrated view on the use of the services of natural, social, and financial capital in production and consumption. As this book focuses on the role of the financial system, Figure 1.7 draws the financing lines (investment and lending) to the main players. The endpoint—LTVC consistent with achieving the SDGs by 2030—is the relevant perspective for all players (financial sector, corporates,

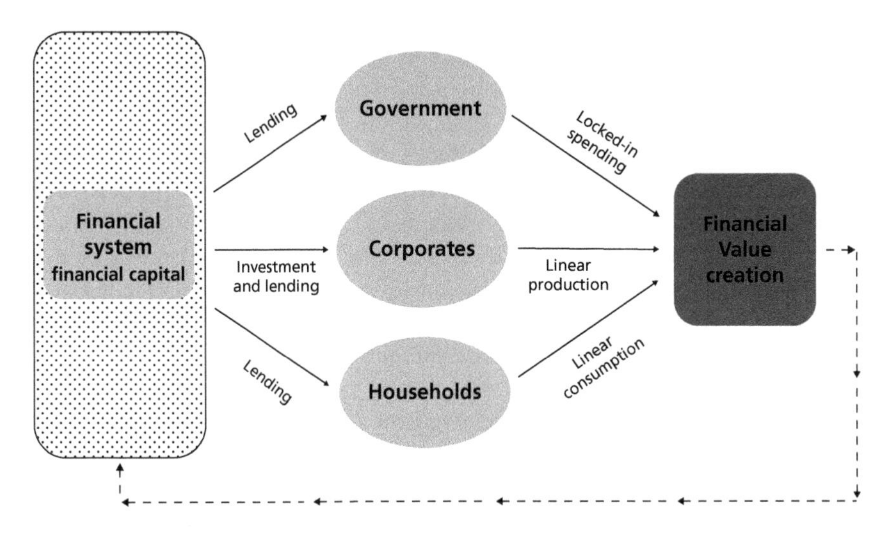

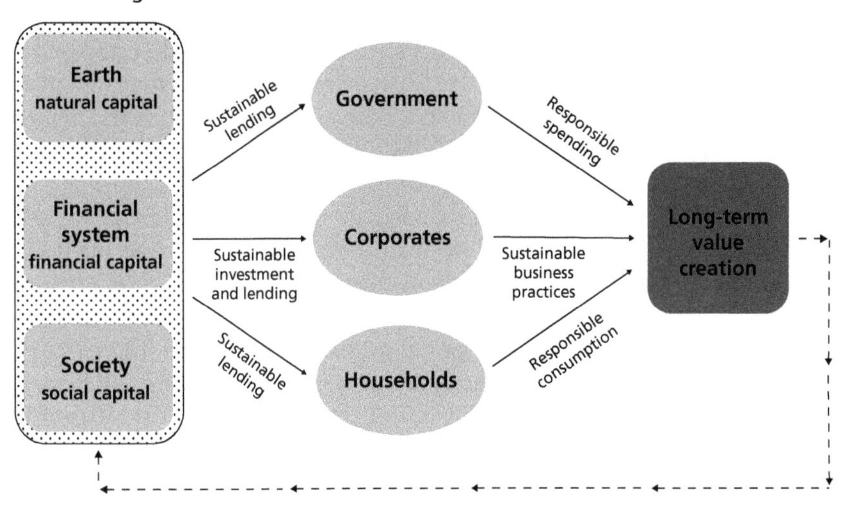

Figure 1.7 Value creation: From an old to a new vision

government, and households) in the system. The feedback loop highlights that LTVC preserves natural, social, and financial capital in the long term.

Corporates play a key role in the transition to a sustainable economy. It is therefore important to broaden their objective from shareholder value to stakeholder value, which integrates financial, social, and environmental value. Another challenge is a behavioural bias towards the short term. Market practices, such as monthly or quarterly performance benchmarking and variable pay, reinforce this short-term bias. A possible cost of financial markets is thus short-termism, with agents in the financial intermediation chain weighing near-term outcomes too heavily at the expense of longer-term opportunities. But sustainability is about the long term. Chapters 3 and 4 explore governance approaches that focus on LTVC.

Some corporates will survive that transition, others will not, because their competitive positions are eroded. Sustainability is therefore also about corporate survival. It is a critical issue to competitive positions, business models, and, ultimately, strategy. The fields of strategy and finance overlap in the areas of valuation and strategic value management. The latter is the practice of ensuring that investment decisions create long-term value. This involves the analysis of a company's value drivers, which in turn are affected by material sustainability issues. Chapter 5 discusses how successful companies can anticipate sustainability issues in their valuation and strategy.

Metrics and data to assess and manage social and environmental issues are not only needed for ex ante decision-making, but also for ex post accountability to facilitate governance. An emerging trend is integrated reporting, whereby companies report on financial, human/social, and natural capitals in an integrated way rather than publishing separate reports: one financial report and one sustainability report. Investors have typically been interested only in the first type of reports. The lack of reliable metrics and data is, to date, a major hurdle in the acceptance of integrated reports. Chapter 6 highlights the need for developing appropriate metrics, collecting relevant data, and assuring the quality of published data in such reports.

Sustainability needs to be incorporated in mainstream finance. Table 1.4 presents how our SF typology developed in this chapter can be applied to various financial instruments and sectors. At the basic level (SF 1.0), exclusion of companies or projects with very negative social or environmental impact is incorporated in the investment, lending, or insurance strategy. The next level (SF 2.0) incorporates ESG factors and risks in the decision-making and manages the integrated value. The advanced level (SF 3.0) starts with an analysis of the social and environmental impact before considering financial returns. While Chapter 7 analyses new investment approaches for LTVC, Chapters 8 to 11 discuss the integration of sustainability in financial instruments and sectors.

Table 1.4 Integration of sustainability in financial instruments and sectors

<table>
<tr><th>SF typology</th><th>Equity
(Chapter 8)</th><th>Bonds
(Chapter 9)</th><th>Banking
(Chapter 10)</th><th>Insurance
(Chapter 11)</th></tr>
<tr><td>SF 1.0</td><td colspan="4">Exclusion</td></tr>
<tr><td>SF 2.0</td><td colspan="4">ESG integration</td></tr>
<tr><td>SF 3.0</td><td>Impact investing</td><td>Green bonds; Social bonds</td><td>Impact lending; Microfinance</td><td>Microinsurance</td></tr>
</table>

Finally, the transition to a sustainable economy requires changing our ways of working. While technical discussions of externalities and policy development dominate the sustainability debate, the real transition challenge is developing integrated thinking and implementing effective transition management (Chapter 12). *Integrated thinking* combines the financial, social, and environmental dimensions: integrated value then becomes the new norm for business and investment decision-making. Organizations are often hierarchical and locked into traditional ways of working; building capacity for sustainable development may be difficult in such structures. Doppelt (2017) outlines a guide for change, which starts with challenging and shifting the dominant business-as-useful mindset across the organization.

1.6 **Conclusions**

Coming from an 'empty' world with abundant natural resources, the Industrial Revolution brought prosperity in the form of economic and population growth. At the same time, this growth—based on production processes dependent on fossil fuels and other natural resources—has created social and environmental challenges. Mass production in a competitive economic system has led to long working hours, underpayment, and child labour, first in the developed world and later the developing world. Social regulations have increasingly been introduced to counter these practices and promote decent work and access to education and health care. However, mass production and consumption is also stressing the Earth system through pollution and depletion of natural resources. Climate change is now the most pressing ecological constraint or planetary boundary. To address these social and environmental challenges in our economic system, the UN has developed the SDGs for 2030. Sustainable development means that current and future generations have the resources needed, such as food, water, health care, and energy, without stressing the Earth system processes.

SF looks at how finance (investing and lending) interacts with economic, social, and environmental issues. This chapter shows how SF has the potential to move from finance as a goal (profit maximization) to finance as a means. In his book *Finance and the Good Society*, Shiller (2012) provides some stimulating examples of how finance can serve society and its citizens. The same could be done to address environmental challenges.

We are in the transition to a low-carbon and more circular economy. The externalities of the current carbon-intensive economy are becoming increasingly clear to the wider public and are leading to action (e.g., moving from fossil fuels to renewable energy). Finance is about anticipating such actions and incorporating expectations in today's valuations for investment decisions. Finance can thus contribute to a swift transition to a low-carbon economy.

Key concepts used in this chapter

Common good refers to what is shared and beneficial for all or most members of a given community.

Environmental issues or ecological issues are issues, abiotic or biotic, that influence living organisms; see *planetary boundaries* for the most critical environmental issues.

Externalities refer to consequences of activities, which affect other (or third) parties without this being reflected in market prices.

Fair financial return preserves at the minimum the (real) value of capital.

Inside-out perspective asks how businesses can reduce their social and environmental impact; this perspective contrasts with the *outside-in perspective.*

Integrated thinking combines the financial, social, and environmental dimensions.

Integrated value is obtained by combining the financial, social, and environmental values in an integrated way (with regard for the interconnections).

Legitimacy theory indicates that corporates aim to legitimize their corporate actions to gain approval from society and thus ensure their continuing existence.

Linear production and consumption system is based on extraction of raw materials (take), processing into products (make), consumption (use), and disposal (waste).

Living wage is a wage for a full-time worker sufficient to provide his or her family's basic needs for an acceptable standard of living; a living wage varies with the local cost of living.

Outside-in perspective asks how business can contribute effectively to solving social and environmental challenges.

Planetary boundaries framework consist of nine planetary boundaries within which humanity can continue to develop and thrive for generations to come; these boundaries include climate change, biosphere integrity, land-system change, freshwater use, biochemical flows, ocean acidification, atmospheric aerosol loading, stratospheric ozone depletion, and novel entities.

Precautionary principle states that an action should not be taken (or a boundary should not be crossed) if the consequences are uncertain and potentially dangerous.

Resilience of a system (e.g. an eco-system or organization) is the adaptive capacity of a system to deal with unpredictable shocks.

Resources abundances refers to the plentiful availability of natural resources like minerals, metal ores, fossil fuels, land and fresh water.

Shareholder value approach means that the ultimate measure of a corporate's success is the extent to which it enriches its shareholders.

Social foundations consist of the 12 top social priorities, grouped into three clusters, focused on enabling people to be: (i) well: through food security, adequate income, improved water and sanitation, housing, and health care; (ii) productive: through education, decent work, and modern energy services; and (iii) empowered: through networks, gender equality, social equity, having a political voice, and peace and justice.

Stakeholder value approach means that a corporate should balance or optimize the interests of all its stakeholders: customers, employees, suppliers, shareholders, and the community.

Sustainable development means that current and future generations have the resources needed, such as food, water, health care, and energy, without stressing processes within the Earth system.

Sustainable finance looks at how finance (investing and lending) interacts with economic, social, and environmental issues.

SUGGESTED READING

Gladwin, T., J. Kennelly, and T. Krause (1995), 'Shifting paradigms for sustainable development: implications for management theory and research', *Academy of Management Review*, 20(4): 874–907.

Hart, O. and L. Zingales (2017), 'Companies should maximize shareholder welfare not market value', CEPR Discussion Paper No. 12186.

Levine, R. (2005), 'Finance and growth: theory, mechanisms and evidence', in: P. Aghion and S. N. Durlauf (eds.), *Handbook of Economic Growth*, Elsevier, Amsterdam, 865–923.

Raworth, K. (2017), *Doughnut Economics: Seven Ways to Think Like a 21st-Century Economist*, Random House Business Books, London.

Steffen, W., K. Richardson, J. Rockström, S. Cornell, I. Fetzer, E. Bennett, R. Biggs, S. Carpenter, W. de Vries, C. de Wit, C. Folke, D. Gerten, J. Heinke, G. Mace, L. Persson, V. Ramanathan, B. Reyers, and S. Sörlinet (2015), 'Planetary boundaries: guiding human development on a changing planet', *Science*, 347(6223): 736–47.

Tirole, J. (2017), *Economics for the Common Good*, Princeton University Press, Princeton, NJ.

UN (United Nations) (2015), 'UN Sustainable Development Goals (UN SDGs)—transforming our world: the 2030 Agenda for Sustainable Development', A/RES/70/1, New York.

REFERENCES

Acemoglu, D. and J. Robinson (2012), *Why Nations Fail*, Crown Business, New York.

Barone, G. and S. Mocetti (2016), 'Inequality and trust: new evidence from panel data', *Economic Inquiry*, 54(2): 794–806.

Bauer, R., K. Koedijk, and R. Otten (2005), 'International evidence on ethical mutual fund performance and investment style', *Journal of Banking and Finance*, 29(7): 1751–67.

Brundtland Report (1987), *Our Common Future: The United Nations World Commission on Environment and Development*, United Nations, New York.

Busch, T., R. Bauer, and M. Orlitzky (2016), 'Sustainable development and financial markets', *Business & Society*, 55(3): 303–29.

Cobb, C. and P. Douglas (1928), 'A theory of production', *American Economic Review*, 18 (Supplement): 139–65.

Coulson, A. (2016), 'KPMG's True Value methodology: a critique of economic reasoning on the value companies create and reduce for society', *Sustainability Accounting, Management and Policy Journal*, 7(4): 517–30.

Daly, H. and J. Farley (2011), *Ecological Economics: Principles and Applications*, Island Press, Washington DC.

Dixon-Fowler, H., D. Slater, J. Johnson, A. Ellstrand, and A. Romi (2013), 'Beyond "does it pay to be green?" A meta-analysis of moderators of the CEP–CFP relationship', *Journal of Business Ethics*, 112(2): 353–66.

Doppelt, B. (2017), *Leading Change Toward Sustainability: A Change-Management Guide for Business, Government and Civil Society*, updated 2nd edn, Routledge, Abingdon.

Dyllick, T. and K. Muff (2016), 'Clarifying the meaning of sustainable business introducing a typology from business-as-usual to true business sustainability', *Organization and Environment*, 29 (2): 156–74.

ECB (European Central Bank) (2015), 'Bank profitability challenges in euro area banks: the role of cyclical and structural factors', *Financial Stability Review*, May, 134–45.

Ferrell, A., H. Liang, and L. Renneboog (2016), 'Socially responsible firms', *Journal of Financial Economics*, 122(3): 585–606.

Friedman, M. (1970), 'The social responsibility of business is to increase its profits', *New York Times Magazine*, 13 September.

GABV (Global Alliance for Banking on Values) (2016), 'Real economy—real returns: a continuing business case for sustainability-focused banking', Research Report, Zeist, http://www.gabv.org/wp-content/uploads/2016-Research-Report-final.pdf, accessed 25 June 2018.

GIIN (Global Impact Investing Network) (2016), 'Annual Impact Investor Survey 2016', Global Impact Investing Network, New York.

Gladwin, T., J. Kennelly, and T. Krause (1995), 'Shifting paradigms for sustainable development: implications for management theory and research', *Academy of Management Review*, 20(4): 874–907.

Hart, O. and L. Zingales (2017), 'Companies should maximize shareholder welfare not market value', CEPR Discussion Paper, DP12186.

Heinkel, R., A. Kraus, and J. Zechner (2001), 'The effect of green investment on corporate behavior', *Journal of Financial and Quantitative Analysis*, 36(4): 431–49.

Holling, C. S. (2001), 'Understanding the complexity of economic, ecological, and social systems', *Ecosystems*, 4(5): 390–405.

IPCC (Intergovernmental Panel on Climate Change) (2014), 'Fifth assessment synthesis report', New York.

Levine, R. (2005), 'Finance and growth: theory, mechanisms and evidence', in: P. Aghion and S. N. Durlauf (eds.), *Handbook of Economic Growth*, Elsevier, Amsterdam, 865–923.

Meadows, D., D. Meadows, J. Randers, and W. Behrens III (1972), *Limits to Economic Growth: A Report for the Club of Rome's Project on the Predicament of Mankind*, Universe Books, New York.

Mercer (2015), 'Investing in a time of climate change', New York, https://www.mercer.com/our-thinking/wealth/investing-in-a-time-of-climate-change.html, accessed 25 June 2018.

National Commission (2011), 'Deep water: the Gulf oil disaster and the future of offshore drilling', National Commission on the BP Deepwater Horizon Oil Spill and Offshore Drilling, US Government, https://www.gpo.gov/fdsys/pkg/GPO-OILCOMMISSION/pdf/GPO-OILCOMMISSION.pdf, accessed 25 June 2018.

Norström, A. V., A. Dannenberg, G. McCarney, M. Milkoreit, F. Diekert, G. Engström, R. Fishman, J. Gars, E. Kyriakopoolou, V. Manoussi, K. Meng, M. Metian, M. Sanctuary, M. Schlüter, M. Schoon, L. Schultz, and M. Sjöstedt (2014), 'Three necessary conditions for establishing effective Sustainable Development Goals in the Anthropocene', *Ecology and Society*, 19(3): 8.

Omran, M. and D. Ramdhony (2015), 'Theoretical perspectives on corporate social responsibility disclosure: a critical review', *International Journal of Accounting and Financial Reporting*, 5(2): 38–55.

Ortiz-de-Mandojana, N. and P. Bansal (2016), 'The long-term benefits of organizational resilience through sustainable business practices', *Strategic Management Journal*, 37(8): 1615–31.

Raworth, K. (2017), *Doughnut Economics: Seven Ways to Think Like a 21st-Century Economist*, Random House Business Books, London.

Renneboog, L., J. ter Horst, and C. Zhang (2008), 'Socially responsible investments: institutional aspects, performance, and investor behavior', *Journal of Banking and Finance*, 32(9): 1723–42.

Riedl, A. and P. Smeets (2017), 'Why do investors hold socially responsible mutual funds?', *Journal of Finance*, 72(6): 2505–50.

Robinson, A., R. Calov, and A. Ganopolski (2012), 'Multistability and critical thresholds of the Greenland ice sheet', *Nature Climate Change*, 2(6): 429–32.

Rockström, J. and P. Sukhdev (2016), 'How food connects all the SDGs', Stockholm Resilience Centre, http://www.stockholmresilience.org/research/research-news/2016-06-14-how-food-connects-all-the-sdgs.html, accessed 25 June 2018.

Rosling, H. (2018), *Factfulness: Ten Reasons We're Wrong about the World – and Why Things Are Better Than You Think*, Sceptre, London.

Schoenmaker, D. (2017), 'From risk to opportunity: a framework for sustainable finance', RSM Series on Positive Change, vol. 2, Rotterdam School of Management, Erasmus University, https://ssrn.com/abstract=3066210, accessed 25 June 2018.

Shiller, R. (2012), *Finance and the Good Society*, Princeton University Press, Princeton, NJ.

Skancke, M. (2016), 'Fossil fuel investments: fossil fuel investment and the broader issue of transitioning to a low-carbon economy', Australian Council of Superannuation Investors, Melbourne.

Steffen, W., K. Richardson, J. Rockström, S. Cornell, I. Fetzer, E. Bennett, R. Biggs, S. Carpenter, W. de Vries, C. de Wit, C. Folke, D. Gerten, J. Heinke, G. Mace, L. Persson, V. Ramanathan, B. Reyers, and S. Sörlinet (2015), 'Planetary boundaries: guiding human development on a changing planet', *Science*, 347(6223): 736–47.

Sutton, P., S. Anderson, R. Costanza, and I. Kubiszewski (2016), 'The ecological economics of land degradation: impacts on ecosystem service values', *Ecological Economics*, 129: 182–92.

Tirole, J. (2017), *Economics for the Common Good*, Princeton University Press, Princeton, NJ.

True Price (2014), 'The business case for true pricing: why you will benefit from measuring, monetizing and improving your impact', Report drafted by True Price, Deloitte, EY, and PwC, 2nd edn, Amsterdam, http://trueprice.org/wp-content/uploads/2015/02/True-Price-Report-The-Business-Case-for-True-Pricing.pdf, accessed 25 June 2018.

UN (United Nations) (2015), 'UN Sustainable Development Goals (UN SDGs)—transforming our world: the 2030 Agenda for Sustainable Development', A/RES/70/1, New York.

UNFCCC (United Nations Framework Convention on Climate Change) (2015), 'Adoption of the Paris Agreement', Paris.

Part II

Sustainability's challenges to corporates

2 Externalities—internalization

Overview

The social and environmental factors identified in Chapter 1 are *externalities*, which affect other parties without these effects being reflected in market prices. As neoclassical models use market prices as relevant signals for decision-making (e.g. investment, production, or consumption decisions), these social and environmental externalities are not incorporated. This chapter discusses how to address this market failure, which hampers sustainable development.

There are several mechanisms to internalize social and environmental externalities. A major method is government intervention through regulation or taxation. Social legislation in the developed world is a successful example of internalizing social externalities. While a very few countries have implemented effective carbon taxes to curb carbon emissions, most countries have no, or very low, carbon taxes. Even worse, fossil fuel subsidies are still widespread and hinder the adoption of renewable energy.

The corporate sector is increasingly working on the internalization of externalities. This chapter explains the integrated value approach, which measures the financial, social, and environmental dimensions, and subsequently calculates the 'true' or integrated price of a product or the integrated value of a company. While companies can do much to internalize non-priced externalities, there is insufficient collective effort. A system perspective towards governance is required to address this shortfall (see Chapter 4). Moreover, government intervention, or the threat thereof, may be needed to address social and environmental externalities.

Although the United Nations (UN) Sustainable Developments Goals Agenda has set a clear timeline to address the main social and environmental externalities by 2030, there are significant political and technological uncertainties about how these externalities will unfold over time. *Scenario analysis* is a process of analysing possible future events by considering alternative possible outcomes under uncertainty. This chapter outlines the process of selecting scenarios (e.g. low, medium, high carbon tax), calculating the discounted cash flows (DCFs) for each scenario and synthesizing the scenario results by weighting the probabilities attached to each. We apply scenario analysis to the valuation of fossil fuel companies, which may become *stranded assets* under a scenario with a high carbon tax and/or a major technological breakthrough in renewable energy production.

Central banks and supervisors can also conduct stress tests of the financial sector using extreme scenarios. A case in point is a carbon stress test, which measures the exposure of financials to carbon emissions in their investment and lending portfolio. The outcome of these stress tests can raise awareness of exposure to major externalities and prompt financial firms to mitigate these exposures.

Learning objectives

After you have studied this chapter, you should be able to:

- explain the concepts of externality and internalization;
- understand the role of government regulation and taxation;
- understand the integrated value approach for measuring externalities;
- explain policy and technology uncertainty;
- use scenario analysis.

2.1 Why externalities matter

Our economic system of production and consumption serves to create welfare for society. The production function shows how factor inputs are converted into product outputs. In the neoclassical tradition, the Cobb–Douglas production function (Cobb and Douglas, 1928) is written as:

$$Q = F(K, L) \tag{2.1}$$

where Q represents the output of (consumption) goods and services, K is physical capital input (the value of machinery, equipment, and buildings), and L is labour input (the total number of person-hours worked). However, the neoclassical production function neglects the use of natural resources, including waste and energy resources, and the impact of the production process on social and human capital.

To address this shortcoming, a first step is to distinguish between funds and flows (Daly and Farley, 2011). Labour and physical capital are funds that transform a flow of resources into a flow of products, but are not themselves physically embodied in the product. Labour and physical capital thus provide fund services, while the flow of resources is that which is being transformed (or used up). A second step is to incorporate *natural resources* (both non-renewable or abiotic resources, such as mineral resources and fossil fuels, and renewable or biological resources, such as timber, fresh water, solar energy, and biomass) into the production function. The ecological economics production function (Daly and Farley, 2011) embodies the fund–flow distinction (funds uppercase; flows lowercase) and accounts for energy use and waste emissions:

$$q + w = F(K, L, N; r, e) \tag{2.2}$$

where q represents flows of (consumption) goods and services, w flows of waste, r flows of natural resources, and e flows of energy. N stands for the fund function of natural capital, like a forest yielding the service of watershed protection or wildlife habitat. The flow function of natural capital yielding a flow of resources is already captured in r (e.g. the timber of a forest). Another example of a natural resource is land, whereby land restoration projects make a clear distinction between flow and fund functions (Ferwerda, 2016). In its fund function, land is the soil, whose supply is inherently fixed and can be primarily financed with green bonds or bank loans (see Chapters 9 and 10). The flow of (ecosystem) services comprises, for example, the annual crops cultivated and harvested by farmers. The entrepreneurial activity of farming is riskier and typically financed by a mix of equity and debt. A final step is to include the social impact of production. The enlarged production function is written as:

$$q + w = F(K, L, N, S, H; r, e) \tag{2.3}$$

where S represents the *social and relationship capital* and H the *human capital* used in the production process (see Chapter 6 for the six capitals). Whereas the social and relationship capital covers social activities, nuisances, or contributions to local communities and relationships within and between communities, the human capital dimension refers to people's competencies, capabilities, and experience and includes issues such as health and safety, gender equality, training, and job satisfaction.

The original Cobb–Douglas production function stresses the substitutability between the production factors. A classical example is investment in advanced machinery, which reduces the need for labour. However, natural resources are complementary and cannot be substituted with labour or physical capital. When producing steel, for example, you cannot reduce the amount of iron ore used as input. The non-substitutability of capitals is a principle of sustainability. Nevertheless, natural resources can be substituted with other natural resources. An example is the light-weighting technique, which uses aluminium instead of steel. This in turn can reduce energy use: aluminium vehicles, for example, are lighter and thus need less energy to be driven. Another example of substitutability is renewable energy, which can replace the use of fossil fuels. Technological development, which is often exponential, plays an important role in the transformation of production processes.

As discussed in Chapter 1, we are in a transition from a linear economy (take, make, use, and waste) to a low-carbon and more circular economy to reduce the reliance on natural resources. A key goal of the sustainable development agenda is to ensure sustainable consumption and production patterns (see goal 12 in Box 2.1). Sustainable production and consumption means that the use of natural resources (N, r), including the flows of energy (e) and waste (w), stay within the regenerative and carrying capacity of the Earth system.

However, *abiotic natural resources* (N^a), such as mineral resources, are finite. The speed of depletion (T in years) of abiotic resources is given by the following equation:

$$T = {N^a}/{D^a} \tag{2.4}$$

where D^a represents the annual global demand or consumption of abiotic resources. Impending exhaustion (T) cannot be easily calculated from current reserves for two reasons. First, the reserve base (N^a) consists of discovered and undiscovered resources. In the case of copper, for example, identified resources as of 2014 are twice as large as the amount projected to be needed through to 2050, indicating that about 70 years ($T \doteq 70$) are left. But estimates of yet-to-be discovered copper resources are up to 40 times more than currently identified resources (Meinert, Robinson, and Nassar, 2016). Next, annual global consumption (D^a) is dependent on several factors. While recycling and substitution reduce world demand for mineral resources, population growth and rising standards of living require new primary supplies of mineral resources.

Figure 2.1 shows the end-of-life recycling rates for metals. The recycling rate for much-used metals such as the ferrous metal iron (Fe—atomic number 26) and the non-ferrous metal aluminium (Al—atomic number 13) is over 50 per cent. In contrast, where materials are used in small quantities in complex products, for example the precious metal tantalum (Ta—atomic number 73) in electronics, recycling is technically much more challenging and amounts to less than 1 per cent in Figure 2.1.

Next, the goal of inclusive economic growth and decent work (goal 8 in Box 2.1) means that social and human capitals (S, H) should be preserved in the production process. The framework of the UN Sustainable Development Goals (SDGs) provides a common language to discuss the capitals (see Box 2.1). How can we incorporate these capitals or factors of the enlarged production function in our decision-making?

The remainder of this chapter deals largely with negative externalities due to ignoring these capitals. For completeness, we stress that there are also positive externalities, such as companies investing in renewable energy, material savings, training their employees, sustainable food production, and/or improvement of health care. At the country level, international cooperation (through trade and other mechanisms) reduces, for example, war.

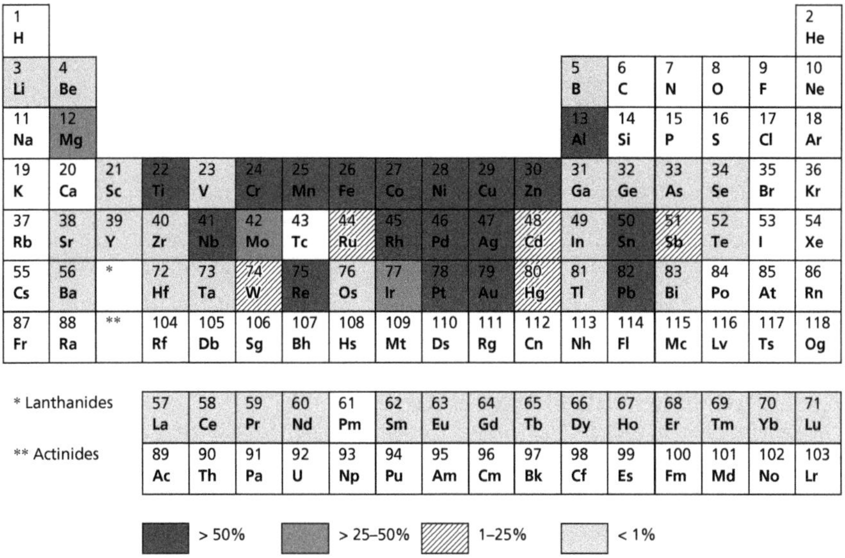

1 H																	2 He
3 Li	4 Be											5 B	6 C	7 N	8 O	9 F	10 Ne
11 Na	12 Mg											13 Al	14 Si	15 P	16 S	17 Cl	18 Ar
19 K	20 Ca	21 Sc	22 Ti	23 V	24 Cr	25 Mn	26 Fe	27 Co	28 Ni	29 Cu	30 Zn	31 Ga	32 Ge	33 As	34 Se	35 Br	36 Kr
37 Rb	38 Sr	39 Y	40 Zr	41 Nb	42 Mo	43 Tc	44 Ru	45 Rh	46 Pd	47 Ag	48 Cd	49 In	50 Sn	51 Sb	52 Te	53 I	54 Xe
55 Cs	56 Ba	*	72 Hf	73 Ta	74 W	75 Re	76 Os	77 Ir	78 Pt	79 Au	80 Hg	81 Tl	82 Pb	83 Bi	84 Po	85 At	86 Rn
87 Fr	88 Ra	**	104 Rf	105 Db	106 Sg	107 Bh	108 Hs	109 Mt	110 Ds	111 Rg	112 Cn	113 Nh	114 Fl	115 Mc	116 Lv	117 Ts	118 Og

* Lanthanides	57 La	58 Ce	59 Pr	60 Nd	61 Pm	62 Sm	63 Eu	64 Gd	65 Tb	66 Dy	67 Ho	68 Er	69 Tm	70 Yb	71 Lu
** Actinides	89 Ac	90 Th	91 Pa	92 U	93 Np	94 Pu	95 Am	96 Cm	97 Bk	98 Cf	99 Es	100 Fm	101 Md	102 No	103 Lr

Legend: > 50%   > 25–50%   1–25%   < 1%

Figure 2.1 Recycling rates for 60 metals

Note: The periodic table of global end-of-life functional recycling rates for 60 metals, with the individual metals categorized into one of four ranges of recycling.

Source: Adapted from Graedel et al. (2011).

BOX 2.1 SOCIAL, HUMAN, AND NATURAL CAPITALS IN THE SDG FRAMEWORK

The UN has developed 17 SDGs, as discussed in Chapter 1. Table 2.1 splits them in 'people' SDGs, which cover basic needs and are linked to social and human capitals (S, H), and 'planet' SDGs, which require urgent action and are linked to natural capital (N, r, e, w).

Table 2.1 Linking SDGs and capitals

SDG	Brief description	Social & human capitals	Natural capital
1	No poverty	X	
2	Zero hunger	X	
3	Good health and well-being	X	
4	Quality education	X	
5	Gender equality	X	
6	Clean water and sanitation		X
7	Affordable and clean energy		X
8	Decent work and economic growth	X	
9	Infrastructure, industry, and innovation	X	
10	Reduced inequalities	X	
11	Sustainable cities and communities	X	
12	Responsible consumption and production	X	X

(continued)

BOX 2.1 CONTINUED

13	Climate action		X
14	Life below water		X
15	Life on land		X
16	Peace, justice, and strong institutions	X	
17	Partnerships for the goals	X	

2.1.1 INTERNALIZING EXTERNALITIES

While an enlarged production function is easily written down, the problem is that many of the social and environmental factors are *externalities* or external effects, which affect other parties without these effects being reflected in market prices. Neoclassical models use market prices as relevant signals for decision-making (e.g. investment, production, or consumption decisions) and thus do not incorporate social and environmental externalities. The shareholder value model in finance as usual and sustainable finance (SF) 1.0 (see Chapter 1) uses these market prices when maximizing profits. There is thus a market failure to account for social and environmental externalities. It should be added that there is also a government failure in the form of lack of policies, and uncertainty about future policies, to deal with these externalities.

What are the consequences of ignoring these externalities? As natural resources are underpriced (only the costs of extraction and, where applicable, mining concessions are counted), the overuse of scarce natural resources, including fossil fuels and waste, in production continues. Moreover, there is an underinvestment in new technologies and infrastructure that rely less on natural resources and more on renewable energy. In his aptly titled book *Why Are We Waiting?*, Stern (2015) argues we need to stop investing in old-type energy and production infrastructures, as such investments add to the installed base for years to come and slow down the transition. On the social side, current labour practices, such as underpayment, discrimination, lack of health and safety procedures, and child labour, may continue.

This chapter reviews the methods for internalizing social and environmental externalities. Chapter 3 provides an overview of the sustainability players, including the instruments at their disposal, forums in which they might work together, and the opportunities and threats they face (see Table 3.1). We identify five main players, which can apply various *internalization mechanisms*:

1. **Government**: A first best solution to internalize externalities is taxation or regulation by the government. Section 2.2 analyses how this can be done.

2. **Civil society**: Non-governmental organizations can raise awareness of social and environmental externalities through a public voice in the media. The aim of public debate is to stimulate other players (government, financials, business, and consumers) to behave responsibly and address externalities. Societal connections, such as families, social clubs, sport clubs, churches, and charitable organizations, also develop civic values. Chapter 3 briefly discusses the role of civil society.
3. **Investors**: Financial institutions can incorporate environmental, social, and governance factors in their investment and lending strategy and engage with corporates in which they invest. Chapters 3, 4, and 7 analyse how investors can engage effectively with corporates. Chapters 8 to 10 discuss the role of various financial institutions in detail.
4. **Corporates**: Corporates can incorporate the costs of externalities into business practices across the value chain of production. Section 2.3 describes how externalities can be measured and priced. Chapter 5 examines how corporates can embrace sustainability in their strategy and change their business models.
5. **Consumers**: Consumers can buy sustainable products and services. Responsible advertising can influence consumer behaviour. Chapter 3 briefly discusses the role of consumers.

To address the problem of ignoring negative externalities and to preserve the *common good* for present and future generations, governments can use taxation or regulation to price or internalize externalities. A case in point is the imposition of carbon taxes to cut carbon emissions (Stern, 2008). But this first best solution is difficult to achieve due to international coordination failure in addressing global challenges, such as climate change. Nevertheless, there are societal forces at work that put pressure on investors and business to internalize social and environmental externalities. To function long term, business is dependent on a vibrant and healthy society. This is the social licence to operate (see Chapter 1). The challenge of sustainable development is to what degree business is able to internalize social and environmental impacts, as illustrated in Figure 2.2.

Chapter 3 discusses barriers to change as well as possible governance solutions to achieve sustainable development. An integrated approach is needed, whereby sustainability is incorporated in business models and financing decisions from a system perspective (i.e. the ecosystem of the Earth). Sections 2.2 and 2.3 describe methods for governments and business to measure and price externalities. Daly and Farley (2011) warn against *economic imperialism*, which seeks to expand the boundary of the economic system until it encompasses the entire ecosystem of the Earth. The challenge is to draw a boundary for applying market-based principles. In some cases, the market is the most effective means of allocating resources. In other cases, the market approach does not work because of the inherent characteristics of some

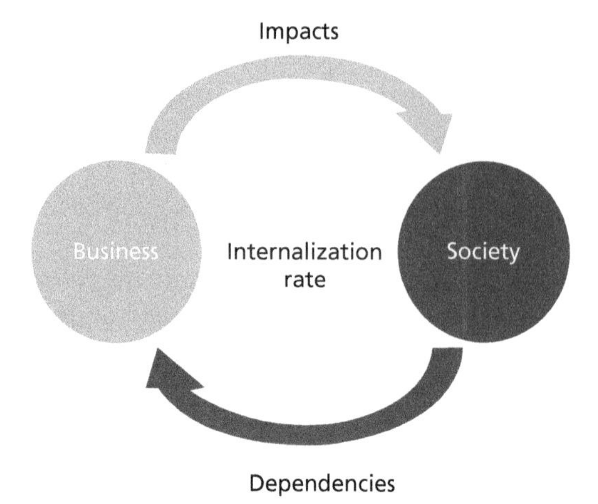

Figure 2.2 Internalization of social and environmental impacts

Source: Adapted from True Price.

environmental goods and services. Examples are in the field of biodiversity loss (treatment of endangered spices, like whales) and land use (preserving land for nature or biological farming).

Starting from the current situation, whereby most environmental externalities are not priced, there is scope for expanding the use of the price mechanism for the allocation of natural resources. But the regenerative and carrying capacity of planet Earth needs to be respected to stay within planetary boundaries, as discussed in Chapter 1.

2.2 **Government intervention**

> *Why Are We Waiting? The Logic, Urgency, and Promise of Tackling Climate Change*
>
> Nicolas Stern

To reduce negative externalities, governments can apply two basic approaches: raising prices through *taxation* to reduce demand and limiting quantity directly through *regulatory quotas* and letting prices adjust. Theoretically, we could get the same result given a demand curve (Daly and Farley, 2011). As demand curves are uncertain and tend to shift, direct quotas provide more certainty of staying within ecological limits of using natural resources and sinks. Where planetary boundaries are becoming very critical, regulation through quota or complete bans (i.e. zero quota) is more appropriate.

2.2.1 ENVIRONMENTAL EXTERNALITIES

An example of an international regulatory approach is the 1987 Montreal Protocol on Substances that Deplete the Ozone Layer. The ozone layer in the Earth's stratosphere filters ultraviolet solar rays that are harmful to humans. In 1987, 24 governments agreed to phase out chlorofluorocarbons (CFCs) by 2000, leading to a long-term recovery of the ozone layer. The Montreal Protocol is a landmark agreement that has successfully reduced the global production, consumption, and emissions of CFCs and included trade sanctions to achieve the stated goals of the treaty (Velders et al. 2007). The treaty negotiators justified the sanctions because depletion of the ozone layer is an environmental problem most effectively addressed at the global level. Without the trade sanctions, there would be economic incentives for non-signatories to increase production, damaging the competitiveness of the industries in the signatory nations as well as decreasing the search for less damaging CFC alternatives.

2.2.1.1 Taxing externalities

Where possible, economists prefer pricing externalities through a *Pigouvian tax*, which reflects the social costs of the damage. The Pigouvian tax is set at the marginal external cost and is a cost-effective method to achieve the targeted reduction. When adjustment costs are higher than the tax, firms pay the tax. By contrast, firms with low adjustment costs find it cheaper to adjust than to pay the tax. The final outcome in an economy with profit-maximizing firms is that the marginal adjustment cost will equalize the tax. Accordingly, Stern (2008) suggests that a carbon tax is an efficient way to achieve the public good of a low-carbon economy. The price signal will then guard the transition towards a low-carbon economy. In a similar way, appropriate pricing of natural resources (virgin materials) helps to avoid depletion and provides an incentive for material savings and recycling efforts.

Some countries have started to implement carbon pricing through carbon taxes or carbon *emissions trading systems* (ETS). The objective of the latter approach (also known as cap-and-trade system) is to cap the total level of carbon emissions. Firms that perform better than expected in reducing their emissions can sell their surplus allowances to larger emitters. In this way, the firms that are more effective in reducing the emissions get rewarded, while the least-effective ones get penalized. This market mechanism, with an interplay between demand and supply of emission allowances, produces a market price for carbon emissions (Bianchini and Gianfrate, 2018). The caps ensure that the required emissions reductions will progressively take place by keeping all the emitters within the boundaries of the pre-allocated carbon budget.

Early adopters of carbon taxes were the Scandinavian countries in the 1990s, which currently have carbon taxes ranging from \$50 to 130 per tCO_2e

(ton carbon dioxide equivalent). The Scandinavian experience shows that carbon pricing can be effective in changing behaviour and reducing carbon emissions. Åkerfeldt and Hammar (2015), for example, report that the gradual increase from €27 per tCO_2e in 1991 to €123 per tCO_2e in 2013 led to a shift in the energy mix from fossil fuels towards biofuels, as well as apartments in Sweden being heated by district heating (fuelled by household waste and various wood residues). The result was a reduction in carbon emissions of 23 per cent, without a negative impact on economic growth. Taxing the resource base of our predominantly brown economy (i.e. coal, oil, gas, and many other minerals) can steer the economy away from resource-intensive growth towards smart-technology industries in renewable energy, clean water, new and better materials, and waste management.

More broadly, 40 national jurisdictions and over 20 cities, states, and regions have put a price on carbon in 2016, covering almost a quarter of global carbon emissions (World Bank, 2016). However, about three quarters of the emissions covered are priced at less than €10 per tCO_2e. A case in point is the European ETS system with a carbon price of €10 per tCO_2e at the time of writing, because of the oversupply of emission allowances. These low prices have limited effect on carbon emissions. The most recent estimates for an effective carbon price are $40–80 per tCO_2e by 2020, rising to $50–100 per tCO_2e by 2030 (Stiglitz and Stern, 2017).

Most governments have thus not (yet) implemented effective carbon prices. There are several reasons for insufficient action. First, there is a coordination failure between national governments, as global warming is a global public good (Barrett, 2008; Tirole, 2017). The free-rider effect prevents action. Secondly, governments have a short horizon of up to four years, the length of the election cycle. Faced with such a short horizon, politicians follow public opinion rather than impose the (currently) unpopular idea of a carbon tax, which only brings benefits in the longer term. Thirdly, there are intergenerational trade-offs between present and future generations. While these generations should be treated equally from an equity perspective, the present generation may care less about future generations. Section 2.3 discusses the appropriate discount factor for dealing with the future. Fourthly, there is uncertainty about the fundamental causes of global warming. Climate sceptics consider the possibility that global warming is not caused by human activity. Box 2.2 discusses optimal carbon tax policy in the case of climate scepticism.

Instead of solely reaching the carbon emission threshold with carbon taxes, Acemoglu and colleagues (2012) propose to reach the R&D threshold above which clean technology becomes more efficient than dirty technology. Their solution to redirect technical change towards cleaner technology is a mix of carbon taxes (to make dirty technology more expensive) and research subsidies for clean technology (to redirect research).

The size of environmental externalities is staggering. And instead of these externalities being priced, fossil fuels are actually subsidized. The International

BOX 2.2 OPTIMAL POLICY AND CLIMATE SCEPTICISM

What is the optimal policy given uncertainty about the fundamental causes of global warming? While the majority scientific view is that human emissions contribute to climate change—reflected in the UN IPCC—climate deniers argue that it is very challenging to measure with precision the impact of human activity on the climate and there is tremendous disagreement about the degree of impact. So, climate deniers would not agree that human activity is a primary contributor to global warming.

But even climate change deniers have some doubt about whether man-made emissions contribute to global warming or not. Prudent science should therefore deal with the error that a model is falsely assumed to be correct. To reflect the two opposing views of the climate–economy interaction—one in which human emissions contribute endogenously to climate change and another in which the climate follows exogenous projections of committed warming—Van der Ploeg and Rezai (2017) propose an agnostic approach to policy which accounts for the scientific uncertainty that climate change deniers could be right after all. Climate change sceptics or agnostics attach a (small) positive probability to climate change deniers being right or, at least, acknowledge the possibility that global warming is not caused by anthropogenic carbon emissions at all.

Using the dynamic integrated model of climate and the economy, Van der Ploeg and Rezai (2017) find that the cost of avoiding the most harmful aspects of climate change is small compared with the cost of inaction. So robust policies, such as doing one's best or minimizing regret under the worst possible outcomes, call for pricing carbon.

Not pricing carbon may benefit current generations by avoiding the economic burden of climate regulation, giving politicians the (dishonest) excuse to avoid painful restructuring of carbon-based industries. Van der Ploeg and Rezai's results, however, discredit this wait-and-see approach. Using modern decision theory, they show that agnostics should decarbonize the economy rapidly as the consequences of erring on the 'wrong' side are too grave. The agnostic policymaker's response to climate change deniers is thus price carbon.

Monetary Fund reports that pre-tax energy subsidies for fossil fuels amount to $333 billion, which is 0.4 per cent of world GDP in 2015 (Coady et al. 2017). These subsidies are counterproductive and a highly inefficient way to provide support to low-income households. With externalities covering environmental damage estimated at $4,150 billion (5.6 per cent of GDP), the post-tax subsidies amount to 6 per cent GDP. Fossil fuel subsidies discourage needed investments in energy efficiency, renewables, and energy infrastructure. So, there is no need to subsidize renewables; it is sufficient to tax fossil fuels appropriately.

2.2.2 SOCIAL EXTERNALITIES

Turning to social externalities, differences among countries are even more pronounced. Developed countries largely internalized these externalities after World War II through regulations on issues such as maximum working hours, health and safety conditions, gender equality, and minimum wage. By contrast, many developing countries do not have social legislation and still experience, for example, underpayment and child labour, as discussed in Chapter 1. The SDGs cover many of these social externalities (see Box 2.1).

Also on the social side, taxes are used to change behaviour. The classical example is taxes on alcohol and tobacco, which have long been an important means of raising revenues for public spending in many countries. There is increasing interest in using taxes on these, and other unhealthy products like sugar-sweetened beverages, to achieve public health goals. If the primary policy goal of a health tax is to reduce consumption of unhealthy products, then evidence supports the implementation of taxes that increase the price of products by 20 per cent or more (Wright, Smith, and Hellowell, 2017).

Summing up, some progress is being made, but substantial environmental as well as social externalities are still not effectively addressed through government regulation or taxation.

2.3 Measuring and pricing externalities

A first step for business towards addressing or mitigating the remaining externalities is to measure and price these externalities, where possible. Attaching a financial value to social and environmental externalities facilitates the optimizing process among the financial (or economic), social, and environmental dimensions (F, S, E), as discussed in Chapter 1. Innovations in technology (measurement, information technology, data management) and science (life-cycle analyses, social life-cycle analyses, environmentally extended input–output analysis, environmental economics) make the monetization of social and environmental externalities possible (True Price, 2014). In this way, the *integrated value* I can be established by summing the financial, social, and environmental values in an integrated way. In the earlier literature, this methodology is labelled total or true value methodology.

The methodology for calculating the integrated value involves measuring, monetizing, and balancing financial and non-financial values (KPMG, 2014; True Price, 2014). Figure 2.3 illustrates the four steps to calculate the integrated value:

1. We start by calculating the financial value and quantifying and monetizing the social and environmental impacts (bar 1).
2. We then internalize the social and environmental externalities and calculate the integrated value as the sum of the values (bar 2).
3. Next, we adjust to account for the combination of the three factors. As explained in Chapter 1, there are several non-linear trade-offs between the

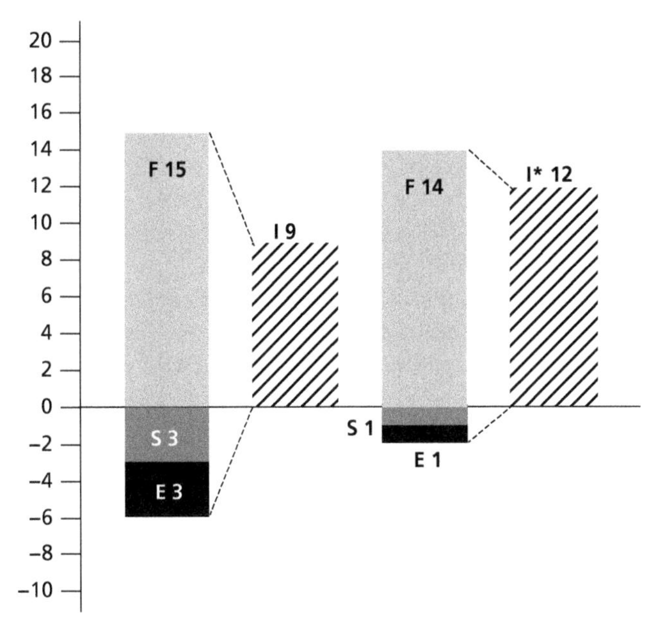

Figure 2.3 From financial value to integrated value

Note: F = financial value; S = social value; E = environmental value; I = integrated value; I* = optimized integrated value. The first two bars illustrate the values based on the original production process; the final two bars show the values based on the optimized production process.

economic, social, and environmental aspects of corporate investment. The monetization helps corporations to find the optimal combination of the three factors. In our example, the corporation is able to reduce both the social and environmental impact from 3 to 1 at an extra cost of 1 (bar 3) by adapting its production process.

4. Finally, we calculate the integrated value I^* (bar 4).

Reducing the social and environmental impact in step 3 is not always costly. With the rapidly declining cost of solar energy for example, we are getting close to the point where the use of renewable energy can reduce carbon emissions without extra costs. It should be recognized that the integrated value methodology has to make assumptions (e.g. about the size of the externalities) and is surrounded by uncertainty (e.g. about the development and/or exact price of externalities).

Our example in Figure 2.3 shows that the internalization of the externalities leads to an increase in the integrated value from 9 (bar 2) to 12 (bar 4). In the traditional finance approach, which maximizes *F* only, the original production process would be continued (bar 1 at 15 is higher than bar 3 at 14) and the additional value would not be realized. When pricing of the externalities and/or reputation damage materialize in the medium term, the old production process becomes obsolete and the new production process becomes more favourable. In the case of medium to long-term investments, the assets used in the original production process might become *stranded assets* (see later in this section) resulting in a loss of financial value. To avoid this risk, companies (and their financiers) might start to internalize the externalities before the government (taxation, regulation), the employees (strike action, talent drain), or the public (reputation, customer strike) do so.

Box 2.3 provides an example of how a sector can apply the integrated value methodology, also labelled true value or true price methodology, to products and make changes over the full value chain. More broadly, the transition to a low-carbon and more circular economy, stimulated by the internalization of social and environmental externalities, involves changes in behaviour and new consumption and production patterns based on sharing (e.g. car sharing) and

BOX 2.3 THE TRUE PRICE OF ROSES FROM KENYA

A true price analysis was conducted to identify a business case for sustainable rose farming. The study covered cut blooms from T-hybrid roses from Lake Naivasha in Kenya and compared roses produced at a conventional farm to those produced at a sustainable farm. Mapping the supply chain showed that the retail prices of roses per stem produced on both types of farms were on average the same (€0.70). The true price, on the other hand, was much lower for the sustainable rose (€0.74) than the conventional rose (€0.92). This difference in true price comes mainly from the environmental impact associated with transporting the roses via airfreight and the social impact in terms of workers' incomes.

The true price analysis identified various projects to reduce environmental and social costs:

- Transport by ship to reduce carbon emissions.
- Solar-powered greenhouse to reduce non-renewable energy use.
- Closed-loop hydroponics to reduce water and fertilizer usage.
- Training in health and safety to improve workers' skills.
- Gender committees to reduce harassment and gender discrimination.
- Payment of a basic living wage to improve the well-being of workers.

The true price analysis maps the costs of each project and its effect on the profit and loss of an average farm. For example, health and safety training would generate about €4,500 profit per hectare, while switching to transport by sea would increase profit by €5,000 per hectare. Better social standards for rose-farm workers and more environmentally friendly growing and transportation techniques are financially feasible, without negatively affecting farm owners' bottom lines.

Some improvements in social standards, such as paying a living wage to workers, were less feasible if farm owners have to bear all the costs. Based on an economic value chain analysis, it was shown that providing a living wage could be possible when a fraction of the costs are borne by wholesale traders, retail traders, and consumers. This strengthened the promotion of better social and environmental standards.

Source: True Price (2014).

minimal use of natural resources (e.g. energy and material savings). These new patterns include both reusing or recycling and using products up to their technical, instead of fashionable, lifetime cycle. Chapter 3 on responsible consumption and Chapter 5 on circular business models discuss this in more detail.

Stranded assets Stranded assets refer to assets that lose their value. Caldecott, Tilbury, and Carey (2014) introduced this term for fossil fuel assets, which may become stranded due to government regulation (e.g. carbon pricing) or technological change (e.g. reduced cost of solar photovoltaic (PV) or wind). It is more widely applicable to carbon-intensive assets, such as real estate or traditional cars. Real estate with a low energy-efficiency label may lose its (collateral) value if measures to improve its energy efficiency are not cost-efficient (see Chapter 10). Diesel cars are, for example, losing their value, as there is a move to ban them from entering city centres in order to reduce pollution levels.

Stranded assets can also happen in other areas. A case in point is land use. Intensive agriculture (with frequent use of fertilizer and irrigation) may cause soil erosion, leading to less or no food production from the degraded land in the future and species loss (e.g. in the Midwest region of the United States or in north-east China). Land can thus become a stranded asset. Several planetary boundaries are then worsened (see Figure 1.2 in Chapter 1): not only land-system change, but also biodiversity, biochemical flows (phosphorus and nitrogen in fertilizer), climate change, and freshwater use. The estimated economic cost of ecosystem services and biodiversity lost because of land degradation is over 10 per cent of annual global GDP (IPBES, 2018). On the social side, land degradation is also a major contributor to mass human migration and increased conflict (IPBES, 2018).

2.3.1 THE MONETIZATION OF EXTERNALITIES: PITFALLS

While the monetization of externalities helps to bring social and environmental externalities into corporate decision-making, there are several caveats to the market-driven calculation of integrated value. First, the calculation is traditionally done on efficiency grounds: the minimal input of resources needed for the maximum output of goods. As discussed in Chapter 1, ecosystem management requires building and maintaining resilience or quality in the system or process so it has the capacity to absorb shocks and to avoid tipping points. So, we propose optimization with scope for adaptive capacity. Some industrial companies use, for example, safety, not only for the protection of the people and the environment but also for the control of the production process (reducing production losses); they thus 'overinvest' in the quality of production facilities and safety procedures. Incorporating adaptive capacity is primarily an issue of taking a sufficiently long horizon extending over the full cycle of the production system or process. In that way, the benefits in terms of shock-absorbing capacity and the costs of extra resources are included. The integrated value approach is based on a medium to long horizon. For pricing of carbon emissions, for example, this long-term approach implies using an effective future carbon price of $50 to 100 per tCO_2e in the calculations (see Section 2.2).

Next, monetization cannot fully express the ethical aspects of externalities, such as human rights or health and safety (KPMG, 2014). The three capitals (financial, social, and environmental) are also not substitutable. More generally, Porritt (2007) distinguishes five types of sustainable capital: natural or environmental capital (stock or flow of energy and materials—both renewable and non-renewable), human capital (people's capabilities, experience, and motivation), social capital (institutions that help to maintain and develop human capital in partnerships with others), manufactured capital (fixed assets and material goods), and financial capital (financing of an organization). Chapter 6 discusses these capitals in more detail.

Finally, working out integrated value can lead to perverse outcomes: the negative environmental impact of deforestation, for example, can be offset by large economic gains; in other words, legitimizing destruction. To avoid these outcomes, we incorporate the constraint that the social-environmental value cannot be reduced compared to its initial value (see equation 1.2 in Box 1.4). Another caveat is the inherent uncertainty (e.g. underlying climate scenarios) that makes pricing difficult.

On the positive side, participation can improve quality and support for the integrated value concept. Coulson (2016) suggests that producers could involve stakeholders in the application of the integrated value methodology to form a more inclusive and pluralist conception of risk and values for social and environmental impacts. Next, the reliability of the input factors (i.e. the size and price of externalities), the underlying calculations, and the reported outcomes are important for the credibility of the integrated value concept. Integrated reporting and certification (Chapter 6) play a key role in the monetization of externalities.

2.3.2 INSUFFICIENT PRIVATE EFFORT

The adoption of sustainable business and finance practices is a major advance towards sustainable development, but it might not be sufficient for two reasons. First, the *fallacy of composition* arises when one concludes that something is true of the whole, at the macro level, from the fact that it is true of every part, at the micro level. Even if individual companies internalize social and environmental externalities, it is not certain that planetary boundaries are not crossed. One example is the current drive of companies to reduce their carbon footprints. This eco-efficiency push is a welcome trend in itself, but the available evidence suggests that the projected trajectories for carbon emissions exceed the allowable carbon budget for staying below 2° Celsius of global warming (eco-effectiveness). Dyllick and Muff (2016) call this discrepancy the 'big disconnect'. Busch, Bauer, and Orlitzky (2016) also make the paradoxical observation that increasing sustainable investment does not necessarily induce sustainable development and call for a system perspective, which we explore in Chapter 4.

There are several reasons for the divergence between the micro and macro outcomes. First, companies and financial institutions use a private discount factor to discount future CFs. Stern (2008) argues that the public discount factor should be very small or zero because the government should value current and future generations equally. Because social and environmental impacts are particularly felt in the long term, private discounting leads to insufficient effort from a social welfare perspective. Next, only about 20 per cent of companies are actively managing their carbon footprints to some extent (see Table 4.3 in Chapter 4). These micro efforts are not enough to keep the carbon emissions within the allowable carbon budget at the macro level.

Secondly, the *boundary problem* compounds the challenge of internalizing externalities. When regulation for one sector is tightened, business will shift to other sectors and countries with fewer or no requirements (Goodhart, 2008). Exemptions in the EU ETS, such as airlines operating between EU and non-EU countries, highlight the boundary problem—as well as the international coordination problem—in environmental regulation. This is an example of carbon leakage. Other examples are national-based regulations for products that companies can circumvent by relocating production to countries with less strict regulations. A solution to this problem might be the use of product or activity-based regulation.

There are limits to what the private sector can achieve. While companies and financial firms are starting to look at social and environmental externalities, there is clearly a role for government to make production and consumption fully sustainable through regulation and taxation of these externalities. The starting point is that much of the transition is driven by private investment, but that investment is threatened by government-induced risk (Stern, 2015). Policies, governance, and institutions create a risk–return balance on the basis of which investors decide whether or not to act. But it is government policy, including the stability and credibility of policy, that creates the framework for that investment and sets out a range of pricing and regulatory instruments to encourage the transition to a low-carbon economy. Stern (2015) adds that making sound policy is not just about the analysis and implementation of incentives, but also about social and personal responsibility and values. Moreover, the role of communities is often undervalued. Only with the involvement of community can we recycle and reuse. Interesting examples of the sharing economy (e.g. car-sharing schemes) are emerging. Chapter 4 explores the role of private coalitions for sustainable production and for SF.

We are in the transition to a low-carbon and more circular economy. The externalities of the current carbon-intensive economy are becoming increasingly clear to the general public (e.g. more catastrophic weather events, such as droughts and flooding in countries close to the equator, and air pollution; see Chapter 11). A case in point is California, where air pollution from heavy traffic in the 1990s prompted environmental regulations and stimulated innovations, for example in electric cars from Tesla and in solar technology. China, India, and Mexico face similar or even worse air pollution, which may at some point prompt stricter environmental regulations in these countries. Finance is about anticipating such events and incorporating expectations into today's valuations, which underpin investment decisions. Finance can thus contribute to a swift transition to a low-carbon economy.

2.4 Scenario analysis

The SDG framework in Box 2.1 identifies the main social and environmental externalities, but there are significant political and technological uncertainties about how these externalities will develop over time.

2.4.1 UNCERTAINTIES ABOUT EXTERNALITIES

2.4.1.1 Policy uncertainty

On the policy side, at which stage of development will emerging economies start adopting labour laws addressing working conditions and banning child labour? When will developed (as well as developing) countries implement an effective carbon tax? Next, might a possible carbon tax be reversed later, as, for example, happened in Australia? Uncertainty about policy intervention increases risk for investors and negatively affects long-term investment planning. A case in point is uncertainty about the trajectory to phase out fossil fuel subsidies and introduce a carbon tax, which complicates investment in energy infrastructure. By contrast, a clear and credible policy path setting out a step-wise implementation of effective carbon taxes fosters investment in renewable energy.

2.4.1.2 Technological uncertainty

Technological uncertainty compounds the policy uncertainty. A case in point is the spectacular rise of solar PV systems, which convert directly solar energy into electricity. Because solar PV generates power from sunlight, power output is limited to times when the sun is shining. Nevertheless, there are several options, such as demand response, flexible generation, grid infrastructure integration, and storage, to deal cost-effectively with this challenge. The rapid spread of renewable energy is a bright spot in the global energy transition towards a low-carbon economy. Despite lower fossil fuel prices, renewable power expanded at its fastest-ever rate in 2016, thanks to supportive government policies and sharp cost reductions.

While being small in absolute terms, electricity from global solar PV increased from 4 TWh (terawatts per hour; 1 terawatt is 1 million watts) in 2005 to 247 TWh in 2015, achieving a 51 per cent annual growth rate, the fastest of all renewable electricity technologies. Germany, until recently the largest producer due to its support for solar PV electricity generation, has increased production from 0.1 TWh in 2000 to 39 TWh in 2015 (IEA, 2016). The country provides an interesting example of policy and technological change reinforcing each other. Currently, China is the largest solar PV electricity generator, with 45 TWh in 2015, which is largely driven by concerns about air pollution and capacity targets that were outlined in the country's 13th five-year plan to 2020 (IEA, 2017).

Figure 2.4 shows how the adoption of solar PV has repeatedly beaten forecasts, indicating a virtuous cycle. The 2007 and 2010 forecasts of the International Energy Agency (IEA) and Greenpeace are consistently lower than the actual outcome (measured as global installed capacity in gigawatt (GW), which is 1 billion watts). But Greenpeace's forecasts are closer to the actual outcome and more optimistic than IEA's forecasts. More generally, Figure 2.4 highlights that our thinking tends to be linear, while the underlying technological development may be exponential.

A famous example of exponential technological growth is Moore's law, which states that the number of transistors per square inch on integrated circuits has doubled every year since their invention. A current example of exponential technical development may be the hydroelectric car, which contains fuel cells that combine hydrogen and oxygen to produce electricity. If the development and adoption of the hydroelectric car were to continue, this would be a major driver of renewable energy (reducing the use of fossil fuels).

Solar, wind, geothermal, hydropower, ocean power, and bioenergy are all sources of renewable energy. The role of renewables continues to increase in the electricity sector, heating and cooling of real estate, and transport sector.

To show the potential of exponential growth for renewable energy, Rockström and colleagues (2017) determine first that the share of renewables in the

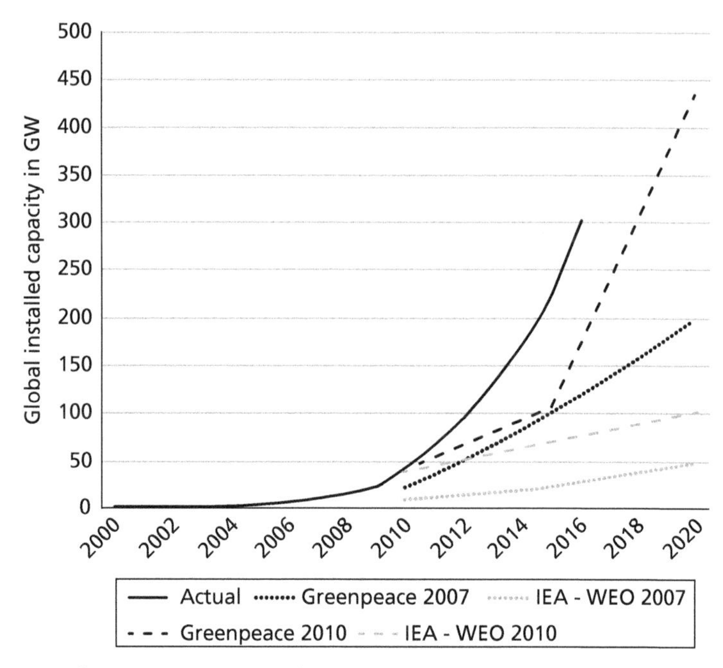

Figure 2.4 Solar power capacity: predictions versus actual

Note: Shows global installed capacity in GW. Depicts forecasts by IEA in its World Energy Outlook (WEO) and Greenpeace in its Energy [R]evolution Report for the use of solar PV and actual use of solar PV. The actual global installed capacity is consistently higher than the forecasts.

Source: Adapted from Greenpeace (2012 and 2015).

energy sector has doubled every 5.5 years based on 2005–15 global trends. Next, they estimate that keeping the doubling time constant in the next three decades would yield full decarbonization (grey area in Figure 2.5) in the entire energy sector by around 2040, with coal use ending around 2030–35 and oil use in 2040–45.

Another way of presenting exponential growth or decline is framing the decarbonization challenge in terms of a global decadal roadmap based on a simple rule of thumb or 'carbon law' of halving gross carbon emissions every decade (Rockström et al. 2017). Figure 2.6 illustrates how such a global carbon law of halving emissions each decade can lead to net-zero emissions around mid-century, a path necessary to limit global warming to well below 2°C.

There is also a dark side to technological change. Weitzman (2013) warns against geoengineering, which is a deliberate large-scale intervention in the Earth's natural systems to counteract climate change. This is an easy and fast way to reduce global temperatures. An example of geoengineering is spraying sulphate aerosols into the atmosphere. This would mimic the reflective particles released from volcanic eruptions, cooling the planet and returning us to

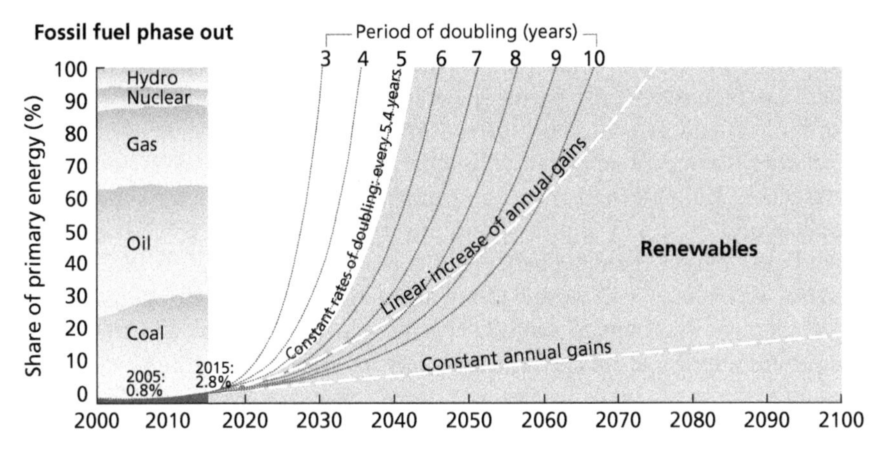

Figure 2.5 Non-linear renewable energy expansion trajectories

Note: Non-linear renewable energy expansion trajectories are based on 2005–15 global trends. Keeping the historical doubling times of around 5.5 years constant in the next three decades would yield full decarbonization (grey area) in the entire energy sector by around 2040.

Source: Rockström et al. (2017).

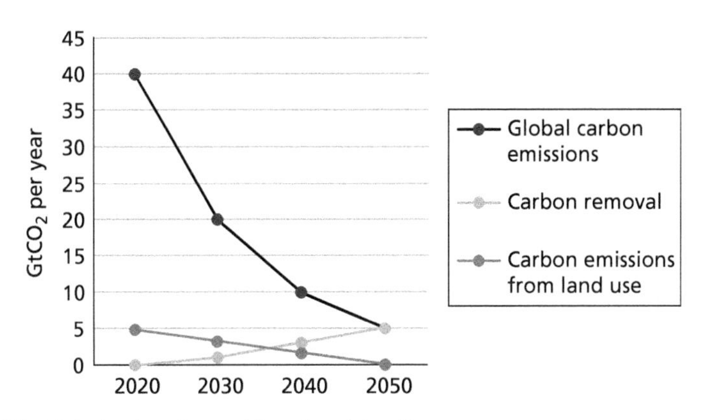

Figure 2.6 Global carbon law guiding decadal pathways

Note: The decadal staircase follows a global 'carbon law' of halving emissions every decade and a complementary fall in land-use emissions, plus it ramps up CO_2 removal technologies.

Source: Adapted from Rockström et al. (2017).

pre-industrial temperatures. Such a project would be cheap: one ton of sulphur dioxide would be sufficient to cancel out the climate effects of almost 30,000 tons of carbon dioxide. Due to the affordability of this project, any single country could unilaterally undertake a geoengineering project. The ease with which geoengineering could be used is, however, a major drawback at the same time. Even if the technology were used responsibly, the aerosols would do nothing to halt ocean acidification and a myriad of other problems associated with carbon emissions. Furthermore, if the aerosol spraying was halted for some reason, the particles would be washed out of the sky within a month or so, and global temperatures would skyrocket faster than ever.

Another source of uncertainty is changes in consumer behaviour and preferences. The determinants of consumers' willingness to buy sustainable products and/or to pay a price premium can change over time. There are several examples of changing behaviour. A well-known example is the decline in social acceptance with regard to buying clothes produced by child labour. These changes can happen swiftly. The introduction of Fairtrade chocolate (minimum wage for small cocoa farmers in West Africa and Latin America) in the late 1990s/early 2000s has led to a rapid consumer adoption. Moreover, there is a circular relationship between production and consumption, as consumers' adoption of low-carbon or clean products is also based on the availability of such products (Ottman, Stafford, and Hartman, 2006).

2.4.2 THE USE OF SCENARIO ANALYSIS

Scenario analysis is a powerful tool to get insight in the possible development of externalities when there is a significant amount of uncertainty. It is a process of analysing possible future events by considering alternative possible outcomes (sometimes called 'alternative worlds'). Thus, scenario analysis, which is one of the main forms of projection, does not try to show one exact picture of the future but alternative scenarios. Another method to deal with uncertainty is stochastic simulation. However, this method can only be used when detailed market data are available and new risks, such as environmental risks, are not (yet) fully priced in (Lo, 2017).

Bianchini and Gianfrate (2018) show how scenario analysis can be applied to corporate valuation for investment purposes. Scenario-based valuation requires at least two scenarios, but very often consist of three (or more): a best case, a most likely case, and a worse case. The number of scenarios should be based on how different the scenarios are, how accurately they can be 'forecasted', and the available amount of time and resources for preparing them. De Ruijter (2014) proposes a strategic approach when creating scenarios for an organization, using the following steps:

1. **Determine the most important uncertainties** for the future and put them into a framework. This can be two axes representing two key uncertainties, but also a decision tree containing the most important questions for the future.
2. **Elaborate the scenarios**: fill them in with the developments, trends, uncertainties, and possible actions of actors from the transactional environment, until each scenario forms a plausible and relevant whole leading to new insights.

3. **Re-present the scenarios** to make possible future situations and the path leading there appealing stories.

Analyst reports are the 'fortune tellers' of the investment communities. They form the underlying analytical basis of many investment decisions and DCF methodology (see Chapter 8 for more details) is used in most analyst reports. And in turn, DCF requires a forecast of future inward CFs, outward CFs, and the terminal value of the investment beyond the projection period (see Figure 2.7). Next, the impact on the risk premium needs to be determined to calculate the discount rate (which is the sum of the risk-free rate and the risk premium). For private investors, more risk or uncertainty leads to a higher discount rate.

This DCF methodology relies on multiyear forecasts. And all forecasting methods, including the use of expert judgement, statistical extrapolation, Delphi and prediction markets, contain fundamental weaknesses (De Ruijter, 2017). Forecasting is not meant to highlight the potentially high impact of rare events. Forecasting often has the explicit assumption of *ceteris paribus* or 'all else is equal', but what if all else is not equal?

We are coming from a period in which externalities are largely not internalized. Forecasting models based on historical data thus underestimate future disruptions, if these externalities become internalized (i.e. *ceteris* non *paribus*). What is the probability of a carbon price of $100? On historical frequency, which is backward looking, the probability is 0 per cent, as it has not happened. But given the political commitments (see Section 2.4.3), this probability is

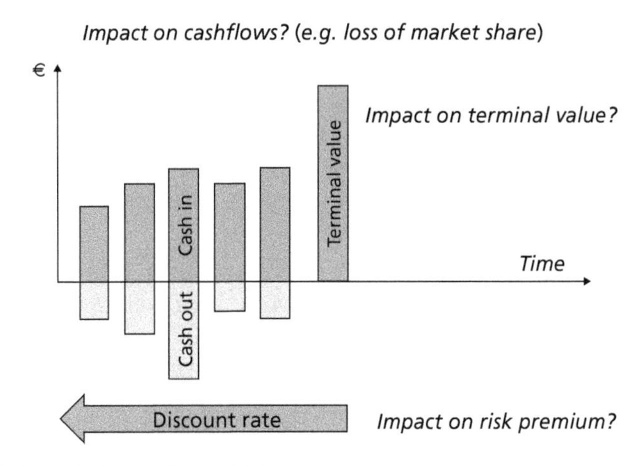

Figure 2.7 Impact of scenarios on DCFs

Note: In each scenario, the impact of the factors on cash flows, terminal value, and risk premium is calculated.

Source: De Ruijter (2017).

positive. The Bayesian probability can be estimated using all available information on, for example, political commitments, changing attitudes towards carbon pricing in society, and new technologies. This is a forward-looking approach, highlighting the downward and upward risks.

The final step is to synthesize the scenario results by weighting the probabilities attached to each scenario, which add up to 100 per cent. In a three-scenario setting, a conceivable assumption is that the most likely scenario has 50 per cent probability and the other two scenarios 25 per cent each. In an example in Section 2.4.3, we show the working of scenario analysis.

2.4.3 CLIMATE MITIGATION SCENARIOS

To illustrating the working of scenario analysis, we apply it to the impact of climate policy on the valuation of a major oil company. In the recent Paris Agreement on climate change, countries have reconfirmed the target of limiting the rise in global average temperatures relative to those prevailing in the pre-industrial world to 2°C and to pursue efforts to limit the temperature increase to 1.5°C. Meeting such targets requires ensuring that the stock of CO_2 and other greenhouse gases in the atmosphere do not exceed a certain limit. The Intergovernmental Panel on Climate Change (IPCC, 2014) estimates that the remaining carbon budget amounts to 900 $GtCO_2$ from 2015 onwards. The speed with which the limit is reached depends on the path of emissions. If current emissions are not drastically cut, the 2°C limit would be reached by 2035 (see vertical dotted line in Figure 2.8).

There are many uncertainties with regard to climate change. First of all, will the world succeed in limiting climate change to 1.5–2 degrees? If so, with what energy system? What role will energy saving, carbon capture and storage, and the different forms of renewable energy play in this? The future of technological innovation is inherently uncertain as is the political will of the global community to address climate change. Public policy is also a driver of technological change, for instance through the amount of R&D invested and as a market maker for clean tech.

Different scenarios are possible, based on the different moment that governments start implementing effective environment policies (Advisory Scientific Committee, 2016). If governments manage an early transition with substantial cuts in carbon emissions starting in 2020, a 'soft landing' is likely (the first dashed curve in Figure 2.8). The 'orderly transition' to a low-carbon economy would be gradual, allowing adequate time for the physical capital stock to be replenished and for technological progress to endogenously contribute to keeping energy costs at bearable levels. The adverse scenario is one of late adjustment starting in 2030, resulting in a 'hard landing' (the last dotted

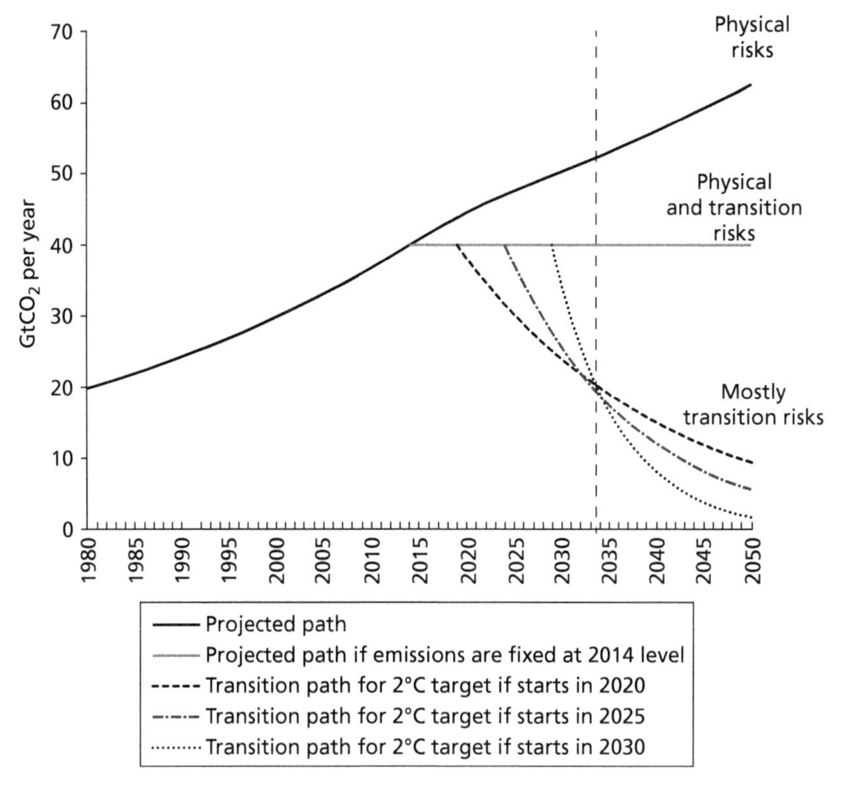

Figure 2.8 Possible trajectories of carbon emissions

Source: Prudential Regulation Authority (2015).

curve in Figure 2.8). In this scenario, the underlying political economy—that is, the short-term political costs of the transition combined with the need for global coordination of emission cuts—leads to belated and sudden implementation of constraints on the use of carbon-intensive energy. This back-loaded policy intervention will force more severe immediate reductions in emissions.

A portfolio manager or loan officer needs to make an assessment of the impact on his entire investment portfolio or loan book in each scenario. In a scenario with government-imposed carbon taxes, for example, the impact is not confined to the big oil companies or utilities that supply electricity. Figure 2.9 indicates that the transport sector—cars, lorries, and airplanes—is responsible for a large part of carbon emissions. Next, real estate, both residential houses and commercial offices, use fossil fuels for heating and cooling. Finally, a substantial proportion of the manufacturing industry is dependent on fossil fuels. All these sectors, which form a large part of the value added in the economy, are thus affected by potential carbon taxes.

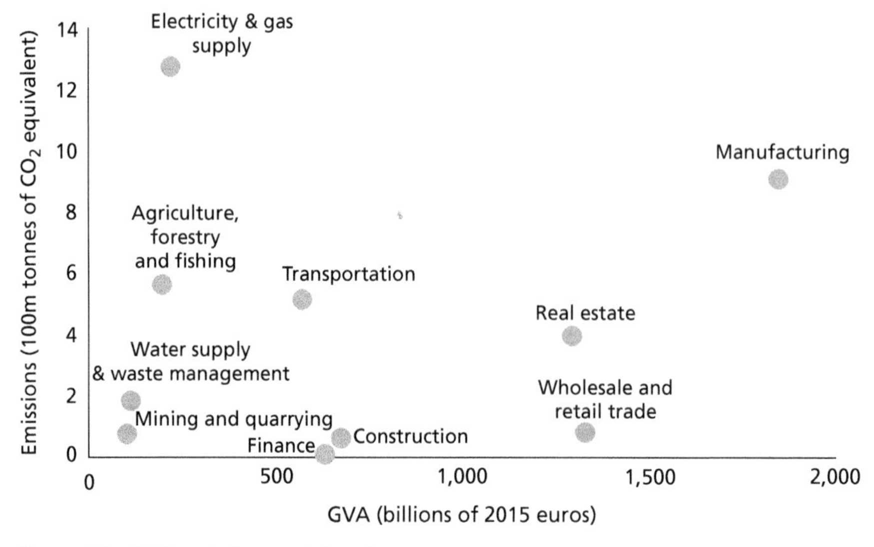

Figure 2.9 GHG emissions and GVA by sector, EU

Note: This graph shows greenhouse gas emissions. Real estate emissions include heating and cooling. GVA is gross value added, taken from Eurostat.

Source: Schoenmaker and Van Tilburg (2016).

Table 2.2 Assumptions used in scenarios

Scenario	Oil price	Cost	EBIT margin
Business as usual	$60 + 2% annual price inflation	2% annual cost inflation	18%
Transition from 2020	As business as usual, but 4% net drop per 2020	2% annual cost inflation; no offset of 2020 price drop	18% until 2019; 13% from 2020
Transition from 2025	As business as usual, but 10% net drop per 2025	2% annual cost inflation; no offset of 2025 price drop	18% until 2024; 7% from 2025
Transition from 2030	As business as usual, but 20% net drop per 2030	2% annual cost inflation; no offset of 2030 price drop	18% until 2029; –4% from 2030

2.4.3.1 Example of impact on an oil company

We can apply these scenarios, as well as a naive 'business-as-usual scenario' to a fictive oil company. We make the following assumptions in Table 2.2. All scenarios start from a $60 oil price in 2018 with 2 per cent annual inflation in both the oil price and the company's cost base. The scenarios are exactly the

Table 2.3 Valuations calculated for scenarios

Scenario	Fair stock price	Upside
Business as usual	$163	30%
Transition from 2020	$115	-8%
Transition from 2025	$94	-25%
Transition from 2030	$0	-100%

same in most other respects (volumes sold, capital expenditures (CAPEX)/ sales, number of shares, leverage, etc.). But they differ in terms of the assumed price shock—driven by the introduction of carbon prices. In the business-as-usual scenario, no carbon price is introduced at all as it is miraculously deemed not necessary. In the three transition scenarios, carbon prices are introduced with varying degrees of speed and shock, that is, early but gradually in the transition from 2020 (allowing the oil company to adapt better) and late but more radically in the transition from 2030 (giving the oil company no chance to recover). This explains the differences in earnings before interest and taxes (EBIT) margins in the four scenarios.

The price shock due to carbon pricing results in the valuations in Table 2.3 (based on a net present value (NPV) analysis, see Chapter 8 for an explanation and examples of NPV analyses) and price upside given the stock's current $126 price.

So, the oil company looks cheap in the business-as-usual scenario, but overvalued (to differing degrees) in the other scenarios. In the transition from 2030 scenario, the company's margins go negative and its terminal value goes negative as well. If that scenario were to happen, the company would go bankrupt and the stock would go to zero. The late transition is the riskiest, as it leads to the steepest drop in oil price and gives the oil company less time to transition towards renewable energies, leading to more stranded assets.

But when would that be priced in? First, there would be several years of good margins and CFs. And more generally: What scenario will happen? And what is the right price for the stock? That all depends. One could arrive at a fair value for the stock by attaching probabilities to the four scenarios. As the left part of Table 2.4 shows, assuming equal probabilities for all four scenarios results in a fair value of $93. The risk is then 26 per cent undervalued at the current price of $126.

Alternatively, one could ask what kind of probabilities the current stock price implies—and the right side of Table 2.4 indicates that the $126 stock price implies a 60 per cent chance of business as usual versus 13–14 per cent for each of the other scenarios. If you feel (like we do) that a 60 per cent of business as usual is an overestimation, then the stock is overpriced.

Table 2.4 Probabilities applied to scenarios

Scenario	Fair stock price	Probability	Weighted price	Probability	Weighted price
Business as usual	$163	25%	$41	60%	$98
Transition from 2020	$115	25%	$29	14%	$16
Transition from 2025	$94	25%	$23	13%	$12
Transition from 2030	$0	25%	$0	13%	$0
Total		100%	$93	100%	$126

Focusing on just one of these four scenarios (implicitly attaching a 100 per cent probability to it) could be a dangerous simplification. Of course, all of this analysis is highly simplified. Many other scenarios could occur. Also, the analysis does not take into account the management's reactions to (anticipated) changes in oil prices, such as cuts or raises in investments, which might ameliorate or worsen the outcomes. The worst outcome for the oil company would be that it continued to believe in business as usual even after a price shock happened—rationalizing it with the fact that in the past oil prices always recovered eventually—albeit after many companies had gone bankrupt.

Reviewing the options, the oil company can, for example, reconsider its business-as-usual strategy and start replacing its ongoing investment (CAPEX) in traditional upstream and downstream facilities by investment in renewables. The analysis in this example of a fictive oil company shows that scenario analysis can be a very valuable tool with which to consider various scenarios and their probabilities.

2.4.4 STRESS TESTING

Central banks and supervisors conduct stress tests of the financial sector, using extreme scenarios, to identify tail risks in the financial system. A case in point is a carbon stress test, which measures the exposure of financials to carbon emissions in their investment and lending portfolio (ASC, 2016; Schoenmaker and Van Tilburg, 2016). The outcome of these stress tests can raise awareness of exposure to major environmental externalities and prompt financial firms to mitigate such exposures. Thomä and Dupre (2017) argue that traditional stress tests based on macro-economic scenarios and a three-year horizon underestimate the transition risk to a carbon-neutral economy. They rightly argue that the impact of climate factors needs to be analysed at the sector level and with longer horizons of up to 20 years, as some physical assets have maturities of 20 years or longer.

Battiston and colleagues (2017) conducted a climate stress test of the financial system. In line with our argument to include all carbon-intensive sectors (see Figure 2.9), they carried out a network analysis of the exposures of financial firms to all climate-relevant sectors. Climate mitigation policies will adversely affect equity holdings in climate-relevant sectors (as equity absorbs losses in the first instance) but less so debt holdings (bonds and loans). The impact of climate policies on assets invested in energy-intensive activities can in principle be either positive or negative depending on the energy source and the technologies used in the production process. Further, in other sectors such as housing, climate policies, and, in particular, energy efficiency, policies can result in an increase or decrease of property values according to the energy source used for heating and electricity and the level of compliance with building requirements on energy-efficiency.

Using empirical data of the Euro area, Battiston and colleagues (2017) show that while direct equity exposures to the fossil fuel sector are small (3–12 per cent of financial firms' market capitalization), the combined equity exposures to climate-policy relevant sectors are large (40–54 per cent) and heterogeneous. The direct exposures are amplified by second-round effects (i.e. indirect exposures to failing financial counterparties in the first round) of 30–40 per cent. These results suggest that climate policies could result in potential winners and losers across financial firms and would not have an adverse systemic impact as long as they are implemented early on and within a stable framework.

Next, Battiston and colleagues (2017) provided the following aggregate exposures on loans as a fraction of banks' capital: fossil and utilities = 11 per cent; energy-intensive = 28 per cent; transport = 16 per cent; and housing (including mortgages) = 281 per cent. Climate policies impacting on the energy-intensive, transport, and/or housing sector would imply increased volatility on large portions of bank loans.

Finally, the question arises of how financial supervisors should treat low-carbon (green) and high-carbon (brown) assets in the *capital adequacy framework*, which determines how much equity capital a bank has to hold against risk-weighted assets. Box 2.4 discusses the proposal of a higher risk weight for brown assets (see also Chapter 10).

2.5 **Conclusions**

This chapter analyses social and environmental externalities, which are absent in the traditional production function. We show how social and natural capital can be incorporated into our decision-making. But what mechanisms can be used to address these important external effects, which affect other parties, without these effects being priced in the market?

BOX 2.4 A BROWN CAPITAL CHARGE?

Runaway climate change is the ultimate systemic risk for banks. To discourage lending to brown assets, a differentiated *capital treatment* of green and brown assets would be helpful. The question is whether green assets should get a lower risk weight or brown assets a higher risk weight.

The European Commissioner Valdis Dombrovskis has announced that he will 'look positively' at a 'green support factor' for bank lending (High-Level Expert Group on Sustainable Finance, 2018). However, Boot and Schoenmaker (2018) argue that it is a bad idea to grant banks extra-low levels of capital if something is 'green'; realizing the extra risk of 'brown' does not make 'green' extra-safe. Endorsing 'lowering capital requirements for certain climate-friendly investments, such as energy-efficient mortgages or electric cars' is asking banks to turn a blind eye on proper risk management, as it is not clear which green technologies will win (i.e. business risk).

Both sides agree that climate risks are material for banks and need to be taken into account in setting capital requirements. Currently this is not the case—an increasingly important risk factor is neglected. Instead of the 'green supporting factor', Boot and Schoenmaker (2018) argue that a much stronger case can be made for a 'brown penalising factor' for fossil-fuel-intensive and -dependent assets. Not only does it give lenders the capacity to withstand losses when the energy transition accelerates, a brown penalizing factor will also discourage further investments that contribute to climate change. Thus the systemic risk of climate change itself would be reduced.

Preferably this would be done through the first pillar of the capital regulation framework that sets minimum capital requirements (Boot and Schoenmaker, 2018). Climate exposures—proxied by the carbon intensity of assets—should be translated into credit risk. This cannot be done using risk models that are based on historical data, as energy transition is an unprecedented development. Rather, scenario studies should be used to quantify the impact of transition.

A major way to internalize externalities is government regulation and taxation. While there are examples of successful regulation, such as social legislation in the developed world and an international treaty banning CFCs to protect the ozone layer, major social externalities in developing countries as well as environmental externalities are not yet effectively regulated or taxed. In particular, effective policies to curb carbon emissions have been elusive, notwithstanding the Paris Climate Agreement to limit global warming to 2° Celsius, and possibly to 1.5° Celsius. Only a very few countries, such as the Scandinavian countries, have implemented an effective carbon tax of $80 to $100.

Business has started to measure and price externalities, where possible. The integrated value can be calculated by combining financial, social, and environmental values in an integrated way. The monetization of these factors helps businesses optimizing the integrated value, for example, by adapting their production process. As old production processes may become obsolete (leading to stranded assets), it is in a business's self-interest to adopt more sustainable practices. Nevertheless, private effort might be insufficient in the absence of government intervention.

The future development of externalities is surrounded by policy and technological uncertainty. Examples of uncertainty are the introduction of carbon taxes overnight by an incoming government, a ban on child labour, an imposition of minimum wages, and a rapid decline in the cost of renewables, such as solar and wind, due to technological innovation (which can grow exponentially). Scenario analysis helps investors to deal with these uncertainties. They can calculate the expected enterprise value of the corporates in which they invest by weighting the discounted CFs under alternative scenarios. Scenario analysis also helps companies to reconsider their strategy and implement actions to prepare for certain situations (as discussed in Chapter 5).

Key concepts used in this chapter

Abiotic resources are non-renewable natural resources, such as mineral resources and fossil fuels; see *natural resources.*

Biological or biotic resources are renewable natural resources obtained from the biosphere, such as timber, animals, fresh water, solar energy, and biomass; see *natural resources.*

Boundary problem indicates that when regulation for one sector is tightened, business will shift to other sectors with less or no requirements.

Capital adequacy requirement is the amount of equity capital a bank has to hold as required by its financial regulator. This is usually expressed as a ratio of equity that a bank must hold as a percentage of risk-weighted assets.

Common good refers to what is shared and beneficial for all or most members of a given community.

Economic imperialism seeks to expand the boundary of the economic system until it encompasses the entire ecosystem of the Earth.

Environmental factors or ecological factors are factors, abiotic or biotic, that influence living organisms; see *planetary boundaries* for the most critical environmental factors.

Emissions trading system, also known as cap-and-trade system, introduces an emission cap (a ceiling on the maximum amount) and permits trading of emission allowances.

Fallacy of composition arises when one concludes that something is true of the whole from the fact that it is true of every part individually.

Externalities refer to consequences of activities that affect other (or third) parties without this being reflected in market prices.

Human capital refers to people's competencies, capabilities, and experience and includes issues such as health and safety, gender equality, training, and job satisfaction.

Integrated value is obtained by combining the financial, social, and environmental values in an integrated way (with regard for the interconnections).

Internalization mechanism refers to a method to 'internalize' or take into account externalities.

Natural resources cover non-renewable or *abiotic resources*, such as mineral resources and fossil fuels, and renewable or *biological resources*, such as timber, fresh water, solar energy, and biomass.

Regulatory quotas are government-imposed limits on quantity.

Pigouvian tax is a tax levied on a market activity that generates negative externalities. The tax is intended to correct an inefficient market outcome and does so by being set equal to the social cost of the negative externalities.

Scenario analysis is a process of analysing possible future events by considering alternative possible outcomes.

Social and relationship capital covers social activities, nuisances, or contributions to local communities and relationships within and between communities.

Stranded assets refer to assets that lose their value. This term is often used for fossil fuel assets, which may become stranded due to government regulation or technological change. It is more widely applicable to carbon-intensive assets or other assets, such as land, which may become stranded due to soil erosion.

SUGGESTED READING

Daly, H. and J. Farley (2011), *Ecological Economics: Principles and Applications*, Island Press, Washington DC.

Dasgupta, P. and P. Ehrlich (2013), 'Pervasive externalities at the population, consumption, and environment nexus', *Science*, 340(6130): 324–8.

Ruijter, P. de (2014), *Scenario Based Strategy: Navigate the Future*, Gower Publishing, Farnham.

Stern, N. (2008), 'The economics of climate change', *American Economic Review: Papers and Proceedings*, 98(2): 1–37.

Sukhdev, P. (2008), 'The economics of ecosystems and biodiversity (TEEB)', Interim Report.

Sukhdev, P. (2011), 'The economics of ecosystems and biodiversity (TEEB)', Final Report.

True Price (2014), 'The business case for true pricing: why you will benefit from measuring, monetizing and improving your impact', Report drafted by True Price, Deloitte, EY, and PwC, 2nd edn, Amsterdam, http://trueprice.org/wp-content/uploads/2015/02/True-Price-Report-The-Business-Case-for-True-Pricing.pdf, accessed 25 June 2018.

REFERENCES

Acemoglu, D., P. Aghion, L. Bursztyn, and D. Hemous (2012), 'The environment and directed technical change', *American Economic Review*, 102(1): 131–66.

Åkerfeldt, S. and H. Hammar (2015), 'CO_2 taxation in Sweden: experiences of the past and future challenges', *Revue Projet Journal* 2015–09.

ASC (Advisory Scientific Committee) (2016), 'Too late, too sudden: transition to a low-carbon economy and systemic risk', Report No. 6 of the Advisory Scientific Committee of the European Systemic Risk Board, Frankfurt.

Barrett, S. (2008), 'Climate treaties and the imperative of enforcement', *Oxford Review of Economic Policy*, 24(2): 239–58.

Battiston, S., A. Mandel, I. Monasterolo, F. Schütze, and G. Visentin (2017), 'A climate stress-test of the financial system', *Nature Climate Change*, 7(4): 283–8.

Bianchini, R. and G. Gianfrate (2018), 'Climate Risk and the Practice of Corporate Valuation', in: S. Boubaker, D. Cummings, and D. Nguyen (eds.), *Research Handbook of Finance and Sustainability*, Edward Elgar, Cheltenham, ch. 23.

Boot, A. and D. Schoenmaker (2018), 'Climate change adds to risk for banks, but EU lending proposals will do more harm than good', Bruegel Blogpost, 16 January, Brussels.

Busch, T., R. Bauer, and M. Orlitzky (2016), 'Sustainable development and financial markets', *Business and Society*, 55(3): 303–29.

Caldecott, B., J. Tilbury, and C. Carey (2014), 'Stranded assets and scenarios', Discussion Paper, Smith School of Enterprise and the Environment, University of Oxford, Oxford.

Coady, D., I. Parry, L. Sears, and B. Shang (2017), 'How large are global fossil fuel subsidies?', *World Development*, 91: 11–27.

Cobb, C. and P. Douglas (1928), 'A theory of production', *American Economic Review*, 18 (Supplement): 139–65.

Coulson, A. (2016), 'KPMG's True Value methodology: a critique of economic reasoning on the value companies create and reduce for society', *Sustainability Accounting, Management and Policy Journal*, 7(4): 517–30.

Daly, H. and J. Farley (2011), *Ecological Economics: Principles and Applications*, Island Press, Washington DC.

Dyllick, T. and K. Muff (2016), 'Clarifying the meaning of sustainable business introducing a typology from business-as-usual to true business sustainability', *Organization and Environment*, 29(2): 156–74.

Ferwerda, W. (2016), '4 returns, 3 zones, 20 years: a holistic framework for ecological restoration by people and business for next generations', RSM Series on Positive Change, Rotterdam School of Management, Erasmus University, http://events.globallandscapesforum.org/wp-content/uploads/sites/2/2017/11/4-Returns-3-Zones-20-Years-A-Holistic-Framework-for-Ecological-Restoration-by-People-and-Business-for-Next-Generations.pdf, accessed 27 June 2018.

Goodhart, C. (2008), 'The boundary problem in financial regulation', *National Institute Economic Review*, 206: 48–55.

Graedel, T., J. Allwood, J.-P. Birat, M. Buchert, C. Hagelüken, B. Reck, S. Sibley, and G. Sonnemann (2011), 'What do we know about metal recycling rates?', *Journal of Industrial Ecology*, 15(3): 355–66.

Greenpeace (2012), 'Energy (r)evolution: a sustainable world energy outlook 2012', Amsterdam.
Greenpeace (2015), 'Energy (r)evolution: a sustainable world energy outlook 2015', Amsterdam.
High-Level Expert Group on Sustainable Finance (2018), 'Financing a sustainable European economy', Final Report, European Union, Brussels.
IEA (International Energy Agency) (2016), 'Key renewable trends', Paris.
IEA (International Energy Agency) (2017), 'Key world energy statistics 2017', Paris.
IPBES (Intergovernmental Science-Policy Platform on Biodiversity and Ecosystem Services) (2018), 'Worsening worldwide land degradation now "critical", undermining well-being of 3.2 billion people', Bonn.
IPCC (Intergovernmental Panel on Climate Change) (2014), 'Fifth assessment synthesis report', New York.
KPMG (2014), 'A new vision of value: connecting corporate and societal value creation', Amsterdam, https://assets.kpmg.com/content/dam/kpmg/pdf/2014/10/a-new-vision-of-value-v1.pdf, accessed 27 June 2018.
Lo, A. (2017), *Adaptive Markets: Financial Evolution at the Speed of Thought*, Princeton University Press, Princeton, NJ.
Meinert, L., G. Robinson Jr, and N. Nassar (2016), 'Mineral resources: reserves, peak production and the future', *Resources*, 5(1): 14.
Ottman, J., E. Stafford, and C. Hartman (2006), 'Avoiding green marketing myopia: ways to improve consumer appeal for environmentally preferable products', *Environment: Science and Policy for Sustainable Development*, 48(5): 22–36.
Porritt, J. (2007), *Capitalism as if the World Matters*, Earthscan, Abingdon.
Prudential Regulation Authority (2015), 'The impact of climate change on the UK insurance sector', Bank of England, London, https://www.bankofengland.co.uk/-/media/boe/files/prudential-regulation/publication/impact-of-climate-change-on-the-uk-insurance-sector.pdf, accessed 27 June 2018.
Rockström, J., O. Gaffney, J. Rogelj, M. Meinshausen, N. Nakicenovic, and H. Schellnhuber (2017), 'A roadmap for rapid decarbonization', *Science*, 355(6331): 1269–71.
Ruijter, P. de (2014), *Scenario Based Strategy: Navigate the Future*, Gower Publishing, Farnham.
Ruijter, P. de (2017), 'Valuing uncertainty using disruptive scenarios and real options', *VBA Journaal*, 33(130): 6–9.
Schoenmaker, D. and R. van Tilburg (2016), 'What role for financial supervisors in addressing environmental risks?', *Comparative Economic Studies*, 58(3): 317–34.
Stern, N. (2008), 'The economics of climate change', *American Economic Review: Papers and Proceedings*, 98(2): 1–37.
Stern, N. (2015), *Why Are We Waiting? The Logic, Urgency, and Promise of Tackling Climate Change*, MIT Press, Cambridge, MA.
Stiglitz, J. and N. Stern (2017), 'Report of the High-Level Commission on Carbon Prices', World Bank Carbon Pricing Leadership Coalition, Washington DC, 29 May.
Thomä, J. and S. Dupre (2017), 'Right direction, wrong equipment: why transitions risks do not fit into regulatory stress tests', Discussion Paper, 2° Investing Initiative, London.

Tirole, J. (2017), *Economics for the Common Good*, Princeton University Press, Princeton, NJ.

True Price (2014), 'The business case for true pricing: why you will benefit from measuring, monetizing and improving your impact', Report drafted by True Price, Deloitte, EY, and PwC, 2nd edn, Amsterdam, http://trueprice.org/wp-content/uploads/2015/02/True-Price-Report-The-Business-Case-for-True-Pricing.pdf, accessed 25 June 2018.

Van der Ploeg, F. and A. Rezai (2017), 'The agnostic's response to climate deniers: price carbon!', CEPR Discussion Paper No. 12468.

Velders, G., S. Andersen, J. Daniel, D. Fahey, and M. McFarland (2007), 'The importance of the Montreal Protocol in protecting climate', *PNAS*, 104(12): 4814–19.

Weitzman, M. (2013), 'The geo-engineered planet', in: I. Palacios-Huerta (ed.), *In One Hundred Years*, MIT Press, Cambridge, MA, 145–64.

World Bank (2016), 'State and trends of carbon pricing 2016', Washington, DC.

Wright, A., K. Smith, and M. Hellowell (2017), 'Policy lessons from health taxes: a systematic review of empirical studies', *BMC Public Health*, 17: 583.

3 Governance and behaviour

Overview

How can corporates steer their business towards sustainable practices? That raises a fundamental question in corporate finance about the objective of the corporate. The current objective is maximizing profit, which boils down to maximizing shareholder value. But the shareholder model is holding companies back from sustainable business practices. An enhanced shareholder view recognizes that it is instrumental to treat the other stakeholders well in order to preserve long-term shareholder value. An alternative view is to broaden the objective of the corporate to optimizing the total or integrated value, which combines financial, social, and environmental values. In that way, the interests of stakeholders are ranked equally.

Such a move to the stakeholder model requires new rules for corporate governance and decision-making on corporate investments to deal with the different interests. Using the total value methodology of Chapter 2, the net present value (NPV) rule can incorporate the social and environmental dimension in its calculation. The sustainability dimension can also be included in executive contracts and compensation. It is, further, important to clarify the fiduciary duty of investors towards their clients. The clarified fiduciary duty encompasses key investment activities, including investment strategy, risk management, asset allocation, governance, and stewardship. Sustainability factors can be incorporated in these activities.

Another obstacle to adopting sustainable practices is short-termism. Short-term market practices are reinforced by the dominance of the efficient markets hypothesis, which has a strong focus on the stock price as a central performance measure for executive and investor performance. Contrary to this neoclassical view, the adaptive markets hypothesis assumes that market efficiency depends on an evolutionary model of individuals adapting to a changing environment. This can explain why new risks, such as carbon risks, are not yet fully priced in.

Possible solutions to counter short-term market practices are a more long-term orientation for the reporting structure (moving away from quarterly reporting), the pay structure for executives (deferred rewards and clawback provisions), and the investment performance horizon (moving away from quarterly benchmarking) and an adoption of incentives for long-term investors. This chapter stresses that these measures need to be designed in an incentive-compatible manner. In this way, executives' and investors' horizons can become more closely aligned and focused on the longer term.

Learning objectives

After you have studied this chapter, you should be able to:

- explain behavioural biases against change;
- understand the changing objective of corporates;
- explain the role of corporate governance steering companies' behaviour;
- explain how markets reinforce short-termism;
- understand the design of incentives for long-term thinking.

3.1 **Behavioural biases against sustainable development**

3.1.1 FROM COMPETITIVE TO COLLABORATIVE CONSUMPTION

The biggest bottleneck for the transition to sustainable development is not technical but societal. Are households and business prepared to change their consumption and production patterns? Responsible consumption and production is a key goal among the 17 Sustainable Development Goals (SDGs). Unbridled consumption leads to depletion or degradation of natural resources. Calculations suggest that if the 6.2 billion people in poor and middle-income countries were to match the consumption patterns of the 1.3 billion people in high-income countries, at least two more Earths would be needed to support everyone on a sustained basis (Dasgupta and Ehrlich, 2013). The consensus among demographers is that world population will be 9.7 billion by 2050 and 11.2 billion by 2100 (World Bank, 2017), making the demands on Earth even more unsustainable.

Current consumption behaviour is based on competitive consumption. Several types of consumption serve as status symbols and there is a tendency for people to try to outdo one another (Dasgupta and Ehrlich, 2013). Competitive consumption (hosting expensive wedding ceremonies and birth celebrations) in developing countries may not have repercussions on the global environment, but it hinders the prospects the poor may have for escaping poverty. In developed countries, competitive consumption has further adverse consequences. Cars, for example, make transportation simple and easy, but choices of the make and vehicle use are driven in many ways by the competitive urge. Moreover, car use is dependent on an underpriced resource: oil. Combining consumption habits and a growing complementary infrastructure (petrol stations, expanded network of highways), we have a spiralling exploitation of natural capital and related environmental externalities. Another consumer habit leading to 'overconsumption' is buying a new model of a consumer good well before the end of the technical lifetime of a currently used consumer good.

Because people try to find ways to relate to one another, they also adopt patterns of consumption that reflect a desire for conformity, not competition. Fads and fashions are brief occurrences, but conformist consumption can be persistent if it serves the need for social belonging. A community may coordinate to settle on one of many alternative behaviour patterns that are ranked identically by all individuals. Presumably, there would be equilibria that are more intensive than others in their use of underpriced natural capital. If each person can be persuaded to believe that others will reduce their consumption of X, every person will follow suit. One way of achieving that assurance would be to nudge one another to opt for a targeted alternative (Dasgupta and Ehrlich, 2013).

A major example of collaborative consumption is the emerging sharing or peer-to-peer economy, whereby participants mutualize access to products or services, rather than having individual ownership. Examples are the sharing (for free or renting out) of cars, bicycles, equipment, houses (Airbnb), and taxis (Uber). The sharing economy may take a variety of forms, including using information technology (i.e. the Internet) to provide individuals with information that enables the optimization of resources through the mutualization of excess capacity in goods and services. A common premise is that when information about goods is shared (typically via an online marketplace), the value of those goods may increase for the business, for individuals, for the community, and for society in general.

3.1.2 BEHAVIOUR OF COMPANIES AND INVESTORS: TOWARDS INTERNATIONALIZATION OF EXTERNALITIES

Chapter 2 shows how business (and households) can measure and monetize externalities. But social and environmental externalities are not static, they can be internalized. What are the mechanisms to internalize these externalities? Table 3.1 provides an overview of the sustainability players, including the instruments at their disposal, forums in which they might work together, and the opportunities and threats they face. While our focus is primarily on the role of companies and investors (asset managers and banks), we also include governments, civil society (non-governmental organizations (NGOs)), and households in Table 3.1 for completeness. The mechanisms

Table 3.1 Players in sustainability

Player	Sphere of influence	Horizon	Mechanisms	Leading organizations and cooperation forums	Opportunities	Threats
Government	Country / global	Up to four years	Strong leadership role • Taxation • Regulation	• United Nations (UN): COP, New York	• Economy-wide impact • Public role in energy and infrastructure	• Shortfall of efforts • Monitoring climate pledges • Policy differences • Free-rider behaviour • Dealing with future generations • Corruption
Civil society	Debate	From MT to LT	Public voice of NGOs • Media • Social capital • Deselection	• Oxfam, Oxford • Amnesty International, London • Greenpeace, Amsterdam • WWF, Washington DC	• Agenda setting • Stimulate citizenship of investors and corporates	• Single issue • Fragmentation • Dependent on goodwill of (local) government
Corporates	Value chain of production	From MT to LT	Key players for transformation • Procurement • Production process	• WEF, Davos • WBCSD, Geneva	• Reputation building • Sound and stable business practices	• Shortfall of efforts • Short-termism: quarterly reporting; shareholder value thinking • Lobbying for status quo • Reliable IR • Relocating production to less strict countries
Investors	Investments	From ST to LT	Long-term investors • Investment strategy • Lending strategy • Engagement	• PRI, London • FCLTGlobal, Boston • GIIN, New York • GABV, Zeist • Equator Principles, London	• Stimulate corporate sustainability • Stewardship and engagement	• Shortfall of efforts • Short-termism: monthly/quarterly benchmarking • Long investment chain • Marking to market • Supervisory treatment of illiquid investments • Alternative sources of finance: retained earnings, non-responsible investors • Monitoring
Households	Consumption	From ST to LT	Ultimate beneficiaries • Buying decisions • Sharing economy • Electing government	Consumer associations	• Steer corporates, utilities, housing • Steer investments • Vote for policies	• Poverty • Lack of trust in government • Environmental degradation • Free-rider behaviour • Human aversion to change

Note: Only a few of the main cooperation forums or large players are listed for illustration purposes. COP = Conference of the Parties (governed by the UN); WWF = World Wildlife Fund; WEF = World Economic Forum; WBCSD = World Business Council for Sustainable Development; PRI = Principles for Responsible Investment (supported by the UN); FCLTGlobal = Focus Capital on the Long-Term Global; GIIN = Global Impact Investing Network; GABV = Global Alliance for Banking on Values; ST = short term; MT = medium term; LT = long term.

for fostering sustainability are easy to understand, such as taxation for government, sustainable production process for companies, or responsible buying decisions for consumers. But there is a big difference between understanding social and environmental externalities and acting on them (i.e. internalizing them). Sections 3.2 to 3.3 explore incentives or opportunities to act.

Moreover, there are strong forces to maintain the status quo, such as lobbying by incumbent companies against change in order to preserve the current value of their assets. A case in point is the lobby of the oil industry against electric cars in California in the 1990s, which was documented in the 2006 film *Who Killed the Electric Car?* (Bedsworth and Taylor, 2007). Another example is the lobbying of the energy-intensive steel industry against the EU's Emissions Trading Scheme. More broadly, the Global Climate Coalition was an international lobbyist group of businesses from 1989 to 2001 that opposed action to reduce carbon emissions and challenged the science behind global warming. Similarly, the Council for Tobacco Research promoted misleading science about the links between tobacco and disease. NGOs, such as the Climate Action Network, play a key role in making counter-arguments, although they cannot match company budgets for lobbying. Another solution is for investors (as part of shareholder engagement) to engage with companies, requesting them to stop their lobby, and, if not successful, to exclude lobbying companies.

Next, companies have behavioural biases, which may lead to corporate scandals. There is no superior corporate governance model, as corporate scandals can and do happen in all major regions. Examples are Enron in the United States, Volkswagen in Europe, and Olympus in Japan (see Box 3.1). These corporate scandals reveal classical agency problems in companies, whereby management has several ways to boost profits and hide problems. The main corporate governance models to mitigate these agency problems are discussed in Section 3.3.

Finally, investors are also subject to behavioural biases, which reinforce current practices. Assets are typically priced as an extrapolation of the recent past, while the value in the long term or the terminal value of projects may be different. Changes, if at all considered, are typically gradual, while revolutionary changes to business models and phase transitions happen and look logical in hindsight. In their seminal work *Superforecasting: The Art and Science of Prediction*, Tetlock and Gardner (2015) use psychology, political science, and the wisdom of crowds to predict possible outcomes of an election, an economic crisis, or even a war. Moreover, *scenario analysis* is a major tool to broaden (and lengthen) the horizon and explore future possible outcomes, as explained in Chapter 2.

How can financial firms steer business towards sustainable practices? That is ultimately a question of governance. The changes require adopting social

BOX 3.1 CORPORATE SCANDALS ACROSS THE WORLD

The collapse of Enron in 2001, the largest corporate bankruptcy at the time in American history, involved the use of accounting loopholes, special purpose entities, and poor financial reporting. In that way, the management (i.e. the chief executive officer and the chief financial officer) of the energy company was able to book energy sales as revenues and hide billions of dollars in debt from failed deals and projects. These practices inflated Enron's accounts and performance. The bankruptcy of Enron also led to the closure of its accountant, Arthur Andersen.

Moving to the German carmaker Volkswagen, the US Environmental Protection Agency found in 2015 that many diesel VW cars being sold in America had a 'defeat device' (software) in their engines that could detect when they were being tested, changing the performance accordingly to improve results. Volkswagen made a major push to sell diesel cars in the USA, backed by a huge marketing campaign proclaiming its cars' low emissions. Volkswagen admitted cheating emissions tests in the USA and paid billions in damages. As a response, there was a major overhaul of VW's management board.

The Olympus scandal started in October 2011 when Michael Woodford was suddenly ousted as chief executive of the international optical equipment manufacturer, Olympus Corporation, when he exposed 'one of the biggest and longest-running loss-hiding arrangements in Japanese corporate history'. Irregular payments for acquisitions had resulted in very significant asset impairment charges in the company's accounts. The corruption scandal involved concealment of more than 117.7 billion yen ($1.5 billion) of investment losses and other dubious fees as well as suspicion of covert payments to criminal organizations. By 2012 the scandal had developed into one of the biggest loss-concealing financial scandals in the history of corporate Japan and had wiped 75 to 80 per cent off the company's stock market valuation. It led to the resignation of much of the board.

and environmental factors in decision-making (Sections 3.2 to 3.3) and moving decision-making from short to long term (Section 3.4). Figure 3.1 highlights these challenges for the shift from traditional finance (the top left cell) to sustainable finance (SF) (covering all nine cells).

3.2 What is the objective of the corporation?

To discuss the role of corporates in sustainable development, we first need to establish the objective of the corporate. The classical shareholder model in finance argues that corporates should maximize shareholder value (e.g. Jensen, 2002). By contrast, the stakeholder model argues that large companies should act in the interests of a broader group of agents than just their shareholders and optimize stakeholder value (e.g. Magill, Quinzii, and Rochet, 2015). The choice of the value maximization function has also consequences for decision-making on corporate investment.

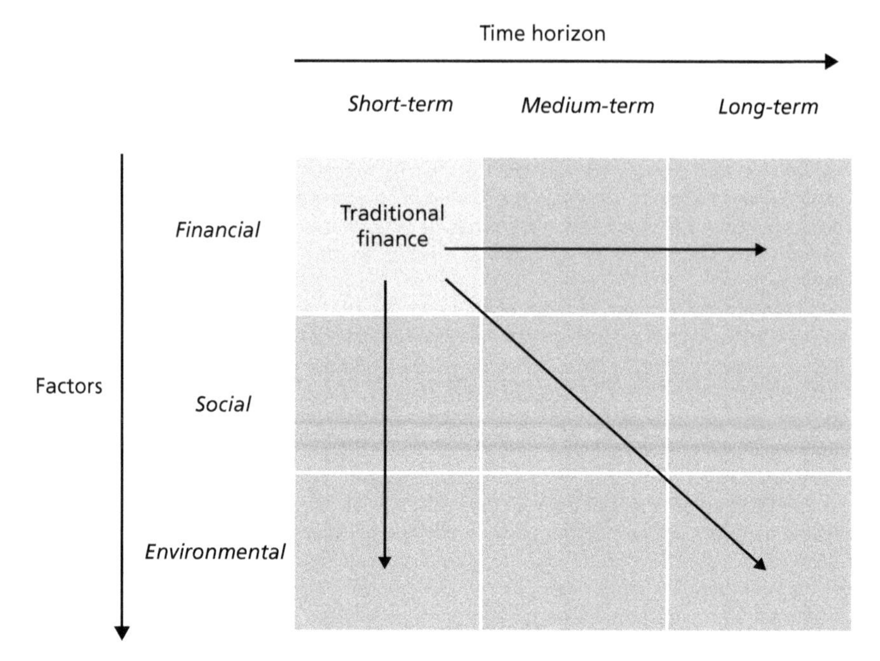

Figure 3.1 Time horizon and factors in SF

Source: Sikken (2014).

3.2.1 SHAREHOLDER MODEL

Shareholders are residual, non-contractual claimants (Jensen and Meckling, 1976). They get paid after all contractual claims to other stakeholders, such as creditors, employees, customers, government, are met. Shareholders thus maximize financial consideration, after the other stakeholders are satisfied. Mehrotra and Morck (2017) discuss several challenges to this shareholder view: contractual issues, public policy, and business ethics.

First, it is difficult to incorporate all possible future circumstances in contracts with stakeholders. Unforeseen circumstances, including externalities, can happen, which give rise to the notion of incomplete contracts (Grossman and Hart, 1986; Hart and Moore, 1990). In such cases, the shareholder interest would override the interests of the other stakeholders in the shareholder model.

Secondly, stakeholders, as organized groups, are better able to lobby government for public policy to address their interests, including externalities, than shareholders, who are dispersed and face the free-riding problem in organizing themselves (Mehrotra and Morck, 2017). According to this view, within public policy stakeholder interests are better covered than shareholder interests. However, major externalities, such as environmental and social (in particular in outsourced production) concerns, are not fully incorporated in public policy.

Thirdly, business ethics concerns are a final line of defence for stakeholders (Mehrotra and Morck, 2017). Obeying the letter of the law regarding the rights of stakeholders can pit shareholder value maximization against social welfare. Where externalities are important, a narrow focus on shareholder value can create scope for managers to make morally dubious decisions. For example, maximizing shareholder value ex ante might justify cutting costs and entertaining acceptably small risks of environmental disasters. Even if such a disaster triggers legal actions that bankrupt the committing corporate, its shareholders are protected by limited liability and so lose only the value of their shares.

Such disasters might be discouraged by exposing directors to personal liability should they occur. But directors usually have liability insurance (see Chapter 11), which limits their personal exposure. Shapira and Zingales (2017) examine why different mechanisms of control, such as legal liability, regulation, and reputation, can all fail to deter socially harmful behaviour. One common reason for the failures of deterrence mechanisms is that the company controls most of the information and its release.

The key question of how to rank shareholder and other stakeholder interests remains. Should shareholder interests come first, or should all interests be put on equal footing?

3.2.2 REFINED SHAREHOLDER VALUE MODEL

Although the shareholder model cannot fully satisfy the interests of stakeholders, there are also problems with stakeholder theory. The manager has to serve all interests. Otherwise, they could design their own objective functions and run their corporations in their own interests (Jensen, 2002). Stakeholder theory thus leaves managers unaccountable, as simultaneously optimizing several objectives is difficult to measure and control.

Jensen (2002) argues that firm value maximization (or shareholder value maximization) is best achieved in practice by catering to all stakeholders—an approach he calls enlightened value maximization. This view defends stakeholder interests as a means to the end goal of shareholder value maximization. But Mehrotra and Morck (2017) show that this argument is flawed. It fails to resolve the many situations of clear conflict between the interests of shareholders and different stakeholders. It also fails to value externalities the corporate may inflict on more distant stakeholders, such as the environment (see Hart and Zingales (2017) in Section 3.2.3 on externalities).

Nonetheless, Mehrotra and Morck (2017) argue that enlightened value maximization (or refined shareholder value) may well be the least bad alternative on offer. In contrast to stakeholder theory, the approach has a single roughly measurable objective—refined shareholder value—while explicitly recognizing that good relations with stakeholders can boost firm value by easing contracting costs and facilitating surplus creation. Box 1.3 in Chapter 1 defines the formal objective function of the refined shareholder value model, which is categorized as SF 1.0.

3.2.3 STAKEHOLDER MODEL

The stakeholder model argues that managers should balance the interests of all stakeholders. Several proposals have come forward on how to balance these interests. Hart and Zingales (2017) make a distinction between shareholder value, which aims for maximization of financial value only, and shareholder welfare, which incorporates social and environmental externalities. An important assumption in their model is that these externalities are not perfectly separable from production decisions. So, companies face a choice in the degree of sustainability in their business model. The mechanism in the Hart–Zingales model to guide that choice is voting by prosocial shareholders on corporate policy.

Magill, Quinzii, and Rochet (2015) also argue that large companies should act in the interests of a broader group of agents than just their shareholders (the stakeholder view). In their model, a large firm typically faces endogenous risks that may have a significant impact on the workers it employs and the consumers it serves. These risks generate externalities on these stakeholders, which are not internalized by shareholders. As a result, in the competitive equilibrium, there is underinvestment in the prevention of these risks.

Magill, Quinzii, and Rochet (2015) suggest that this underinvestment problem can be alleviated if firms are instructed to maximize the total welfare of their stakeholders rather than shareholder value alone (stakeholder equilibrium). The stakeholder equilibrium can be implemented by introducing new property rights (employee rights and consumer rights) and instructing managers to maximize the integrated value of the company (the value of these rights plus the shareholder value). But how can this approach be practically implemented?

A new business language is emerging around 'the integrated value' of the company. Traditional financial reports record assets, liabilities, and profits only on the basis of financial and manufactured capitals (financial value). Integrated financial reports broaden this range to six capitals, by adding human, social, intellectual, and natural capitals, reflecting social and environmental value (see Chapter 6 on integrated reporting (IR)). These capitals incorporate social and environmental externalities and are expressed in money.

This single language of IR enables managers to analyse the trade-offs for decision-making.

The corporate sector can thus play an important role in achieving the SDGs through long-term value creation (LTVC). The concept of LTVC means that a company aims to optimize its financial, social, and environmental value in the long term (Dyllick and Muff, 2016; Tirole, 2017). The optimization requires a careful balancing of the three dimensions whereby interconnections and trade-offs are analysed but none should deteriorate in favour of the others. Box 1.4 defines the formal objective function for optimizing the integrated value in the stakeholder model, which is categorized as SF 2.0.

It should be noted that the production and publication of integrated balance sheets and integrated profit and loss accounts (IP&L) is work in progress. Standards for the new capitals are emerging but auditing of the new information has just been started. Furthermore, there is no consensus on the monetization of social and environmental values. Since monetization has several pitfalls (see Chapter 2), some argue separate key performance indicators (KPIs) should be designed. The financial value can then be expressed in financial KPIs, while the social and environmental values are expressed in non-financial KPIs (e.g. payment of living wages, health and safety conditions, gender balance, material savings, carbon-neutral production, zero net deforestation). This approach comes closer to SF 3.0, which optimizes social and environmental value subject to minimum financial value (see Box 1.5 for the formal objective function).

3.2.4 HOW TO TAKE STRATEGIC DECISIONS THAT ANTICIPATE INTERNALIZATION OF EXTERNALITIES?

The internalization of externalities is a dynamic process that is not easy to navigate. Some externalities are already internalized through best business practices at companies, for example, energy and material savings in the production process and cultivating an inspired workforce. Further externalities may be internalized in the future under pressure from government interaction, such as regulation and tax, societal pressure, and technological developments, like low-cost solar and wind energy (True Price, 2014). Companies can incorporate externalities by connecting the relevant social and environmental dimensions to their business model. That is in line with the Hart–Zingales and Magill–Quinzii–Rochet models, which assume that the externalities are connected to a company's production process.

Chapter 5 on strategy discusses the value driver adjustment (VDA) approach, which incorporates the social and environmental dimensions in the NPV rule for investment decisions and valuation. The VDA approach allows for adjustments to both CFs and the discount rate in the NPV calculation (Schramade, 2016).

3.3 Corporate governance mechanisms

Disconnects between the owners or shareholders of a company, the managers of a company, and the society in which the company operates can and do happen. There is a key role for *corporate governance*, which refers to the mechanisms, relations, and processes by which a company is controlled and directed. It involves balancing the many interests of the stakeholders of a company. Modern insights from corporate governance go beyond financial factors.

As corporate ownership varies around the world, so do corporate governance challenges. Anglo-Saxon countries typically have companies with dispersed shareholders and active share trading in stock markets. La Porta, Lopez-de-Silanes, and Shleifer (1999) indicate that the United Kingdom, the United States, Australia, and Canada fit this picture. The shareholder model (SF 1.0) is the leading model in these common law countries. In this setting, the classical *agency theory* focuses on conflicts of interests between owners (i.e. shareholders) as principals and managers as agents (Jensen and Meckling, 1976). Does the manager put in enough effort? Does he or she act in the interest of the shareholder? Solutions are found in the control and incentivization of managers. Examples are contracts for a limited term (typically four years) and performance-related pay (see Section 3.4). A strong element of the shareholder model is the accountability of management and the scope for correction, such as the removal of management or takeover of the company in case of underperformance. At the same time, the focus can be too heavily on short-term shareholder interests only.

By contrast, mainland Europe and Asia have more companies with controlling shareholders, which may disadvantage minority shareholders. A case in point is the illegal business practice of *tunnelling*, whereby a controlling shareholder directs company assets to himself or herself for personal gain (e.g. to other parts of their business group) at the expense of minority shareholders (Bae, Kang, and Kim, 2002). Strong shareholder protection measures are then a solution to protect minority shareholders. The controlling shareholder, often the family or the state, can directly appoint the manager (La Porta, Lopez-de-Silanes, and Shleifer, 1999). In these civil law countries, the market for corporate control is less active and management is held less accountable and is more entrenched than in common law countries. As a result, intervention in underperforming companies can be delayed. The civil codes typically embrace the interest of a broad set of stakeholders, notably employees.

Liang and Renneboog (2017) find that legal origin—interpreted as systems of social control of economic life—helps explain cross-country variation in companies' environmental, social, and governance (ESG) activities. ESG scores are higher in civil law countries than in common law countries. These higher ESG scores reflect social preferences for good corporate behaviour and a stakeholder orientation. Such social preferences are more embedded in rule-based mechanisms that restrict firm behaviour ex ante and which are more prevalent in civil law countries. By contrast, ex post judicial settlement mechanisms are more important in common law countries. The common law tradition emphasizes shareholder primacy and a private market-oriented strategy of social control, and perhaps because of this emphasis, it is also less stakeholder-oriented (Liang and Renneboog, 2017).

As legislation is less flexible than corporate governance codes, which can be regularly updated, corporate governance best practices are typically enshrined in the latter. The leading countries have a corporate governance committee or council with members drawn from industry, investors, trade unions, and universities. These corporate governance codes have started to address the narrow shareholder perspective and short-termism in financial markets. Interesting examples are the recent adjustment of the Dutch corporate governance code, which now includes LTVC for its various stakeholders as an objective of companies, and the UK corporate governance and stewardship codes, which stress the long-term perspective.

3.3.1 INCORPORATING SUSTAINABILITY INTO CORPORATE GOVERNANCE

The challenge is to combine the best of both worlds: the accountability of the shareholder model in which a takeover is possible in case of structural underperformance and the broad approach of the stakeholder model that incorporates all interests. Box 3.2 reports on a recent takeover battle between the shareholder model (SF 1.0) and the stakeholder model (SF 2.0). The aftermath of the aborted takeover generated a debate on the 'protection' of companies with stakeholder models against the aggressive bids of shareholder model companies. Without protection, financial considerations (F) would always dominate over social and environmental considerations (S+E). This would imply a bias towards SF 1.0. General defences against takeovers, such as certified shares or priority shares with friendly shareholders, can reduce market discipline on the management, which in turn might decrease the stock price of the company.

We propose a *societal cost-benefit analysis*, which includes financial, social, and environmental factors, based on the total or true value methodology described in Chapter 2 (De Adelhart Toorop, De Groot Ruiz, and Schoenmaker, 2017). It is the responsibility of the management of both the acquiring and target company to conduct this test to obtain the integrated value of the joint companies. Similar to the way that an investment bank decides whether the terms of a merger or acquisition are fair, an independent

BOX 3.2 THE ABORTED TAKEOVER OF UNILEVER BY KRAFT HEINZ

In February 2017, Kraft Heinz, the US food company, attempted a takeover of Unilever, the European food company (*Financial Times*, 2017). A deal would have brought together two companies with radically different business models and cultures. With a portfolio of slower-growing brands, Kraft Heinz is heavily concentrated in the USA and underpinned by debt-financed deals. It implemented aggressive cost-cutting strategies to generate margin expansion that allowed it to repay the debt and bolster shareholder returns; this is the shareholder model framework. Meanwhile, Unilever is better known for strong brands and its presence in some of the biggest emerging markets. Under its chief executive, Paul Polman, Unilever attempted to focus on better balancing of profitability with social and environmental sustainability—the stakeholder model.

This was a big takeover battle. Kraft Heinz offered $143 billion for Unilever, but Unilever did not want to give up its sustainable business model. In the end, Warren Buffett, the financier behind Kraft Heinz, did not approve a hostile takeover and halted Kraft Heinz from further bidding for Unilever.

advisor would give a fairness opinion on the outcome of the societal cost–benefit test. A Commercial Division of the Court or a Take-Over Panel (as in the United Kingdom) would only approve a takeover or merger if and when this cost–benefit test showed an improvement in the integrated value for society (in comparison to the integrated value of the stand-alone companies). When necessary the Court or Panel could appoint experts to recalculate the societal cost–benefit test.

It should be acknowledged that conducting such a societal cost–benefit test is administratively cumbersome and requires detailed information. With the advance to IR this information will become more readily available. This highlights again the importance of IR (see Chapter 6).

A societal test is consistent with a trend towards broadening the responsibility of investors and lenders. The High-Level Expert Group on Sustainable Finance (2018) recommends clarifying the *fiduciary duty* of institutional investors and their asset managers. Fiduciary duty sets out the responsibilities that financial institutions owe to their beneficiaries and clients. Clarified duties would encompass key investment activities, including investment strategy, risk management, asset allocation, governance, and stewardship. Making it clear in the relevant directives that sustainability factors must be incorporated in these activities can ensure that the clarified duty is effective. The clarified duty would also require that all participants in the investment chain proactively seek to understand the sustainability interests and preferences of their clients, members, or beneficiaries (as applicable) and to provide clear disclosure of the effects, including the potential risks and benefits, of incorporating them into investment mandates and strategies.

3.3.2 GOVERNANCE MODELS

What are the consequences of the stakeholder model for professional management and the sources of equity and debt? We adopt the principal–agent model to analyse human behaviour. This model asks how self-interested managers can be influenced to take the right decisions. The legal practice is that both common and civil law jurisdictions already require managers to optimize the interests of the corporation. The difference between the shareholder and stakeholder model may thus matter less in practice than in theory (Mehrotra and Morck, 2017).

Common law courts typically uphold the business judgement rule, which bars courts from second-guessing decisions made in the normal course of running a business. This allows managers to favour other stakeholders over shareholders by holding their decisions to a 'reasonable man' standard. If a reasonable man might have done the same in their place, the managers may not be second-guessed. Company law in civil law regimes typically requires (executive) directors to act in the interests of the corporation.

Several governance mechanisms can be introduced:

- **Executive contracts and compensation packages**: Sustainability can be specified as KPI in the contract and included in the compensation package. Indicators are the ranking in a sustainability index (e.g. the Dow Jones Sustainability Index) or the profit derived from the IP&L account.
- **Type of shareholders**: Hart and Zingales (2017) introduced the concept of prosocial shareholders, who care about social and environmental issues. Knauer and Serafeim (2014) argue that companies can attract long-term investors by committing to integrated thinking and IR. Several institutional investors, notably pension funds, have a long investment horizon and rank social and environmental factors as important as financial returns (De Jong et al. 2017).
- **Creditors**: A company's debt-to-equity ratio changes when moving to an integrated balance sheet based on six capitals (see Chapter 6 for a stylized example). More broadly, assets, liabilities, and profits in an integrated report are different from those in a traditional financial report. This has major consequences for the ratios that the company as borrower is required to stay at or above (e.g. debt-to-equity ratio or interest coverage ratio). These ratios are part of loan and bond covenants.
- **Non-executive/supervisory board monitoring**: The supervisory board (or non-executive directors) can monitor the appropriate balancing of stakeholder interests through the management (i.e. executive directors). An example is the Dutch structure regime for large companies with an important role for the supervisory board. It is already common practice to have an

audit committee (drawn from the supervisory board or from non-executive directors) to monitor a company's financial reports. The remit of the audit committee could be widened to the integrated reports. Alternatively, a separate sustainability committee could monitor the creation of social and environmental value (and avoidance of social and environmental externalities) by management.

3.3.3 ORGANIZATION FORMS

The stakeholder model may lead to other solutions for the organizational form of companies. While several governance mechanisms, such as executive compensation, IR, and type of shareholders, can be adopted for public companies, other non-profit organizational forms are also possible. An important question is whether these alternative organizational forms can be scaled up.

A first alternative to the publicly listed company is the private company. As public companies have difficulties resolving agency problems between investors and managers, private companies financed by debt and private equity are gaining in importance (Kahle and Stulz, 2017). As single shareholder, the private equity holder appoints the management and can intervene directly in the company. The private equity model can easily be scaled up, as institutional investors are an important source of capital for private equity. Other sources are family offices and individual investors. While the tension between shareholders and other stakeholders is still present in private equity, some family offices are adopting LTVC as an investment goal (De Jong et al. 2017).

A second organizational form is the cooperation, which is created by groups of people, such as customers or suppliers, working together for common or mutual benefit instead of profit. The interests of the major stakeholders (i.e. customers or suppliers) are then fully aligned with the company in the cooperation model. A major drawback, however, is that a cooperation cannot raise equity beyond its members. The lack of access to external equity can become a constraint on expansion when the cooperation grows or makes a loss (eroding equity).

A third organizational form is the B corporation, which is a certified company meeting certain social and environmental standards. B corporation certification is a private certification issued to for-profit companies by B Lab, a global non-profit organization. To be granted and to preserve certification, companies must receive a minimum score for 'social and environmental performance'. However, B corporation has no legal status (unlike the benefit corporation, which is a legal form conferred by state law in the USA).

A fourth organizational form is the social enterprise or foundation with a social and/or environmental goal (e.g. a hospital promoting health care). These social enterprises or foundations are non-profit, but need to satisfy the minimum financing condition to continue their operations. The societal impact comes first at these organizations. A major challenge is the governance, as external pressure (from shareholders) is absent.

A fifth organizational form is a governmental organization with a public objective. There are variations from a full governmental organization to a (majority) government-owned company or a private company with government intervention (strict regulations or Pigouvian taxes; see Chapter 2). The advantage of governmental organizations is that they are run for the public good. But the challenge is to operate efficiently in the public domain, as the profit motive is missing. Moreover, governmental organizations are dependent on the public budget for expansion, which may lead to underinvestment when public finances are tight.

3.3.4 ENGAGEMENT

Moving to shareholder influence, how can investors exert influence on companies in which they invest? Institutional investors have two choices for action when they become unhappy with an investee company: (i) they can engage with management to try to institute change ('voice' or direct intervention); or (ii) they can leave the company by selling shares ('exit' or divestment) or threaten to leave. As argued in Section 1.4.1, divestment has limited impact because another investor buys the shares. *Engagement* refers to investors' dialogue with investee companies on a broad range of ESG issues.

In a survey of 143 investors, McCahery, Sautner, and Starks (2016) reported that institutional investors, mostly very large ones with a long-term focus, find voice—especially when conducted behind the scenes—very important: 63 per cent of the respondents have engaged in direct discussions with management in the last five years and 45 per cent have had private discussions with a company's board outside of management's presence. The investor's horizon makes a difference. Long-term investors intervene more intensively than short-term investors. Furthermore, investors who choose engagement do so more often because of concerns over a company's corporate governance or strategy than over short-term issues. These findings support the view that interventions are not primarily conducted by short-term, 'myopic' activists who intend solely to reap short-term gains. Chapter 4 discusses how institutional investors can increase their impact by forming coalitions to foster joint engagement.

3.4 **Horizon: Moving from short-term to long-term thinking**

The *tragedy of the horizon* is a major obstacle to SF (Carney, 2015). The costs of action are borne now, while the benefits remain in the future. The impact of economic activity on society, and even more so on the environment, is typically felt in the long term, which is discounted. By contrast, the horizons that managers and investors in traditional finance work to are often short term, resulting in excessive or myopic discounting (see Section 3.4.5).

As indicated in the right-hand column of Table 3.1, several practices reinforce *short-termism* (which we deal with in the remainder of Section 3.4):

- Quarterly financial reporting by companies.
- Variable pay systems based on annual results.
- Monthly or quarterly benchmarks for measuring investor performance.
- Marking-to-market of investments.
- Supervisory treatment of illiquid investments.

These practices make the transition to SF difficult. There is a trade-off between using markets as a disciplining device for managers and investors and designing measures or incentives that foster their long-term behaviour. A common theme behind these practices is the widely accepted *efficient markets hypothesis*, which states that stock prices incorporate all relevant information and thus on average reflect the long-term fundamental value of the firm (Fama, 1970). The efficient markets hypothesis reinforces the focus on stock price as a central performance measure for executive and investor performance.

An alternative to the efficient markets hypothesis is the *adaptive markets hypothesis* (Lo, 2004; 2017). Contrary to the neoclassical view that individuals maximize expected utility and have rational expectations, an evolutionary perspective makes considerably more modest claims. The degree of market efficiency depends on an evolutionary model of individuals adapting to a changing environment. Prices reflect as much information as dictated by the combination of environmental conditions and the number and nature of distinct groups of market participants, each behaving in a common manner and having a common investment horizon. For example, retail investors, institutional investors, market makers, and hedge fund managers can be seen as distinct groups with differing investment horizons. If multiple groups (or the members of a single highly populous group) are competing within a single market, that market is likely to be highly efficient. If, on the other hand, a small number of groups are active in a given market, that market will be less efficient. The adaptive markets hypothesis can explain why new risks, such as environmental risks, are not yet fully priced in, because not enough investors are examining them.

Andersson, Bolton, and Samama (2016) argue that there is little awareness of carbon risk among (institutional) investors and it is thus not priced by the market. Hong, Li, and Xu (2016) investigated whether stock markets efficiently price risks brought on or exacerbated by climate change. Their findings support regulatory concerns that markets that are inexperienced with climate change underreact to such risks. These authors thus call for corporate exposure to climate risks to be disclosed.

3.4.1 QUARTERLY FINANCIAL REPORTING

There is ample evidence that the majority of firms view quarterly earnings as the key metric for an external audience, more so than underlying CFs (Graham, Harvey, and Rajgopal, 2005). The pressure created by a high reporting frequency to continuously achieve a strong share price induces managers to adopt a short-term perspective (myopia) in choosing the firm's investments. Such pressures disappear when the reporting frequency is decreased. Infrequent reports could provide better incentives for project selection decisions even though they provide less information to the capital market (Gigler et al. 2014). Nevertheless, timely publication of information that has a material impact on a firm's performance remains important.

Barton and Wiseman (2014) recommend focusing on metrics like economic value added over ten years, R&D efficiency, patent pipelines, and multiyear return on capital investments. More generally, the nature of financial reporting should be broadened. IR is a process founded on integrated thinking within a firm that results in a regular integrated report about value creation over time and related communications covering aspects of value creation. IR facilitates transparency of social and environmental aspects. The current process is largely bottom-up with the exception of South Africa, which already requires IR: some firms have started to publish integrated reports. However, the quality and reliability of the reported information varies significantly. To speed up this process, the Financial Stability Board set up the Bloomberg Task Force to provide a set of voluntary, consistent disclosure recommendations for companies to use to provide information to investors, lenders, and insurance underwriters about their climate-related financial risks (TCFD, 2017). At some point, best practices need to be incorporated into binding international accounting standards, adopted by the International Accounting Standards Board and supported by the International Organization of Securities Commissions. Finally, integrated reports would need to be audited, according to these future standards, to provide assurance of the reported information.

Faced with a large percentage of investors that chase short-term returns, companies could benefit by attracting investors with longer-term horizons and providing incentives that are more consistent with the long-term strategy of the company. Knauer and Serafeim (2014) argue that there is no need for companies to take their investor base as a 'given'. One promising way of attracting long-term investors is a commitment to integrated thinking and the adoption of IR, which provides companies with a means of credibly communicating the commitment of its top leadership to dispersing integrated thinking across the organization and to building strong relationships with important external stakeholders.

3.4.2 VARIABLE PAY SYSTEMS

Executive directors' bonuses based on annual results or paid in stock options reinforce the focus on short-term results (Edmans, Fang, and Lewellen, 2017). More broadly, executives are primarily concerned with the direct impact of investments during their tenure, as current performance is a key factor for their career prospects. To address this short-term bias, a more long-term-orientated pay structure for executives can be introduced. The *deferred reward principle* suggests that pay for exerting effort in the current period is spread over current and future periods to achieve intertemporal risk-sharing. The payment of all or part of a bonus can thus be deferred and made contingent on subsequent events, such as the completion of a major strategy or project when the full impact of the investment becomes clear. Also the vesting period (or the lock-up period) for equity compensation can be lengthened, even after retirement. Another powerful tool is *clawback provisions* in executive compensation whereby an employer takes back money that has already been disbursed, sometimes with an added penalty (Bolton and Samama, 2013). Clawback provisions can be activated in case of fraud or accounting errors, but also in cases where subsequent losses show in hindsight that the executives received excess compensation.

3.4.3 QUARTERLY PERFORMANCE BENCHMARKING

Fund managers are evaluated on a regular basis against performance benchmarks. The quarterly relative performance monitoring to which many funds and fund managers are subject results in the adoption of short-termist attitudes and approaches to the management of funds (Baker, 1998). Moreover, a greater proportion of institutional investors simply pursue passive, broad asset-class-allocation investment strategies, which means that a smaller fraction of shareholders is informed about any individual firm and its fundamental long-term value.

To overcome short-term interests, performance evaluation should be aligned with the time horizon of the investment strategy and underlying investments. Chapter 7 discusses performance measures based on a three or five-year moving average. Lengthening the investment horizon facilitates the engagement of (institutional) investors with companies. It is important to distinguish intended holding periods from observed holding periods. An investor could have a very long intended holding period but might still decide to terminate a position early based on new long-term information (Edmans, 2017).

3.4.4 MARKING-TO-MARKET

Market prices give timely signals that can aid decision-making. But in the presence of distorted incentives and illiquid markets there are other harmful effects that inject artificial volatility into prices, which distorts real decisions. When markets are only imperfectly liquid in the sense that sales or purchases affect the short-term price dynamics, the illiquidity of the secondary market causes another type of inefficiency (Plantin, Sapra, and Shin, 2008). A bad outcome for the asset will depress fundamental values somewhat, but a more damaging effect comes from the negative externalities generated by other firms selling. Under a mark-to-market regime, the value of someone's assets depends on the prices at which others have managed to sell their assets. When others sell, observed transaction prices are depressed more than is justified by the fundamentals exerting a negative effect on all others, but especially on those who have chosen to hold on to the asset. Anticipating this negative outcome, a short-horizon investor will be tempted to pre-empt the fall in price by selling the asset itself. However, such pre-emptive action will merely serve to amplify the price fall. In this way, the mark-to-market regime generates an endogenous volatility of prices that impedes the resource allocation role of prices. This process comes into effect particularly during times of crises.

The alternative, the historical cost regime, also leads to inefficiencies, as there are no adjustments for subsequent changes in the market values of assets. Assessing the pros and cons, Plantin, Sapra, and Shin (2008) found that the damage done by marking to market is greatest when claims are: (i) long-lived; (ii) illiquid; and (iii) senior. For trading of junior assets in liquid markets, such as traded stocks, marking to market is superior to historical cost in terms of the trade-offs. But for senior, long-lived, and illiquid assets and liabilities, such as bank loans and insurance liabilities, the harm caused by distortions can outweigh the benefits. Banks loans are, for example, typically carried at historic or nominal value, with deduction of expected credit losses (i.e. impairments).

In the aftermath of the global financial crisis in 2007, the international accounting standard for financial instruments (IAS 39) was amended to exempt financial instruments from fair value accounting, when they are managed based on amortized cost in accordance with a financial firm's business model. To keep the appropriate perspective, the fair value discussion focuses on a subset of assets (i.e. financial instruments) and on unusual circumstances. Shleifer and Vishny (2011) show the case of fire sales, where fair value accounting reinforces the downward spiral and is thus counterproductive. The unusual circumstances should be confined to these instances when the markets are clearly illiquid, otherwise undue forbearance or tolerance may arise. The benefit of fair value accounting is that management and regulators get a clear signal from the markets prompting them to act. Several studies (e.g. Laux and Leuz, 2010) argue that fair value accounting did not play a major role in the financial crisis.

3.4.5 SUPERVISORY TREATMENT

Liquid investments, which can be traded and thus marked-to-market daily, carry a relatively low supervisory capital charge, as financial firms can divest these assets at short notice. The supervisory treatment is based on marking-to-market, liquidity, and efficient market measures. By contrast, private market and direct investments carry a higher capital charge to cater for the 'risk' that the investment cannot be liquidated at short notice. Environmental projects typically have a long horizon and cannot be measured frequently: results are visible only after a certain period of time has passed. Land restoration projects, for example, have a horizon of 20 years (Ferwerda, 2016). Other examples are infrastructure projects, such as energy, road, or coastal defence infrastructure projects. When regulated financial institutions keep hold of an investment to maturity, ways to avoid or reduce the need for a supervisory surcharge for illiquidity can be found by measuring the potential and the risk of a project over the full cycle of that project (e.g. using scenario analysis) rather than on a daily mark-to-market basis.

In summary, a possible cost of financial markets is short-termism, with agents in the financial intermediation chain giving near-term outcomes too much weight at the expense of longer-term opportunities. There is evidence that stock prices in the United Kingdom and the United States have historically over-discounted future dividends by 5 to 10 per cent, suggesting significant evidence of myopia (Davies et al. 2014). Possible incentive-compatible solutions to counter short-termism would be more long-term-orientated pay structures for executives (e.g. clawback provisions and deferred rewards). Moreover, the reliance on mark-to-market valuations should be reduced.

3.5 **Guidelines governing SF**

Social and environmental externalities are by their nature not incorporated in the decisions taken by companies and investors. As most externalities play out in the medium to long term, the problem is aggravated by the short horizon to which executives and investors work. Moreover, the efficient markets hypothesis, which states that stock prices incorporate all relevant information and thus reflect the fundamental value of the firm, reinforces the focus on stock price as a central performance measure for executive and investor performance.

Based on the review of the challenges in this chapter, Schoenmaker (2017) developed the following guidelines to govern SF. These guidelines are to be used from different perspectives: companies, investors, and supervisors.

1. *Company perspective*

- Move from shareholder to stakeholder model, whereby a company balances the interests of all its stakeholders: customers, employees, suppliers, shareholders, and the community.
- More broadly, corporates should strive for LTVC for the common good (i.e. what is shared and beneficial for all or most members of a given community).
- Executive contracts should include sustainability indicators (e.g. IP&L and/ or ranking in sustainability index).

2. *Lengthening executive and investors horizons*

- To counter short-termism, executive and investor horizons should be aligned to the long term.
- On the executive side, a more long-term-orientated reporting structure (moving away from quarterly reporting) and pay structure for executives (e.g. deferred rewards and clawback provisions) would reduce short-termism.
- More generally, IR by companies facilitates social and environmental transparency and thus increases the accountability of executives.
- On the investment side, a more long-term investment performance horizon (moving away from quarterly benchmarking) would promote long-term investment.

3. *Investor engagement with corporates*

- To become a force for LTVC, long-term (institutional) investors should build investor coalitions to cooperate on engagement with corporates on social and environmental issues (see Chapter 4).

4. *Market efficiency and liquidity*

- Raise awareness of alternative theories of market efficiency.
- The dominant view of liquidity (the degree to which an asset can be quickly bought or sold in the market without affecting the asset's price) favours listed securities and is based on the efficient markets hypothesis.
- An alternative view is the adaptive markets hypothesis, which implies that the degree of market efficiency depends on an evolutionary model of individuals adapting to a changing environment. That can explain why new risks, such as environmental risks, are not (yet) fully priced in.

5. *Supervisory treatment*

- Reduce the supervisory bias towards favouring 'liquid' investments (which are listed) and allow for 'buy and hold' investments.
- Financial institutions should be stress-tested to identify overexposure to and concentration in carbon-intensive assets. These carbon stress tests make use of various climate scenarios, including the adverse scenario of late adjustment resulting in a 'hard landing', and have a long horizon over which adverse events could occur.

3.6 **Conclusions**

This chapter examines behavioural challenges in the transition to sustainable development. The first challenge is to broaden the objective of the corporate from shareholder value to stakeholder or integrated value. The latter incorporates social and environmental value as well as financial value in the objective function. This broadened objective function leads to new corporate governance mechanisms (including new contracts for managers) and new decision-making rules for corporate investment.

The second challenge is to move from short-term to long-term thinking. This chapter reviews several incentives to align executive and investor horizons over the longer term. On the executive side, incentive-compatible measures include a more long-term-orientated financial reporting structure (moving away from quarterly reporting) and an executive pay structure with deferred rewards and clawback provisions. On the investment side, the investment performance horizon should go beyond the current standard of quarterly benchmarking.

Key concepts used in this chapter

Adaptive markets hypothesis implies that the degree of market efficiency depends on an evolutionary model of individuals adapting to a changing environment.

Agency theory looks at conflicts of interest between people with different interests in the same assets. An important conflict is that between shareholders and managers of companies.

Clawback provision is a provision in executive compensation whereby an employer takes back money that has already been disbursed.

Corporate governance refers to the mechanisms, relations, and processes by which a company is controlled and is directed. It involves balancing the many interests of the stakeholders of a company.

Deferred reward principle states that pay (reward) for exerting effort in the current period is spread over the current and future periods to achieve intertemporal risk-sharing.

Efficient markets hypothesis states that stock prices incorporate all relevant information and thus on average reflect the long-term fundamental value of the firm.

Engagement refers to investors' dialogue with investee companies on a broad range of ESG issues.

Externalities refer to consequences of activities that affect other (or third) parties without this being reflected in market prices.

Fiduciary duty sets out the responsibilities that financial institutions owe to their beneficiaries and clients. The expectation is to be loyal to beneficiary interests, prudent in handling money, and transparent in dealing with conflicts.

Integrated value is obtained by combining the financial, social, and environmental values in an integrated way (with regard for the interconnections).

Long-term value creation refers to the goal of companies that optimize financial, social, and environmental value in the long run.

Shareholder model means that the ultimate measure of a corporate's success is the extent to which it enriches its shareholders.

Short-termism refers to the myopic behaviour of executives and investors who focus on the short term.

Societal cost–benefit analysis or test refers to the analysis of the joint financial, social, and environmental values in the case of a corporate takeover. This test is based on the *total or true value methodology*.

Stakeholder model means that a corporate should balance or optimize the interests of all its stakeholders: customers, employees, suppliers, shareholders, and the community.

Sustainable development means that current and future generations have the resources needed, such as food, water, health care, and energy, without stressing the Earth system processes.

Sustainable finance looks at how finance (investing and lending) interacts with economic, social, and environmental issues.

Tragedy of the horizon refers to the situation where the costs of (sustainable) action are borne now, while the (social and environmental) benefits remain in the future.

Tunnelling is a practice whereby a controlling shareholder directs company assets to himself for personal gain (e.g. to other parts of his business group) at the expense of the minority shareholders.

SUGGESTED READING

Carney, M. (2015), 'Breaking the tragedy of the horizon: climate change and financial stability', Speech at Lloyd's of London, 29 September.

Hart, O. and L. Zingales (2017), 'Companies should maximize shareholder welfare not market value', CEPR Discussion Paper No. 12186.

Jensen, M. (2002), 'Value maximization, stakeholder theory, and the corporate objective function', *Business Ethics Quarterly*, 12(2): 235–56.

Lo, A. (2017), *Adaptive Markets: Financial Evolution at the Speed of Thought*, Princeton University Press, Princeton, NJ.

Mehrotra, V. and R. Morck (2017), 'Governance and stakeholders', in: B. Hermalin and M. Weisbach (eds.), *The Handbook of the Economics of Corporate Governance*, vol. 1, Elsevier, Amsterdam, 637–84.

REFERENCES

Andersson, M., P. Bolton, and F. Samama (2016), 'Hedging climate risk', *Financial Analysts Journal*, 72(3): 13–32.

Bae, K., J. Kang, and J. Kim (2002), 'Tunneling or value added? Evidence from mergers by Korean business groups', *Journal of Finance*, 57(6): 2695–740.

Baker, M. (1998), 'Fund managers' attitudes to risk and time horizons: the effect of performance benchmarking', *European Journal of Finance*, 4(3): 257–78.

Barton, D. and Wiseman, M. (2014), 'Focusing capital on the long term', *Harvard Business Review*, 92(1/2): 44–51.

Bedsworth, L. and M. Taylor (2007), 'Learning from California's zero-emission vehicle program', *California Economic Policy*, 3(4): 1–20.

Bolton, P. and F. Samama (2013), 'L-shares: rewarding long-term investors', *Journal of Applied Corporate Finance*, 25(3): 86–97.
Carney, M. (2015), 'Breaking the tragedy of the horizon: climate change and financial stability', Speech at Lloyd's of London, 29 September.
Dasgupta, P. and P. Ehrlich (2013), 'Pervasive externalities at the population, consumption, and environment nexus', *Science*, 340(6130): 324–8.
Davies, R., A. Haldane, M. Nielsen, and S. Pezzini (2014), 'Measuring the costs of short-termism', *Journal of Financial Stability*, 12: 16–25.
De Adelhart Toorop, R., A. De Groot Ruiz, and D. Schoenmaker (2017), 'Maatschappelijke toetsing overnames is nodig' [Societal test of takeovers is necessary], *ESB*, 102 (4752): 360–3.
De Jong. A, D. Schoenmaker, M. Gruenwald, and A. Pala (2017), 'Large shareholders in corporate governance', Research for the Monitoring Committee Corporate Governance, Rotterdam School of Management, Erasmus University, Rotterdam.
Dyllick, T. and K. Muff (2016), 'Clarifying the meaning of sustainable business introducing a typology from business-as-usual to true business sustainability', *Organization and Environment*, 29 (2): 156–74.
Edmans, A. (2017), 'The answer to short-termism isn't asking investors to be patient', *Harvard Business Review*, July.
Edmans, A., V. Fang, and K. Lewellen (2017), 'Equity vesting and investment', *Review of Financial Studies*, 30(7): 2229–71.
Fama, E. (1970), 'Efficient capital markets: a review of theory and empirical work', *Journal of Finance*, 25(2): 383–417.
Ferwerda, W. (2016), '4 returns, 3 zones, 20 years: a holistic framework for ecological restoration by people and business for next generations', RSM Series on Positive Change, vol. 1, Rotterdam School of Management, Erasmus University, http://events.globallandscapesforum.org/wp-content/uploads/sites/2/2017/11/4-Returns-3-Zones-20-Years-A-Holistic-Framework-for-Ecological-Restoration-by-People-and-Business-for-Next-Generations.pdf, accessed 27 June 2018.
Financial Times (2017), 'Kraft Heinz drops $143bn pursuit of Unilever', 20 February.
Gigler, F., C. Kanodia, H. Sapra, and R. Venugopalan (2014), 'How frequent financial reporting can cause managerial short-termism: an analysis of the costs and benefits of increasing reporting frequency', *Journal of Accounting Research*, 52(2): 357–87.
Graham, J., C. Harvey, and S. Rajgopal (2005), 'The economic implications of corporate financial reporting', *Journal of Accounting and Economics*, 40(1): 3–73.
Grossman, S. and O. Hart (1986), 'The costs and benefits of ownership: a theory of vertical and lateral integration', *Journal of Political Economy*, 94(4): 691–719.
Hart, O. and J. Moore (1990), 'Property rights and the nature of the firm', *Journal of Political Economy*, 98(6): 1119–58.
Hart, O. and L. Zingales (2017), 'Companies should maximize shareholder welfare not market value', CEPR Discussion Paper No. 12186.
High-Level Expert Group on Sustainable Finance (2018), 'Financing a Sustainable European Economy', Final Report, European Union, Brussels.
Hong, H, F. Li, and J. Xu (2016), 'Climate risks and market efficiency', NBER Working Paper No. 22890.

Jensen, M. (2002), 'Value maximization, stakeholder theory, and the corporate objective function', *Business Ethics Quarterly*, 12(2): 235–56.
Jensen, M. and W. Meckling (1976), 'Theory of the firm: managerial behavior, agency costs, and ownership structure', *Journal of Financial Economics*, 3(4): 305–60.
Kahle, K. and R. Stulz (2017), 'Is the US public corporation in trouble?', *Journal of Economic Perspectives*, 31(3): 67–88.
Knauer, A. and G. Serafeim (2014), 'Attracting long-term investors through integrated thinking and reporting: a clinical study of a biopharmaceutical company', *Journal of Applied Corporate Finance*, 26(2): 57–64.
La Porta, R., F. Lopez-De-Silanes, and A. Shleifer (1999), 'Corporate ownership around the world', *Journal of Finance*, 54(2): 471–517.
Laux, C. and C. Leuz (2010), 'Did fair value accounting contribute to the financial crisis?', *Journal of Economic Perspectives*, 24(1): 93–118.
Liang, H. and L. Renneboog (2017), 'On the foundations of corporate social responsibility', *Journal of Finance*, 72(2): 853–910.
Lo, A. (2004), 'The adaptive markets hypothesis: market efficiency from an evolutionary perspective', *Journal of Portfolio Management*, 30(5): 15–29.
Lo, A. (2017), *Adaptive Markets: Financial Evolution at the Speed of Thought*, Princeton University Press, Princeton, NJ.
McCahery, J., Z. Sautner, and L. Starks (2016), 'Behind the scenes: the corporate governance preferences of institutional investors', *Journal of Finance*, 71(6): 2905–32.
Magill, M., M. Quinzii, and J.-C. Rochet (2015), 'A theory of the stakeholder corporation', *Econometrica*, 83(5): 1685–725.
Mehrotra, V. and R. Morck (2017), 'Governance and stakeholders', in: B. Hermalin and M. Weisbach (eds.), *The Handbook of the Economics of Corporate Governance*, vol. 1, Elsevier, Amsterdam, 637–84.
Plantin, G., H. Sapra, and H. Shin (2008), 'Marking-to-market: panacea or Pandora's box?', *Journal of Accounting Research*, 46(2): 435–60.
Schoenmaker, D. (2017), 'From risk to opportunity: a framework for sustainable finance', RSM Series on Positive Change, vol. 2, Rotterdam School of Management, Erasmus University, https://papers.ssrn.com/sol3/papers.cfm?abstract_id=3066210, accessed 28 June 2018.
Schramade, W. (2016), 'Bridging sustainability and finance: the value driver adjustment approach', *Journal of Applied Corporate Finance*, 28(2): 17–28.
Shapira, R. and L. Zingales (2017), 'Is pollution value-maximizing? The Dupont case', CEPR Discussion Paper No. 12323.
Shleifer, A. and R. Vishny (2011), 'Fire sales in finance and macroeconomics', *Journal of Economic Perspectives*, 25(1): 29–48.
Sikken, B. J. (2014), Lecture Series Finance & Sustainability, Duisenberg school of finance, Amsterdam.
TCFD (Task Force on Climate-related Financial Disclosures) (2017), 'Recommendations of the Task Force on Climate-related Financial Disclosures: final report (Bloomberg Report)', Financial Stability Board, Basel.
Tetlock, P. and D. Gardner (2015), *Superforecasting: The Art and Science of Prediction*, Random House, New York.

Tirole, J. (2017), *Economics for the Common Good*, Princeton University Press, Princeton, NJ.

True Price (2014), 'The business case for true pricing: why you will benefit from measuring, monetizing and improving your impact', Report drafted by True Price, Deloitte, EY, and PwC, 2nd edn, Amsterdam, http://trueprice.org/wp-content/uploads/2015/02/True-Price-Report-The-Business-Case-for-True-Pricing.pdf, accessed 25 June 2018.

World Bank (2017), 'World development indicators 2017', Washington DC.

4 Coalitions for Sustainable Finance

Overview

This short intermezzo chapter discusses the increasing role of institutional investors in corporate governance. They currently manage 65 per cent of equity holdings. By acting jointly in a coalition, institutional investors can become a force for change in companies. New evidence shows that collaboration among active investors is instrumental in increasing the success rate of social and environmental engagements with companies. Also on the banking side and on the corporate side, coalitions are emerging. These coalitions take a collective or system approach towards sustainability.

Such a system approach goes back to Ostrom (1990), who suggests that private coalitions can cooperate to provide a common good. An example of collective action is a reduction target for carbon emissions agreed among a group of investors and/or corporates. Another example is minimum social and environmental standards agreed among international banks for project financing. In this chapter, the design principles for effective coalitions are analysed. It appears that not only a common objective and clear membership rules but also monitoring and sanctions (i.e. enforcement of the rules) are key features of an effective coalition.

This intermezzo chapter discusses the emerging coalitions for sustainable finance (SF), which have only very recently been established. Growing membership and sharpening of the internal rules can turn these coalitions in agents of transformational change (see Chapter 12).

Learning objectives

After you have studied this chapter, you should be able to:

- understand the role of institutional investors;
- explain the functioning of private coalitions;
- understand the mechanisms used to increase the effectiveness of coalitions.

4.1 The increasing role of institutional investors

Institutional investors play an increasing role in the investment landscape (Darvas and Schoenmaker, 2018). *Institutional investors* are (large) financial institutions that manage investments (equities, bonds, and alternative assets) for clients and beneficiaries. Traditional investors include investment funds, pension funds, and insurance companies. Alternative institutional investors include sovereign wealth funds, hedge funds, and private equity. As professional parties, institutional investors have the means and knowledge to engage with companies. Figure 4.1 shows that the size of traditional institutional investors has increased from 67 per cent of GDP in 1990 to 230 per cent of GDP in 2016. Institutional investment is expected to rise further due to ageing, reduction of social security, and increased wealth (Darvas and Schoenmaker, 2018).

Institutional investors have become important players in the stock market (Çelik and Isaksson, 2014). Table 4.1 shows that their share of equity holdings has increased to around 65 per cent across developed countries. Traditional institutional investors (investment funds, pension funds, and insurers) own 58 per cent of equity holdings and alternative institutional investors (sovereign wealth funds and hedge funds) another 7 per cent. Institutional investors are thus the dominant shareholders of companies.

Section 4.2 discusses how institutional investors can increase their impact by forming coalitions to foster joint engagement.

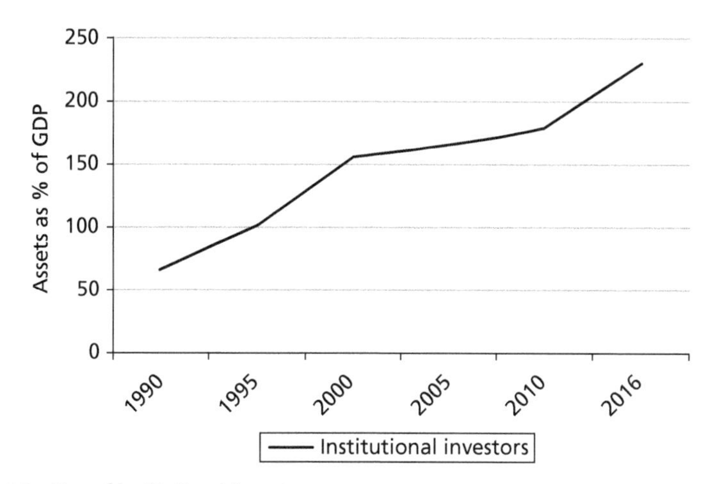

Figure 4.1 Rise of institutional investors

Note: Assets of institutional investors (pension funds, insurers and investment funds) of 15 large EU countries, Switzerland, and the United States as % of GDP.

Source: Authors' calculations based on ECB (2017) and OECD (2017).

Table 4.1 Share of institutional investors in equity

Type of institutional investor	Amount (in US$ trillion)	Share in equity markets
Investment funds	24.0	41.1%
Investment funds (excl. pension funds/insurers)	11.2	19.1%
Pension funds and insurance companies	22.9	39.1%
Traditional institutional investors	**34.1**	**58.2%**
Sovereign wealth funds	3.3	5.6%
Hedge funds	0.9	1.6%
Alternative institutional investors	**4.2**	**7.2%**
Total institutional investors	**38.3**	**65.4%**

Note: Pension funds and insurers invest directly in equity and indirectly via investment funds. This indirect investment is deducted from the equity managed by investment funds to avoid double counting. As only data for institutional investors in developed countries is available, the share is calculated as a percentage of developed equity markets. The figures are for 2016.

Source: Authors' calculations based on OECD (2017) and SIFMA (2017).

4.2 A system approach towards sustainability

A classic problem in environmental economics is the *tragedy of the commons*. This refers to the situation within a shared-resource system, when individual users acting independently according to their own self-interest behave contrary to the common good of all users by depleting that resource through their collective action. Common resources not only refer to natural resources, which can be depleted or degraded, but also the use of the atmosphere or hydrosphere as sinks, a practice which can be overused. A standard approach to preserving a *common good* is government taxation or regulation (top row of Table 3.1 in Chapter 3) or the vesting of private property rights. However, an exclusive regulatory approach towards curbing carbon emissions has been elusive to date.

Ostrom (1990) looks beyond centralized regulation by external authorities or private property rights as the means to govern common pool resources. She offers design principles for how common resources can be governed sustainably and equitably in a community. The central idea is to build coalitions in which members spontaneously develop rules to govern the use of the common good in question, to monitor members' behaviour, to apply graduated sanctions for rule violators, and to provide accessible means for dispute resolution.

In sum, the essence of a coalition is that membership is voluntary, but members must follow internal rules. The key to building an effective and inclusive coalition is to define clear group boundaries, whereby the major parties are covered, and to ensure that those affected by the rules can participate in modifying the rules (Ostrom, 1990). As suggested in Chapter 1, the rules governing the use of a common good, such as the available carbon budget, should follow a system approach.

Thurm, Baue, and Van der Lugt (2018) point out that current sustainability practices are too incremental and fail to take such a system approach. As a result, we simply do not know whether individual companies are doing enough, or not. Instead, Thurm and colleagues (2018) argue that one should pursue context-based sustainability, which connects the nano (personal), micro (organization), meso (industry or portfolio), and macro (system) levels to determine individual company contributions. Starting from what is needed at the system level, one can determine the thresholds that should not be crossed, and the allocations of resources that individual companies are allowed to use. Thurm, Baue, and Van der Lugt (2018) call for strong improvements in reporting (Reporting 3.0) to ensure that such thresholds and allocations can be determined. So far, their movement named Reporting 3.0 has mobilized over 6,000 people ('positive mavericks') to drive change in their respective organizations and to share best practices.

McElroy (2008) has developed the footprint method to measure the sustainability performance of an organization. He defines the sustainability quotient as follows:

$$SP = AI/NI \tag{4.1}$$

where SP represents the sustainability performance, AI the net actual impact on the carrying capacities of vital capitals (such as human or natural capital) and NI the normative impact on the carrying capacities of vital capitals. The sustainability quotient can be applied to the ecological ceilings and social foundations (see Section 1.2 in Chapter 1). The SP scores work in the following way:

- for ecological quotients: $SP \leq 1$ are sustainable, $SP > 1$ are unsustainable.
- for societal quotients: $SP \geq 1$ are sustainable, $SP < 1$ are unsustainable.

The innovation of this system approach is that a company's actual impact is measured against its normative impact (derived from system thresholds). Environmental, social and governance (ESG) ratings (see Chapter 7) measure only the impact of a company (the numerator), but without relation to system thresholds (the denominator). The sustainability quotient puts a company's performance in the appropriate context of the social or ecological system.

4.2.1 EXAMPLE OF CARBON BUDGET

The efforts to limit climate change, one of the key United Nations (UN) Sustainable Development Goals, provide an illustration of the proposed system approach. Currently, countries make climate pledges within the framework of the annual conferences of the parties (COPs) to the United Nations Framework Convention on Climate Change (UNFCCC, 2015). The Paris Agreement is an example of a coalition—at the country level—as a means to govern shared resources. The aggregated climate pledges so far (technically called the nationally determined contributions) still imply likely global warming of more than 2°C (UNFCCC, 2016), but there is an expectation that countries will increase their pledges over time (the *ratchet effect*) as part of predefined five-year review cycles.

For instance, within the overall COP framework, companies could introduce a global sub-COP framework with a downward trajectory of corporate carbon budgets under the auspices of the World Economic Forum (WEF) or the World Business Council for Sustainable Development (WBCSD) (see Tables 4.2 and 4.3). Private and public corporations (including utilities) would be included. The starting point could be the pledged carbon reductions of the largest companies (e.g. the Fortune 500). The Bloomberg principles for climate-related financial disclosures could be used for yearly reporting and monitoring of corporate progress (TCFD, 2017). This system approach would thus be based on a mix of top-down calculation of the overall sustainable carbon budget (the denominator in Equation 4.1) and bottom-up declarations of carbon reduction intentions by companies (the numerator in Equation 4.1).

As part of their intensifying corporate governance approach, long-term asset owners and asset managers, such as pension funds and insurers, can stimulate companies to operate within 'system' boundaries and can hold them accountable (Clift et al. 2017). To ensure that companies stay within these boundaries or budgets, asset managers also need to report the carbon footprint (as well as other environmental and social dimensions) of their investments. Furthermore, asset managers need to cooperate on joint investor engagement with companies by forming investor coalitions on long-term sustainable investment (McNulty and Nordberg, 2016).

4.3 **Coalitions for SF**

Several investor coalitions on long-term sustainable investment have recently emerged. These coalitions include the Principles for Responsible Investment (PRI), Focusing Capital on the Long-Term Global (FCLTGlobal), the Global Impact Investing Network (GIIN), and the Global Alliance for Banking on

Values (GABV). Neal and Warren (2015) find that long-term investors and investors who are less concerned about stock liquidity (see Chapter 3) intervene more intensively at investee companies.

Table 4.2 describes the two main coalitions for asset managers, banks, and corporates by outlining their total size, main members, and size of the reference group they belong to (respectively, global assets under management (AUM), global banking assets, and Fortune 500 total revenues). Some of the coalitions are very small in comparison to their benchmark, with a few members making up most of the coalition's total size (for example FCTL Global or GABV). Others are very big, with the five biggest members representing less than 30 per cent of the total coalition (for example PRI, Equator Principles, WEF).

This overview shows that the coalition members are drawn from North America, Europe, and Asia. These coalitions thus have the potential to become a global force for change. The long-term focus of these coalitions would include avoiding environmental and social hazards, which materialize over the medium to long term, and grasping the opportunities offered by low-carbon investment, which pays off in the long term. Engagement is a very powerful tool to improve social and environmental standards in the corporate sector where social and environmental externalities are caused (Skancke, 2016). The ultimate aim is to steer business towards truly sustainable practices (i.e. long-term value creation (LTVC)) spurred by a macro perspective.

The largest asset manager, BlackRock, with global investments at $5.1 trillion in 2016, is a member of both investor coalitions. In an annual letter to CEOs of large companies, Larry Fink, the chief executive at BlackRock, focused on LTVC. From the 2017 annual letter, we take the following extracts for illustration purposes:

Each year, I write to the CEOs of leading companies in which our clients are shareholders. These clients, the vast majority of whom are investing for long-term goals like retirement or a child's education, are the true owners of these companies. As a fiduciary, I write on their behalf to advocate governance practices that BlackRock believes will maximize long-term value creation for their investments.

Last year, we asked CEOs to communicate to shareholders their annual strategic frameworks for long-term value creation and explicitly affirm that their boards have reviewed those plans. Many companies responded by publicly disclosing detailed plans, including robust processes for board involvement. These plans provided shareholders with an opportunity to evaluate a company's long-term strategy and the progress made in executing on it.

BlackRock engages with companies from the perspective of a long-term shareholder. Since many of our clients' holdings result from index-linked investments—which we cannot sell as long as those securities remain in an index—our clients are the definitive long-term investors. As a fiduciary acting on behalf of these clients, BlackRock takes corporate governance particularly seriously and engages with our voice,

Table 4.2 Main coalitions for SF

Panel A. Asset managers

	PRI	AUM ($ billion)	% of coalition	Coverage in %		FCLT Global	AUM ($ billion)	% of coalition	Coverage in %
1	BlackRock	5,117	8%		1	BlackRock	5,117	52%	
2	Vanguard Group	3,814	6%		2	State Street Global Advisors	2,446	25%	
3	UBS	2,771	4%		3	APG	498	5%	
4	State Street Global Advisors	2,446	4%		4	Schroders	490	5%	
5	Allianz Asset Management	2,086	3%		5	CPPIB	279	3%	
	Others	45,766	74%			Others	982	10%	
	Total PRI	**62,000**	**100%**	**38%**		**Total FCLT Global**	**9,812**	**100%**	**6%**
	Total global AUM	**163,000**		**100%**		**Total global AUM**	**163,000**		**100%**

Panel B. Banks

	Equator Principles	Assets ($ billion)	% of coalition	Coverage in %		GABV	Assets ($ billion)	% of coalition	Coverage in %
1	JPMorgan Chase	2,491	5%		1	Group Credit Cooperative	26	23%	
2	HSBC Holdings	2,375	5%		2	Vancity	18	16%	
3	BNP Paribas	2,190	5%		3	Amalgamated Bank NY	18	16%	
4	Bank of America	2,188	5%		4	Triodos Bank	14	12%	
5	Bank of Tokyo	1,982	4%		5	GLS Bank	5	4%	
	Others	34,733	76%			Others	30	28%	
	Total Equator Principles	**45,959**	**100%**	**30%**		**Total GABV**	**110**	**100%**	**0.07%**
	Global banking assets	**152,961**		**100%**		**Global banking assets**	**152,961**		**100%**

Panel C. Corporates

	WEF	Revenues ($ billion)	% of coalition	Coverage in %		WBCSD	Revenues ($ billion)	% of coalition	Coverage in %
1	Walmart	482	6%		1	Walmart	482	9%	
2	Shell	272	3%		2	Shell	272	5%	
3	Volkswagen	237	3%		3	Volkswagen	237	5%	
4	Toyota	237	3%		4	Toyota	237	5%	
5	BP	226	3%		5	Apple	234	4%	
	Others	7,123	83%			Others	3,769	72%	
	Total WEF	**8,577**	**100%**	**31%**		**Total WBCSD**	**5,230**	**100%**	**19%**
	Fortune 500 total revenues	**27,634**		**100%**		**Fortune 500 total revenues**	**27,634**		**100%**

Note: The table shows the share of the largest five members in each coalition (3rd column). The 4th column indicates the coverage of the coalition in the reference group (i.e. the relevant sector). The figures are for end 2016. See Table 4.3 for more information on calculation and sources.

Source: Schoenmaker (2017).

> and with our vote, on matters that can influence the long-term value of firms. With the continued growth of index investing, including the use of ETFs [exchange traded funds] by active managers, advocacy and engagement have become even more important for protecting the long-term interests of investors.
>
> As we seek to build long-term value for our clients through engagement, our aim is not to micromanage a company's operations. Instead, our primary focus is to ensure board accountability for creating long-term value. However, a long-term approach should not be confused with an infinitely patient one. When BlackRock does not see progress despite ongoing engagement, or companies are insufficiently responsive to our efforts to protect our clients' long-term economic interests, we do not hesitate to exercise our right to vote against incumbent directors or misaligned executive compensation.
>
> Environmental, social, and governance (ESG) factors relevant to a company's business can provide essential insights into management effectiveness and thus a company's long-term prospects. We look to see that a company is attuned to the key factors that contribute to long-term growth: sustainability of the business model and its operations, attention to external and environmental factors that could impact the company, and recognition of the company's role as a member of the communities in which it operates. A global company needs to be local in every single one of its markets.
>
> BlackRock also engages to understand a company's priorities for investing for long-term growth, such as research, technology and, critically, employee development and long-term financial well-being. The events of the past year have only reinforced how critical the well-being of a company's employees is to its long-term success.

However, there is a gap between what executives of asset managers say in public letters, where they stress the need for long-term orientation and broad notions of value creation, and the focus on the current year and financial metrics by their investment analysts and portfolio managers (High-Level Expert Group on Sustainable Finance, 2017).

4.3.1 REASONS TO JOIN COALITIONS FOR SF

But why would an investor, bank, or company join a coalition? A major reason to join is that members can seize the opportunities of the transition towards a sustainable economy and are thus intrinsically—or even just instrumentally—motivated to work on LTVC. Remember, the long-term focus of these coalitions usually includes avoiding social and environmental hazards, which materialize over the medium to long term. These issues are harder to capture in a traditional short-term profit-maximizing approach to finance. However, all organizations—especially large ones—are complex. There are various complementary reasons why any given organization might decide to join a coalition:

- **Peer effect**: The size of the coalition and the membership of key competitors push other peers to join to avoid a competitive disadvantage in the long term.

- **Outside pressure**: Consumers and non-governmental organizations can prompt an organization to align its corporate social responsibility principles to those of the coalition.
- **Reputation**: An organization may want to join a coalition in order to be identified as a leader in sustainable practices or just to improve the perception of its corporate identity—in some cases this may become a marketing operation.
- **Risk avoidance**: A company might be incentivized to join in order to avoid the risk of stranded assets (Litterman, 2015).
- **Collective advocacy**: A coalition is stronger than individual entities in pushing governments to clarify their agendas and lobby for sustainable change. This can help coalition members reduce policy-related uncertainty over the future value of assets (Skancke, 2016).
- **Collective engagement**: Dimson, Karakaş, and Li (2015) provide evidence that collaboration among activist investors is instrumental in increasing the success rate of social and environmental engagements. Coalitions of long-term investors are thus a major force for change through collective engagement with companies.

We recommend further research on building effective coalitions for SF in parallel with regulatory initiatives to address social and environmental externalities. Private and public initiatives can reinforce each other. Private action can pave the way for public rules and taxes. In turn, public endorsement can strengthen private coalitions. To start this broad research agenda, an initial assessment of the main coalitions for SF is provided in Table 4.3. For asset management, we look at PRI, FCLTGlobal, and GIIN. For banking, the Equator Principles for project finance and GABV are included. For companies, WEF and WBCSD are analyzed.

Even if a new coalition has a clear joint mission or ideology, many issues and undesirable incentives can arise. This can lead the coalition to self-destruct or underperform. The most obvious risk is free riding, whereby an organization enjoys (part of) the benefits of a coalition's membership without observing its principles and rules. The pioneering work of Ostrom (1990) on the design of institutions for governing common resources can be applied in this context to understand what principles should be followed by a coalition for a proper and effective functioning. In order to make an initial assessment, we follow the design principles developed by Ostrom. Thus we assess each coalition on the following features:

1. **Clearly defined boundaries**: What percentage of the relevant sector is covered by the coalition?
2. **Membership rules restricting the use of the common good**: How ambitious is the vision of SF that the coalition applies? Scores range from 1.0 to 3.0, with 3.0 being the most advanced—see Table 1.3 in Chapter 1.

Table 4.3 Coalitions for SF

Coalition	Coverage (in %)	SF typology	Collective-choice arrangement	Monitoring	Graduated sanctions or rewards	Conflict-resolution mechanisms
PRI	38.0%*	1.0/2.0	Yes, six principles for responsible investment and mandatory reporting	Yes, assessment reports	Only for the board	No
FCLT Global	6.0%*	1.0/2.0	No, but collective goal to encourage long-term behaviour in business and investment	Partly, demonstrated commitment to LTVC for new members	No	No
GIIN	0.05%*	3.0	Partly, activities to support impact investing	No	No	No
Equator Principles	30.0%†	1.0/2.0	Yes, principles setting out a framework for managing environmental and social risk in projects	Yes, requirement to report; Equator Principles Association assesses compliance with reporting requirements, but does not verify content	No, compliance with principles responsibility of members	No
GABV	0.07%	2.0/3.0	Yes, principles of sustainable banking	Yes, scorecard to measure the economic, social, and environmental impact of banks	No	No
WEF	31.0%	1.0/2.0	No, but mission based on stakeholder theory, which stresses accountability to all parts of society	No	Only for the managing board	No
WBCSD	18.9%	1.0/2.0	Yes, principles of sustainable development	Yes, council reviews and benchmarks annual sustainability report of members	Yes, cessation of membership in case of non-adherence	Partly, crisis management

Notes: The two or three main coalitions are shown for each group (asset managers, banks, corporates). PRI = Principles for Responsible Investment (supported by the UN); FCLTGlobal = Focus Capital on the Long-Term Global; GIIN = Global Impact Investing Network; GABV = Global Alliance for Banking on Values; WEF = World Economic Forum; WBCSD = World Business Council for Sustainable Development. The coverage is calculated as follows: the assets of members as percentage of global AUM at conventional, alternative, and private wealth funds—for asset managers; the assets of member banks as percentage of global banking assets—for banks; and the revenues of member Fortune 500 corporates as percentage of total revenues of Fortune 500 corporates—for corporates. The SF typology (1.0, 2.0, and 3.0 from Table 1.3 in Chapter 1) is based on the author's assessment. The information is correct as of end 2016.

* Confining the analysis to global AUM of conventional funds at $109 trillion (instead of global AUM of all funds at $163 trillion), PRI members' assets are 57 per cent of global AUM; FCLTGlobal members' assets 9 per cent; and GIIN members' assets 0.07 per cent.

† Ninety-one banks have officially adopted the Equator Principles, covering over 70 per cent of international project finance debt in emerging markets.

Source: Website of respective coalitions and authors' calculations and assessment based on Schoenmaker (2017).

3. **Collective choice arrangements:** Can individuals or organizations affected by the coalition's operational rules and principles participate in the modification of these rules and principles?
4. **Monitoring:** Is there effective reporting on progress towards meeting the rules and principles, with assessment of the extent to which these rules and principles are followed?
5. **Sanctions and rewards:** How are violations of coalition rules and principles punished and how is compliance rewarded?
6. **Conflict resolution mechanism:** Do coalition members and their officials have rapid access to low-cost local arenas to resolve conflicts between members or between members and officials?

As we see, there is clearly an inverse relationship between the quality of the SF typology and the size of the coalition. Table 4.3 shows that the larger coalitions—covering 20 to 40 per cent of the relevant reference group—sit somewhere between SF 1.0 and 2.0. These coalitions thus include social and environmental factors in their decision-making, albeit alongside the financial factor, but do not give priority to them over profits.

However, it is interesting to note that coalition members tend to progressively tighten coalition principles in subsequent versions, providing a dynamic component—some sort of virtuous cycle. However, not all coalitions even have clear principles guiding the behaviour of their members. PRI and WBCSD have well-defined sustainability principles, which are monitored and are also closer to SF 2.0 than the other coalitions (FCLTGlobal, the Equator Principles, and WEF). Conversely, coalitions adopting SF 3.0 put social and environmental factors first, with financial factors as a viability constraint. The coverage of these advanced coalitions is very small, with less than 1 per cent of the relevant group covered. We classify GABV between SF 2.0 and 3.0, because GABV stresses the triple bottom line (2.0)—people, planet, and profit—as well as social and environmental challenges (3.0).

A key question for the effectiveness of these coalitions is the monitoring of the coalition members. Here the picture is very diverse. Some coalitions, such as the Equator Principles Association (see also Weber, 2017), leave monitoring and reporting explicitly to members, while the WBCSD explicitly reviews and benchmarks its members' annual sustainability reports. Organizations need to map their whole scope tree and monitor not only their direct impact on society and environment but also that of their clients and of the full value chain. Reporting is a powerful mechanism that provides incentives for concrete action, often even without the threat of sanctions. However, the latter are even more effective and some coalitions do have a sanction/reward system in place. But this is often to a limited extent (for example, only for the board). The WBCSD instead threatens to expel members that do not meet the 'membership conditions' and is the only coalition with a conflict-resolution mechanism. The lack of a system that ensures enforceability is a clear weak spot of many coalitions.

Finally, because short-termism is one of the main barriers to SF (see Chapter 3), these coalitions should adopt a long-term focus and allow time for new solutions to develop and flourish without quarterly benchmarking.

4.4 Conclusions

This short intermezzo chapter shows how institutional investors can increase their impact by forming coalitions to promote joint engagement. In this way, investors can increase their leverage on corporates and foster sustainable business practices. Private coalitions on sustainability can run in parallel with government initiatives and regulations on sustainability, reinforcing each other.

Further research on the design of effective coalitions is recommended. This research could examine the common objective, membership rules, peer monitoring, and sanctions. These coalitions on SF have the potential to pave the way for transformational change, as discussed in Chapter 12.

Key concepts used in this chapter

Coalition for sustainable finance is a group of like-minded organizations (investors, banks, or companies) that form a non-profit platform or coalition to pursue sustainable business and finance practices.

Common good refers to what is shared and beneficial for all or most members of a given community.

Corporate governance refers to the mechanisms, relations, and processes by which a company is controlled and is directed. It involves balancing the many interests of the stakeholders of a company.

Engagement refers to investors' dialogue with investee companies on a broad range of ESG issues.

Externalities refer to consequences of activities, which affect other (or third) parties without this being reflected in market prices.

Institutional investors are (large) financial institutions that manage investments (equities, bonds, and alternative assets) for clients and beneficiaries. Traditional investors include investment funds, pension funds, and insurance companies. Alternative institutional investors include sovereign wealth funds, hedge funds, and private equity.

Long-term value creation refers to the goal of companies, which optimize financial, social, and environmental value in the long run.

Ratchet effect refers to escalations in price or production that tend to self-perpetuate. Once prices have been raised, it is difficult to reverse these changes, because people tend to be influenced by the previous best or highest level.

Tragedy of the commons refers to the situation within a shared-resource system, where individual users acting independently according to their own self-interest behave contrary to the common good of all users by depleting that resource through their collective action.

SUGGESTED READING

Dimson, E., O. Karakaş, and X. Li (2015), 'Active ownership', *Review of Financial Studies*, 28(12): 3225–68.

Ostrom, E. (1990), *Governing the Commons: The Evolution of Institutions for Collective Action*, Cambridge University Press, Cambridge.

REFERENCES

Çelik, S. and M. Isaksson (2014), 'Institutional investors and ownership engagement', *Financial Market Trends*, 2013(2): 93–114.

Clift, R., S. Sim, H. King, J. L. Chenoweth, I. Christie, J. Clavreul, C. Mueller et al. (2017), 'The challenges of applying planetary boundaries as a basis for strategic decision-making in companies with global supply chains', *Sustainability*, 9(2): 279.

Darvas, Z. and D. Schoenmaker (2018), 'Institutional investors and development of Europe's capital markets', in: D. Busch, E. Avgouleas and G. Ferrarini (eds.), *Capital Markets Union in Europe*, Oxford University Press, Oxford, 395–412.

Dimson, E., O. Karakaş, and X. Li (2015), 'Active ownership', *Review of Financial Studies*, 28(12): 3225–68.

ECB (European Central Bank) (2017), 'Structural financial indicators 2017', Frankfurt.

High-Level Expert Group on Sustainable Finance (2017), 'Financing a sustainable European economy', Interim Report, European Union, Brussels.

Litterman, B. (2015), *Climate Risk: Tail Risk and the Price of Carbon Emissions*, John Wiley & Sons Inc., New York.

McElroy, M. (2008), *Social Footprints: Measuring the Social Sustainability Performance of Organizations*, Thetford Center, Vermont, USA.

McNulty, T. and D. Nordberg (2016), 'Ownership, activism and engagement: institutional investors as active owners', *Corporate Governance: An International Review*, 24(3): 346–58.

Neal, D. and G. Warren (2015), 'Long-term investing as an agency problem', CIFR Paper No. 063/2015, Centre for International Finance and Regulation, Sydney.

OECD (Organisation for Economic Co-operation and Development) (2017), 'OECD institutional investor statistics 2017', Paris, http://www.oecd.org/publications/oecd-institutional-investors-statistics-2225207x.htm, accessed 28 June 2018.

Ostrom, E. (1990), *Governing the Commons: The Evolution of Institutions for Collective Action*, Cambridge University Press, Cambridge.

Schoenmaker, D. (2017), 'From risk to opportunity: a framework for sustainable finance', RSM Series on Positive Change, vol. 2, Rotterdam School of Management, Erasmus University, https://papers.ssrn.com/sol3/papers.cfm?abstract_id=3066210, accessed 28 June 2018.

SIFMA (Securities Industry and Financial Markets Association) (2017), 'The SIFMA fact book 2017', New York, https://www.sifma.org/wp-content/uploads/2016/10/US-Fact-Book-2017-SIFMA.pdf, accessed 28 June 2018.

Skancke, M. (2016), 'Fossil fuel investments: fossil fuel investment and the broader issue of transitioning to a low-carbon economy', Australian Council of Superannuation Investors, Melbourne.

TCFD (Task Force on Climate-related Financial Disclosures) (2017), 'Recommendations of the Task Force on Climate-related Financial Disclosures: final report (Bloomberg Report)', Financial Stability Board, Basel.

Thurm, R., B. Baue and C. van der Lugt (2018), 'Blueprint 5 The Transformation Journey: A Step-By-Step Approach to Organizational Thriveability and System Value Creation', Reporting 3.0, Berlin.

UNFCCC (United Nations Framework Convention on Climate Change) (2015), 'Adoption of the Paris Agreement', Paris.

UNFCCC (United Nations Framework Convention on Climate Change) (2016), 'Aggregate effect of the intended nationally determined contributions: an update', Marrakech, https://unfccc.int/resource/docs/2016/cop22/eng/02.pdf, accessed 28 June 2018.

Weber, O. (2017), 'Equator Principles reporting: factors influencing the quality of reports', *International Journal of Corporate Strategy and Social Responsibility*, 1(2): 141–60.

5 Strategy and intangibles—changing business models

Overview

Business models and practices are important for sustainability, because social and environmental externalities are generated primarily in the corporate sector.

This chapter examines how companies can consider sustainability in their business models. Corporate sustainability goes well beyond corporate social responsibility (CSR), which is mostly about limiting harm. Rather, companies play a key role in the transition to a sustainable economy. Some will survive that transition, others will not, as their competitive positions are eroded. Sustainability is therefore also about corporate survival. It is a critical issue with regard to:

- Competitive positions: What position does the company occupy in a market, relative to its competition?
- Business models: How does the company create and deliver value?
- Intangibles: What resources does the company have that have no clear physical or financial embodiment?
- Strategy: What is the company's plan for achieving desirable outcomes?

In this chapter, we examine how these relations work and consider examples of sustainability issues at several companies. It should be emphasized that the materiality (or lack thereof) of sustainability issues varies per industry, and also within industries, depending on the nature of the industry, the specific company's business model, and local conditions.

Companies that manage their material sustainability issues well are more likely to protect their competitive positions, adapt their business models, and grow their intangible assets. The better their strategy anticipates the importance of sustainability issues, the more likely they are to be successful both in long-term value creation (LTVC) and in making the transition to a more sustainable economy. Section 5.5 formulates guidelines for LTVC.

Learning objectives

After you have studied this chapter, you should be able to:

- explain how companies can prepare for the transition to a sustainable economy;
- explain why and how companies should connect sustainability to their competitive position, business model, intangible assets, and strategy;
- loosely connect corporate sustainability performance with corporate financial performance;
- identify the materiality of sustainability issues.

5.1 Preparing for transformational change

Moving to a more sustainable economy implies system change, which is inherently complex. Holling (2001) describes such system change as a panarchy, consisting of hierarchies and adaptive cycles. Each level evolves at its own pace and is protected from above by larger and slower levels, and invigorated from below by faster, smaller cycles of innovation. Panarchy is a conceptual framework to account for the dual characteristics of complex systems: stability and change. It studies how economic growth and human development depend on ecosystems and how they interact.

For companies, this requires an integrative view on corporate sustainability, as Hahn and colleagues (2015) argue (see also Chapter 1). They stress the need for simultaneous integration of the economic, environmental, and social (EES) dimensions, without a priori emphasizing one over another. Firms need to accept tensions in corporate sustainability and pursue different sustainability aspects simultaneously, even if they seem to contradict each other. In a similar vein, Porter and Kramer (2011) propose a shift from CSR to corporate shared value, because firms need to (and will be forced to) internalize their externalities. Dyllick and Muff (2016) distinguish different generations of business sustainability, with only a few companies having yet reached business sustainability 3.0, which means starting with sustainability challenges (not economic concerns), creating value for the common good (not just shareholders), and taking an outside-in view (rather than inside out). Table 5.1 illustrates the business sustainability typology, which mirrors our sustainable finance (SF) typology in Table 1.3.

Making the transition is a major change management challenge (see Chapter 12). Whether a company can achieve business sustainability 3.0 depends on factors such as culture and the dialogue in the board. Here, the trap of groupthink looms: poor decision-making in a group can happen when members strive for unanimity above their motivation to realistically appraise alternative courses of action (Janis, 1971). To avoid this trap, boards should

Table 5.1 The business sustainability typology

Business sustainability typology	Concerns (What?)	Values created (What for?)	Organizational perspective (How?)
Business as usual	Economic concerns	Shareholder value	Inside out
Business sustainability 1.0	Three-dimensional concerns	Refined shareholder value	Inside out
Business sustainability 2.0	Three-dimensional concerns	Triple bottom line	Inside out
Business sustainability 3.0	Starting with sustainability challenges	Creating value for the common good	Outside in
Key shifts involved	1st shift: broadening the business concern	2nd shift: expanding the value created	3rd shift: changing the perspective

Source: Dyllick and Muff (2016).

strive for diversity in members' backgrounds and skill sets and ensure that the right questions are asked. This might help to overturn the organizational perspective from inside out to outside in. An outside-in perspective starts with the societal challenges (outside) and considers how the company (inside) can contribute to solving them.

To what extent companies are preparing for transformational change can be gauged from both their words and their actions. For example, some energy companies are still in denial about climate change and the impending shift away from fossil fuels—this is visible in the fact that they do not talk about that shift nor act on it. Others do talk about that shift, but it is clear from their actions (i.e. continued investment in expensive oil fields) that they assume the shift will be very gradual and will not happen any time soon. Still others take more action and shift their investments away from coal and oil to gas, which is less polluting, but which is still a fossil fuel. Just a few are like the utilities SSE (United Kingdom) and EDP (Portugal), which are explicit about the future of clean energy and, accordingly, allocate their capital expenditure towards renewable energy. These utilities have managed to adopt an outside-in perspective.

The winning companies will be the ones that lead the adaptation process of their industry, while the losers will be the ones that remain in denial. However, the most advanced sustainability approaches will not always win either, as they may not match economic reality. As long as a new technology is too expensive, and its superior performance does not pay off in economic terms, it will not create a viable business model. Launching new, more sustainable business models can be very risky, just as not becoming more sustainable can be risky. In some industries sustainability issues are less pressing and therefore less relevant for long-term survival. Still, the biggest winners will be those that not only adapt within their own industry but also provide solutions for other industries. The opportunities to do so are there, but they need to be taken. That is where strategy comes in.

5.2 Theories of competitive position, business models, intangibles, and strategy

A company does not operate in isolation. Schramade (2016) argues the extent to which a company can survive and thrive depends on varying factors, such as its competitive position in the markets where it operates, the design and fit of its business models, and how it builds intangible assets. Intangible assets are assets without physical or financial embodiment. These factors culminate in the company's choice and execution of its strategy, that is, the company's plan to achieve its desired outcomes (see Figure 5.1).

In fact, Lev (2017) argues that a sustainable competitive edge is crucial for achieving the ecological, sociological, environmental, and business meanings of sustainability. As he puts it: 'Without a sustainable competitive advantage, a business enterprise will not be able to devote the resources required to be environmentally or socially sustainable.'

5.2.1 COMPETITIVE POSITION

> In business, I look for economic castles protected by unbreachable 'moats'.
>
> Warren Buffett
>
> Warren Buffett is the classic example of a long-term investor who looks beyond the noise of short-term news items. Rather, he prefers buying enduring businesses. In the epigraph quoted, the castle is the business and the moat is the company's competitive advantage.

The competitive position of a company is the position it occupies in a market relative to its competitors. If that competitive position is strong, the

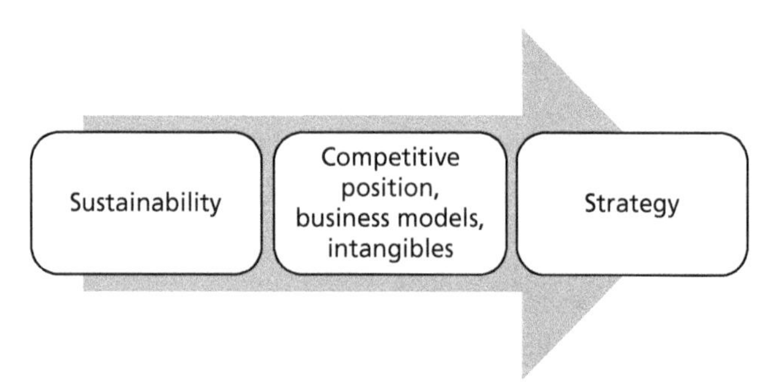

Figure 5.1 Linking sustainability and strategy

Source: Adapted from Schramade (2016).

company is said to have a competitive advantage. Porter (1985) distinguishes three generic competitive strategies:

1. **Cost leadership**: Lower cost than competitors.
2. **Differentiation**: Differ from the competition by type of activities or by way those activities are executed.
3. **Focus**: Offer products to selected market segments, not industry wide.

Porter argues that a company can only perform better than its competitors if it offers more value to customers (differentiation or focus) or the same value at lower cost (cost leadership) or both. These generic strategies have been criticized for lacking specificity and being limiting. It is also not clear how to achieve these. It is good to know that you want to achieve differentiation, but how do you go about it?

Another way of framing is that competitive advantage is achieved and maintained by the successful deployment of strategic assets, which share three attributes (Lev, 2017):

- They are *valuable*: They create or contribute to the creation of a stream of net economic benefits.
- They are *rare*.
- They are *difficult to imitate*.

But still, what are the sources of strategic assets?

5.2.1.1 Sources of competitive advantage

The academic literature (e.g. Porter, 1990; Wernerfelt, 1984) has identified several, partly overlapping, sources of competitive advantage. Many of these sources can also be considered sustainability issues, intangibles, or underlying value drivers. These sources can be classified in four broad groups:

1. resources;
2. knowledge;
3. human capital;
4. networks

5.2.1.2 Resources

Resources, and in particular natural resources (e.g. Porter, 1990), have for many years been regarded as key sources of wealth for companies and other organizations, such as states. States have gone to war over resources and resources are still a source of friction between states, especially if they relate to energy (oil), water, or food. Box 5.1 provides an example of a company that has a competitive advantage based on its resources.

BOX 5.1 RIO TINTO'S COMPETITIVE EDGE FROM PHYSICAL RESOURCES

Rio Tinto is a mining company mainly active in iron ore. The company's iron ore mines in western Australia are the lowest cost in the world, thanks to high-grade iron ore and strong infrastructure. As a result, the company's iron ore profit margins are consistently higher than those of its peers.

More recently, data have been recognized as key resources, which is reflected in the fact that data-intense companies such as Alphabet (Google) and Facebook are now among the largest companies in the world. Their rise has yielded increased concerns over data privacy and market power, with some people already calling for these companies to be broken up or regulated like utilities.

The resource-based view of the company (e.g. Barney, 1991; Wernerfelt, 1984) takes a much wider and more intangible view of firm resources. It says that the application of a set of (tangible or intangible) resources is the basis of competitive advantage. This advantage can only be sustained if the valuable resources are not perfectly mobile, not easily imitated, and hard to substitute.

5.2.1.3 Knowledge

Technology can bring significant competitive advantage, because it may allow companies to produce better-performing or cheaper products. But knowledge is not just technology, it also encompasses processes (doing things better). Moreover, knowledge is potentially more valuable if others have less of it, for example, in the presence of information asymmetries (Nayyar, 1990). Hall (1993) emphasizes intangible resources, that is, non-physical and non-financial resources that provide a durable competitive advantage, for example resulting from the possession of relevant capability differentials. This ties into the resource-based view mentioned in section 5.2.1.2.

Often, valuable knowledge is tacit and hard to exploit or export. To make full use of tacit knowledge, the company needs to codify it. Box 5.2 provides an example of a competitive advantage from knowledge.

BOX 5.2 NOVOZYMES' COMPETITIVE ADVANTAGE FROM R&D

Novozymes is a Danish enzyme maker that replaces traditional chemicals with enzymes (proteins that act as catalysts) in, for example, washing powders, and baking and agricultural products. Its enzymes provide better performance at lower temperatures and hence lower energy costs and lower emissions. As a result, the company grows twice as fast and at double the profit margin compared to ordinary chemicals companies.

5.2.1.4 Human capital and culture

Pfeffer (1994) argues that traditional sources of success—product and process technology, protected or regulated markets, access to financial resources, and economies of scale—have become weaker than in the past, since the rate of change has gone up. This leaves organizational culture and capabilities, derived from how people are managed, as comparatively more vital. He points out that the five best-performing stocks over the 1972–92 period were of companies that operated in very tough (i.e. overall poorly performing) industries. These companies stood out because they were able to manage their workforce more effectively, which is a hard skill to imitate. After all, the success that comes from managing people effectively is often not as visible or transparent from the outside as it is within the company itself. It is often hard to comprehend the dynamics of a particular company and how it operates because the way people are managed often fits together in an organizational system. It is easy to copy one thing but much more difficult to copy numerous things.

In a similar vein, Barney (1986) argues that culture can drive superior performance. But, unfortunately, studies of culture are unable to describe how less successful firms can modify their cultures to achieve competitive advantage. Barney identifies three conditions for culture to drive competitive advantage: (i) cultures have to be valuable (resulting in stronger value drivers); (ii) rare; and (iii) hard to imitate. That is, the same conditions that characterize strategic assets.

Investment consultants Coburn Ventures (Coburn, 2016) argue that a strong culture is not the same as a successful culture. Rather, the success of a culture depends on the context in which the company operates. For example, a very aggressive corporate culture can work in the phase of high growth and then become counterproductive in the phase of restructuring. Another problem with culture is that it is hard to capture from the outside. Guiso, Sapienza, and Zingales (2015) find that a company's 'advertised' values can be very different from the 'real' values as perceived by their employees.

5.2.1.5 Networks/access

To achieve a competitive position in a market, a company needs to have access to that market. Such access can be restricted in several ways. First of all, market access might be limited or even blocked by government regulation, allowing incumbents to hold a strong competitive position. There can be good reasons for such regulation, for example minimum quality standards. But often it is simply rent seeking by local elites, as is typically the case in many emerging markets (see, for example, Acemoglu and Robinson, 2012). Secondly, market access might be limited by a lack of awareness or visibility. Many markets are small and specialized. Thirdly, customers might be sticky and hard to pull away from incumbents. This is the case if switching costs for clients are high (due to a lot of hassle, lack of transparency, or long-term/combined contracts for example).

Network effects might also arise from scale, in that networks become more valuable as they get bigger. Think of social media such as LinkedIn or Facebook that became more interesting to both advertisers and users as more users participated. In addition, companies might also benefit from specialized supplier networks (Dyer, 1996), which allow them to develop superior skill sets and generate strong financial returns.

5.2.1.6 Competitive position and financial performance

A firm's competitive position is typically reflected in its financial performance: companies with strong competitive positions tend to have a strong financial performance. Their superior products or lower costs show up in strong value drivers: higher sales growth, higher profit margins, and a higher return on investment. Schramade (2016) argues that performance on material sustainability issues should follow a similar causality, with a competitive edge on a sustainability issue resulting in stronger value drivers. In the end, strong value drivers are underpinned by strong competitive advantages such as the ones mentioned in sections 5.2.1.1-5. These can be industry specific, company specific, business unit specific, or location specific. But high growth in itself is not sufficient. Chan, Karceski, and Lakonishok (2003) find that high margins tend to be much more viable than high sales growth. After all, high growth puts strain on an organization (unlike high margins) and there are limits to market size, and hence limits on growth.

5.2.2 BUSINESS MODELS

Great business models can reshape industries and drive spectacular growth. A case in point is the iPhone, which transformed mobile phones into portable computers. But it is often hard to design a strong business model. Johnson, Christensen, and Kagermann (2008) point out that many companies find business model innovation difficult and managers often do not understand their existing business model well enough to know when it needs changing, or how. Box 5.3 provides an example of a company that did not change its business model in time.

5.2.2.1 What is a business model?

A business model is the representation of how a company creates and delivers value. Or, as Osterwalder and Pigneur (2010) put it: 'a business model

BOX 5.3 DOLLAR SHAVE CLUB VERSUS GILLETTE

Gillette enjoyed decades of high profit margins thanks to its model of providing cheap razors and expensive blades. However, as it was overearning, it basically invited in new entrants, and Dollar Shave Club came in with a subscription model that undercut Gillette.

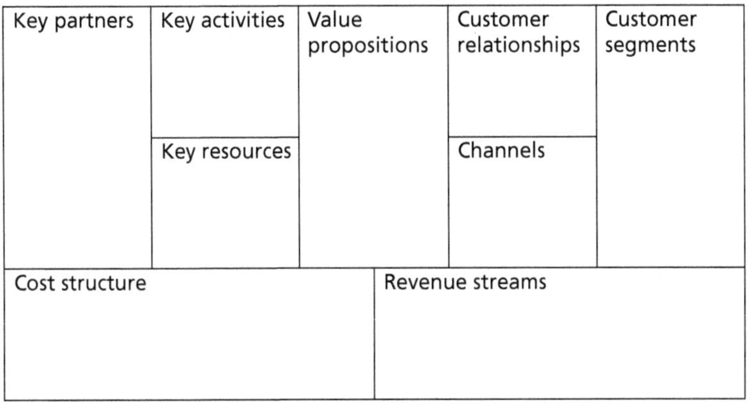

<table>
<tr><td rowspan="2">Key partners</td><td>Key activities</td><td rowspan="2">Value propositions</td><td>Customer relationships</td><td rowspan="2">Customer segments</td></tr>
<tr><td>Key resources</td><td>Channels</td></tr>
<tr><td colspan="3">Cost structure</td><td colspan="2">Revenue streams</td></tr>
</table>

Figure 5.2 The business model canvas

Source: Adapted from Osterwalder and Pigneur (2010).

describes the rationale of how an organisation creates, delivers and captures value'. This becomes clearer if one considers the elements of a business model. Osterwalder and Pigneur (2010) have done so with their business model canvas, which distinguishes nine elements, as illustrated in Figure 5.2. The business model canvas outlines the building blocks for the activities and enables businesses to focus on operational and strategic management and on marketing.

Similarly, Johnson and colleagues (2008) argue that a successful business model has three components:

1. **A customer value proposition**: The model helps customers perform a specific 'job' that alternative offerings do not address.
2. **A profit formula**: The model generates value for the company through factors such as the revenue model, cost structure, margins, and/or inventory turnover.
3. **Key resources and processes**: The company has the people, technology, products, facilities, equipment, and brand required to deliver the value proposition to targeted customers. The company also has processes (training, manufacturing, services) to leverage those resources.

Of course, these elements are reminiscent of the sources of competitive advantage considered in Section 5.2.1.1. There is no single best business model. Slywotzky and Morrison (1997) distinguish dozens of business models that can be successful provided that they fit the circumstances. Given that circumstances can change, business models need to adapt.

It should be noted that the business model descriptions given are profit-centric and have been criticized for ignoring sustainability issues. Joyce and Paquin (2016) therefore propose a triple-layered business model canvas, which extends the original business model canvas by adding two layers:

- an environmental layer—based on a lifecycle perspective; and
- a social layer—based on a stakeholder perspective.

5.2.2.2 Reinventing business models

As mentioned, companies have difficulty in reinventing their business models. Chesbrough (2010) asserts that 'While companies may have extensive investments and processes for exploring new ideas and technologies, they often have little, if any, ability to innovate the business models through which these inputs will pass.' He argues that there are barriers to business model experimentation, because this conflicts with existing interests within the firm, locked-in investments, and high cash flows (CFs) from existing business. For example, car companies have apparently stated that building electric cars is easy. But they have refrained from doing so as this would cannibalize the existing model with its high margins from replacement parts. However, this might turn out to be a costly mistake. The ability to adapt one's business model can be crucial to corporate survival, especially in changing circumstances.

5.2.3 INTANGIBLES AND MATERIALITY

A century ago, the balance sheet of a firm was a pretty good indicator of firm value. This is no longer the case, with the switch from agriculture and basic industries to services and advanced industries. Most listed firms are priced much higher than their book values. That is not a sign of overvaluation (at least not necessarily), but it indicates that the value of firms has shifted from tangible assets, such as land, buildings, and machinery, and financial assets, to intangibles, such as human capital, processes, data, and innovation. This is particularly so in research and development (R&D)-intense sectors such as health care and information technology and/or in services sectors such as consultancy. Figure 5.3 shows that the intangibles of the Standard & Poor's (S&P) 500 companies have increased from 17 per cent of market value in 1975 to 87 per cent in 2015.

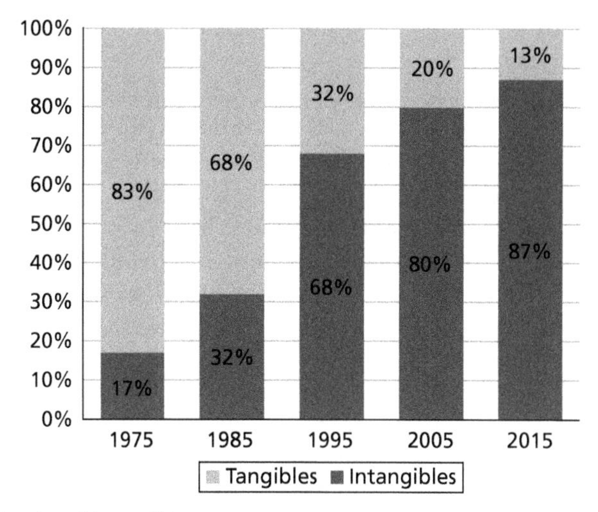

Figure 5.3 The rise of intangibles

Note: The tangible and intangibles are measured as a percentage of the market value of the S&P 500 companies.

Source: Ocean Tomo, LLC.

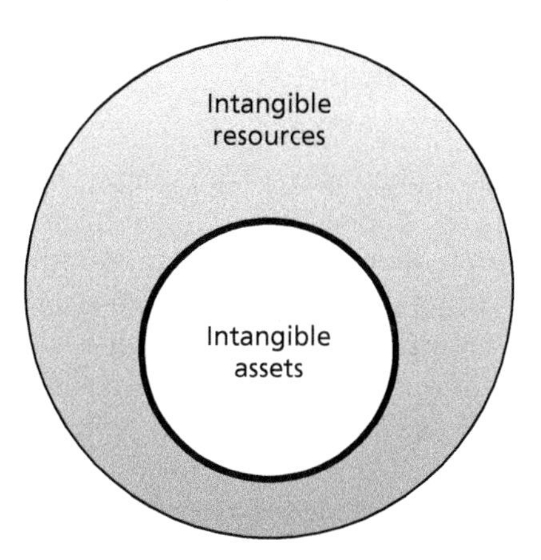

Figure 5.4 Intangible resources versus intangible assets

5.2.3.1 Intangible resources versus intangible assets

It is important to distinguish intangible resources from intangible assets, as the latter is a much narrower concept. Intangible assets are only those intangible resources that meet the criteria of an asset (see Figure 5.4).

According to the International Accounting Standards Board (IASB, 2010), 'An asset is a resource controlled by the enterprise as a result of past events and from which future economic benefits are expected to flow to the enterprise.'

An asset is thus a claim towards future benefits, or to put it differently, a cash-generating unit.

Among assets, intangible assets are those claims towards future benefits that do not have a physical or financial embodiment (Lev, 2000). Often-used synonyms for intangible assets are intellectual property and knowledge assets. Intangible assets meet the criteria of an asset, that is, that the resource is controlled by the enterprise and that future benefits can be estimated. But many intangible resources do not meet these criteria and are thus not capitalized as assets. As a result, they do not show up on the balance sheet. But they may be included, explicitly or implicitly, in company valuations, provided that investors have sufficient confidence in their eventual cash-generating abilities. As an example, most R&D does not show up in the balance sheet, except capitalized R&D expenses (if the company so chooses) or R&D that has already resulted in revenue streams, for example by means of royalties. This is problematic, as important sources of value creation are not reported. Moreover, intangibles tend to be much harder to manage than tangible assets, which makes it even more critical they are well understood.

Intangibles come in many guises and Lev (2000) distinguishes three major nexuses of intangibles:

- innovation/discovery;
- organizational practices/designs;
- human resources.

These nexuses are often intertwined. For example, strong human resources are needed for a company to be innovative. In addition, the nexuses are often the source of more visible strengths such as brands. After all, a strong brand typically results from doing something right, such as providing more reliable or more innovative products. Not surprisingly, these three nexuses are reminiscent of the sources of competitive advantage mentioned in section 5.2.1.1. They are also strongly related to the six capitals of integrated reporting that are discussed in Chapter 6.

Companies can have large intangible assets on their balance sheet that are called goodwill. Goodwill is the price paid in an acquisition in excess of the book value of assets. This is not necessarily a good reflection of the real value of the intangible resources. After all, the company might have paid too much or too little for the acquired company. Goodwill is thus not an intangible resource in itself, but it is rather an intangible asset that is a reflection of underlying intangible resources.

5.2.3.2 Materiality

A criterion that applies to both intangible assets and the wider concept of intangible resources is that of materiality. In accounting, materiality is a

Figure 5.5 Types of materiality

concept relating to the importance of an amount, transaction, or discrepancy. Accounting materiality is too narrow though, because it applies only to assets, not to intangible resources that are not assets. Therefore, it is worthwhile introducing the adjacent concepts of market materiality and business materiality. Market materiality refers to anything that significantly moves the stock market price of a company, including noise that turns out to be irrelevant otherwise. Business materiality refers to anything that significantly affects the company's ability to operate its business model and its future cash-generating capacity.

Figure 5.5 shows that the three materiality concepts may or may not overlap with each other at various instances and over time. For example, a bottleneck in a factory might evolve over a few months' time from a business issue (lower production) to one that is picked up by the market (the stock price drops) to an accounting issue (lower profitability). But market materiality might also precede business materiality, for example if a rise in car demand results in a stock price rise now, new machine orders (business materiality) later, and profitability (accounting materiality) much later.

The various concepts are typically blurred, with people using the term 'intangibles' to refer to all three types and more, such as stakeholder materiality and media materiality. More and more companies have started presenting a materiality matrix that outlines those sustainability issues that they consider most material, often assessed in cooperation with stakeholders. Figure 5.6 gives the materiality matrix of Novozymes (see Box 5.2). Such materiality matrices tend to differ a great deal between companies and industries.

Khan, Serafeim, and Yoon (2016) find that firms that do well on material sustainability issues tend to outperform in terms of stock price, while those that do well on immaterial sustainability issues tend to underperform. Green washing (i.e. pretending to be more sustainable than one actually is) does not pay off and the market detects it at some point. Examples of companies that

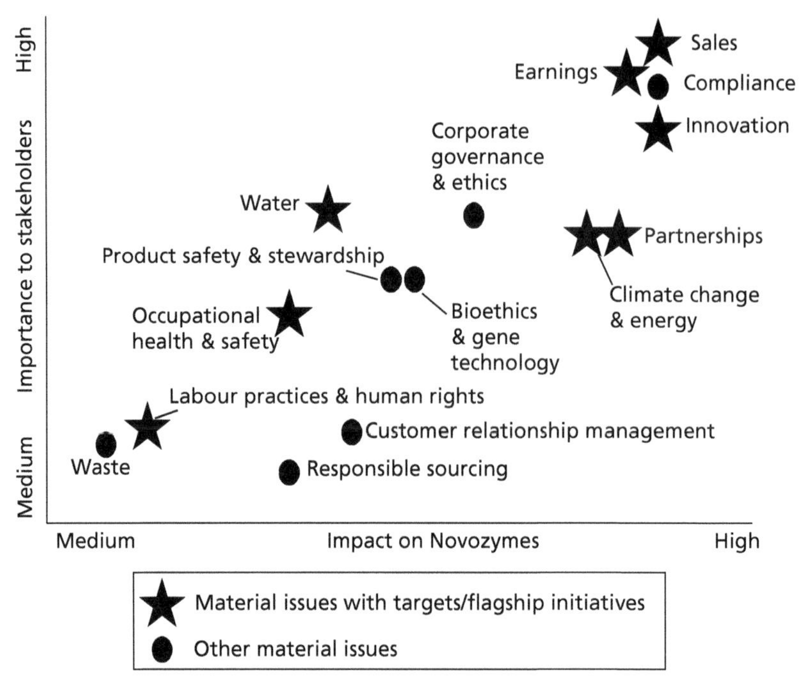

Figure 5.6 Novozymes' materiality matrix

Source: Novozymes 2016 Annual Report.

BOX 5.4 ANGLO AMERICAN'S FAILURE TO MAINTAIN INTANGIBLES

South African mining company Anglo American has a long history of technical expertise and strong project execution. However, because the associated intangible human resources were neglected, many people left the firm and much of its corporate memory was lost. The result was weak execution on projects. The Minas Rio iron ore project in Brazil turned out especially disastrous: originally planned to be built for around $2.5 billion, the project was delivered years over time and about $10 billion over budget. Local conditions were not sufficiently analysed and the company failed to apply for necessary environmental permits. While Anglo had high scores with sustainability ratings agencies, and scored well on many immaterial issues, it failed spectacularly on its most material sustainability issues: local stakeholder management and environmental management.

performed well on immaterial issues but failed on the material issues include VW (dieselgate) and Anglo American (see Box 5.4). These findings and examples highlight the need to focus on material issues—regardless of their nature and whether they are an asset or not. This might seem obvious, but in practice companies and sustainability analysts alike fail to prioritize.

5.2.3.3 **Problems with intangibles**

Those differences between intangibles resources do matter in other ways: some are reported (assets), some are not (not assets). Moreover, the reported intangible assets may be reported in an inconsistent way. This is partly a result of accounting shortcomings. But Lev (2000) suggests that the problem lies deeper: 'the information failures concerning intangibles are deeply rooted in their economic attributes: high risk, lack of full control over benefits and absence of markets'. He adds that 'Intangibles are frequently embedded in physical assets and labour, leading to considerable interaction between tangible and intangible assets in the creation of value. These interactions pose serious challenges to the measurement and valuation of intangibles.' Moreover, he mentions the politics of intangibles disclosure as a complicating factor, saying that 'corporate executives and auditors currently have few, if any, incentives to expand the information available about intangibles'. After all, it is in the interest of corporate executives to maintain information asymmetries with shareholders and other stakeholders, as it allows them to stay in power and maximize their incomes.

Haskel and Westlake (2017) argue that intangibles have four economic characteristics that are changing the economy. That is, they:

1. represent a sunk cost;
2. generate spillovers—also known as externalities;
3. are often scalable; and
4. tend to have synergies with one another.

The combination of these characteristics can easily result in industry concentration, that is, 'winner takes all' markets in which a few companies seize the vast majority of economic profits. This is typically not good for equality.

5.2.3.4 **Intangibles and finance**

Intangibles are highly relevant for finance and valuation, but also problematic to assess. As Figure 5.4 explains, intangible resources that are not intangible assets may show up in a company's valuation, while remaining invisible on that company's balance sheet. However, the degree to which they do show up is questionable (see also the three types of balance sheets in Section 6.3 of Chapter 6). In fact, as Lev (2000) argues, economic theory predicts and empirical evidence confirms that deficiencies in the disclosure of intangibles are associated with the following:

- excessively high cost of capital;
- systematic undervaluation ('lemons discount');
- excessive gains to officers of R&D-intensive companies from trading in the stocks of their employers;

- continuous deterioration in the usefulness of financial information;
- manipulation of financial information through intangibles.

To counter these deficiencies, Lev (2000) recommends the use of a so-called value chain scorecard. This is an information system based on non-financial indicators, to be used for both internal decision-making and disclosure to investors. It reports every step of the investment process. Unfortunately, Lev's advice was not heeded and the value chain scorecard was not widely adopted. However, it does resemble later recommendations by the International Integrated Reporting Council, which are discussed in Chapter 6.

5.2.4 STRATEGY

> If one does not know to which port one is sailing, no wind is favourable.
>
> Seneca

Corporate history is littered with companies that once held leading positions but failed as they did not see their markets change and/or were not able to adapt their strategy. Examples are Research In Motion, the producer of BlackBerry, Nokia in mobile phones, and Kodak in photography.

The concept of strategy originates in the military, with practice going back thousands of years. The word itself is derived from the Greek *strategos*, or 'the art of the general'. A strategy can be described as the plan chosen to achieve a desired future state. This still leaves a lot open for interpretation. Hambrick and Fredrickson (2001) argue that many companies think they have a strategy while in fact they do not. For a so-called strategy to be really a strategy, they claim it needs to have five parts:

1. **Arenas**: In which markets is the company going to be active?
2. **Vehicles**: How is it going to get there?
3. **Differentiators**: How can the company win in the marketplace?
4. **Staging**: What will be the speed and sequence of moves?
5. **Economic logic**: How will returns be obtained?

Sustainability issues can change the strategic environment. Therefore, each of the five parts can be affected by, or even be based on, sustainability issues. As Schramade (2017) argues, the United Nation's (UN's) Sustainable Development Goals (SDGs, see also Box 2.1 in Chapter 2) offer companies an opportunity to adopt sustainable business models and strategies. As governments have ambitious targets on realizing the 17 SDGs to make the world more sustainable by 2030, companies with negative social and environmental externalities face intensifying pressure to change, while solutions providers can benefit from higher sales growth, higher profit margins, and lower risk.

BOX 5.5 STRATEGIC CHOICES BY BMW

German carmaker BMW is well known for its premium-brand high-performance cars. It is also one of the more forward-looking and sustainability-minded carmakers. In 2007, BMW management realized that the world was changing and that margins were eroding. To better deal with changing customer behaviour and trends such as sustainability, urbanization, and regulation, the company decided to focus on mobility rather than just cars. The 2007 Number ONE strategy aimed to better benefit from opportunities beyond car production, looking more closely at the vehicle life cycle and industry value chain. In practice, this resulted in the development of the i-series electric cars, which were developed with revolutionary materials and built to be all-electric.

Moreover, with investors' fiduciary duty increasingly encompassing sustainability (see Chapter 3), businesses are under increasing pressure to incorporate this. Box 5.5 provides an example of a forward-looking strategy addressing environmental concerns.

5.2.4.1 Strategy and finance

The fields of strategy and finance overlap in the areas of valuation and strategic value management. The latter is the practice of ensuring that investment decisions create value, in the sense of having positive net present values (NPVs), that is, returns on capital exceeding the cost of capital (see Koller, Goedhart, and Wessels (2015) for an elaborate discussion). This practice involves the analysis of value drivers, which in turn can be affected by material sustainability issues. At a group level, it also involves allocating capital to those divisions or business units with the best projects.

5.3 Typical material sustainability issues

As suggested in Section 5.2 and highlighted by corporate scandals (see, for example, the Deepwater oil spill of BP in Box 1.1), sustainability can have a large impact on competitive positions, intangibles, business models, and strategy. This concerns not only risks, but also opportunities. It is important for companies to identify these issues in order to capture opportunities and avoid being blindsided by risks. Unfortunately, there is no undisputed classification of sustainability issues. They are typically classified as ESG (environmental, social, and governance issues) or EES (e.g., Hahn et al. 2015). However, these abbreviations have been criticized for lack of completeness.

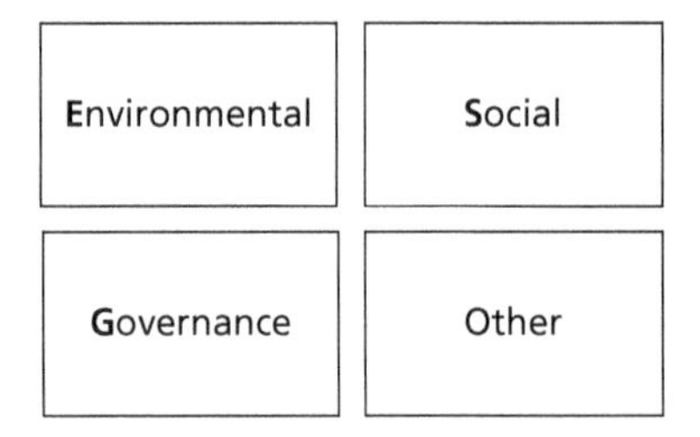

Figure 5.7 Sustainability issues

Nevertheless, this book follows the widely used ESG classification and puts the unclassifiable in the bucket 'other'. We thus distinguish:

1. environmental issues;
2. social issues;
3. governance issues;
4. other issues.

Figure 5.7 illustrates these four categories. It should be emphasized that their materiality (or lack thereof) varies per industry, and also within industries, depending on the nature of the industry, the specific company's business model, and local conditions. For example, a mining company faces very different issues to a pharmaceutical company. And less obviously, a gold miner in Africa faces different issues from an iron ore miner in Australia. The latter is, for example, much less exposed to labour issues (due to being in iron ore rather than gold mining) and less to the management of local stakeholders (due to being in Australia rather than Africa). These differences can be existential as companies might lose their licence to operate or their markets might get destroyed.

5.3.1 E FOR ENVIRONMENTAL ISSUES

The environment is ultimately the most important sustainability issue at the planetary level. As former UN Secretary-General Ban Ki-moon (at the 21st UN Climate Summit, 7 December 2016) put it: 'There can be no Plan B, because there is no Planet B.' At the company level, several environmental issues can be distinguished, such as climate strategy, greenhouse gas emissions, water, land use, reuse of raw materials, environmental management, and product stewardship. Companies such as Volkswagen (fuel emissions software) and BP (the Deepwater oil spill, discussed in Box 1.1) have stumbled on environmental issues. But there are opportunities too: companies such as Novozymes with biological solutions or Tesla with electric cars are transforming value chains with environmentally friendly alternatives. Other companies provide simpler solutions like light-weighting or renewable energy. Solar production is, for example, growing exponentially, as discussed in Chapter 2.

5.3.2 S FOR SOCIAL ISSUES

Both internally and externally, social issues can be very material. On the internal side, think of human capital (employees), health and safety, management, and culture. On the external side, important issues are the management of local stakeholders, social issues in the supply chain, brands, and trust. Here again there are risks and opportunities. Mining companies, such as Anglo American and Barrick, lost billions of dollars due to poor management of local stakeholders. In July 2017, the US Food and Drug Administration announced limits on nicotine content in cigarettes and all major tobacco companies saw their stock prices drop significantly that day. Airbag maker Takata (previously a $2 billion market-cap company) went bankrupt in 2017 after safety issues in its airbags resulted in a recall of millions of cars. Conversely, companies can establish sustainable competitive advantage by careful brand management or by tapping the potential of its workforce. Edmans (2012) finds that firms with higher employee satisfaction also perform better on the stock market. Another example of positive social impact is the production of medical equipment.

5.3.3 G FOR GOVERNANCE ISSUES

Corporate governance is ultimately about ensuring that a company is run in a decent way and that shareholders receive a return on their investment (Shleifer and Vishny, 1997). Governance comprises elements such as ownership structure, management compensation, voting structure and rules, business ethics, and a supervisory board. Companies with stronger corporate governance tend to have higher valuations and lower cost of capital (e.g. Gompers, Ishii, and Metrick, 2003). Moreover, Shrivastava and Addas (2014) find evidence that high-quality corporate governance itself can engender high sustainability performance, that is, strong G drives strong S and E. In emerging markets, corporate governance tends to be weaker, partly reflecting weaker country governance.

5.3.4 OTHER ISSUES

There are other issues that are not captured in E, S, or G. 'Other' does not mean unimportant though. Think of innovation and supply chains. Hendricks and Singhal (2005) find that companies with supply chain disruptions tend to underperform in the stock market, often for a long time. For example, when Nippon Shokubai had an explosion at its acrylic acid plant in September 2012, its stock price fell by 13 per cent in a day. Since acrylic acid is a key raw material for nappies, many nappy producers were affected as well. Section 6.3 in Chapter 6 provides examples of indicators of ESG issues.

5.3.5 MAPPING MATERIAL ISSUES

Companies often deal with ESG issues in isolation rather than taking a holistic approach (see Chapter 1). Also, they are not always aware which issues are material to their business. Many issues are potentially material for a company, but few are actually material in a specific case. To investigate what their most material issues are, companies can both undertake internal research and engage in stakeholder dialogues. This can result in a materiality matrix (such as the one shown in Figure 5.6), which may or may not be reported to the outside world. Or one could devise a stakeholder impact map, which outlines the company's main stakeholders, their main goals, and the way the company helps or hurts them. Tables 5.2 and 5.3 provide examples for a pharmaceutical company and a social media company—as filled out by the authors and their students.

As a pharmaceutical company operates in very different circumstances to a social media company, it also has different stakeholders, with different goals and impacts. Only the shareholders and the employees are similar in both cases. Governments are present in both stakeholder impact maps, but

Table 5.2 Stakeholder impact map for a pharmaceutical company

	Patients	Governments	Shareholders	Employees	Doctors & hospitals	Insurers
Positive impact	Treatment & possible cure	Population health	High prices & high growth, new drugs drive share price	Remuner-ation & job fulfilment	Good treatment outcomes	Fewer other costly treatments
Negative impact	High cost	Fees (prices) paid	High R&D costs, high risk	Perhaps company reputation	High prices	High prices
Short-term goals	Survival, affordability & accessibility	Reduce health-care costs	Maximize financial return	Good work–life balance and pay	Doctors to get perks; hospitals minimize costs	Minimize costs
Long-term goals	Better health outcomes at decent prices to them	Better health outcomes at decent prices to them	Maximize financial return	Personal development & financial security	Better health outcomes at decent prices to them	Better health outcomes at decent prices to them

Table 5.3 Stakeholder impact map for a social media company

	Users	Advertisers	Shareholders	Employees	Governments
Positive impact	Connect people, widen their opportunity to express themselves	Reach users in a targeted way, save costs elsewhere	High growth drives share price	Remuneration & job fulfilment	Reach people
Negative impact	Privacy, addiction		Unease at high multiples (valuation)	Perhaps company reputation	Might affect public opinion in a way that undermines government; fake news
Short-term goals	Connect & share	Get more customers	Maximize financial return	Good work–life balance and pay	Control of information, data security; battle fake news
Long-term goals	A good life	Better understanding of customer needs	Maximize financial return	Personal development & financial security	Protect the state and the people

with very different impact and goals. When analysing such stakeholder impact maps, one should pay special attention to the frictions between the various goals and impacts, both within the same stakeholder and across stakeholders. Those frictions can be a good indication of the problems (or opportunities) ahead.

Chapter 8 shows that such stakeholder maps are a good starting point for integrating sustainability into investment decisions, for example, by means of the value driver adjustment approach (see Schramade, 2016).

5.4 Circular business models

An important transformation is the change from linear to circular business models. While raw materials are wasted at the end of a product's lifespan in the linear model (Panel A of Figure 5.8), a circular economy is restorative or regenerative by intention and design. A circular economy narrows material loops. Raw materials keep their value in the circular production and consumption economy (Panel B of Figure 5.8). The idea of a circular economy is inspired by eco-systems in which the waste of one system is food for another. Circular businesses aim to retain a product's added value for as long as

Panel A: The value hill in a linear economy

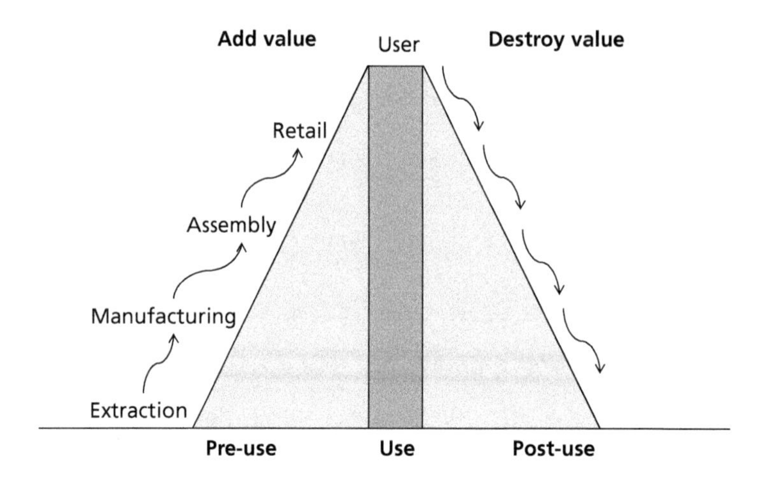

Panel B: The value hill in a circular economy

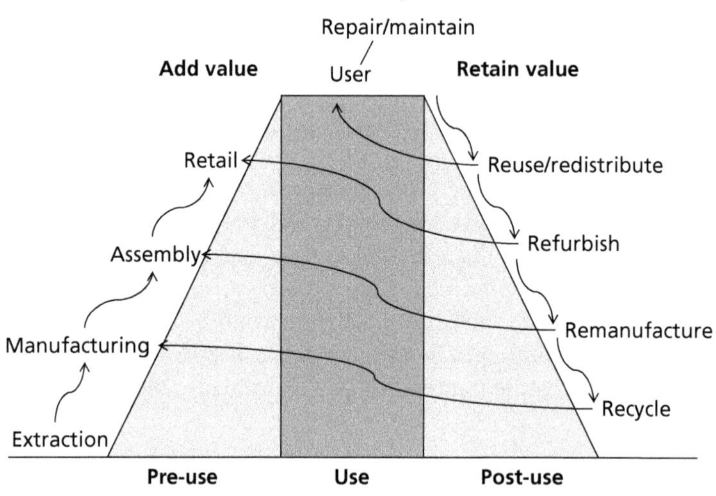

Figure 5.8 The value hill of raw materials

Source: Circle Economy (2016)

possible, if not forever. In the context of the value hill, value is added while the product moves 'uphill' and circular strategies keep the product at its highest value (top of the hill) for as long as possible. Products are designed to be long lasting and are suitable for maintenance and repair, thus slowing resource loops and prolonging the use phase of the product. When a product is ready to start its downhill journey, it is done as slowly as possible so that its useful

BOX 5.6 CIRCULAR DESIGN—FAIRPHONE

Fairphone is an example of circular design. The Fairphone (second edition) is an Android smartphone that is built with longevity in mind and is the first modular phone on the market. Designed for reparability, spare parts are offered in an online shop together with instructions on how to replace broken elements. Consequently, the design of the product has changed the relationship between consumers and their phones.

The materials used support local economies and include conflict-free minerals from the Democratic Republic of the Congo to stimulate alternative solutions. Fairphone works closely with manufacturers that want to invest in employee well-being. They believe that factory workers deserve safe conditions, fair wages, and worker representation.

Source: Circle Economy (2016).

resources can still be of service to other systems, as illustrated in Panel B of Figure 5.8 (Circle Economy, 2016).

The transition to a circular economy and its corresponding differences in the way businesses are organized have two main challenges. The first is the need for a business to maintain control over its resources. This means that products need to be tracked and returned once they are no longer in use. The second challenge is to preserve a product at its highest value and optimize its residual value. There are several circular business strategies on the value hill (Circle Economy, 2016).

The path that products take while travelling up and down the value hill is divided in three phases. The pre-use phase (mining, production, distribution) is displayed on the left in Panel B of Figure 5.8 as value is added in every step and the product moves uphill. Circular design business models are focused on prolonging the use phase (e.g. product longevity), accounting for end-of-life suitability (e.g. modularity), minimizing resource-intensiveness and reusing existing products, components, or materials. Box 5.6 provides an example of circular design.

The second phase is the in-use phase and is depicted at the top of the hill in Panel B of Figure 5.8. Here the value of a product is at its highest. Business models in this category seek to optimize the use of the product by providing services or add-ons to extend lifetime of a product or provide ways to improve its productivity. A much-explored business model is the product-service-system model, where companies create bundles of products and services that are of greater value together than they are alone and provide business with greater control over their resources. These models are organized through leasing, renting, pay-per-use, or performance-based business models, which allow the ownership to remain with the service provider. Examples of other models in this category are sharing platforms or life extension strategies (Stegeman, 2015). Box 5.7 gives an example of optimal use. The move from the sales model in the linear economy to the product as a service model in the

BOX 5.7 OPTIMAL USE—BUNDLES

This example is of a product as a service model optimizing the use of products. Bundles developed a pay-per-wash business model that focused on selling packages of washing cycles ('bundles') instead of washing machines.

By attaching a device to their washing machines the company is able to maintain ownership of the machines while monitoring their usage. Statistics gathered from the machine are displayed on the Wash-App, which provides the customer with insights into the overall cost of doing their laundry, including energy, water, and detergent consumption. This not only reduces the costs for the customer, but also extends the life of the machine.

Source: Circle Economy (2016).

circular economy provides challenges for financing. Chapter 10 discusses the financing of circular business models.

The third phase is the post-use phase, where the product loses value as it moves downhill. However, by feeding the complete product or its components back into a previous phase (e.g. by providing second-hand products they flow directly back into the use phase), value is retained.

Bocken, Ritala, and Huotari (2017) investigate the introduction of the circular economy concept in business. They find that the closing and slowing material loops are applied most among large companies. Business models contributing to closing loops, which refer to (post-consumer waste) recycling, are commonplace. For instance, industrial symbiosis models are growing in popularity. Industrial symbiosis is an association between two or more industrial facilities or companies in which the waste or by-products of one become the raw materials for another.

Slowing loops is about retaining the product value as long as possible. Examples of business models include the mentioned product-service-system models, the classic long-life model, and business models that extend the product value through remanufacturing. Although remanufacturing (and maintenance) as a strategy could significantly mitigate energy use and emissions, while contributing to job creation and economic growth, industry innovation in this field is still slow.

Recent research has started to question the core of the circular economy, namely, whether closing material and product loops does in fact prevent primary production. Zink and Geyer (2017) argue that circular economy activities can increase overall production, which can partially or fully offset their benefits. Because there is a strong parallel to energy efficiency rebound, Zink and Geyer have termed this effect 'circular economy rebound'. Circular economy rebound occurs when circular economy activities, which have lower per-unit-production impacts, also cause increased levels of production, reducing their benefit.

5.5 Long-term value creation and the purpose of the firm

The previous sections have shown that material ESG issues can have profound effects on business models and competitive positions. Upward and Jones (2016) distinguish between weakly and strongly sustainable business models. Profit-orientated companies have a tendency to adopt weakly sustainable business models. The move to strongly sustainable business models requires companies not only to take care of the financial viability of their business model, but also to define and measure social benefits and environmental regeneration. They have to manage the integrated value (IV) of the company (see Chapter 3).

This, along with continuous technological disruption, makes value creation even harder and less obvious than perceived. Even more fundamentally, the purpose of the firm comes into question. As a company moves from simply maximizing financial value to maximizing IV (I = F + S + E; see Table 1.3), serious questions need to be asked regarding what the company wants to achieve, and where and how it can best accomplish this.

5.5.1 THE PURPOSE OF THE FIRM

What are companies for? According to Friedman (1970), the answer is simple: companies should maximize profitability, as that is what their owners (shareholders) want. In practice, however, companies are not just run or started in order to make as much money as possible. They operate in a societal context in which much more is expected from them than just this. Often, companies are started because their founder identifies a large unmet need or has invented a brilliant technological innovation. For example, the founder of Lever Bros (now Unilever) wanted to popularize cleanliness and hygiene in 1890s England.

Hart and Zingales (2017) give theoretical footing to this by building a theoretical model of the company's objective function when shareholders are prosocial and externalities are not perfectly separable from production decisions. They disagree with Friedman's (1970) influential statement that companies should simply maximize profits. Rather, Hart and Zingales (2017) argue that the ultimate shareholders of a company are ordinary people who are concerned about money, but not just about money: 'If consumers and owners of private companies take social factors into account and internalise externalities in their own behaviour, why would they not want the public companies they invest in to do the same?'

The classical Friedman answer would be to separate money-making activities from ethical activities. That may be correct for charity, which can be separated from the company (and be done by shareholders themselves), but it is not possible for the externalities that emanate from a company's core activities. Those have to be taken care of by the company. Hence, Hart and Zingales (2017) argue that companies should maximize shareholder welfare (which we label in this book as stakeholder value or IV) instead of shareholder value (see Chapters 1 and 3).

Maximizing IV is a good goal, but still less fundamental than a company's purpose. They are related though. With a clear purpose it also becomes clear how IV is to be maximized. How companies define or find their purpose is a matter of deeply questioning why the company exists. This can be very easy and obvious, but it can also be a very lengthy and painful process. Maximizing IV is the much more mundane matter of operationalizing that purpose. Having a purpose is immensely rewarding: it brings clarity of vision, a better alignment of activities and strategy, and better-motivated employees.

5.5.2 PURSUING LTVC

Based on the discussions in Chapters 3 and 5, we formulate the following guidelines for a company pursuing LTVC:

1. Make the company's purpose a key part of corporate strategy. After all, the purpose should tell you in which direction you are going.
2. Integrate sustainability and externalities in all functional business areas, including investment decisions (see an example on long-term capital budgeting in section 5.5.2.1) and reporting (see Chapter 6).
3. Communicate long-term goals clearly with all stakeholders, including customers, employees, and investors, and balance the goals (see Box 5.8).
4. Deliver what you promise and adapt to changing circumstances.

BOX 5.8 LTVC AT KPN

Dutch telecom operator KPN could maximize short-run return on invested capital (ROIC) by cutting operating costs (e.g. marketing costs for new customers) and capital investments (e.g. large investments in new network technology), which would look wonderful for short-term minded shareholders. However, it would also effectively kill its business, as ROIC would soon drop sharply as market share and product margins fall. To restore market share, KPN would have to spend more than the initial costs and investments needed to pursue its long-term strategic goals.

The company therefore manages five goals: shareholders, customers, employees, society, and environment. It has KPIs on all five and reports on each one of them every quarter, which should give a much better understanding of long-term value drivers than the old reporting system did. The net promoter score for customers is especially found to be very powerful. Equity analysts are slow to adapt though. Their interest in the non-financial indicators is low but rising, management says. Figure 5.9 shows the importance of balancing the goals. This balanced approach puts KPN's business on a more solid and less volatile footing.

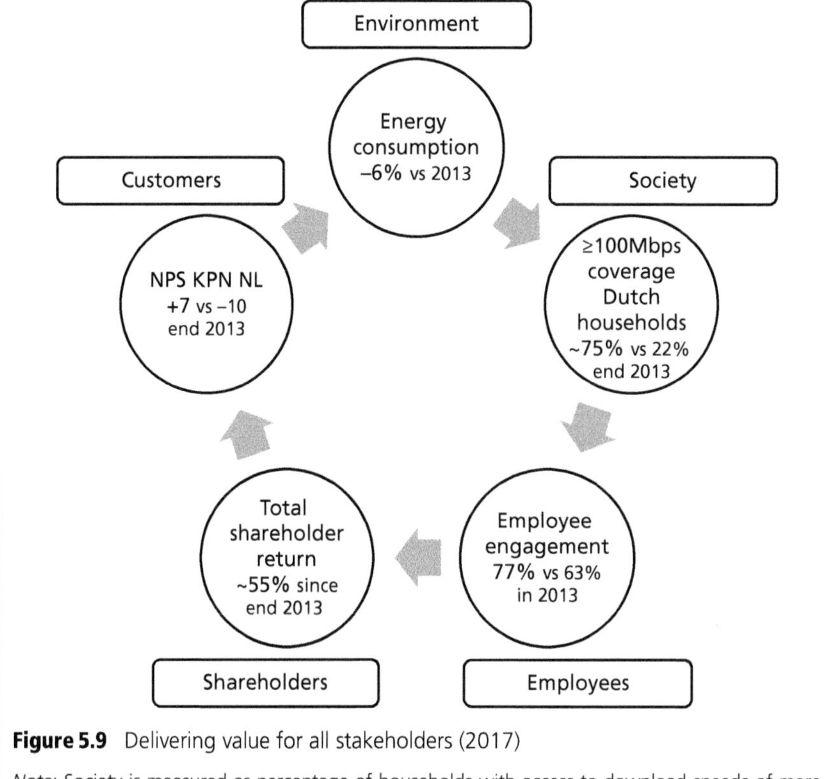

Figure 5.9 Delivering value for all stakeholders (2017)

Note: Society is measured as percentage of households with access to download speeds of more than 100 megabits per second.
Source: KPN presentations.

5. Build and maintain your key long-term intangibles to achieve transformational change.
6. Focus performance measurement on the long term and on meeting the company's overall purpose. In communications with capital markets, stop reporting and guiding on quarterly performance.
7. Base incentives for management and employees on meeting long-term objectives and get rid of short-term variable pay.

5.5.2.1 Example of long-term capital budgeting

A few years ago, we met a board member of a consumer goods corporation known for its advanced integration of sustainability issues. We asked him how his board integrated sustainability into their investment decisions and his answer was sobering: they simply split the list of proposals into sustainability projects and all other projects. For the former group, they even take projects with a negative NPV, since not doing them is not an option. The good thing about that approach is that sustainability is at least prioritized. But this is not integration, as it is still unknown how valuable these sustainability efforts are and whether they really should happen. It also means that top management fails in really making middle management change their approach. And that is what sustainability leadership is about: a multiyear change process.

Suppose a mining company considers building a $2bn desalination plant as its flagship mine is in a high water stress area. The desalination plant allows it to turn salty seawater into fresh water instead of using scarce local fresh water for the mining process. If the company builds the desalination plant, it will enjoy no additional CFs. If it does not build the plant, it will likely lose its licence to operate the mine. Table 5.4 shows a primitive NPV for the mining company.

With a $2.2bn negative NPV, the project looks financially unattractive. However, this primitive analysis ignores the benefit of keeping the CFs from the mine that would otherwise be lost. Say that without the desalination plant, the mine (and its average annual CF of $1.1bn) would certainly be lost by 2021. Table 5.5 calculates the correct NPV.

That is, building a $2bn desalination plant would yield $7.4bn in value. That might still be an underestimation as it does not even include positive side effects such as better relations with local stakeholders, which might in turn reduce the mine's cost of capital.

One could also do scenario analysis on this (see Chapter 2). Assume that losing the licence to operate the mine in 2021 is not a certainty but a probability. Then the NPV actually becomes a weighted average of the two NPV calculations shown in Table 5.6.

So, from a purely financial perspective, if the probability of losing the licence to operate the mine is over 23 per cent, the company should build

Table 5.4 Primitive NPV analysis of a mining company

	2018	2019	2020	2021	2022	2023	2024	2025	2026
Net investment in the desalination plant	−2,000	−20	−20	−20	−20	−20	−20	−20	−20
Operating costs of the desalination plant	−15	−15	−15	−15	−15	−15	−15	−15	−15
Free cash flow	−2,015	−35	−35	−35	−35	−35	−35	−35	−35
Continuing value									−438
Discount factor	0.909	0.827	0.751	0.683	0.621	0.564	0.513	0.466	0.466
Present value	−1,832	−29	−26	−24	−22	−20	−18	−16	−204
NPV	−2,191								

Table 5.5 Correct NPV analysis of a mining company

	2018	2019	2020	2021	2022	2023	2024	2025	2026
Net investment in the desalination plant	−2,000	−20	−20	−20	−20	−20	−20	−20	−20
Operating costs of the desalination plant	−15	−15	−15	−15	−15	−15	−15	−15	−15
Saved CF from the otherwise lost mine	0	0	0	1,100	1,100	1,100	1,100	1,100	1,100
Free cash flow	−2,015	−35	−35	1,065	1,065	1,065	1,065	1,065	1,065
Continuing value									13,313
Discount factor	0.909	0.827	0.751	0.683	0.621	0.564	0.513	0.466	0.466
Present value	−1,832	−29	−26	727	661	601	546	497	6,209
NPV	7,354								

Table 5.6 Probabilities of scenarios and weighted NPV

Probability of losing the licence	Saved CF	No saved CF	Total, weighted NPV
0%	0	−2,191	−2,191
10%	735	−1,972	−1,237
20%	1,471	−1,753	−282
30%	2,206	−1,534	672
40%	2,942	−1,315	1,627
50%	3,677	−1,096	2,581
60%	4,412	−876	3,536
70%	5,148	−657	4,491
80%	5,883	−438	5,445
90%	6,619	−219	6,400
100%	7,354	0	7,354

the plant (see Figure 5.10). However, even at lower probabilities it probably makes sense given the not yet included positive side effects.

5.6 **Conclusions**

Corporate sustainability goes well beyond CSR. Companies play a key role in the transition to a sustainable economy. Some will survive that transition, others will not, as their competitive positions are eroded. Sustainability is therefore also about corporate survival. It is a critical issue to competitive

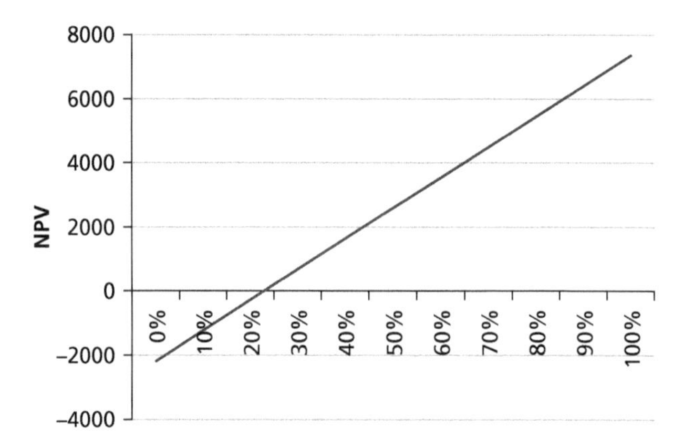

Figure 5.10 NPV at various probabilities of losing the license to operate

Note: The x-axis indicates the probability of the scenario in which the mining company loses its licence to operate.

positions, business models, intangible assets, and, ultimately, strategy. For many corporate executives, it is not obvious that these issues are connected as they often lack the tools to analyse them properly.

Companies that manage their sustainability issues well are more likely to protect their competitive positions, adapt their business models, and grow their intangible assets. The better their strategy anticipates the importance of sustainability issues, the more likely companies are to be successful in making the transition to a more sustainable economy. It is key to preparing companies for the future, including scenarios where a government may implement sustainability policies overnight without compensating incumbent companies.

It is important to identify material sustainability issues, which may differ across companies and industries. Chapter 8 highlights evidence that a company's general ESG ratings have no clear impact on its financial performance, while material ESG factors lead to superior financial performance.

Key concepts used in this chapter

Assets (in general) are things of value.

Assets (in accounting) are cash-generating units.

Business model is the representation of how a company creates and delivers value.

Circular economy is an industrial system that is restorative or regenerative by intention and design.

Competitive position is the position a company occupies in a market, relative to its competitors.

ESG stands for environmental, social, governance.

Green washing refers to pretending to be more sustainable than is actually the case.

Human capital represents the skills, knowledge, and experience of an individual or group in terms of their value to the company.

Intangible assets are assets that have no physical or financial embodiment (the subset of intangible resources that qualify as assets for accounting purposes).

Intangible resources are resources that are not tangible assets (and not necessarily *intangible assets*).

Materiality indicates relevant and significant information.

Materiality matrix is a matrix that maps the materiality of issues on two axes, typically one axis for the company's business and another for the company's stakeholders.

Network effect is a phenomenon whereby a product or service becomes more valuable as more people use it.

Panarchy is a conceptual framework to account for the dual characteristics of complex systems—stability and change; it studies how economic growth and human development depend on ecosystems and how they interact.

Resource-based view refers to an academic school of thought that says that the application of a set of resources is the basis of competitive advantage.

Stakeholder impact map is a matrix that outlines the goals and interests of various stakeholders.

Strategic assets are assets that are valuable, rare, and difficult to imitate.

Strategy is the plan chosen to achieve a desired future state.

Sustainable competitive advantage is the state in which a company survives and prospers in a competitive environment over the long run.

SUGGESTED READING

Dyllick, T. and K. Muff (2016), 'Clarifying the meaning of sustainable business introducing a typology from business-as-usual to true business sustainability', *Organization and Environment*, 29 (2): 156–74.

Lev, B. (2017), 'Evaluating sustainable competitive advantage', *Journal of Applied Corporate Finance*, 29(2): 70–5.

Osterwalder, A. and Y. Pigneur (2010), *Business Model Generation: A Handbook for Visionaries, Game Changers, and Challengers*, John Wiley & Sons, New York.

Porter, M. and M. Kramer (2011), 'The big idea: creating shared value', *Harvard Business Review*, 89(1–2): 62–77.

Schramade, W. (2016), 'Bridging sustainability and finance: the value driver adjustment approach', *Journal of Applied Corporate Finance*, 28(2): 17–28.

REFERENCES

Acemoglu, D. and J. Robinson (2012), *Why Nations Fail*, Crown Business, New York.

Barney, J. (1986), 'Organizational culture: can it be a source of sustained competitive advantage?', *Academy of Management Review*, 11(3): 656–65.

Barney, J. (1991), 'Firm resources and sustained competitive advantage', *Journal of Management*, 17(1): 99–120.

Bocken, N., P. Ritala, and P. Huotari (2017), 'The circular economy: exploring the introduction of the concept among S&P 500 firms', *Journal of Industrial Ecology*, 21(3): 487–90.

Chan, L., J. Karceski, and J. Lakonishok (2003), 'The level and persistence of growth rates', *Journal of Finance*, 58(2): 643–84.

Chesbrough, H. (2010), 'Business model innovation: opportunities and barriers', *Long Range Planning*, 43(2): 354–63.

Circle Economy (2016), 'Master circular business with the value hill', Utrecht, https://www.circle-economy.com/master-circular-business-with-the-value-hill/, accessed 29 June 2018.

Coburn, P. (2016), *Culture*, Coburn Ventures, New York.

Dyer, J. (1996), 'Specialized supplier networks as a source of competitive advantage: evidence from the auto industry', *Strategic Management Journal*, 17(4): 271–91.

Dyllick, T. and K. Muff (2016), 'Clarifying the meaning of sustainable business introducing a typology from business-as-usual to true business sustainability', *Organization and Environment*, 29(2): 156–74.

Edmans, A. (2012), 'The link between job satisfaction and firm value, with implications for corporate social responsibility', *Academy of Management Perspectives*, 26(4): 1–19.

Friedman, M. (1970), 'The social responsibility of business is to increase its profits', *New York Times Magazine*, 13 September.

Gompers, P., J. Ishii, and A. Metrick (2003), 'Corporate governance and equity prices', *Quarterly Journal of Economics*, 118(1): 107–56.

Guiso, L., P. Sapienza, and L. Zingales (2015), 'The value of corporate culture', *Journal of Financial Economics*, 117(1): 60–76.

Hahn, T., J. Pinkse, L. Preuss, and F. Figge (2015), 'Tensions in corporate sustainability: towards an integrative framework', *Journal of Business Ethics*, 127(2): 297–316.

Hall, R. (1993), 'A framework linking intangible resources and capabilities to sustainable competitive advantage', *Strategic Management Journal*, 14(8): 607–18.

Hambrick, D. and J. Fredrickson (2001), 'Are you sure you have a strategy?', *Academy of Management Executive*, 15(4): 48–59.

Hart, O. and L. Zingales (2017), 'Companies should maximize shareholder welfare not market value', CEPR Discussion Paper No. 12186.

Haskel, J. and S. Westlake (2017), *Capitalism without Capital: The Rise of the Intangible Economy*, Princeton University Press, Princeton, NJ.

Hendricks, K. and V. Singhal (2005), 'An empirical analysis of the effect of supply chain disruptions on long-run stock price performance and equity risk of the firm', *Production and Operations Management*, 14(1): 35–52.

Holling, C. S. (2001), 'Understanding the complexity of economic, ecological, and social systems', *Ecosystems*, 4(5): 390–405.

IASB (International Accounting Standards Board) (2010), 'Conceptual framework for financial reporting', London.
Janis, I. (1971), 'Groupthink', *Psychology Today*, 5(6): 43–6.
Johnson, M., C. Christensen, and H. Kagermann (2008), 'Reinventing your business model', *Harvard Business Review*, 86(12): 57–68.
Joyce, A. and R. Paquin (2016), 'The triple layered business model canvas: a tool to design more sustainable business models', *Journal of Cleaner Production*, 135: 1474–86.
Khan, M., G. Serafeim, and A. Yoon (2016), 'Corporate sustainability: first evidence on materiality', *Accounting Review*, 91(6): 1697–724.
Koller, T., M. Goedhart, and D. Wessels (2015), *Valuation: Measuring and Managing the Value of Companies*, 6th edn, John Wiley & Sons, New York.
Lev, B. (2000), *Intangibles: Management, Measurement, and Reporting*, Brookings Institution Press, Washington DC.
Lev, B. (2017), 'Evaluating sustainable competitive advantage', *Journal of Applied Corporate Finance*, 29(2): 70–5.
Nayyar, P. (1990), 'Information asymmetries: a source of competitive advantage for diversified service firms', *Strategic Management Journal*, 11(7): 513–19.
Osterwalder, A. and Y. Pigneur (2010), *Business Model Generation: A Handbook for Visionaries, Game Changers, and Challengers*, John Wiley & Sons, New York.
Pfeffer, J. (1994), 'Competitive advantage through people', *California Management Review*, 36(2): 9–28.
Porter, M. (1985), *Competitive Advantage: Creating and Sustaining Superior Performance*, Free Press, New York.
Porter, M. (1990), 'The competitive advantage of nations', *Harvard Business Review*, 68(2): 73–93.
Porter, M. and M. Kramer (2011), 'The big idea: creating shared value', *Harvard Business Review*, 89(1–2): 62–77.
Schramade, W. (2016), 'Bridging sustainability and finance: the value driver adjustment approach', *Journal of Applied Corporate Finance*, 28(2): 17–28.
Schramade, W. (2017), 'Investing in the UN Sustainable Development Goals: opportunities for companies and investors', *Journal of Applied Corporate Finance*, 29(2): 87–99.
Shleifer, A. and R. Vishny (1997), 'A survey of corporate governance', *Journal of Finance*, 52(2): 737–83.
Shrivastava, P. and A. Addas (2014), 'The impact of corporate governance on sustainability performance', *Journal of Sustainable Finance & Investment*, 4(1): 21–37.
Slywotzky, A. and D. Morrison (1997), *The Profit Zone*, Times Business, Random House, New York.
Stegeman, H. (2015), 'The potential of the circular economy', Rabobank, Utrecht, https://economics.rabobank.com/publications/2015/july/the-potential-of-the-circular-economy/, accessed 29 June 2018.
Upward, A. and P. Jones (2016), 'An ontology for strongly sustainable business models: defining an enterprise framework compatible with natural and social science, *Organization & Environment*, 29(1): 97–123.
Wernerfelt, B. (1984), 'A resource-based view of the firm', *Strategic Management Journal*, 5(2): 171–80.
Zink, T. and R. Geyer (2017), 'Circular economy rebound', *Journal of Industrial Ecology*, 21(3): 593–602.

6 Integrated reporting—metrics and data

Overview

Financial reporting serves an important role as a means of communication between corporate management and the company's stakeholders, including investors. It faces the challenge of painting a reliable picture of economic reality, which has become increasingly problematic. Since the 1970s, complexity has increased and intangibles have become a more important part of a company's asset base (see Chapter 5). As traditional reporting falls short in dealing with intangibles and complexity, calls for improvement are being made. The most concrete proposal so far is integrated reporting (IR).

This chapter outlines why reporting matters, how it falls short, and how IR might be an improvement. IR is about understanding how an organization creates integrated value and how its activities affect the capitals (intellectual, human, social, and natural capitals, as well as financial capital) it relies upon for this. It does so by at least partly addressing the shortcomings of traditional financial reporting, such as the latter's scant inclusion of intangibles. This chapter gives examples of how IR is applied by leading companies. It also illustrates what an IR balance sheet could look like. IR moves from two capitals (financial and manufactured) to six capitals (adding intellectual, social and relationship, human and natural).

Ultimately, IR facilitates integrated thinking, which takes into account the connectivity and interdependencies between factors that affect an organization's ability to create integrated value over time; it combines financial, social, and environmental dimensions.

IR is applied by an increasing number of companies, but it is still far from widespread. Moreover, some criticize it for being too focused on investors and auditors and not enough on society. Still, the approach is promising and has strong advantages, such as increased meaning and better insight into management's decision-making quality. As it is still in an early stage of adoption, it requires further development and the benchmarking of best practices.

IR is facilitated by the increasing availability of data on human, social, and natural capitals, such as data on gender in boards, living wages, and carbon emissions. The emergence of sustainability data providers is discussed. While sustainability or environmental, social, and governance (ESG) data is thus becoming available, the challenge for companies and investors is to distinguish between material ESG dimensions (i.e. relevant for a particular company) and immaterial ESG dimensions. Only the material ESG dimensions matter for valuation and investment analysis, as discussed in Chapters 7 and 8.

Learning objectives

After you have studied this chapter, you should be able to:

- describe the benefits and limitations of traditional reporting;
- explain the emergence and relevance of IR;
- outline the obstacles IR faces;
- illustrate the characteristics of an integrated report;
- understand the range of sustainability data.

6.1 Financial reporting: merits and limitations

Financial reporting matters and is valuable for communication with the outside world and performance measurement of businesses, but it increasingly struggles to meet the needs of users.

6.1.1 WHY REPORTING?

As the joint stock corporation gained popularity, a need arose to report on performance to shareholders. Over the centuries, accounting has become increasingly sophisticated to facilitate better decision-making, external monitoring, and more complex transactions. While accounting standards—to make reporting across companies more comparable—started at the national level, they are currently set at the international level. The International Accounting Standards Board (IASB) issues internal accounting standards, under the name of International Financial Reporting Standards (IFRS).

Eccles and Saltzman (2011) claim that financial reporting has institutional legitimacy, thanks to a variety of factors:

- measurement, reporting, and auditing standards;
- effective enforcement mechanisms, including courts of law for redress of fraud in the financial statements;
- sophisticated internal control and measurement systems; and
- information technologies that enable the rapid capture and aggregation of data.

6.1.2 LIMITATIONS TO REPORTING

However, reporting also faces numerous challenges and problems. For example, different user needs make alignment and comparability hard. Investors tend to be forward looking, but reporting is backward looking. A board is held accountable for the past but should be prepared for the future. In addition, reporting is focused on physical and financial assets, not intangibles (see Chapter 5). As Lev (2017) puts it: 'strategic assets are very different from the kinds of assets that are reported by accountants on corporate balance sheets'. Strategic assets are those that bring competitive advantage. Moreover, there are a lot of inconsistencies in reporting, such as different ways for recording items like sales and inventories, while intangibles are often not, or only partially, capitalized and reported as assets. This means that important sources of corporate value creation are often not reported. Also, some aspects of reporting are mandatory while others are voluntary. And there are differences in regulation between countries and institutions. Complexity makes it hard to understand reports and often makes them very long.

Eccles and Saltzman (2011) point to the difficulty of finding the most relevant information, the time lag in issuing reports, and the paucity of information about the risks being taken by the company to create value for shareholders. Moreover, they argue that 'Questions about whether a financial report presents a "true and fair view" of a company cannot be adequately answered, because the reports do not contain information on non-financial performance that can determine a company's long-term financial picture.' Similarly, Gray (1993) argues that traditional accounting and reporting actively support and encourage unsustainable organizations. The misleading information, which does not provide a full view of ESG risks and opportunities, leads to inaccurate budgeting, costings, and decision-making, which undermines the ability of companies to survive in the long term.

Two decades ago, Lev and Zarowin (1999) found evidence that the usefulness of reported earnings, CFs, and book (equity) values had been deteriorating over the last twenty years of the 20th century. They argued:

> Whether driven by innovation, competition, or deregulation, the impact of change on firms' operations and economic conditions is not adequately reflected by the current reporting system. The large investments that generally drive change, such as restructuring costs and R&D expenditures, are immediately expensed, while the benefits of change are recorded later and are not matched with the previously expensed investments. Consequently, the fundamental accounting measurement process of periodically matching costs with revenues is seriously distorted, adversely affecting the informativeness of financial information. We argue that it is in the accounting for intangibles that the present system fails most seriously to reflect enterprise value and performance, mainly due to the mismatching of costs with revenues. We demonstrate the adverse informational consequences of the accounting treatment of intangibles by

documenting a positive association between the rate of business change and shifts in R&D spending, and an association between the decrease in the informativeness of earnings and changes in R&D spending.

Since the late 1990s, more and more companies have started to publish stand-alone corporate social responsibility (CSR) reports. Dhaliwal and colleagues (2011) find that such companies have lower analyst forecast errors, indicating not just better non-financial reporting, but better financial reporting as well. Hummel and Schlick (2016) find that superior sustainability performers choose to undertake high-quality sustainability reporting to signal their better performance to the market, while weak performers prefer to hide their weakness by not being transparent. While some companies are very advanced, it is still far from clear how non-financial reporting is best done. Eccles, Krzus, and Ribot (2015) argue that a measurement and reporting infrastructure is needed for non-financial performance.

6.2 **Non-financial metrics, data, and value drivers**

What kind of non-financial data, targets, and key performance indicators can be used for IR? The ESG factors are discussed in turn. These factors are relevant for human, social, and natural capitals in the integrated report (see Section 6.3).

6.2.1 EXAMPLES OF METRICS IN E (ENVIRONMENTAL DIMENSION)

CO_2 emissions are probably the most widely used metric on the environmental side (natural capital). Several companies nowadays report on their scope 1, scope 2, and scope 3 emissions. The Greenhouse Gas (GHG) Protocol (WRI, 2015) distinguishes between direct emissions from sources that are owned or controlled by the reporting entity and indirect emissions that are a consequence of the activities of the reporting entity, but occur at sources owned or controlled by another entity. The GHG Protocol further categorizes these direct and indirect GHG emissions into three scopes to which we add a fourth scope:

- **Scope 1**: All direct GHG emissions of an organization.
- **Scope 2**: Indirect GHG emissions from consumption of purchased electricity, heat, or steam.
- **Scope 3**: Other indirect emissions—the full corporate value chain emissions from the products they buy, manufacture, and sell (e.g. if a car manufacturer sells cars, this represents the emissions of the cars in use).
- **Scope 4**: Reductions in clients' scope 3 achieved by a company's smart solutions (e.g. if a company helps a truck manufacturer to significantly reduce emissions of its vehicles). This scope is not (yet) in the GHG Protocol.

Table 6.1 provides an example of the carbon footprint of a major company, Philips, which reports in line with the GHG Protocol. The reduction in scope 2 emissions is driven by increased use of renewable electricity. Philips has started a carbon neutrality programme by compensating for carbon emissions.

Some companies have started to report on scope 4, that is, the emissions they have avoided by taking action (see Box 6.1 for an example). Moreover, some advanced companies such as Unilever, DSM, and Microsoft, use internal carbon prices to set incentives for CO_2 reductions. Admittedly, this is a simple binary metric, namely, whether they have an internal carbon price or not, but it signals a strong commitment. Sustainability ratings agencies like Sustainalytics (see Section 6.4) track whether companies have the right systems in place for the management of emissions or toxic materials. Water, waste, and energy use are also increasingly reported, and are typically scaled to company sales to make the numbers at least somewhat comparable to those of peers.

Table 6.1 Operational carbon footprint by scope

	2013	2014	2015	2016	2017
Scope 1	44	40	39	42	38
Scope 2	114	109	106	121	58
Scope 3	654	594	612	658	751
Total (scopes 1 to 3)	812	743	757	821	847
Emissions compensated by carbon offset projects	0	0	0	0	220
Net operational carbon emissions	812	743	757	821	627

Note: Figures given in kilotons CO_2-equivalent for Philips.
Source: Philips Annual Report 2017.

BOX 6.1 EMISSIONS SAVED BY NOVOZYMES

In its 2017 annual report Novozymes stated that it had saved its clients 76 million tons of CO_2 and that it aims to raise that number to 100 million tons. There is a clear link to the value drivers, as reductions in CO_2 emissions are generated by using less energy, and hence have lower input costs. As a result, Novozymes creates a lot of value for its clients and is able to generate sales growth and margins that are both twice as high as that of the overall chemical industry (see Box 5.2 in Chapter 5).

6.2.2 EXAMPLES OF METRICS IN S (SOCIAL DIMENSION)

Social metrics (relevant for human and social capitals) are typically harder to distinguish than environmental metrics, but they are being recorded. For example, most metals and mining companies report accident frequency rates and local stakeholder programmes. Some companies, across many industries, report on human capital by disclosing employee engagement data or attrition rates. External human capital data is available as well, in the form of Glassdoor or Indeed scores. Glassdoor and Indeed are recruitment agencies that also provide scores on companies. In consumer industries especially, brand valuations or net promoter scores (NPS) are used. Supplier standards seem to be on the rise, with companies formulating standards that their suppliers and the suppliers of their suppliers need to meet. A few companies also report on social impact—see, for example, Philips' target of improving 3 billion lives (see Table 6.4).

6.2.3 EXAMPLES OF METRICS IN G (GOVERNANCE DIMENSION)

Governance indicators include shareholder structures, board composition, board independence, management compensation, governance committees, voting rights, share classes, and codes of conduct. There are plenty of data points available, but interpreting them is the hard part as the relevance of these indicators depends on the context, that is, the other indicators.

6.2.4 RELATION TO THE VALUE DRIVERS

There is sparse but increasing evidence that material E, S, and G issues can affect the value drivers of a company. As mentioned in Chapter 5, Khan, Serafeim, and Yoon (2016) find that firms that do well on material sustainability issues tend to outperform in terms of stock price, while those that do well on immaterial sustainability issues tend to underperform. There is also evidence specifically on E (e.g. Derwall et al. 2005), S (e.g. Edmans, 2011), and G (e.g. Gompers, Ishii, and Metrick, 2003). In addition, Dhaliwal and colleagues (2011) find a reduced cost of equity for firms with superior CSR performance that initiate voluntary CSR disclosures.

More intuitively, one could also map the ESG issues that are likely to affect the value drivers for a certain company or industry. For example, at Novozymes, growth and margins are driven by innovation, which depends in turn on human capital. Figure 6.1 illustrates the value drivers of Novozymes.

At a mining company, the drivers are very different. Management of local stakeholders and environmental management are key to the firm's licence to operate, and drive its ability to achieve decent margins and maintain capital discipline. Mining companies use a lot of capital to build and maintain mines

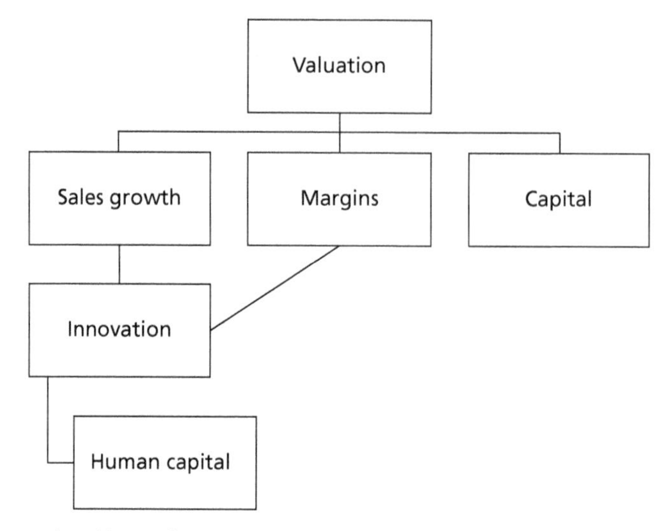

Figure 6.1 Value drivers of Novozymes

Note: The scheme shows the value drivers in a bottom-up way.

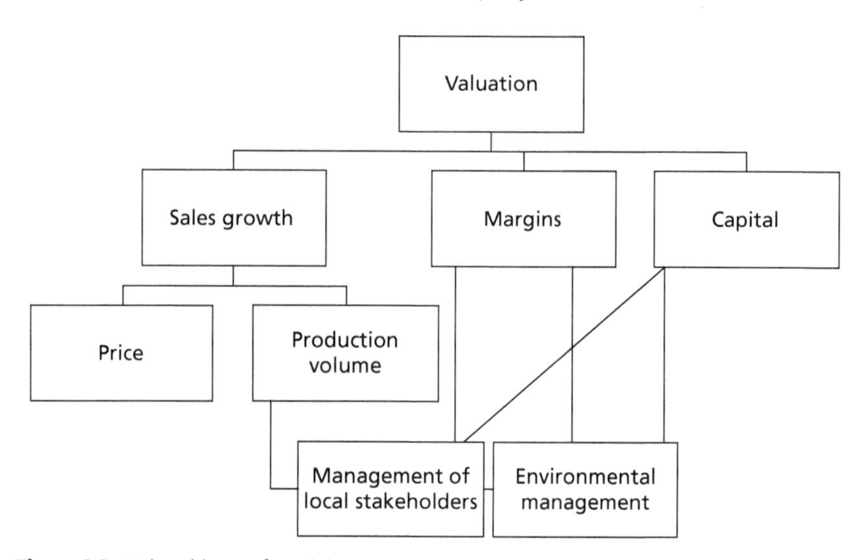

Figure 6.2 Value drivers of a mining company

Note: The scheme shows the value drivers in a bottom-up way.

that tend to be in operation for decades. All of that is wasted if the company loses its licence to operate due to environmental problems or unresolved local stakeholder conflict. For example, miners Barrick and Anglo American lost billions of dollars on their Pascua Lama and Minas Rio projects. Figure 6.2 shows the value drivers of a mining company.

6.3 The emergence of IR

The emergence of IR is an evolution of corporate reporting. In the 1990s, companies started to publish non-financial information on social and environmental dimensions in a separate CSR report. This is a reflection of a silo approach: the financial report for investors and the CSR report for 'society'. The switch to integrated thinking is nicely captured in the title of a seminal book *One Report: Integrated Reporting for Sustainable Strategy* (Eccles and Krzus, 2010). IR combines financial and non-financial reporting. The first integrated reports started to appear in the early 2000s, but the IR movement only gained traction in the second decade of this century. In 2010, the International Integrated Reporting Council (IIRC) was founded, with the explicit mission to achieve global adoption of IR. Other milestones were the founding of the Sustainability Accounting Standards Board (SASB) in 2011 and the G4 guidelines issued by the Global Reporting Initiative (GRI) in 2013. These organizations differ in their approaches, with the IIRC being more principles based, the GRI more standards based, and the SASB very industry specific.

The remainder of Section 6.3 focuses mainly on the IIRC's framework, as it is the easiest to apply across industries, followed by a summary of the GRI and SASB frameworks. Most of the criticism levelled at the IIRC is also applicable to the approaches of the GRI and the SASB. Table 6.2 provides an overview of the various IR frameworks and compares them with the traditional financial reporting framework (IFRS). An important element of these frameworks is the definition of materiality, which gives guidance on what is relevant to a company and should therefore be reported.

6.3.1 WHAT IS IR?

The basics of IR have been laid out extensively in a 2013 report by the IIRC, called 'The international <IR> framework'. In the report, an integrated report is defined as 'a concise communication about how an organisation's strategy, governance, performance and prospects, in the context of its external environment, lead to the creation of value over the short, medium and long term'. However, Eccles and Saltzman (2011) define an integrated report as a single document that presents and explains a company's financial and non-financial—ESG—performance. In practice, it often is a mix of those two definitions. The move from traditional financial reporting to IR is in line with the move from sustainable finance (SF) 1.0, which focuses on the financial dimension, to SF 2.0 and 3.0, which also incorporate social and environmental dimensions (see Chapter 1).

Table 6.2 Comparing reporting frameworks

	IFRS (Global)	<IR> (Global)	GRI (Global)	SASB (USA)
Audience	All existing and potential investors, lenders, and other creditors	Providers of financial capital and others interested in the organization's ability to create value	All stakeholders	Investors of those companies that engage in public offerings of securities registered under the Securities Act
Subject matter and report purpose	Financial performance and position	Value creation over time (short, medium, and long term)	Sustainability impact (economic, environmental, social, and governance)	Sustainability impact (environment, social capital, human capital, business model and innovation, leadership and governance)
Nature of materiality definition	*Information* is material if omitting it or misstating it could influence decisions that users make based on financial information about a specific reporting entity. Relevance is based on the nature and/or magnitude of the items to which the information relates in the context of an individual entity's financial report	Multistep process: • Relevant issues affect strategy, governance, performance, prospects and are discussed by the *board* • Disclosure of material matters based on user need, and guiding principles	Organization-driven materiality The *report* should cover aspects that: • reflect the organization 's significant ESG impacts; or • substantively influence the assessments and decisions of stakeholders	SASB identifies a minimum set of sustainability *topics* that have a significant impact on most, if not all, companies in an industry and which (depending on the specific operating context) are likely to be material to a company within that industry; guided by the materiality definition adopted by US securities laws
Disclosure form	Financial statements	Integrated report	Sustainability (GRI) report	For use in reports filed with the SEC

Source: Compiled by the authors; based on IASB, IIRC, GRI, and SASB.

6.3.1.1 Vision of the IIRC

The IIRC (2013) states that its 'long term vision is a world in which integrated thinking is embedded within mainstream business practice in the public and private sectors, facilitated by Integrated Reporting (<IR>) as the corporate reporting norm'. IR is thus a means to, and an expression of, the real goal: integrated thinking, which combines financial, social, and environmental dimensions. Again, this is a transition process.

Integrated thinking means taking into account the connectivity and interdependencies between the factors that affect an organization's ability to create value over time. For example, the ability of a biotech company to continue to generate breakthrough new products depends on the quality of its innovation process, which in turn depends on the quality of its human capital. It is argued that the more that integrated thinking is embedded into an organization's activities, the more naturally the connectivity of information will flow into management reporting, analysis, and decision-making. This should also lead to better integration of the information systems that support internal and external reporting and communication, including preparation of the integrated report.

In terms of sustainability accountability, Oliver, Vesty, and Brooks (2016) suggest that organizations should be open about the sustainability of their activities to the community. Sustainability awareness would thereby help senior managers and policymakers to deal with the broader implications of corporate activity on society and the planet. The integrated thinking approach helps them to break away from silo thinking (see Chapter 12).

IR moves from two capitals (financial and manufactured) to six capitals (adding intellectual, social and relationship, human and natural). All organizations depend on various forms of capital for their success. In the IR framework, the capitals comprise financial, manufactured, intellectual, human, social and relationship, and natural capital (IIRC, 2013):

1. **Financial capital** is the pool of funds that is available to an organization for use in the production of goods or the provision of services and obtained through financing, such as debt, equity, or grants, or generated through operations or investments (retained earnings).
2. **Manufactured capital** comprises manufactured physical objects that are available to an organization for use in the production of goods or the provision of services, including buildings and equipment.
3. **Intellectual capital** (often called intangibles) includes intellectual property, such as patents, copyrights, and software, and 'organizational capital', such as tacit knowledge, systems, procedures, and protocols.
4. **Human capital** covers people's competencies, capabilities, and experience, and their motivations to innovate. It includes job satisfaction and health and safety conditions.
5. **Social and relationship capital** refers to the institutions and the relationships within and between communities, groups of stakeholders, and other networks, and the ability to share information to enhance individual and collective well-being.
6. **Natural capital** refers to all renewable and non-renewable environmental resources, ecological services (e.g. water purification or climate stabilization), and processes that provide goods or services that support the past, current, or future prosperity of an organization.

Figure 6.3 depicts the six capitals. Financial and manufactured capitals are those that organizations most commonly report on. IR takes a broader view by

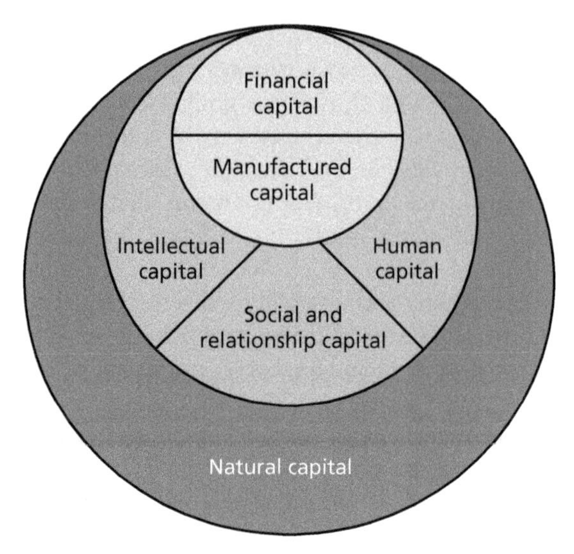

Figure 6.3 The six capitals in IR

Source: Adapted from IIRC (2013).

also considering intellectual, social and relationship, and human capitals (all of which are linked to the activities of humans) and natural capital (which provides the environment in which the other capitals sit). Not all capitals are equally relevant or applicable to all organizations. While most organizations interact with all capitals to some extent, these interactions might be relatively minor or so indirect that they are not sufficiently important to include in the integrated report.

6.3.1.2 The IIRC's approach

The IIRC (2013) has defined the following principles, which should guide the preparation, information content, and presentation of the integrated report:

- **Strategic focus and future orientation**: Insight into the organization's strategy, and how it relates to the organization's ability to create value in the short, medium and long term, and to its use of and effects on the capitals.
- **Connectivity of information**: A holistic picture of the combination, interrelatedness, and dependencies between the factors that affect the organization's ability to create value over time.
- **Stakeholder relationships**: Insight into the nature and quality of the organization's relationships with its key stakeholders, including how and to what extent the organization understands, takes into account, and responds to their legitimate needs and interests.

- **Materiality**: Disclose information about matters that substantively affect the organization's ability to create value over the short, medium, and long term.
- **Conciseness**: Too lengthy reports reduce the chances of a user finding the information that he or she needs.
- **Reliability and completeness**: Include all material matters, both positive and negative, in a balanced way and without material error.
- **Consistency and comparability**: The information should be presented: (i) on a basis that is consistent over time; and (ii) in a way that enables comparison with other organizations to the extent it is material to the organization's own ability to create value over time.

Next, the IIRC identifies eight content elements that should be included in an integrated report:

1. **Organizational overview and external environment**: What does the organization do and what are the circumstances under which it operates?
2. **Governance**: How does the organization's governance structure support its ability to create value in the short, medium, and long term?
3. **Business model**: What is the organization's business model and how does the organization create value?
4. **Risks and opportunities**: What are the specific risks and opportunities that affect the organization's ability to create value over the short, medium, and long term, and how is the organization dealing with them?
5. **Strategy and resource allocation**: Where does the organization want to go and how does it intend to get there?
6. **Performance**: To what extent has the organization achieved its strategic objectives for the period and what are its outcomes in terms of effects on the capitals?
7. **Outlook**: What challenges and uncertainties is the organization likely to encounter in pursuing its strategy, and what are the potential implications for its business model and future performance?
8. **Basis of presentation**: How does the organization determine what matters to include in the integrated report and how are such matters quantified or evaluated?

6.3.1.3 The GRI's reporting standards

The GRI is an organization that provides a complementary IR framework. Compared to the IIRC, it seems much more rule based than principle based, which in our view makes reporting according to the GRI more rigid than reporting according to the IIRC. The GRI requires things that are material to society—the 'sustainability context'—to be reported. For example, in a water-scarce area a company reports on water even if it has a small impact.

The GRI's 2016 reporting standards (GRI, 2016) are formulated in a 443-page document, which consists inter alia of:

- GRI 101 Foundation. This is the starting point for using the set of GRI standards. GRI 101 sets out the reporting principles for defining report content and quality.
- GRI 102 General Disclosures. GRI 102 is used to report contextual information about an organization and its sustainability practices.
- GRI 103 Management Approach. This part is used to report information about how an organization manages a material topic.

Following a stakeholder approach, the GRI focuses on reliable, relevant, and standardized information to stakeholders; investors are not privileged. The standards offer greater comparability than the principle-based approach of the IIRC. The GRI's reporting standards also give guidance on dealing with stakeholders. The principle of stakeholder inclusiveness calls on the reporting organization to identify its stakeholders and explain how it has responded to their reasonable expectations and interests. Stakeholders are defined as 'entities or individuals that can reasonably be expected to be significantly affected by the reporting organisation's activities, products, or services; or whose actions can reasonably be expected to affect the ability of the organisation to implement its strategies or achieve its objectives'. Organizations are encouraged to undertake systematic stakeholder engagement, which should result in ongoing learning and increased accountability.

6.3.1.4 The SASB's industry materiality approach

The SASB aims to develop and disseminate sustainability accounting standards. It does so by developing industry-specific metrics and recommendations that should allow better comparison and benchmarking. As of 2018, the SASB has developed sustainability accounting standards for 79 industries in 11 sectors. The SASB's approach is materiality focused. The criteria for selecting material topics are (SASB, 2017):

- relevant across an industry;
- potential to affect value creation;
- actionable to companies;
- of interest to investors;
- reflective of stakeholder consensus.

6.3.2 IR IN PRACTICE

It is difficult to determine to what extent IR is actually practised, since it is not mandatory. An exception is South Africa, where IR has been obligatory on an 'apply or explain' basis for firms on the Johannesburg stock exchange since 2010 (Eccles and Krzus, 2014). Elsewhere, IR is voluntary. So why do companies do it? Eccles and Saltzman (2011) list a number of reasons for issuing integrated reports:

They include a commitment to sustainability, defined broadly in financial and ESG terms; a belief that an integrated report is the best way to communicate to shareholders and other stakeholders how well a company is accomplishing these objectives; and a recognition that integrated reporting is an important discipline for ensuring that a company has a sustainable strategy.

Still, this is just anecdotal. Dumay and colleagues (2016) find that most published IR research presents normative arguments for IR and that there is little research examining IR practice. An exception is the paper by Barth and colleagues (2017), who find that IR is positively associated with both stock liquidity (measured using bid-ask spreads) and firm value (measured using Tobin's Q). Their findings are consistent with IR achieving its dual objective of improved external information and better internal decision-making.

6.3.2.1 Examples of companies practising IR

The first companies to issue an integrated report were Novozymes in 2002, Natura in 2002, and Novo Nordisk in 2004. Since then, many have followed. Recent noteworthy reports include those of Novozymes (with CO_2 reduction targets benefiting clients; see Box 6.1) and AkzoNobel, which shows business model visualizations for each of its business segments, as well as a true value pilot of its Brazilian operations, which highlights the societal costs and benefits of those operations.

But what does it mean to have an integrated report? Philips was an early adopter, starting to undertake integrated reports from 2008. Tables 6.3 and 6.4 compare the Philips 2016 Annual Report to a typical non-integrated annual report along two dimensions: the IIRC's seven guiding principles and the eight elements of an integrated report. These tables illustrate that Philips' integrated report offers substantially more non-financial information than a traditional financial report, but there is scope for improvement towards IR goals.

6.3.2.2 Imagining a six capitals balance sheet

To illustrate the shortcomings of traditional accounting, we consider the stylized example of a mining company's balance sheet. The traditional balance sheet shows what such a balance sheet typically looks like when simplified to the largest assets and liabilities classes. Of course, there are other assets and liabilities on a mining company's balance sheet, but for purposes of comparison, they do not matter for Figure 6.4.

Table 6.3 Comparison of Philips using the seven guiding principles of an integrated report

Principle	Application by Philips	Typical application
1. Strategic focus and future orientation	√ describe the path to value creation; 'roadmap to win'	~ vague statements, often in the CEO's letter to shareholders
2. Connectivity of information	√ there is quite a bit of cross-referencing	*X* limited
3. Stakeholder relationships	√ Philips explicitly refers to its stakeholders and to its multi-stakeholder projects	*X* not discussed
4. Materiality	√ Philips reports a materiality matrix that rates 27 E, S, and G issues on business impact versus importance to stakeholders	*X* not discussed what is material
5. Conciseness	*X* report is still (too) long with 226 pages	*X* lengthy documents that attempt to minimize legal risks
6. Reliability and completeness	~ Philips reports 'sustainability statements', which includes references to stakeholders and a materiality matrix, as well as data and targets on items such as lives improved, circular revenues, carbon footprint, waste recycling, and supplier sustainability. The company refers to natural capital and financial capital, but not to the other four capitals	~ reliable but far from complete
7. Consistency and comparability	√ comparability of data versus other years is good, but comparability with other companies is limited	~ decent consistency, but low comparability

Note: √ indicates that the company's report does a good job at reporting according to this principle; ~ means that the principle is met to some degree; *X* means that the principle is not met.

Source: Interpretation by authors based on Philips Annual Report 2016.

A problem with the traditional balance sheet is that it does not capture the value of the company's assets. Cash, and to a lesser extent inventory, are probably pretty close to real values, but property, plant and equipment (PPE) can be far off the mark, especially if the assets are old but in a good state. A market value balance sheet (see Figure 6.5) partly addresses this issue by taking the Net Present Value (NPV) of projects.

But the problem is that the market is not necessarily right, and certainly not all the time, as evidenced by price fluctuations. For example, the mining company's stock price might be depressed by low commodity prices, or inflated by high commodity prices, which the market may incorrectly price in to continue for a long time. Moreover, the market price is likely to ignore the externalities that the company generates (see Chapter 2). This problem is addressed in the six capitals balance sheet (see Figure 6.6). As of yet, we are not aware of a company that has published such a balance sheet.

Table 6.4 Comparison of Philips using the eight elements of an integrated report

Elements	Application by Philips	Typical application
1. Organizational overview and external environment	√ description of performance by business segment	~ some description
2. Governance	√ sections on management, the supervisory board, committees, and executive compensation	~ such structures are often described
3. Business model	~ Philips uses the concept of business model 11 times in its report, for example referring to the transformation of its business model from transactional to one of long-term partnerships. However, it does not give a visualization of the model.	***X*** limited description and not visualized
4. Risks and opportunities	√ the CEO letter is quite explicit on this. In the rest of the report, the emphasis is clearly more on risk (mentioned 399 times) than on opportunities (32 times)	~ usually described, but often in rather legal terms
5. Strategy and resource allocation	√ well discussed	***X*** some description
6. Performance	√ financial statements and sustainability statements with historical results and targets for the future, including an impact target of improving the lives of 3 billion people a year by 2025	***X*** usually only financial statements
7. Outlook	√ well discussed	~ increasingly so, but often rather generic statements on macro expectations
8. Basis of presentation	√ Philips states that it prepared its integrated annual report in line with the IIRC framework; and that for its sustainability information, it followed the GRI Standards–Comprehensive Option	√ The report typically refers to IFRS, generally accepted accounting principles, or a local accounting standard

Note: √ indicates that the company's report does a good job at reporting according to this principle; ~ means that the principle is met to some degree; *X* means that the principle is not met.

Source: Interpretation by authors based on Philips Annual Report 2016.

On the asset side, the NPV of projects is replaced by the sum of financial capital, manufactured capital, social and relationship capital, human capital, and intellectual capital, which add up to 13,500 instead of 12,000. Apparently, the market underestimates the long-term value of the firm's assets. However, the market also underestimates the long-term liabilities in the form of negative natural capital, which at 4,500 is nine times higher than the 500 environmental

Traditional balance sheet (based on historical cost accounting)

Cash	800	Interest-bearing debt	1,500
Inventory	200	Environmental liabilities	500
Property, plant, and equipment (PPE)	4,000	Equity	3,000
Total assets	5,000	Total liabilities	5,000

Figure 6.4 Example of a company's traditional balance sheet

Market value balance sheet (based on current market prices)

NPV of projects	12,000	Interest-bearing debt	1,500
		Environmental liabilities	500
		Equity	10,000
Total assets	12,000	Total liabilities	12,000

Figure 6.5 Example of a company's market value balance sheet

Six capitals balance sheet (based on estimated long-term values)

Financial capital (Cash+ inventories)	1,000	Negative financial capital (debt)	1,500
Manufactured capital (PPE at replacement cost)	7,500	Negative natural capital (liabilities)	4,500
Social and relationship capital	1,500	Equity (integrated value)	7,500
Human capital	500		
Intellectual capital	3,000		
Total assets	13,500	Total liabilities	13,500

Figure 6.6 Example of a company's six capitals balance sheet

liabilities on the traditional and market value balance sheets. As a result, equity is much lower than on the market value balance sheet, though still higher than on the traditional balance sheet. The equity in an integrated report represents the integrated value of a company (see Chapter 3).

The other result is that the company's debt–equity ratio increases from 0.2 ([1,500 + 500]/10,000) on a market value basis to 0.8 ([1,500 + 4,500]/7,500) on a six capitals basis, that is, from 'safe' to 'risky'. The six capitals balance sheet gives the best representation of the mining company's fair value and situation. The company and its investors thus get a better picture of the potential and the risks of the company, which may have a bearing on the stock price and the required return. However, there is one major drawback: arriving at the values of each of the six capitals is no trivial matter, as they each hinge on a series of assumptions.

6.3.3 INCENTIVES AND HURDLES TO IR

Whether a company chooses to implement IR depends on several factors. Incentives include a genuine desire to report more accurately to stakeholders; the belief that stronger external reporting can stimulate stronger internal reporting and set the performance bar higher; and financial benefits, such as a lower cost of capital due to higher transparency (Dhaliwal et al. 2011) and a higher valuation and stock liquidity (Barth et al. 2017). Another reason is building a reputation as a sustainable company. Examining the mandatory IR regime in South Africa, Steyn (2014) finds that managers are more motivated by the legitimizing aspect of advancing corporate reputation and stakeholder needs in compiling the integrated report than satisfying investor needs. This highlights the importance of integrated reports for stakeholder dialogue.

Companies may also cater to investor needs. Shefrin and Statman (1984) point out that companies may pay dividends simply because investors want them to. This is the so-called catering effect, which could also apply to IR. Knauer and Serafeim (2014) argue that companies can attract long-term investors by committing to integrated thinking and IR. They illustrate this with the case of Shire, a biotech company where the percentage of long-term shareholders increased after the company undertook IR. Furthermore, 'keeping up with the Joneses' can play a role. Companies that observe certain behaviour from their peers may be tempted to copy that behaviour.

But there are also several barriers to doing IR, such as behavioural challenges, as people tend to favour doing things the way they have always done them (status quo bias; see Chapter 12 on change management). Companies may also worry about disclosing information that is too competitively sensitive. And misunderstandings play a role: some companies seem to think that IR is about disclosing all information in one place and at the same time. There may also be legal barriers in that IR may entail disclosures that enhance the likelihood of the company being sued. Moreover, companies may not have the data required to do IR (see Section 6.4 on emerging sustainability data).

Table 6.5 Benefits and costs of IR

Benefits	Costs
• Greater clarity about the relationship between financial and non-financial performance and how this affects value creation • Better internal decision-making for a sustainable strategy • Deeper engagement and improved relationships with shareholders and stakeholders • Lower reputation risk • Improved measurement and control systems for non-financial information • Greater employee engagement • More committed customers who care about sustainability	• Preparation costs related to the collection and analysis of new data • Infrastructure investments in new information systems and data sets • New processes and control systems • People with analytics skills • Assurance from third parties • Potential proprietary disclosure costs and revelation of competitive information

Source: Institute of Management Accountants (2016).

Another problem is that much of the information in integrated reports cannot yet be certified by auditors, as there is lack of relevant auditor skills and international standards are not yet in place. Auditors and sustainability data providers (see Section 6.4) play an important role in the assurance of integrated reports. Table 6.5 provides an overview of the benefits and costs of IR.

A final shortcoming is that IR primarily looks at the company's performance on the six capitals with little reference to the overall social or ecological system. IR basically measures the net impact of a company on its capitals (the numerator in Equation 4.1 in Chapter 4) without relation to the relevant system threshold (the denominator in Equation 4.1 in Chapter 4). To make a judgement on a company's sustainability, it is not sufficient to know, for example, that it made an improvement on its carbon footprint (eco-efficiency). Rather, it is important to know that a company's carbon footprint stayed within its carbon budget (eco-effectiveness). While the IRRC mentions the system perspective, only 5 per cent of companies make any mention of ecologic limits, and only 0.3 per cent integrate such limits into their strategy and product development (Bjørn et al., 2017).

6.3.4 SUCCESS OR FAILURE?

The jury is still out whether IR is a success or a failure. On the bright side, Eccles and Saltzman (2011) argue that both stakeholders and shareholders are paying increasing attention to IR. However, they concede that questions exist about the reliability of the information reported by companies: 'For the most part, having any type of third-party assurance on non-financial information in the report, let alone on the entire integrated report, is voluntary. And even when assurance is provided, it is not done with the same degree of rigour as the audit of a financial report.'

Another positive is increased meaning. Adams and Simnett (2011) argue that IR results in more meaningful reporting: 'Integrated Reporting is a new reporting paradigm that is holistic, strategic, responsive, material and relevant across multiple time frames.'

Moreover, IR could provide better insight into management decision-making quality. In fact, Churet and Eccles (2014) interpret IR as a proxy for management quality:

> Companies that are able to articulate the relevance of sustainability issues to their long-term business success are likely to be those that are best equipped to address these issues internally. We therefore consider integrated reporting to be a useful proxy for the overall quality of management, which increasingly involves managing intangible assets while also taking account of any negative effects (or 'externalities') on the environment and society.
>
> Integrated thinking also implies an ability to find an optimal balance between managing short-term business imperatives and on-going value creation.

In fact, Ortiz-de-Mandojana and Bansal (2016) find that companies that adopt responsible social and environmental practices have lower financial volatility, higher sales growth, and higher chances of survival over a 15-year period.

Dumay and colleagues (2016) are less enthusiastic and claim that IR is too investor focused. Similarly, but more extremely, Flower (2015) considers IR an outright failure. In his view, while the IIRC was founded with the principal objective of promoting sustainability accounting, it has effectively abandoned this in its 2013 framework. He bases that conclusion on two considerations. First, the IIRC's concept of value is 'value for investors' and not 'value for society'. Secondly, the IIRC places no obligation on firms to report harm inflicted on entities outside the firm (such as the environment) where there is no subsequent impact on the firm.

While there is merit in those two considerations, Flower's conclusions seem harsh. Value for society is not a fully developed concept yet, and the obligation to report harm inflicted on entities outside the firm begs the question as to what exactly harm is and how sizeable that harm needs to be for it to be reported. In due time, we come to an understanding of this. But to get there we probably need evolution rather than revolution.

Flower (2015) also concludes that the IIRC's proposals will have little impact on corporate reporting practice because of their lack of force. He regards the composition of the IIRC's governing council as problematic, as it is dominated by the accountancy profession and multinational enterprises, which he claims are determined to control an initiative that threatens their established position. In effect, he argues, the IIRC has been the victim of 'regulatory capture'. Thomson (2015) is also critical of IR. He argues that IR reduces sustainability into five sources of corporate value, but sources of value that need to be better managed in order to increase the wealth of individual investors not society's prosperity. It will thus not improve the management of social or natural capital.

Perego, Kennedy, and Whiteman (2016) provide a more balanced perspective. Based on expert interviews, they conclude that IR is a fragmented field and that most companies have a weak understanding of its business value. However, they also conclude that challenges are to be expected given that IR is still in the early stages of adoption and that insightful experience exists in several firms. Perego, Kennedy, and Whiteman (2016) envision a future development of IR that will be informed by 'a systematic, rigorous research approach that gathers expert opinions on the relevant implications for standard setting bodies, report preparers and report users'. Indeed, not all IR is the same, and Melloni, Caglio, and Perego (2017) find that IR by weak financial performers tends to be less concise and less balanced than that of strong financial performers, which suggests 'impression management' on the side of the weak performers. Finally, these authors argue that as IR is a relatively new idea, lead time is required to achieve full potential in disclosure quality.

6.4 Sustainability data providers

Current regulations and management control systems already collate much of the data needed for an integrated report. The European emissions trading system (see Chapter 2), for example, requires companies to collect data on carbon emissions. There are also civil society initiatives. CDP, formerly the Carbon Disclosure Project, runs a global disclosure system that enables companies, cities, states, and regions to measure and manage their environmental impacts (climate change, water, and forests). CDP has built a comprehensive collection of self-reported environmental data, such as the carbon data reported by Philips in Table 6.1.

Sustainability data is also produced by external data providers. The kind of data they provide can be classified as:

- raw data versus scores/ratings/advice;
- topic focused versus comprehensive.

Table 6.6 provides some examples of data providers along these classifications. Raw data can range from carbon emissions to the gender of board members. Getting a uniformly measured and defined number on a metric for thousands of companies can be very valuable for putting a company's performance in perspective. Scores or ratings are typically based on data reported by companies, with companies getting points for the presence of certain

Table 6.6 Examples of sustainability data providers

	Raw data	Scores/ratings/advice
Topic focused	Southpole (emissions data)	Equileap (gender equality ratings) Glass Lewis, ISS (shareholder voting advice)
Comprehensive	RepRisk (tracking news on companies)	MSCI, Sustainalytics, RobecoSAM, oekom (all company scores and ratings)

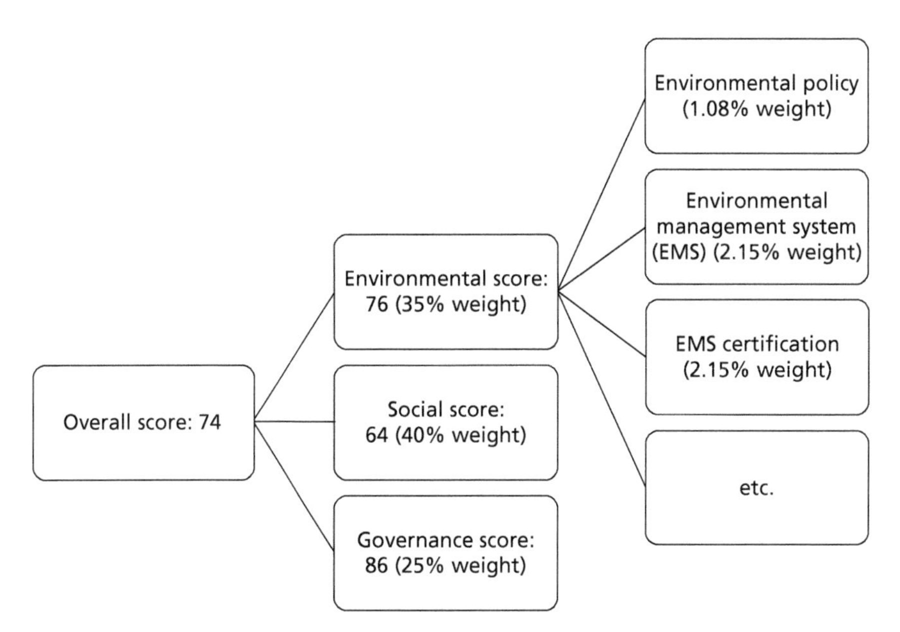

Figure 6.7 Example of a company's sustainability scoring by a sustainability rating agency

policies or for improvements in indicators, while being punished for 'controversies', that is, negative events that indicate poor performance. Scores on those many individual items are added up and weighted to reach an overall company score. For example, a typical Sustainalytics company score is a weighted average of that company's scores on dozens of individual items. Figure 6.7 provides an example of a sustainability scoring.

Topic-focused data providers have expertise in a specific area and try to have the deepest and best data on that topic. Comprehensive data providers, such as MSCI, Sustainalytics, or oekom, need to have expertise on all topics as they provide companies with an overall sustainability profile by scoring them on all topics. They thus typically require more scale and staff than topic-focused data providers. It is interesting to link the ESG score to the United Nations (UN) Sustainable Development Goals (SDGs). The oekom ESG Impact Assessment, for example, offers investors a comprehensive range of impact data relating to companies' product portfolios and production processes. These data enable quantification of a company's contribution towards sustainable development and attainment of the UN SDGs.

Sustainability data providers provide valuable services as they tend to provide previously unavailable data and also make sustainability data more comparable. Moreover, the scores stimulate competition between companies with regard to better reporting.

There are limitations as well. The data provided is just a fraction of the ideal amount, and is typically not sufficient to assess whether a company is prepared for the transition to a more sustainable economy. Moreover, whereas both data and ratings are just starting points for analysis, many investors are tempted to take them at face value and regard them as the final verdict on a company (see Chapter 7 for more on this). Likewise, many investors automatically vote according to the voting recommendations of proxy advisors ISS and Glass Lewis. The challenge is to distinguish between material and immaterial sustainability issues.

Finally, competition among data providers is fierce and will likely propel the amount and quality of available data in the years to come. Meanwhile, accessibility of data is also increasing as they become available through mainstream investor channels like the Bloomberg terminal.

6.5 Conclusions and future outlook

IR, which combines financial, social, and environmental dimensions, is applied by an increasing number of companies, but it is still far from widespread. Moreover, some criticize it for being too focused on investors and auditors and not enough on society. Still, the approach is promising and has strong advantages, such as increased meaning and better insight into management's decision-making quality. IR facilitates integrated thinking, which takes into account the connectivity and interdependencies between factors that affect an organization's ability to create integrated value over time.

As IR is still in an early stage of adoption, it needs further development and benchmarking of best practices. The Philips example shows what kind of meaningful extra information can be disclosed in an integrated report in comparison to a traditional financial report. The Novozymes and mining examples illustrate how material sustainability issues can be linked to value drivers, and hence become more clearly relevant for long-term value creation (Chapter 5) for all stakeholders, including shareholders. To reach SF 2.0 and 3.0, more is needed: eventually all six capitals will have to be present in the financial statements, that is, in the balance sheet, the income statement, and the CF statement. This chapter illustrates what that can look like for a balance sheet, and how dramatically that can change such a statement and its interpretation.

In future, we are likely to see advances in IR practices as companies and frameworks compete to deliver the best reporting. Whether that results in convergence remains to be seen. Scenario analysis might become a regular part of corporate reporting. The Bloomberg Task Force on Climate-related Financial Disclosures (TCFD, 2017) recommends companies to report their likely financial outcomes in a scenario of two degrees global warming (versus the current trajectory of four degrees). See also Section 2.4 in Chapter 2. This should result in better transition preparedness (Chapter 5). There are also developments to connect the six capitals of the IR framework with the SDGs (Adams, 2017). In that way, a company's contribution to sustainable development can directly be assessed.

Next, external data may become more important. Data about companies does not need to come only from the companies themselves, but may also come from clients (e.g. NPSs), suppliers, regulators, or transactions.

Currently, only two (financial and manufactured) of the six capitals are really reported on in annual reports. The returns on the other four are often indirectly visible in the profit and loss (P&L) account with a time lag. For example, a company with strong innovation will reap higher sales growth and margins, which will be visible in the P&L account—though without a label that says they were generated by innovation. Ideally, a stage will be reached where we can measure and report the integrated value and return of all six capitals. However, it will be a long road, as lots of hurdles will have to be overcome, including behavioural ones. The adoption of IR is thus also a major change management challenge (see Chapter 12).

Key concepts used in this chapter

Accounting is the process of keeping financial accounts.

Assurance refers to third-party verification of information.

Balance sheet is a statement of the assets, liabilities, and equity capital of an organization.

Catering is adjusting company policies to satisfy investors.

Financial reporting is the process of producing reports that disclose an organization's financial status.

Integrated reporting refers to concise communication about how an organization's strategy, governance, performance, and prospects, in the context of its external environment, lead to the creation of value over the short, medium, and long term.

Integrated thinking refers to taking into account the connectivity and interdependencies between factors that affect an organization's ability to create value over time; it combines financial, social, and environmental dimensions.

Six capitals are the types of capital distinguished by the IIRC, namely financial, manufactured, intellectual, social and relationship, human and natural capital.

SUGGESTED READING

Eccles, R. and M. Krzus (2014), *The Integrated Reporting Movement*, Wiley & Sons, Hoboken, NJ.

IIRC (International Integrated Reporting Council) (2013), 'The international <IR> framework', London, http://integratedreporting.org/wp-content/uploads/2015/03/13-12-08-THE-INTERNATIONAL-IR-FRAMEWORK-2-1.pdf, accessed 29 June 2018.

Knauer, A. and G. Serafeim (2014), 'Attracting long-term investors through integrated thinking and reporting: a clinical study of a biopharmaceutical company', *Journal of Applied Corporate Finance*, 26(2): 57–64.

Lev, B. (2017), 'Evaluating sustainable competitive advantage', *Journal of Applied Corporate Finance*, 29(2): 70–5.

Melloni, G., A. Caglio, and P. Perego (2017), 'Saying more with less? Disclosure conciseness, completeness and balance in integrated reports', *Journal of Accounting and Public Policy*, 36(3): 220–38.

Oliver, J., G. Vesty, and A. Brooks (2016), 'Conceptualising integrated thinking in practice', *Managerial Auditing Journal*, 31(2): 228–48.

REFERENCES

Adams, C. (2017), 'The Sustainable Development Goals, integrated thinking and the integrated report', Working Paper, IIRC, London.

Adams, S. and R. Simnett (2011), 'Integrated reporting: an opportunity for Australia's not-for-profit sector', *Australian Accounting Review*, 21(3): 292–301.

Barth, M., S. Cahan, L. Chen, and E. Venter (2017), 'The economic consequences associated with integrated report quality: capital market and real effects', *Accounting, Organizations and Society*, 62: 43–64.

Bjørn, A., N. Bey, S. Georg, I. Røpke, and M. Hauschild (2017), ' Is Earth recognized as a finite system in corporate responsibility reporting?', *Journal of Cleaner Production*, 163: 106–17.

Churet, C. and R. Eccles (2014), 'Integrated reporting, quality of management, and financial performance', *Journal of Applied Corporate Finance*, 26(1): 56–64.

Derwall, J., N. Guenster, R. Bauer, and K. Koedijk (2005), 'The eco-efficiency premium puzzle', *Financial Analysts Journal*, 61(2): 51–63.

Dhaliwal, D., Z. Li, A. Tsang, and G. Yang (2011), 'Voluntary nonfinancial disclosure and the cost of equity capital: the initiation of corporate social responsibility reporting', *Accounting Review*, 86(1): 59–100.

Dumay, J., C. Bernardi, J. Guthrie, and P. Demartini (2016), 'Integrated reporting: a structured literature review', *Accounting Forum*, 40(3): 166–85.

Eccles, R. and M. Krzus (2010), *One Report: Integrated Reporting for Sustainable Strategy*, Wiley & Sons, Hoboken, NJ.

Eccles, R. and M. Krzus (2014), *The Integrated Reporting Movement*, Wiley & Sons, Hoboken, NJ.

Eccles, R. and D. Saltzman (2011), 'Achieving sustainability through integrated reporting', *Stanford Social Innovation Review*, 9(3): 56–61.

Eccles, R., M. Krzus, and S. Ribot (2015), 'Meaning and momentum in the integrated reporting movement', *Journal of Applied Corporate Finance*, 27(2): 8–17.

Edmans, A. (2011), 'Does the stock market fully value intangibles? Employee satisfaction and equity prices', *Journal of Financial Economics*, 101(3): 621–40.

Flower, J. (2015), 'The international integrated reporting council: a story of failure', *Critical Perspectives on Accounting*, 27: 1–17.

Gompers, P., J. Ishii, and A. Metrick (2003), 'Corporate governance and equity prices', *Quarterly Journal of Economics*, 118(1): 107–56.

Gray, R. (1993), 'Foreword to *Business and Green Accountability*', in: L. Grayson, H. Woolston, and J. Tanega (eds.), *Business and Green Accountability*, KPMG, London, v–vi.

GRI (Global Reporting Initiative) (2016), 'Consolidated set of GRI sustainability reporting standards', Amsterdam, https://www.globalreporting.org/standards/gri-standards-download-center/consolidated-set-of-gri-standards/, accessed 29 June 2018.

Hummel, K. and C. Schlick (2016), 'The relationship between sustainability performance and sustainability disclosure: reconciling voluntary disclosure theory and legitimacy theory', *Journal of Accounting and Public Policy*, 35(5): 455–76.

IIRC (International Integrated Reporting Council) (2013), 'The international <IR> framework', London, http://integratedreporting.org/wp-content/uploads/2015/03/13-12-08-THE-INTERNATIONAL-IR-FRAMEWORK-2-1.pdf, accessed 29 June 2018.

Institute of Management Accountants (2016), 'Integrated reporting', Montvale, NJ, https://www.imanet.org/-/media/0830fcd907cd41a7bd760b8900fe7b94.ashx, accessed 29 June 2018.

Khan, M., G. Serafeim, and A. Yoon (2016), 'Corporate sustainability: first evidence on materiality', *Accounting Review*, 91(6): 1697–724.

Knauer, A. and G. Serafeim (2014), 'Attracting long-term investors through integrated thinking and reporting: a clinical study of a biopharmaceutical company', *Journal of Applied Corporate Finance*, 26(2): 57–64.

Lev, B. (2017), 'Evaluating sustainable competitive advantage', *Journal of Applied Corporate Finance*, 29(2): 70–5.

Lev, B. and P. Zarowin (1999), 'The boundaries of financial reporting and how to extend them', *Journal of Accounting Research*, 37(2): 353–85.

Melloni, G., A. Caglio, and P. Perego (2017), 'Saying more with less? Disclosure conciseness, completeness and balance in integrated reports', *Journal of Accounting and Public Policy*, 36(3): 220–38.

Oliver, J., G. Vesty, and A. Brooks (2016), 'Conceptualising integrated thinking in practice', *Managerial Auditing Journal*, 31(2): 228–48.

Ortiz-de-Mandojana, N. and P. Bansal (2016), 'The long-term benefits of organizational resilience through sustainable business practices', *Strategic Management Journal*, 37(8): 1615–31.

Perego, P., S. Kennedy, and G. Whiteman (2016), 'A lot of icing but little cake? Taking integrated reporting forward', *Journal of Cleaner Production*, 136(Part A): 53–64.

SASB (Sustainability Accounting Standards Board) (2017), 'SASB rules of procedure', San Francisco, https://www.sasb.org/wp-content/uploads/2017/02/SASB-Rules-of-Procedure.pdf, accessed 29 June 2018.

Shefrin, H. and M. Statman (1984), 'Explaining investor preference for cash dividends', *Journal of Financial Economics*, 13(2): 253–82.

Steyn, M. (2014), 'Organisational benefits and implementation challenges of mandatory integrated reporting: perspectives of senior executives at South African listed companies', *Sustainability Accounting, Management and Policy Journal*, 5(4): 476–503.

TCFD (Task Force on Climate-related Financial Disclosures) (2017), 'Recommendations of the Task Force on Climate-related Financial Disclosures: final report (Bloomberg Report)', Financial Stability Board, Basel.

Thomson, I. (2015), 'But does sustainability need capitalism or an integrated report': a commentary on *The International Integrated Reporting Council: A Story of Failure* by J. Flower', *Critical Perspectives on Accounting*, 27: 18–22.

WRI (World Resources Institute) (2015), 'Greenhouse Gas Protocol', Washington DC.

Part III

Financing sustainability

7 Investing for long-term value creation

Overview

The financial system has an important role to play with regard to the sustainability transition challenge. In that transition, companies are increasingly adopting the goal of long-term value creation (LTVC), which integrates financial, social, and environmental value. This chapter explores how the financial system can move from a traditional investment (and lending) approach that maximizes financial value subject to risk, often in a narrow and short-term way, towards investing for LTVC that optimizes financial, social, and environmental value subject to risk.

The optimization requires a careful balancing of the three dimensions whereby none should deteriorate in favour of the others. While Chapters 8 to 10 provide evidence that investors and banks can adopt these new investment and lending policies without sacrificing return, this chapter analyses the underlying rationale for investing for LTVC. The traditional investment approach builds on the neoclassical paradigm of efficient markets and portfolio theory. The efficient markets hypothesis (EMH) assumes that all information is incorporated in stock prices, suggesting passive investing while portfolio theory spans the financial return and risk space, but does not include social and environmental issues in its equations. That leaves no room for the societal allocation role of finance. Moreover, the excessive diversification of portfolio theory creates a free-rider problem with regard to the monitoring of corporate managements.

The adaptive markets hypothesis (AMH) provides a better framework, as it recognizes the limitations to market efficiency and the need for market participants to adapt to new information, such as social and environmental factors. As a first step investors (and lenders) are increasingly using environmental, social, and governance (ESG) ratings to incorporate social and environmental dimensions. However, these external ratings rely on scanty and sometimes conflicting data and provide limited information on material ESG factors.

This chapter proposes an active investment approach, based on fundamental analysis of companies' ESG factors and engagement with investee companies on material ESG factors. The aim is to uncover and realize companies' social

Table 7.1 Traditional versus long-term investing

Dimension	Traditional investing	Investing for LTVC
Typology	SF 1.0	SF 2.0
Market framework used	EMH	AMH
Pricing of social (S) and environmental (E) dimension	Irrelevant or already priced in	Priced as market participants learn
Value maximization	*Max FV*	*Max IV = FV + SEV*
Value indicator	Earnings per share	Sophisticated discounted cash flow with scenarios for internalization
Investment chains	Long and complicated	Short and simple
Portfolios	Very diversified	More concentrated
Dialogues with corporates	Limited	Deep
Performance horizon	12 months	Years or decades

Note: The sustainability typology (1.0 and 2.0) is taken from Chapter 1. FV = financial value (F), IV = integrated value, and SEV = social–environmental value (S+E), as introduced in Chapter 1.

and environmental value along with their financial value. Fundamental investing leads to more concentrated portfolios and alternative measures of investment performance (away from market benchmarks). The incorporation of ESG information into stock prices is an adaptive process, in which success is dependent on the number of fundamental analysts and the quality of their learning. Table 7.1 summarizes traditional and long-term investment approaches.

In institutional investment, there is often a long chain of parties that sit between the ultimate provider of capital (typically someone investing for his or her retirement) and the ultimate user of capital (typically a company or project). These long and complicated investment chains mean that incentives are distorted, the horizon gets shorter with each extra party in the chain, and meaningful information is lost along the chain.

This chapter identifies six conditions for investing for LTVC: (i) long investment horizons; (ii) active management in concentrated portfolios; (iii) effective engagement with companies; (iv) performance analysis of value added in the real economy; (v) long-term alignment of the mandates of asset owners and asset managers; and (vi) keeping the investment chain short. These conditions are very much related to each other.

Learning points

After you have studied this chapter, you should be able to:

- explain the (over)reliance on market metrics in traditional finance;
- discuss what the obstacles to adaptation are and how they can be overcome;
- explain the key differences between active and passive investment approaches;
- identify the different parties, and their role, in the investment chain;
- list and understand the conditions for LTVC by investors;
- contrast traditional performance measures with alternative ones.

7.1 (Over)reliance on market metrics

The corporate sector plays an important role in achieving the UN Sustainable Development Goals (SDGs) through LTVC. LTVC means considering the financial, social, and environmental value of companies in the long run (see Chapters 3 and 5). However, most investment approaches, based on the neoclassical paradigm of efficient markets and portfolio theory, only capture the financial value in their financial risk and return space. The financial system needs to adapt and explore new investment approaches to capture the social and environmental dimensions as well (see Sections 7.2 and 7.3).

The efficient markets hypothesis (EMH) and portfolio theory have been so influential since the 1960s that they pervade the language and thinking of asset management. Business schools embraced the ideas of efficient markets and portfolio theory and trained millions of students in this way of thinking. As they became the mantra of business schools, these theories also established the separation of finance and ethics. As discussed in Chapter 1, traditional finance is consistent with the argument of Friedman (1970) that 'the business of business is business'. In this view, it is the task of the government to take care of social and environmental concerns. This separation between finance and societal concerns is especially true in the USA (Simon, 2017) but it applies to the entire global financial system, which is dominated by US asset managers and US investment banks. It is second nature for investors to think and communicate in market benchmarks and market risks. This affects the functions of pricing, allocation, and performance measurement in the investment process.

7.1.1 PRICING

The EMH assumes that all relevant information of a company is incorporated in that company's stock or market price (Fama, 1970). Investors cannot systematically beat the market. The market is supposed to be so efficient that it immediately incorporates all relevant new information, making it impossible for investors to benefit from superior insights or information. While there are differences in risk–return profiles across assets, these assets are assumed to be priced accordingly. Arbitrage makes sure that prices stay correct: abnormally high return assets immediately attract more fund flows, which drive up prices and reset expected returns back to the market rate. As a result, in the world of efficient markets, all information is incorporated in stock prices. This suggests everyone should undertake passive investing, as there are no benefits from active investing. As explained in Chapter 3, the narrow financial risk–return thinking has led to a strong focus on the stock price as the central performance measure for executive and investor performance.

However, there is plenty of evidence that markets are not always efficient. Whereas the EMH assumes perfectly rational investors, a vast body of behavioural finance literature has shown since the 1970s that people (including investors) are far from rational (e.g. the early work by Tversky and Kahneman (1973), the review article by Barberis and Thaler (2003), and *The Myth of the Rational Market* by Fox (2009)). The efficiency of markets has also been questioned by strong evidence on the momentum factor, which shows that stocks that have done well over in past few months tend to continue to do well over the next several months (Jegadeesh and Titman, 1993). Behavioural finance indicates that such lack of rationality has important implications for financial markets, which can be seriously overvalued or undervalued for extended periods of time. Furthermore, these behavioural anomalies have now been supplemented by sustainability anomalies (e.g. Khan, Serafeim, and Yoon, 2016) as discussed in Chapters 5 and 8.

7.1.2 ALLOCATION

The capital asset pricing model (CAPM), built on modern portfolio theory (Markowitz, 1952), stresses that risk is an inherent part of higher reward. Importantly, risk and return characteristics should not be considered in isolation per security, but by how much the investment affects the overall portfolio's risk and return. One can construct an efficient frontier of optimal portfolios that maximize expected return for a given level of risk, leading to an efficient economic allocation. In a textbook such as that by Elton and colleagues (2014), the CAPM expresses the expected return on company i's stock $E[R_i]$ as follows:

$$E[R_i] = R_f + \beta_i \ (E[R_m] - R_f) \tag{7.1}$$

whereby R_f is the risk-free rate, β_i the sensitivity of the stock to the market portfolio, and $E[R_m]$ the expected return on the market portfolio. In the CAPM, the only relevant variable to determine a stock's return is its sensitivity to the market, which is called systematic risk. The non-systematic or idiosyncratic risk is not priced. In equilibrium, all investors hold the market portfolio, which is replicated in the market index. It suffices to adopt a passive investment approach by investing in the market index. That is a very strong idea indeed. But the problem is the narrow view on financial risk and return, ignoring the social and environmental dimensions. Even the measure of financial risk is rather narrow, as it is based solely on the volatility of past stock returns, which do not necessarily capture the fundamental risks of the companies in the portfolio.

7.1.3 PERFORMANCE MEASUREMENT

Performance measurement is also well versed in the language of portfolio theory. The traditional way to measure performance is the benchmarking of an investor's returns to those of the relevant market index, which is confined to the financial risk and return dimension. Market benchmarks are indices, such as the MSCI World Index or the MSCI All Country World Index, that consist of a basket of the largest companies by market capitalization in a certain market (i.e. the global stock market, a regional market like developed Asia, or a sector such as real estate). The underlying idea is that the index represents 'the market'. When assessing a fund manager's performance, his or her performance will be measured against such a benchmark (was it higher or lower over the past five years, three years, one year, six months, one month, and one day?), correcting for the amount of risk the fund manager took in achieving that result.

Measures for such market risk-taking include beta, tracking error, information ratio, and Sharpe ratio. Table 7.2 provides a numerical example. Beta (β) is an indication of a portfolio's (or a stock's) exposure to general market movements. Equation 7.1 indicates that beta is measured as price volatility versus the volatility of the market, or more technically, as the covariance between the returns on the portfolio and the market, divided by the variance of the market's return. A beta higher than one means that the portfolio is more volatile than the market, while a beta below one means the portfolio is less volatile. Investors can position themselves accordingly if they have a strong conviction that the market will rise or fall. Hence, portfolio returns in a context of high betas in rising markets (or low betas in falling markets) are interpreted as resulting from taking a market view and market risk, rather than from good stock picking. With a beta of 0.82, the fund manager in Table 7.2 has a rather defensive style.

The tracking error is the difference between the price behaviour of a portfolio and of a benchmark, reported as a standard deviation percentage difference. The thinking is that a high tracking error indicates risk-taking versus the benchmark, and is only desirable if the portfolio's returns are accordingly higher than the benchmark's returns. The fund manager in Table 7.2 has a tracking error of 2.6 per cent, which is not very high.

Table 7.2 Example of fund performance metrics

	Portfolio price end of year	Market price end of year	Portfolio returns (R_p)	Market returns (R_m)	Excess returns over market	Risk-free rate (R_f)	Excess returns over risk-free rate	Expected return given beta	Alpha (α)
2006	76	210							
2007	82	222	7.3%	5.5%	1.8%	4.0%	3.3%	5.2%	2.1%
2008	54	140	−34.5%	−37.0%	2.5%	3.0%	−37.5%	−30.0%	−4.5%
2009	67	177	24.9%	26.5%	−1.6%	1.0%	23.9%	22.0%	2.9%
2010	78	204	15.8%	15.1%	0.7%	2.0%	13.8%	12.8%	3.0%
2011	84	208	8.3%	2.1%	6.2%	1.0%	7.3%	1.9%	6.4%
2012	98	241	17.2%	16.0%	1.2%	1.0%	16.2%	13.4%	3.8%
2013	127	319	28.8%	32.4%	−3.6%	1.0%	27.8%	26.9%	1.9%
2014	148	363	16.4%	13.7%	2.7%	1.0%	15.4%	11.5%	4.9%
2015	156	368	5.4%	1.4%	4.0%	1.0%	4.4%	1.3%	4.1%
2016	178	412	14.7%	11.9%	2.8%	1.0%	13.7%	10.0%	4.7%
Full period			133.9%	95.8%	38.1%				
Annualized			8.9%	6.9%	1.9%	1.6%	7.3%	6.0%	2.9%
Variance			3.0%	3.6%					
Covariance with market return			2.9%						
Beta (β)			0.82						
Tracking error					2.6%				
Information ratio					0.73				
Sharpe ratio							2.39		

Note: Yearly returns are calculated as yearly percentage price changes. The excess return over the market is the portfolio's return minus the market's returns. The excess return over the risk-free rate is the portfolio's return minus the risk-free rate. The expected portfolio return R_p given its beta, is calculated as $R_f + \beta_p \cdot (R_m - R_f)$. Alpha ($\alpha$) is calculated as the portfolio return minus its expected return given its beta. Beta (β) is the ratio of the covariance of the portfolio returns and market returns (2.9 per cent) to the variance of market returns (3.6 per cent). The TE is the standard deviation of excess returns over the market. The information ratio is the ratio of the annualized excess returns (1.9 per cent) to the TE (2.6 per cent). The Sharpe ratio is the ratio of the annualized excess return over the risk-free rate to the variance of portfolio returns.

A related measure is the information ratio. This is the ratio of a portfolio's excess returns over the benchmark to the tracking error. If a fund has a high information ratio (say between 0.4 and 1), that can be interpreted as sustained good performance by the fund manager. With an information ratio of 0.7, the fund manager in Table 7.2 is a strong performer. Next, the Sharpe ratio is different from the aforementioned risk metrics, in that it does not measure risk against the wider market, but against a risk-free rate. It is defined as the average return earned in *excess* of the risk-free rate per unit of portfolio risk. Of course, this does create a new problem, namely what to assume for the risk-free rate.

Summing up, the various performance measures relate a portfolio's return to the market return (or the risk-free rate return), which is calculated in a financial risk–return space. In this view, there is no need to analyse the companies in the portfolio themselves, only the sensitivity of the portfolio's return to the market. The social and environmental dimensions are not included in these performance measures. Section 7.2 discusses attempts to include the social and environmental dimensions by adding so-called ESG factors to the market metrics.

7.1.4 LONG INVESTMENT CHAINS

Long investment chains exacerbate the reliance on market metrics, as each party wants to monitor the investment performance of the next party in the chain. Along the chain, a lot of valuable information is lost. In institutional investment, there is a long and complicated chain of parties that sit between the ultimate provider of capital (typically someone investing for his or her retirement) and the ultimate user of capital (typically a company or project). In their simplest form, such investment chains look like Figure 7.1.

But in practice, such chains are much more complicated than suggested by Figure 7.1, because beneficiaries have investments with multiple asset owners (pension funds of current and past employment, several insurance products) and multiple asset managers. In an investment chain, there is a principal–agent relationship between the parties at each link, with implications for allocation and performance. The investment performance of the asset manager is, for example, measured against a clearly articulated market benchmark (see Box 7.1).

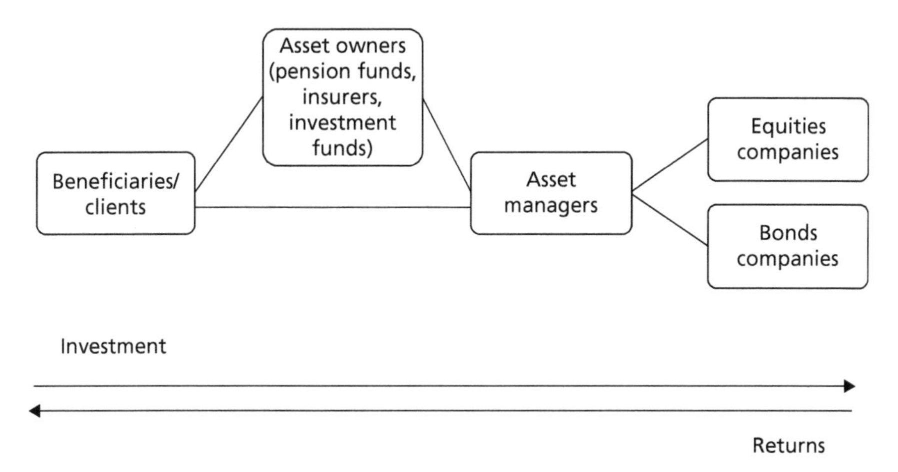

Figure 7.1 A stylized investment chain

BOX 7.1 NORWEGIAN SOVEREIGN WEALTH FUND

A case in point of passive investing is the investment strategy and related performance measurement practice followed by the Norwegian Ministry of Finance, the owner of the Norwegian Government Pension Fund, which had close to $1 trillion in assets in 2017. The Norges Bank Investment Management is the asset manager of the Fund. The Ministry of Finance specifies benchmark indices comprised of a broad range of equities and bonds that the Fund is supposed to track (Kapoor, 2017). The equity benchmark is the FTSE Global All Cap Index, comprising 7,103 listed companies, and the bond benchmark is the Barclays Global Aggregate Index, consisting of 9,487 bonds from 1,926 issuers.

The Ministry of Finance further specifies that the TE (deviation from these indices) should be no more than 1 per cent, which gives very little scope for active portfolio management by Norges Bank Investment Management. The outcome is that the Norwegian Fund owns small stakes of about 2 per cent in thousands of companies. This case is illustrative for asset management. Vanguard, the US investment fund with about $4 trillion in global assets under management (AUM), also follows a passive benchmark strategy. As a result, there is little or no societal allocation role for these investments.

Investment decisions are often made across multilayered asset owner organizations supported by multiple consultants and ratings agencies. A pension fund, for example, typically has a long chain:

- beneficiaries (pensioners and future pensioners);
- governing board;
- chief executive officer and/or chief investment officer;
- asset class heads;
- supporting functions such as finance, accounting, legal, and compliance;
- external and internal asset managers.

Delegated investment management—with multiple parties in the investment chain—causes agency problems between the asset owner or principal on the one hand and the delegated asset manager or agent responsible for making investment decisions on the other. Investment objectives, risk appetite, incentives, horizons, and knowledge are typically not fully aligned, neither across nor within organizations. These problems are exacerbated when investing for the long term, where the pay-off is distant and often highly uncertain (Neal and Warren, 2015). The human reflex is to battle such uncertainty by focusing on short-term metrics that can be measured.

Problems arise from differences in investment horizons, a tendency to evaluate and reward based on short-term results, and a failure to commit. While an institutional investor might wish to pursue a long-term investment strategy for its beneficiaries, it might also use a quarterly benchmark to evaluate its asset managers internally. Furthermore, an institutional investor might appoint internal and external gatekeepers to benchmark them against each other. In such a setting, it is very difficult to avoid tactical investment decisions aimed at short-term investment gains. Neal and Warren (2015) propose that long-term investors should aim to create an environment in which all principals and agents along the chain of delegation are aligned, engaged, and incentivized to work towards long-term outcomes and committed to investing for the long run (see Section 7.3).

7.2 **Including ESG factors: The limitations of current approaches**

Several efforts have been made to supplement the market metrics with ESG ratings and ESG indices. But they only help to some extent. Like corporate social responsibility on the corporate side, they do not address the core of the issue but rather consider ESG as something besides financial and business models, instead of something that is part of what drives these. That is also how most investment professionals have been using ESG ratings and ESG indices: as yet another indicator that may look good or bad, but which barely affects their investment decisions. These practices follow partly from the market-based approach to investing (see Section 7.1) and partly from limitations of ratings.

To distinguish companies' sustainability profiles, ESG ratings have been invented and added to the investor's toolbox. ESG ratings agencies such as MSCI, Sustainalytics, and oekom (see Chapter 6) score thousands of firms on several sustainability metrics within the E (economic), S (social), and G (governance) domains. They provide scores and reports at the company level, to be used by investors who subscribe to their services. The advantage of these ratings is that they provide investors with a quick approximation of a firm's ESG quality, just like a price–earnings ratio provides investors with a quick view on a firm's valuation (see Chapter 8). However, just like valuation multiples, ESG ratings are imprecise shortcuts that can be incorrect at the company level. They can make more sense at the portfolio or market level, where random errors may cancel each other out. But even then, one should be vigilant of systematic errors.

7.2.1 DESIGN LIMITATIONS

ESG ratings have a number of limitations by design. First, ratings want to be too many things to too many people. They have little focus on material issues (i.e. issues that are relevant to the investee companies), although it is crucial for investment purposes to focus on material issues (Khan, Serafeim, and

Yoon, 2016). Secondly, the ratings are based on reported data and policies, which are only a fraction of what is needed for a good assessment and are sometimes even conflicting (Tirole, 2017). Thirdly, scores are 'industry neutral' and based mainly on operations, barely taking into account the products of the companies in question. As a result, tobacco and coal mining companies can gain very high scores in spite of the nature of their products. Finally, there are too many stocks (as many as 70) covered per analyst, which also makes an in-depth assessment unlikely. While the ESG ratings agencies do aim to address these design limitations, they seem trapped by their own frameworks, which they are reluctant to change because they want to maintain consistency in their data.

The design limitations result in several problems that reduce the relevance of ratings to investors. One such problem is the existence of biases in scores, for example, on size (as they favour large companies with big sustainability staff departments). Another problem is that the 'industry-neutral' approach results in ratings that are intuitively wrong—as the least bad companies in very unsustainable industries (say coal or tobacco) still get very high scores and can be named sustainability leaders. The lack of focus on material issues means that a materially negative (and potentially fatal) issue is easily cancelled out by high scores on immaterial items, resulting in serious mistakes, which would have been spotted in a diagnosis by a seasoned analyst.

For example, the software fraud at Volkswagen was not very surprising given the major governance issues at the firm, with fighting shareholders and the local government pushing to maximize financial returns (F) and employment (S) at the expense of environmental standards (E). These issues were well flagged, but Volkswagen nevertheless got very high ratings with most of the ESG ratings agencies as it ticked many positive boxes on other issues. This also happened at other firms like Toshiba. Yet other firms, especially small ones, get low ratings as they do not put enough information on their policies in the public domain, or they get misclassified and compared with the wrong kind of firms. Hence, it is not surprising to see a lack of correlation in scores between rating agencies. Across 1,600 stocks in the MSCI World benchmark, Howard (2016) finds a correlation of 26 per cent between the scores assigned by the two largest rating agencies. Based on survey data, Mooij (2017b) concludes that 'reporting fatigue, a lack of convergence and the (sometimes) poor quality and transparency have made the ESG rating industry more vice than virtue in the adoption of responsible investment'.

In sum, ESG ratings need to get better. Investors should not accept them as a definitive assessment of a company's sustainability quality, but rather as a starting point for analysis. What is more, they should reconsider some of their core assumptions to really embed ESG in their investment process.

7.2.2 CURRENT STATE OF PLAY

Chapter 8 provides an overview and in-depth discussion of ESG strategies. The current state of play is that among institutional investors that follow ESG strategies about half of them only use ESG ratings for negative screening—that is, to exclude companies with very negative externalities (sustainable finance (SF) 1.0). The other half applies ESG ratings for positive screening, such as best-in-class and thematic investing (Eccles, Kastrapeli, and Potter, 2017). Because of their design limitations, the use of ESG ratings for positive screening can be labelled as SF 1.5. Moreover, investors ultimately continue to rely on metrics like TEs and returns versus market benchmarks. The ratings are simply added to these metrics. The next stage is full ESG integration (SF 2.0), which is discussed in Section 7.3.

7.3 **The solution: an active investment approach**

This section proposes an active investment approach, based on fundamental analysis of companies' ESG factors and engagement with investee companies on material ESG factors. The aim is to uncover and realize companies' social and environmental value in tandem with their financial value. The incorporation of ESG information into stock prices is an adaptive process, dependent upon the number of fundamental analysts, how their decisions are determined by ESG factors, and the quality of their learning. The remainder of this section considers the same functions as in Section 7.1 (pricing, allocation, and performance measurement), but through the lens of their potential in active investment management, and adds engagement to the list.

7.3.1 PRICING: FROM EMH TO AMH

The AMH provides an alternative description of markets (Lo, 2004; 2017), as highlighted in Chapter 3. Lo (2004) puts it like this: 'Based on evolutionary principles, the Adaptive Markets Hypothesis implies that the degree of market efficiency is related to environmental factors characterising market ecology such as the number of competitors in the market, the magnitude of profit opportunities available, and the adaptability of the market participants.' Thus, unlike the EMH, the AMH allows for path dependencies, systematic changes in behaviour, and varying risk preferences. It also means that the current state of markets, maximizing financial return subject to risk only, may not last. The changing practices of market participants could result in social and environmental factors being priced in. But it will be an evolutionary process to get there.

The speed of the process depends on the number of fundamental analysts covering these factors. The AMH can explain why new risks, such as environmental risks, are not yet fully priced in, because not enough investors are examining these new risks (see Chapter 3 for further discussion and evidence).

7.3.2 ALLOCATION (1): FROM ESG FACTORS TO FUNDAMENTAL ESG ANALYSIS

In such an adaptive process, the social and environmental dimensions would be incorporated into investment allocation. First of all, an investment analyst would need to investigate the materiality of ESG factors and their impact on an investee company (see Chapter 5). As the UN SDGs are about transition, true sustainability investing should mean investing in transition. Hence, an investor needs to know how well or ill prepared an investee company is: Can the company's business model be adapted to a sustainable economy? Such preparedness can be assessed at the company level and hitherto only in a diagnostic way. This means that one needs an expert, such as a fundamental analyst, to make a judgement call as to a company's preparedness. As we lack objective and scalable metrics for preparedness, it is very challenging to make an assessment at the portfolio or market level. Existing metrics and classifications do not yet suffice.

Private equity operates more or less in this way. Private equity investors research companies and analyse future prospects (which could include transition preparedness), while taking a step away from financial markets, short-term metrics, and portfolios. This means deviating substantially from benchmarks. This is a path taken not just by sustainability investors, but also by several investors looking for better 'alpha opportunities' in less well-known companies that are not covered by several sell-side analysts (see Chapter 8). Cremers and Pareek (2016) show that investing away from the benchmark (with high active share, as they call it) combined with a patient investment strategy (with holding duration of over two years) generates, on average, an outperformance of over 2 per cent per year. Moreover, Van Nieuwerburgh and Veldkamp (2010) find evidence for the theory of information advantage. The investor who can first collect information systematically deviates from holding a diversified portfolio (see Section 7.3.3).

Another implication of a renewed focus on companies and their preparedness is that the traditional tools do not suffice. Investors have to look at companies through a different lens and go beyond traditional financial statement analysis. Inserting some ESG ratings does not measure companies' preparedness for transition, as already argued. Rather, one needs to adopt new tools and data (and often invent them) to really assess the mentioned transformational challenge. This includes considering social and environmental externalities, investigating governance and behaviour, and making an educated

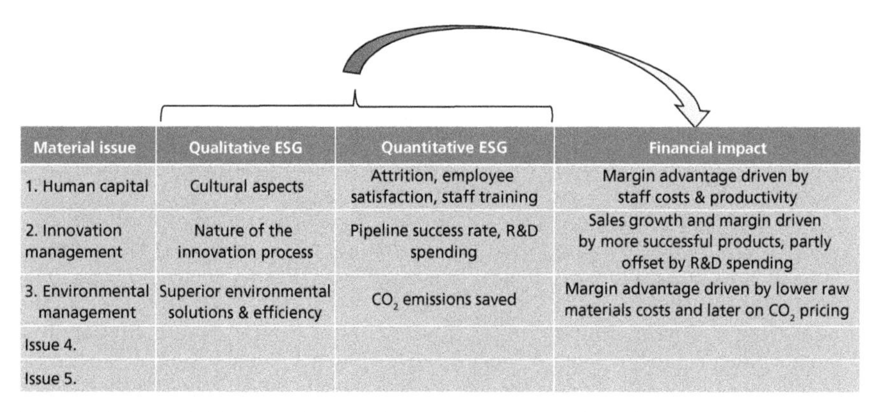

Material issue	Qualitative ESG	Quantitative ESG	Financial impact
1. Human capital	Cultural aspects	Attrition, employee satisfaction, staff training	Margin advantage driven by staff costs & productivity
2. Innovation management	Nature of the innovation process	Pipeline success rate, R&D spending	Sales growth and margin driven by more successful products, partly offset by R&D spending
3. Environmental management	Superior environmental solutions & efficiency	CO_2 emissions saved	Margin advantage driven by lower raw materials costs and later on CO_2 pricing
Issue 4.			
Issue 5.			

Figure 7.2 Financial impact of qualitative and quantitative ESG information

Note: The first step is identifying the company's material ESG issues. The second step is assessing those issues in both qualitative and quantitative ways to arrive at their financial impact (the final step). R&D = research and development.

Source: NN Investment Partners.

guess about their impact on companies' strategies and business models. That, in turn, requires an in-depth fundamental analysis of companies. Figure 7.2 provides a simplified illustration of such ESG analysis at the company and industry level. An analyst starts by identifying the company's material ESG issues and subsequently assesses those issues in both qualitative and quantitative ways to arrive at their financial impact (see Chapter 8).

Such transition preparedness analysis is impossible with a passive investment approach and nearly impossible with a quant approach. There are several reasons for this. First, ratings are of limited use, as argued in Section 7.2.1. Secondly, there is a lack of universally relevant indicators. For quant and passive approaches to be meaningful in assessing transition preparedness, they require indicators that 'work' at the market level, that is, are relevant across companies and sectors. But so far these indicators are rare because materiality is industry or even company specific. Where quant ESG is successful, it is mostly at tracking short-term ESG momentum—the incremental change on ESG performance (Kaiser, 2017)—often without a theoretical model or clear thought behind it, let alone a view on transitions. Hence, it is complementary to fundamental analysis rather than an alternative to it.

Although transition preparedness analysis is possible with an active approach, unfortunately only very few analysts undertake this (Cappucci, 2017; Mooij, 2017a). Ironically, this is partly because the low relevance of ratings has made many analysts overly sceptical of ESG. Unfortunately, that scepticism does not stimulate them to dig deeper themselves. The fact that very few undertake transition preparedness analysis and that a quant approach does not include this, is also an opportunity for very good financial

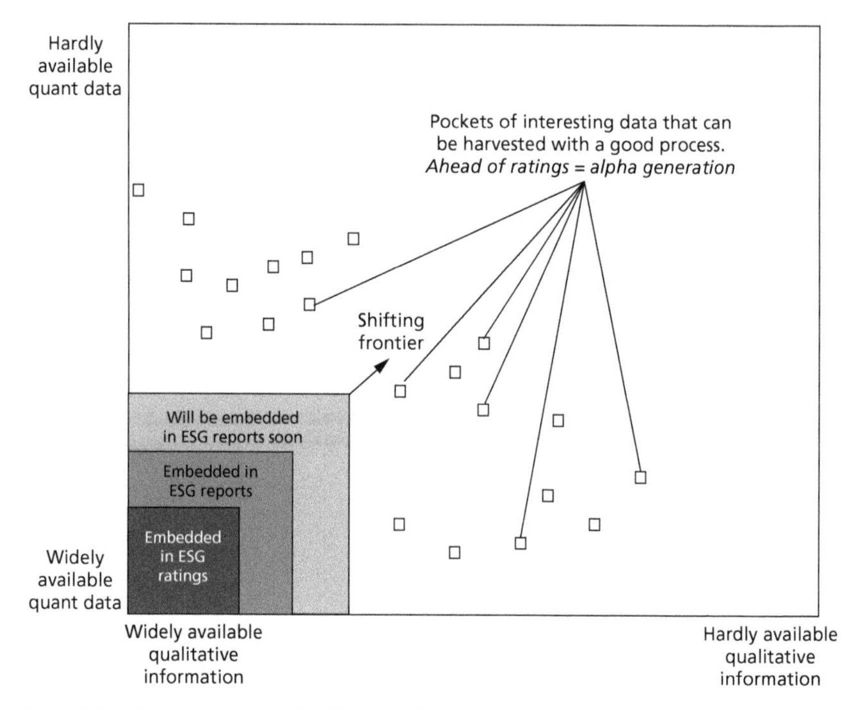

Figure 7.3 The increasing availability of ESG data

performance (alpha generation in Figure 7.3)—just like any use of valuable additional tools and data that most other market participants do not use. This is adaptation at work. Over time, quant and even passive approaches will get better at this, as ratings are expected to improve. Figure 7.3 provides a dynamic picture of the availability of qualitative and quantitative ESG data. The lack of available data is very large now, but should diminish over time in line with the AMH, with pockets of poorly used (and poorly available) data as inefficiencies and opportunities to be exploited.

ESG integration can be complemented by engagement with investee companies (see Section 7.3.4) to reap the full benefits of ESG research. However, for that to happen, we need a change of governance and incentives in the investment chain, which is currently overly long and complicated.

7.3.3 ALLOCATION (2): FROM DIVERSIFIED TO MORE CONCENTRATED PORTFOLIOS

In active management, allocation not only differs in the type of analysis, but also in the concentration of portfolios. By its nature, thorough fundamental ESG analysis can be done for a limited number of companies only, resulting in more concentrated portfolios. In a large cross-country study of security holdings of institutional investors, Choi and colleagues (2017) find that concentrated investment strategies in international markets result in excess risk-adjusted returns, conditional on an information advantage. Institutional investors concentrate holdings in their home market and selected foreign markets and industries as if they possess an information advantage. Institutional investors with higher learning capacity (i.e. skilled investors) form more concentrated portfolios. These results suggest, in contrast to traditional asset pricing theory and in support of information advantage theory, that concentrated investment strategies can be optimal.

Statman (2004) shows that a well-diversified stock portfolio needs to include just 50 to 100 stocks to eliminate idiosyncratic or unsystematic variance of stock returns. There are smaller benefits of diversification beyond those 100 stocks, but they are exhausted when the number of stocks surpasses 300 stocks (see Figure 7.4). Risk management should monitor that the stocks are not overly correlated (reducing their diversification potential) and are spread over sectors and countries. Moreover, diversification gains are mainly driven by a well-balanced allocation over different asset classes, such as equities, bonds, and alternative investments (i.e. real estate, private equity, hedge funds, commodities, and infrastructure) (see, for example, Jacobs, Müller, and Weber, 2014). Thus, for diversification it is more important to have a concentrated portfolio in each asset class than to have a very diversified portfolio (beyond 100 securities) in a single asset class.

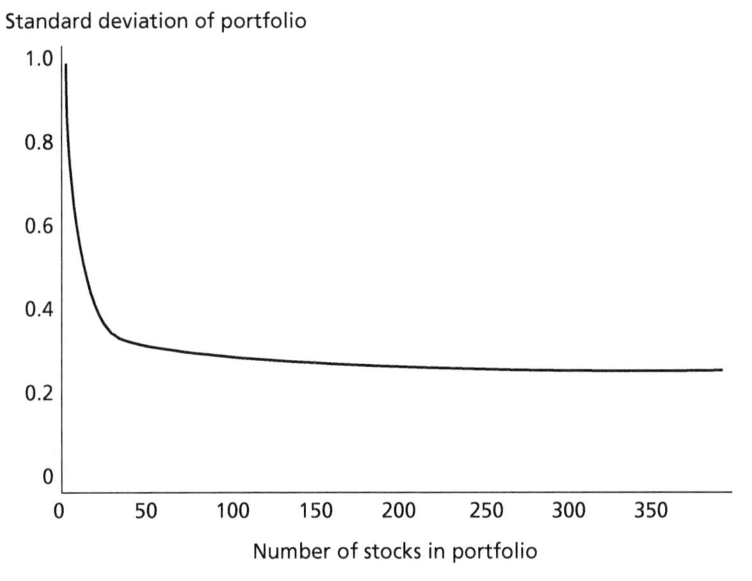

Figure 7.4 Diminishing benefits from diversification

Source: Statman (2004).

Moreover, diversification comes at a cost, especially in the supposedly low-cost passive investment strategy (which charges low fees). First, diversification reduces selectiveness, which disappears almost completely in passive strategies. In passive investing, it is not possible to invest only in the subset of companies that are able and willing to shift towards sustainable business models. However, it is possible to build passive investments on ESG-adjusted indices that exclude the really bad industries, such as coal and tobacco. This negative screening is a rather crude measure, but does steer investment away from the worst companies (SF 1.0).

Secondly, the larger the number of stocks owned, the harder it becomes to have sufficient knowledge about, and really engage with, multiple companies in the portfolio. Thirdly, on an aggregated level, widely diversified portfolios result in inadequate monitoring of corporate management teams. A free-rider problem arises as small percentage stakes mean that few investors have sufficient incentives to monitor management.

7.3.4 ENGAGEMENT

Another element of an active investment approach is effective engagement with investee companies in the long term, both behind the scenes by meeting with companies and in the annual general meeting by voting (McCahery, Sautner, and Starks, 2016). Investors and companies can exchange not only funds, but also ideas on how best to put these funds to work. Even the companies that are already on a journey to becoming more sustainable still need help in developing the most useful and cost-effective disclosure practices. And while lots of investors want companies to provide more and better disclosure of their ESG exposures, they tend to shy away from giving explicit recommendations. So, investors need to become more active in communicating their demands and preferences for information (Higgins et al. 2017).

However, such engagement is costly. It requires the human resources, expertise, and time of asset managers, ideally delivered in cooperation with portfolio managers, investment analysts, and sustainability specialists. This is only feasible in a concentrated and actively managed portfolio: 100 stocks can be followed and engaged in by a small team of people who work closely together. Engagement needs to be actively managed to allow the investment case knowledge of portfolio managers and investment analysts to be integrated into the engagement.

In practice, this happens at very few financial firms. Rather, engagement is typically done at the group level for a small percentage of the holdings and by a team of engagement specialists that lack knowledge of the firms' investment cases and hence miss important points, resulting in engagement on matters that are often not material. As passive portfolios typically have thousands of stocks, the best a passive asset owner can do in practice is to vote for all those companies along the guidelines of a proxy advisor and undertake engagement with a few dozen companies, albeit typically disconnected from the investment case, materiality, and transition preparedness analyses.

Interestingly, new evidence is emerging that financial and societal considerations are converging. In an empirical test of institutional investors' ESG strategies, Dyck and colleagues (2018) find growing importance of financial motivations behind investors' push for social and environmental performance.

7.3.5 ALTERNATIVE MEASURES OF PERFORMANCE (1): FINANCIAL

Investors face an information problem when judging the performance of their fund manager. One way of mitigating that problem is by benchmarking fund performance, either to others in the industry or to an industry-wide index. That is an important reason why relative return benchmarking and index-tracking is commonplace (Haldane, 2014). The resulting problem is that funds are reduced to a few simple backward-looking metrics, which give incentives for taking shortcuts without real accountability. However, those metrics, such as in Table 7.2, are not entirely without merit. So what can be done with them? A possible solution lies in using those same metrics in a more flexible, slightly adapted way, while being cognisant of their limitations (e.g. only measuring the financial dimension). For example, instead of measuring performance against a single benchmark, one could use:

- a range of indices instead of a single one;
- a peer group of comparable competitor funds;
- an absolute return target, possibly corrected for an absolute risk metric.

Table 7.3 shows what the first two performance measures look like for the fund we considered in Table 7.2. The fund outperforms the market index across all three time periods, but the degree to which it beats the underlying sector indices differs over time. This may be related to its own sector exposures. As to its peer group: the fund beats only one out of its five peers over the past year, but four out of five peers over the longer horizons. Next, there is one peer fund that is superior across all three time frames.

An absolute return is appealing as it is often more closely aligned with the goals of the beneficiaries, which are typically in the realm of building capital over the long run rather than beating indices. For the fund we are studying, the absolute return target could, for example, be 7 per cent over five-year cycles, as shown in Table 7.4. Jordà and colleagues (2017) find a long-term average return on equity of about 7 per cent in a cross-country study.

Interestingly, the absolute return target looks tougher for the fund than the relative targets examined in Table 7.3. Clearly, in spite of the fund's strong

Table 7.3 Fund performance against a range of indices and a peer group

	Previous year	Previous 3 years	Previous 5 years
Cumulative fund performance	14.7%	40.7%	112.4%
Cumulative performance of the overall market index	11.9%	29.0%	98.1%
Sector indices			
Healthcare Index	−2.7%	30.3%	117.4%
Consumer Staples Index	5.4%	30.3%	82.1%
Information Technology Index	13.9%	44.9%	113.5%
Utilities Index	16.3%	42.8%	63.8%
Materials Index	16.7%	14.3%	65.1%
Energy Index	27.4%	−7.3%	21.3%
Consumer Discretionary Index	600%	28.0%	127.0%
Industrials Index	18.9%	27.3%	106.7%
Financials Index	22.8%	39.3%	143.4%
Telecom Services Index	23.5%	31.5%	73.5%
% sector indices beaten	40%	80%	60%
Peer group of funds			
Peer fund 1	17.9%	25.8%	93.2%
Peer fund 2	7.9%	22.7%	89.4%
Peer fund 3	17.2%	42.5%	113.3%
Peer fund 4	14.8%	30.8%	99.1%
Peer fund 5	15.5%	31.5%	99.8%
% peers beaten	20%	80%	80%

Note: The three- and five-year performance numbers are cumulative.

Table 7.4 Fund performance on an absolute return basis

Year	Portfolio price end of year	Portfolio returns	7% absolute return target met over this year	Annualized absolute return over the past 5 years	7% absolute return target met over the past 5 years
2006	76				
2007	82	7.3%	yes	N/A	N/A
2008	54	−34.5%	no	N/A	N/A
2009	67	24.9%	yes	N/A	N/A
2010	78	15.8%	yes	N/A	N/A
2011	84	8.3%	yes	1.9%	no
2012	98	17.2%	yes	3.8%	no
2013	127	28.8%	yes	18.8%	yes
2014	148	16.4%	yes	17.1%	yes
2015	156	5.4%	no	14.9%	yes
2016	178	14.7%	yes	16.3%	yes

performance against indices and peers (see Table 7.3), it takes quite a few years to shed the very weak absolute performance of 2008 of −34.5 per cent (i.e. a value loss of over one third). In spite of returns higher than 7 per cent in each of the years 2009–12, the annualized returns over five years in 2011 and 2012 are still below 7 per cent. On a yearly basis, the picture looks better as the fund manages to hit or exceed its 7 per cent target in eight out of ten years. However, this is less impressive than the fund's performance versus the index. The absolute return target is not the holy grail of performance measurement, but simply switching perspective and putting performance in a wider context is valuable.

7.3.6 ALTERNATIVE MEASURES OF PERFORMANCE (2): NON-FINANCIAL

It is important to also measure non-financial performance, as we aim for optimization of the financial, social, and environmental dimensions given risk. There are several ways to do this:

1. performance on specific key performance indicators (KPIs);
2. externality valuation methods;
3. contribution to global sustainability goals.

7.3.6.1 Performance on specific KPIs

Investors increasingly consider company performance on specific KPIs pertaining to the components of E, S, and G. For example, on E, many companies now report their scope 1, 2, and 3 CO_2 emissions (see Chapter 6), and these data are fed into the Bloomberg data system, which is available to a large proportion of the institutional investment community (Bloomberg, 2013). To a lesser extent, this also applies to water and waste data (Bloomberg, 2015). On S, there is increasing reporting of data points such as employee attrition, percentage of women in the workforce, job creation, and safety data like lost time injury frequency rates (LTIFR). On G, there is, for example, the number of independent directors, gender balance, and voting rules to consider.

It is good that such data is increasingly becoming available and indeed analysed. But there are also limitations to analysing performance on specific KPIs. First, each one of the KPIs is too narrow individually. As they pertain to specific components of performance, their meaning on a stand-alone basis is inherently insufficient to obtain a holistic view of sustainability performance. Secondly, KPIs are very hard to compare across companies and industries. The 'normal' values of KPIs are very much affected by the nature of a firm's activities, and also by the differing boundaries of firms. For example, safety issues are much more of a concern for metals and mining companies than for financial institutions. The latter have negligible LTIFR rates, whereas the former do post lost time or even fatalities from workplace accidents. But large differences in LTIFR rates can also be observed within metals and mining, as rates tend to be higher in underground mines, in more labour-intense mines, and in less developed countries. So, if a certain mining company decides to divest a business unit that operates in such a higher LTIFR rate environment, its overall LTIFR rate will dramatically improve without actually making an improvement in safety conditions. Thus, it is not simply difficult to compare such KPIs across companies within industries or across industries, it is also hard to compare them for the same company over time. The comparison can be done, but it requires diligent work by an experienced analyst who takes all the relevant circumstances into account.

Thirdly, the KPIs in question may not measure all that should be measured. For example, reporting of scope 1, 2, and 3 carbon emissions is becoming more common, but provides an incomplete overview of emission patterns. Those emissions give an impression of the current footprint of companies, but they do not indicate to what extent companies succeed in avoiding emissions elsewhere in the chain (labelled scope 4 in Chapter 6). Very few companies do report on this, and one such company that does is Novozymes, which states in its 2017 annual report that it helps clients to save 76 million tons of CO_2. That is, 76 million tons of CO_2 are not emitted but would have been emitted by Novozymes' clients if they had used alternative products. For Novozymes, and quite a few other companies, these emissions saved are a multitude of their own emissions and indicative of the sizeable solutions they provide for achieving a more sustainable economy. Seeing these wider numbers reported, in addition to the carbon emissions of the company itself, would be very valuable. Fourthly, it is not clear if performance on certain KPIs means a sufficient contribution to achieving a more sustainable model.

In sum, it is good that these KPIs are measured and reported, but they are in their infancy and results should be used with caution.

7.3.6.2 Externality valuation frameworks

Whereas specific KPIs tend to be quite narrow, the analysis of externalities offers a more holistic perspective. In recent years, new frameworks have been developed that try to measure and value companies' externalities. Examples of such frameworks are True Price and True Value, as discussed in Chapter 2. The methodology for calculating the integrated value involves measuring, monetizing, and balancing financial and non-financial values. Box 7.2 explains how the True Value methodology can be applied to obtain the integrated value, which this book introduces as the new norm for investment decisions and performance.

True Price (2014) argues that the monetization of social and environmental externalities by a company leads to better decisions, more innovation, and an

BOX 7.2 KPMG'S TRUE VALUE METHODOLOGY

In 'A new vision of value', KPMG (2014) argues that the disconnect between corporate and societal value creation is disappearing as externalities are increasingly being internalized. KPMG identifies three interconnected drivers of the increasing rate of internalization: (i) regulation and standards; (ii) stakeholder action; and (iii) market dynamics. For organizations to explore the implications of these internalization processes, KPMG sets out its True Value approach as a three-step process:

1. **Assess the company's 'true' earnings** by identifying and quantifying its material externalities. The gap between accounting earnings and 'true' earnings can be visualized in a 'true' earnings bridge, which shows several positive and negative externalities.
2. **Understand future earnings at risk** by analysing exposure to the three drivers of internalization. Think, for example, of higher taxes on carbon-intense production (regulatory force), lost production due to stakeholder action, or lost sales due to shortages of key inputs (market dynamics). Exposures are mapped by doing scenario analysis.
3. **Create corporate and societal value** by developing business cases that capture value-creation opportunities and reduce risk. This involves identifying potential investments to reduce negative externalities or to increase positive externalities. For these investment opportunities, the True Value net present value (NPV) is calculated: this includes the likely future returns from internalized externalities. The outcome of that True Value NPV is total financial and social value. Alternative investment opportunities can be compared using the so-called marginal True Value curve.

Source: KPMG (2014).

enhanced reputation. These are valuable effects indeed. But there are also disadvantages. First, an externality analysis is very time-consuming and takes about a year to complete. As a result, few examples of True Price/True Value analysis are available so far, which severely limits investor relevance. An investor-friendly shortcut to valuing externalities would be most welcome, but probably requires analysts to first gain a good deal of experience undertaking the full version.

Secondly, the methods have been criticized for allowing pluses and minuses to be cancelled out, that is, to compensate negative impacts with positive impacts. Thirdly, as with KPIs, it is not clear whether strong performance on a certain externality means a sufficient contribution to achieving a more sustainable model. Box 7.2 describes how KPMG's True Value is applied in three steps, which illustrates the kind of thinking required for assessing transition preparedness. In this book, we use the concept of integrated value instead of total value or true value, as they have the same meaning.

7.3.6.3 Contribution to global sustainability goals

The problem with both specific KPIs and the valuation of externalities is that it is not clear what level of performance is good enough. A company might do better on KPIs or have more positive externalities than peers, but that does not necessarily mean that it is doing well enough to contribute to achieving a sustainable business model. The bigger context is missing. The 17 UN SDGs, discussed in Chapter 1, are global sustainability goals that do provide such a context.

As the SDGs were set as late as 2015, companies have only just begun to report on them. As a result, aggregate corporate data are not yet available, so it is not yet possible to measure corporate contribution to the goals. Nevertheless, Schramade (2017) argues that, even with such poor data, it is possible for investors to get a sense of the SDGs' exposure of their portfolios by simply tagging companies and industries to the goals. This can be done by assessing whether a certain company or industry is likely to have a positive, neutral, or negative impact on each of the SDGs or on a combination of them. Schramade (2017) estimates that just under 20 per cent of companies and industries are SDG positive, just over 20 per cent of them are SDG negative, and 60 per cent are SDG neutral. This method allows investors to assess how a company performs on the social and environmental dimension and to what extent it is prepared for the transition to a sustainable economy.

7.3.7 THE IDEAL INVESTMENT CHAIN

Building on our stylized investment chain in Figure 7.1, Figure 7.5 contrasts the ideal and the current investment chain. The middle column illustrates the ideal investment chain from a SF perspective. The asset owner (e.g. a pension fund or a retail client) is a long-term investor, who cares about financial, social, and environmental returns. The asset owner appoints an asset manager, who invests on his or her behalf. The asset owner asks the asset manager to report on financial and ESG returns, including carbon-related financial disclosures of the invested companies. The asset manager is also actively engaging with the company to promote sustainable business practices.

The final party in the investment chain is the company, which ideally has a board that has adopted a sustainable business model and applies integrated reporting (IR). Closing the circle, the integrated report provides the necessary information on financial, social, and environmental values to the asset manager, who can report back to the asset owner. All parts of the chain are expected to understand the important aspects of SF and its nuances. As a result, they are not easily fooled by ratings.

This ideal investment chain does not exist in practice, so the right column of Figure 7.5 is a more realistic representation of current investment chains. First, there are multiple parties in the chain: both within each nexus of the chain and

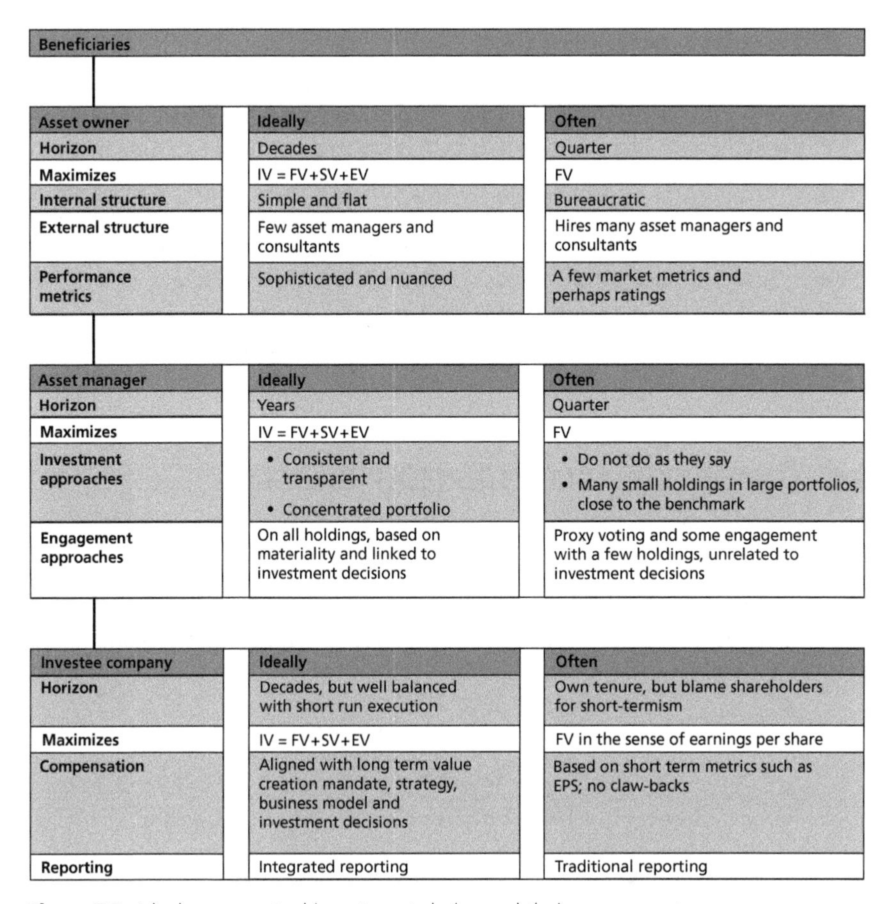

Figure 7.5 Ideal versus actual investment chains and their components

Note: IV = integrated value, FV = financial value (F), SV = social value (S), and EV = environmental value (E).

across multiple nexuses (an asset manager may delegate the investment to another asset manager and so on). An example of the latter is an asset manager for a pension fund, who invests in a hedge fund or private equity. There may be so many delegates that monitoring becomes very difficult. Secondly, performance metrics tend to be narrow. For example, the performance of the asset manager is often measured against a clearly articulated benchmark (see Box 7.1). Thirdly, incentives are shorter term than desirable given fiduciary duty and investment goals. The High-Level Expert Group on Sustainable Finance (2018) recommends incorporating sustainability in the fiduciary duty of institutional investors (and their asset managers) towards their beneficiaries and clients (see Chapter 3).

7.4 Conditions for LTVC

Section 7.3 provides the building blocks for investing for LTVC. How can LTVC be achieved? The short answer is that investors should facilitate firms in their LTVC process, as described in Chapters 3 and 5. The longer answer is that investors can realize long-term investment returns by investing in and engaging with companies that are capable of adding value over the long term, thereby having a positive effect on the value of their portfolios and on society. In a survey of large shareholders in corporate governance, De Jong and colleagues (2017) distil six conditions for investors to enable them to pursue an investment strategy aimed at LTVC (see Figure 7.6).

7.4.1 CONDITION 1: LONG INVESTMENT HORIZONS

With LTVC in mind, it does not make sense to buy stocks 'for a ride' of just a few months or even weeks. Rather, one should buy stocks with a multiyear horizon (five+ years), both in terms of intended holding period and in terms of confidence in the sustainability of the business model (Amel-Zadeh and

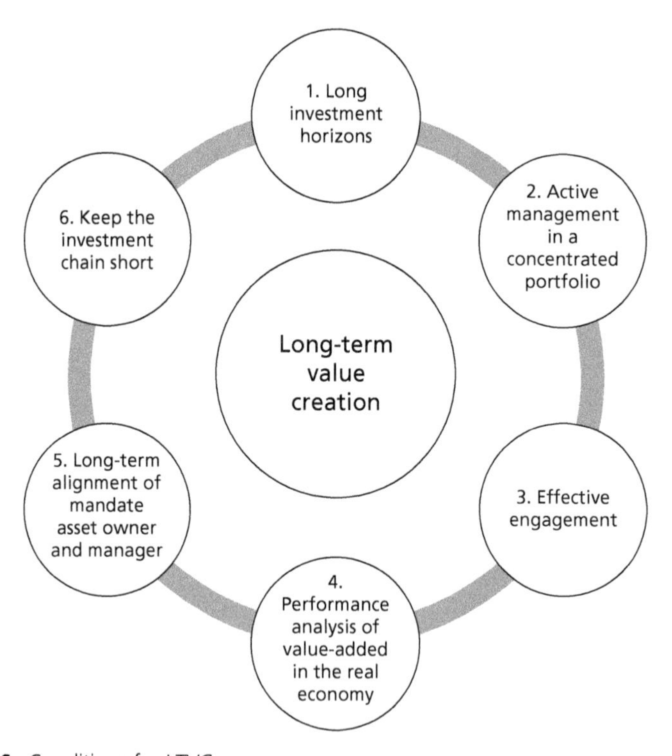

Figure 7.6 Conditions for LTVC

Source: Adapted from De Jong et al. (2017).

Serafeim, 2018). It is important to distinguish intended holding periods from observed holding periods. The latter may simply be a result of a very passive investment stance. An active investor could have a very long intended holding period but might still decide to terminate a position early based on new long-term information (Edmans, 2017).

7.4.2 CONDITION 2: ACTIVE MANAGEMENT OF A CONCENTRATED PORTFOLIO

The second condition is an active investment strategy, with regard to a concentrated portfolio, as described in Section 7.3. That allows for the kind of in-depth fundamental ESG-integrated analysis that can provide an information advantage. It is also a necessary, though not sufficient, condition for effective engagement (see Section 7.4.3: condition 3). Concentrated portfolios stand in contrast to the prescription of the CAPM that every investor would hold a portfolio of all securities available in the market (Elton et al. 2014). Many institutional investors still partially follow that prescription by investing in passive index products. Fortunately, there are also asset owners that deviate from that prescription by investing in a concentrated portfolio—as illustrated in Box 7.3 by the example of Swedish pension fund Alecta.

7.4.3 CONDITION 3: EFFECTIVE ENGAGEMENT

The third condition is effective engagement with invested companies in the long term, both behind the scenes by meeting with companies and in the annual general meeting by voting (McCahery, Sautner, and Starks, 2016). This requires human resources, expertise, and time. By building on the fundamental analysis conducted in the investment process, important synergy benefits can be reaped, making engagement more effective and efficient than stand-alone engagement strategies. Early evidence shows that institutional investors have a positive impact on investee companies' social and environmental performance (Dyck et al. 2018).

7.4.4 CONDITION 4: PERFORMANCE ANALYSIS OF VALUE ADDED IN THE REAL ECONOMY

The fourth condition for LTVC is performance analysis based on companies' value added in the real economy (both financial value and social and environmental value). By contrast, a passive benchmark strategy (with minimum tracking error) does not allow (large) deviations from the market benchmark. However, the development of alternative performance measures is still in its infancy, as discussed in Section 7.3.

7.4.5 CONDITION 5: LONG-TERM ALIGNMENT OF THE MANDATES OF ASSET OWNERS AND MANAGERS

The fifth condition is alignment of the mandates of the asset owner or client and the asset manager in the long term. De Jong and colleagues (2017) indicate that asset managers are primarily motivated by their beneficiaries (asset owners or clients) to pursue LTVC, but the incentives in place are often not aligned. Another important motive for long-term behaviour by asset managers is the investment belief that LTVC has a positive impact on shareholder returns. This belief is something that typically has to grow within asset managers, with a clear tone from the top and the right incentives for people to act upon.

7.4.6 CONDITION 6: KEEP THE INVESTMENT CHAIN SHORT

The sixth and final condition is to keep the investment chain (between parties and within parties) as short as possible, as each player in the investment chain adds complexity and may hold the next player accountable to a shorter period. As a result, valuable information might be lost. The investment chain is similar to a manufacturing supply chain: outsourcing may bring benefits from specialization but also increases vulnerability. Figure 7.7 illustrates the alignment in the investment chain on LTVC (FCLTGlobal, 2015). The asset owner provides a long-term mandate to the asset manager and commits to a long-term horizon. The asset manager has an active ownership stake (as part of a concentrated portfolio) and engages with companies in the long term.

Illustrating the working of the six conditions, Box 7.3 provides an example of a large pension fund, Alecta, which applies these conditions. Alecta's investment strategy is focused on LTVC.

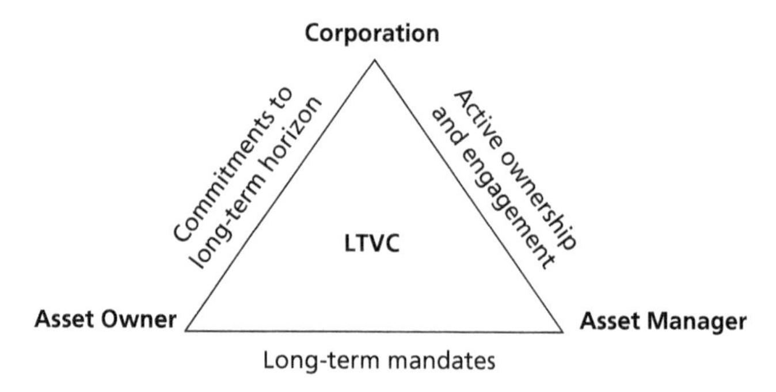

Figure 7.7 Alignment in the investment chain on LTVC

Source: Adapted from FCLTGlobal (2015).

BOX 7.3 INVESTING FOR LTVC AT ALECTA

Alecta is a large Swedish pension fund with AUM of €81 billion in 2016. The pension fund adopts a 15- to 20-year perspective on the asset side and applies ESG integration in its investment process.

Alecta's asset management model is based on the active management of a limited number of shareholdings (104 listed shareholdings in 2016). This active management is achieved through independent in-house analysis, focusing on the absolute return and risks of investments using a five-year average. This has significant advantages compared with index management. Each investment decision is preceded by a sustainability review of the company being considered. When Alecta invests in a company, it often becomes one of the largest shareholders, which enables it to engage in a close dialogue with and influence the company in the desired direction.

Alecta's total management costs are 0.09 per cent of AUM, of which investment management costs are 0.02 per cent. Alecta can keep its operating costs very low, because it has cut out (expensive) external asset managers and consultants. The asset mix and return are as follows at end 2016:

Investments	Market value (in EUR billion)	Share	Total return (in %)	
			2016	2012–16
Shares	34.8	43%	7.2%	15.9%
Debt securities	40.1	50%	3.1%	4.5%
Real estate	5.7	7%	9.2%	11.8%
Total investments	80.6	100%	5.2%	9.1%

Source: Alecta Annual Report 2016.

7.5 **Conclusions**

The financial system is instrumental in achieving the much needed transition to a sustainable economy. But to truly fulfil that societal role, investors have to move away from the current maximization of financial value towards SF 2.0, which optimizes financial, social, and environmental value in an integrated way. This requires doing fundamental research into the investee companies. While several financial institutions aim to move to SF 2.0, traditional investment approaches are still built on the concepts of efficient markets and portfolio theory. Moreover, long and complicated investment chains exacerbate reliance on market metrics.

Portfolio theory does not include social and environmental issues in its equations and leaves no room for a societal allocation role of finance. Its excessive diversification creates a free-rider problem with regard to the monitoring of corporate managements. ESG ratings are developed to distinguish companies' sustainability profiles, but these external ratings are very imprecise shortcuts. Investors need to analyse the investee company and its business model for real ESG integration. The incorporation of ESG information into stock prices is an adaptive process, dependent on the number of fundamental analysts.

Long and complicated investment chains mean that incentives are distorted, meaningful information is lost along the chain, and the allocation role of finance is hampered. This chapter identifies several conditions for LTVC. These conditions not only imply long investment horizons and active management in concentrated portfolios, but also alternative ways to measure performance, both in financial and non-financial ways. These alternative ways are available, but are not yet widely used.

The upcoming chapters study how to incorporate sustainability in equity investing (Chapter 8), bond investing (Chapter 9), and banking (Chapter 10).

Key concepts used in this chapter

Adaptive markets hypothesis implies that the degree of market efficiency depends on an evolutionary model of individuals adapting to a changing environment.

Alpha is a measure of the active return on an investment and measures the performance of an investment compared with a suitable market index.

Active investing refers to a portfolio management strategy where the manager makes specific investments instead of investing in the benchmark (see *passive investing*).

Asset owner is the ultimate owner of an investment asset; asset owners can be retail clients or institutional investors (who invest on behalf of beneficiaries).

Asset managers choose what assets to buy, manage these assets, and collect the cash flows from these assets for asset owners.

Benchmarking in investment is the process of measuring an investment portfolio's performance against a market index.

Beta is an indication of a portfolio's (or a stock's) exposure to general market movements.

Delegated investment management is the assignment of day-to-day investment decisions and implementation to a third-party provider—typically either an investment consultant or asset manager.

Efficient markets hypothesis states that stock prices incorporate all relevant information and thus on average reflect the long-term fundamental value of the firm.

Engagement refers to the investor dialogue with companies to ascertain and improve their ESG quality.

ESG ratings are ratings that try to assess the quality of a company's management of E, S, and G.

Fiduciary duty sets out the responsibilities that financial institutions owe to their beneficiaries and clients. The expectation is to be loyal to beneficiary interests, prudent in handling money, and transparent in dealing with conflicts.

Fundamental analysis is an approach to investing based on obtaining a good understanding of a company's business model and valuation.

Information ratio is the ratio of a portfolio's excess returns over the benchmark to the volatility of those returns (see *tracking error*); the information ratio measures a portfolio manager's ability to generate excess returns relative to a benchmark, but also attempts to identify the consistency of the investor.

Investment chain refers to the parties that sit between the ultimate provider of capital (typically someone investing for his or her retirement) and the ultimate user of capital (typically a company or project); asset owners and asset managers are key players in the investment chain.

Key performance indicator is a measurable value that demonstrates how effectively a company is achieving key business objectives; companies use KPIs at multiple levels to evaluate their success at reaching targets.

Long-term value creation refers to the goal of companies, which optimize financial, social, and environmental value in the long run.

Market index represents an entire stock market and thus tracks the market's changes over time.

Passive investing is an approach to investing that buys widely diversified portfolios, often made up of entire market indices, and limits the amount of buying and selling, so as to steadily build wealth over time.

Performance measure refers to an indicator to measure the success of an investment portfolio on return and risk, often related to a benchmark.

Portfolio theory refers to a *theory* on how risk-averse investors can construct *portfolios* to optimize or maximize expected financial return based on a given level of market risk.

Sharpe ratio is the ratio of the annualized excess return over the risk-free rate to the variance of portfolio returns; it differs from other performance measures in that it does not measure risk against the wider market but against a risk-free rate.

Tracking error is the difference in price behaviour of a portfolio and of a benchmark, reported as a standard deviation percentage difference.

Transition preparedness analysis is an analysis aimed at assessing to what extent a company is prepared for the transition to a more sustainable economy.

SUGGESTED READING

Choi, N., M. Fedenia, H. Skiba, and T. Sokolyk (2017), 'Portfolio concentration and performance of institutional investors worldwide', *Journal of Financial Economics*, 123(1): 189–208.

Dyck, A., K. Lins, L. Roth, and H. Wagner (2018), 'Do institutional investors drive corporate social responsibility? International evidence', *Journal of Financial Economics*, forthcoming.

Eccles, R., M. Kastrapeli, and S. Potter (2017), 'How to integrate ESG into investment decision-making: results of a global survey of institutional investors', *Journal of Applied Corporate Finance*, 29(4): 112–23.

Lo, A. (2017), *Adaptive Markets: Financial Evolution at the Speed of Thought*, Princeton University Press, Princeton, NJ.

McCahery, J., Z. Sautner, and L. Starks (2016), 'Behind the scenes: the corporate governance preferences of institutional investors', *Journal of Finance*, 71(6): 2905–32.

Neal, D. and G. Warren (2015), 'Long-term investing as an agency problem', CIFR Paper No. 063/2015, Centre for International Finance and Regulation, Sydney.

REFERENCES

Amel-Zadeh, A. and G. Serafeim (2018), 'Why and how investors use ESG information: evidence from a global survey', *Financial Analysts Journal*, 74(3): 1–17.

Barberis, N. and R. Thaler (2003), 'A survey of behavioral finance', in: G. Constantinides, M. Harris, and R. Stulz (eds.), *Handbook of the Economics of Finance*, vol. 1, part 2, Elsevier Publishers, Amsterdam, 1053–128.

Bloomberg (2013), 'Bloomberg carbon risk valuation tool', New York, https://data.bloomberglp.com/bnef/sites/4/2013/12/BNEF_WP_2013-11-25_Carbon-Risk-Valuation-Tool.pdf, accessed 2 July 2018.

Bloomberg (2015), 'Water risk valuation tool: integrating natural capital limits into financial analysis of mining stocks', New York, https://www.bbhub.io/sustainability/sites/6/2015/09/Bloomberg_WRVT_09162015_WEB.pdf, accessed 2 July 2018.

Cappucci, M. (2017), 'The ESG integration paradox', Working Paper, https://ssrn.com/abstract=2983227, accessed 2 July 2018.

Choi, N., M. Fedenia, H. Skiba, and T. Sokolyk (2017), 'Portfolio concentration and performance of institutional investors worldwide', *Journal of Financial Economics*, 123(1): 189–208.

Cremers, M. and A. Pareek (2016), 'Patient capital outperformance: the investment skill of high active share managers who trade infrequently', *Journal of Financial Economics*, 122(2), 288–306.

De Jong. A, D. Schoenmaker, M. Gruenwald, and A. Pala (2017), 'Large shareholders in corporate governance', Research for the Monitoring Committee Corporate Governance, Rotterdam School of Management, Erasmus University, Rotterdam.

Dyck, A., K. Lins, L. Roth, and H. Wagner (2018), 'Do institutional investors drive corporate social responsibility? International evidence', *Journal of Financial Economics*, forthcoming.

Eccles, R., M. Kastrapeli, and S. Potter (2017), 'How to integrate ESG into investment decision-making: results of a global survey of institutional investors', *Journal of Applied Corporate Finance*, 29(4): 112–23.

Edmans, A. (2017), 'The answer to short-termism isn't asking investors to be patient', *Harvard Business Review*, 18 July.

Elton, E., M. Gruber, S. Brown, and W. Goetzmann (2014), *Modern Portfolio Theory and Investment Analysis*, 9th edn, Wiley, Hoboken, NJ.

Fama, E. (1970), 'Efficient capital markets: a review of theory and empirical work', *Journal of Finance*, 25(2): 383–417.

FCLTGlobal (Focus Capital on the Long-Term Global) (2015), 'Long-term portfolio guide: reorienting portfolio strategies and investment management to focus capital on the long term', FCLTGlobal, Boston.

Fox, J. (2009), *The Myth of the Rational Market: A History of Risk, Reward, and Delusion on Wall Street*, Harper Business, New York.

Friedman, M. (1970), 'The social responsibility of business is to increase its profits', *New York Times Magazine*, 13 September.

Haldane, A. (2014), 'The age of asset management', Speech at London Business School, 4 April.

Higgins, K., J. White, A. Beller, and M. Schapiro (2017), 'The SEC and improving sustainability reporting', *Journal of Applied Corporate Finance*, 29(2): 22–31.

High-Level Expert Group on Sustainable Finance (2018), 'Financing a sustainable European economy', Final Report, European Union, Brussels.

Howard, J. (2016), 'Painting by numbers: the difficulties of measuring sustainability', Market Insights, Schroders, London, http://www.schroders.com/en/nordics/professional-investor/nordic-insights/expert-magazine/painting-by-numbers—the-difficulties-of-measuring-sustainability/, accessed 2 July 2018.

Jacobs, H., S. Müller, and M. Weber (2014), 'How should individual investors diversify? An empirical evaluation of alternative asset allocation policies', *Journal of Financial Markets*, 19(1): 62–85.

Jegadeesh, N. and S. Titman (1993), 'Returns to buying winners and selling losers: implications for stock market efficiency', *Journal of Finance*, 48(1): 65–91.

Jordà, O., K. Knoll, D. Kuvshinov, M. Schularick, and A. Taylor (2017), 'The rate of return on everything, 1870–2015', CEPR Discussion Paper No. 12509.

Kaiser, L. (2017), 'Style, momentum and ESG investing', Working Paper, https://ssrn.com/abstract=2993843, accessed 2 July 2018.

Kapoor, S. (2017), 'Investing for the future', Re-Define Discussion Paper, Report to Norwegian Church Aid.

Khan, M., G. Serafeim, and A. Yoon (2016), 'Corporate sustainability: first evidence on materiality', *Accounting Review*, 91(6): 1697–724.

KPMG (2014), 'A new vision of value: connecting corporate and societal value creation', Amsterdam, https://assets.kpmg.com/content/dam/kpmg/pdf/2014/10/a-new-vision-of-value-v1.pdf, accessed 2 July 2018.

Lo, A. (2004), 'The adaptive markets hypothesis: market efficiency from an evolutionary perspective', *Journal of Portfolio Management*, 30(5): 15–29.

Lo, A. (2017), *Adaptive Markets: Financial Evolution at the Speed of Thought*, Princeton University Press, Princeton, NJ.

McCahery, J., Z. Sautner, and L. Starks (2016), 'Behind the scenes: the corporate governance preferences of institutional investors', *Journal of Finance*, 71(6): 2905–32.

Markowitz, H. (1952), 'Portfolio selection', *Journal of Finance*, 7(1): 77–91.

Mooij, S. (2017a), 'Asset owners and the diffusion of responsible investment: what explains the low rate of adoption?', Working Paper, Oxford University.

Mooij, S. (2017b), 'The ESG initiative industry: vice or virtue in the adoption of responsible investment?', Working Paper, Oxford University.

Neal, D. and G. Warren (2015), 'Long-term investing as an agency problem', CIFR Paper No. 063/2015, Centre for International Finance and Regulation, Sydney.

Schramade, W. (2017), 'Investing in the UN Sustainable Development Goals: opportunities for companies and investors', *Journal of Applied Corporate Finance*, 29(2): 87–99.

Simon, M. (2017), *Real Impact: The New Economics of Social Change*, Nation Books, New York.

Statman, M. (2004), 'The diversification puzzle', *Financial Analysts Journal*, 60(4): 44–53.

Tirole, J. (2017), Economics for the Common Good, Princeton University Press, Princeton, NJ.

True Price (2014), 'The business case for true pricing: why you will benefit from measuring, monetizing and improving your impact', Report drafted by True Price, Deloitte, EY, and PwC, 2nd edn, Amsterdam, http://trueprice.org/wp-content/uploads/2015/02/True-Price-Report-The-Business-Case-for-True-Pricing.pdf, accessed 25 June 2018.

Tversky, A. and Kahneman, D. (1973), 'Availability: a heuristic for judging frequency and probability', *Cognitive Psychology*, 5(2): 207–32.

Van Nieuwerburgh, S. and L. Veldkamp (2010), 'Information acquisition and portfolio under-diversification', *Review of Economic Studies*, 77(2): 779–805.

8 Equity—investing with an ownership stake

Overview

Sustainability matters more to equity investors than most of them realize. As Chapter 5 shows, material sustainability issues can make or break companies and their business models. As residual claimholders, equity investors are more heavily exposed than other investors. They bear most of the risk when companies fail and they also reap most benefits when companies succeed. Therefore, they have strong incentives to help companies achieve the conditions for long-term value creation (LTVC) described in Chapters 5 and 7.

However, most equity investors fail to properly take material sustainability issues into account. Even if they are interested, they typically lack the frameworks and incentives to really integrate sustainability into their investment decisions (see Chapter 7). This chapter sketches how they can achieve this. It starts by looking at the basics of equities. Subsequently, it considers in what ways sustainability matters to equity investors and presents the increasing academic evidence in this field.

Next, the chapter discusses why investors should undertake environmental, social, and governance (ESG) integration and the extent to which they actually do this. The focus then shifts to describing how ESG integration can practically be done to achieve sustainable finance (SF) 2.0, where it is argued that fundamental equity analysis—through a deeper understanding of investee companies and their valuation drivers—is the approach most suited to ESG integration. Quant and passive investing approaches are currently held back by lack of data and tend to waver between SF 1.0 and 2.0. However, these approaches should ultimately be complementary as all three of them find new ways of identifying valuable ESG information.

Finally, this chapter describes impact investing, whereby social and environmental impact is the first investment criterion. Impact investing is essentially an extreme form of sustainability integration into equity investing, that is, SF 3.0. Table 8.1 summarizes the different ESG approaches.

Table 8.1 Classification of ESG approaches in equity investing

	Exclusionary ESG screening in equities	ESG integration in equities	Impact equity investing
Typology	SF 1.0	SF 2.0	SF 3.0
Goal	*Max* FV *s.t.* SEV^{min}	*Max* $IV = FV + SEV$	*Max* SEV *s.t.* FV^{min}
First investment criterion	Financial return (F)	Depends on the strategy	Impact (positive S+E)
Ratings	Foundation of the approach	Part of the data to be considered	Not available
Products versus operations	Operations focus	Operations and products focus	Products first, then operations
Investment universe	Very large, the worst dropout	The worst 20–30% of companies in terms of S and E dropout	Only the best 10–30% of companies in terms of S and E

Note: The sustainability typology (1.0, 2.0, and 3.0) is taken from Chapter 1. FV = financial value (F), IV = integrated value, and SEV = social-environmental value (S+E), as introduced in Chapter 1.

Learning objectives

After reading this chapter, you should be able to:

- explain the state of play on ESG integration, which can potentially improve both financial and non-financial returns;
- understand how fundamental equity investing brings a deeper understanding of companies, their value drivers, and their investment case;
- explain that fundamental equity investing is more inductive to ESG integration than quant and passive investment approaches;
- explain that impact investing is an extreme form of ESG integration that takes societal impact as the first selection criterion.

8.1 Basics of equities

Stock markets have captured the imagination of the masses at least since the spectacular rise and fall of the South Sea Company in the 1720s. Global stock markets reached a market capitalization of $70 trillion in 2016 (SIFMA, 2017), which is about 90 per cent of global GDP. They perform the important societal function of steering equity finance towards productive means. The emergence of the joint stock company has been a great innovation for spreading risk over a large number of shareholders with residual claims and limited liability. Up to that point, an investor could lose more than the capital he or she put in.

It lowered financial hurdles (such as liquidity) and helped in steering capital towards productive means.

8.1.1 TYPES OF EQUITY

Stock markets trade public equity, but equity can be private as well. In fact, most equity in most companies starts as private and remains private. Only larger companies scale up to become public, as only then do the benefits of listing in terms of risk-sharing start to outweigh the relatively high costs of listing (due to information disclosure requirements). In some ways private equity investing is instructive for public equity investing: because private equity lacks standardized data, ratings, and daily pricing, it has not become a victim of benchmark thinking reducing companies and portfolios to a few market metrics, as discussed in Chapter 7. Private equity needs to undertake fundamental analysis of investee companies, which is a good starting point for SF 2.0 and 3.0. To what extent that happens is beyond the scope of this chapter, which focuses on public equity.

The way one invests in public equity can be classified in active versus passive investing. Passive investing refers to investments in indices or exchange traded funds (which mimic an index), whereas active approaches tend to be either fundamental (i.e. based on analysis of financial statements, business models, etc.) or quant (i.e. based on factors in a model or algorithm). The attraction of passive investing is that it limits the costs of both trading and analysis. However, it also means there is a very limited scope for the societal allocation role of finance, as discussed in Chapter 7. In fact, as passive investing relies on efficient markets, it is dependent on the presence of sufficient fundamental and quant investors to keep markets efficient. Figure 8.1 provides a classification of public and private equities investing.

The remainder of this chapter is on all three types of public equity investing, with a strong emphasis on fundamental equity strategies, as those are best able

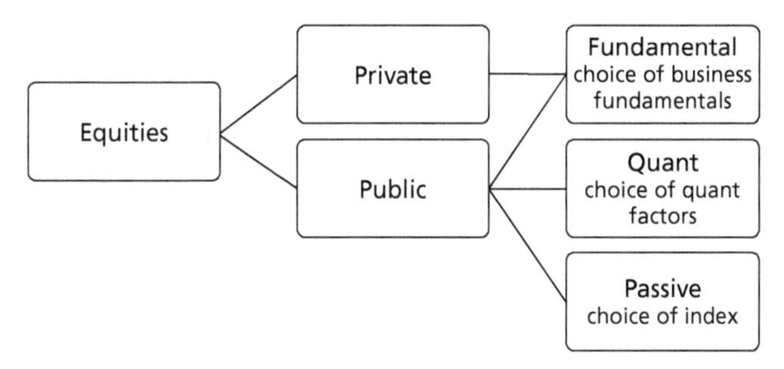

Figure 8.1 Classification of equities investing

to undertake ESG integration. Fundamental investors research a company, which enables them to identify material ESG issues and to estimate their impact on the company's valuation. Fundamental equity strategies are thus those with the most potential of achieving SF 2.0. Traditional financial theory has paid limited attention to fundamental equity investing, as it does not fit efficient markets and portfolio theory very well (see Chapter 7), and it is hard to capture in econometric analysis. That is unfortunate, as fundamental analysis is needed to assess the preparedness of companies for the transition to a more sustainable economy.

8.1.2 EQUITY VALUATION AND ITS DRIVERS

There are several methods for determining (or better, estimating) the value of equity. One can distinguish two types of valuation methods:

- absolute valuation methods; and
- relative valuation methods.

In the case of relative valuation, often called multiples valuation, a stock value P (or more generally, an asset's value) is derived from the given (market) value of another comparable stock. For example, a fast-moving consumer goods company such as Unilever might be valued by taking its earnings per share EPS and multiplying that number with the average price earnings P/E ratio of its peer group:

$$P = EPS * \frac{P}{E} \tag{8.1}$$

So, in this method, when Unilever's EPS is €2.8 and its peers trade at a P/E of 20, then Unilever's fair stock value P is 20 x €2.8 = €56. The problem with relative valuation is that it relies on fair valuation of the comparable assets, which in practice are not necessarily priced correctly. Another disadvantage is that it can be quite hard to find companies that are comparable, meaning that there are no perfect substitutes for a company. Each of its competitors is for instance active in different geographies, different segments, and serves different customers, which may impact the P/E ratio. Absolute valuation methods such as the discounted cash flow (DCF) model avoid this problem by valuing assets on the basis of their discounted future CFs. In a textbook like Berk and DeMarzo (2014), the formula for company value V_0 at $t = 0$ is given as follows:

$$V_0 = \frac{FCF_1}{(1 + WACC)} + \frac{FCF_2}{(1 + WACC)^2} + \ldots + \frac{FCF_N + V_N}{(1 + WACC)^N} \tag{8.2}$$

where FCF represents the free cash flow, $WACC$ the weighted average cost of capital, and V^N the terminal value at $t = N$, which may in turn be valued with a DCF. Note that V_0 in the DCF formula is the enterprise value of the company to all financiers, that is, the value of debt and equity together. Equity holders are residual claimholders, who receive income only after the debt holders have been paid. In effect, equity is an option on the company (Black and Scholes, 1973).

FCF is the CF left to be distributed to financiers after all positive net present value (NPV) investments have been made. It is calculated as cash from operations minus cash into investments. It is important to use FCF rather than earnings, which is much more easily manipulated, as is visible in accruals (i.e. differences between net earnings and operating cash flow (OCF), driven for example by revenues or expenses that have been earned or incurred but not yet recorded in the company's accounts). The weighted average cost of capital (WACC) is the rate of return demanded by the company's financiers (of both equity and debt) and is derived from the expected return on an asset with similar risk.

Koller, Goedhart, and Wessels (2015: 30) simplify the formula as follows:

$$V_0 = \frac{FCF_1}{WACC - g} \tag{8.3}$$

where g is the constant growth rate of the company's *FCF*. A DCF valuation crucially relies on assumptions to be made on future FCF and on the cost of capital, as well as on their elements. This gives a behavioural problem, because analysts often simply extrapolate recent historical numbers or short-term forecasts into infinity (while the company is exposed to internal and external changes, which impact the company).

The DCF example in Table 8.2 illustrates how this works. The top part lists the inputs (e.g. a sales growth of 6 per cent and an earnings before interest and taxes (EBIT) margin of 11 to 12 per cent) and the components (sales, EBIT, and taxes) to calculate the FCF (see the note at Table 8.2 for explaining the abbreviations and the basis of the calculations). First, taxes are deducted from EBIT to obtain the net operating profit less adjusted taxes (NOPLAT). Next, depreciation is added (no cash outflow) and investment is deducted (cash outflow) to obtain the FCF. The columns represent the years: the shaded grey area from 2018 to 2026 are the assumptions made by the analyst in order to arrive at the forecasted CFs (all other data in Table 8.2 are given historical numbers or calculated based on inputs). The middle part contains the discount factor (based on the WACC of 8 per cent) to discount the FCF to the present value. The enterprise value is the sum of the present values. Next, net debt is deducted to obtain the equity value. The bottom part outlines the capital side: net working capital, invested capital, and return on invested capital (ROIC).

Some argue that short-termism is not an issue, as stocks incorporate over a decade of CFs in their pricing. However, we disagree, as the CF forecasts can

Table 8.2 DCF valuation with the value drivers—analyst extrapolation

WACC = 8%
Terminal value growth = 2%

	FY2014	FY 2015	FY 2016	FY 2017	12/31/18	12/31/19	12/31/20	12/31/21	12/31/22	12/31/23	12/31/24	12/31/25	12/31/26
Sales growth	6%	11%	6%	7%	6%	6%	6%	6%	6%	6%	6%	6%	2%
EBIT margin	11%	12%	12%	12%	12%	12%	12%	12%	12%	12%	12%	12%	12%
Tax rate	20%	21%	30%	29%	28%	28%	28%	28%	28%	28%	28%	28%	28%
Depreciation/sales	6%	5%	5%	5%	5%	5%	5%	5%	5%	5%	5%	5%	5%
CAPEX/sales	6%	6%	6%	6%	6%	6%	6%	6%	6%	6%	6%	6%	5%
NWC/sales	9%	9%	9%	8%	8%	8%	8%	8%	8%	8%	8%	8%	8%
Sales	6233	6910	7348	7856	8327	8827	9357	9918	10513	11144	11813	12521	12772
EBIT	691	807	906	937	993	1053	1116	1183	1254	1329	1409	1493	1523
Taxes on EBIT	138	172	276	269	278	295	312	331	351	372	394	418	427
NOPLAT	553	635	630	668	715	758	804	852	903	957	1014	1075	1097
Depreciation	361	377	352	405	416	441	468	496	526	557	591	626	639
Gross CF	914	1012	982	1073	1131	1199	1271	1348	1428	1514	1605	1701	1735
CAPEX	399	430	458	472	500	530	561	595	631	669	709	751	639
Increase in NWC	37	33	32	28	40	42	44	47	50	53	56	59	21
Gross investment	436	463	490	500	539	572	606	642	681	722	765	811	660
FCF	478	549	492	573	592	628	666	705	748	793	840	891	1076
Terminal Value													17930
period, in years					1	2	3	4	5	6	7	8	8
Discount factor					0.926	0.858	0.794	0.735	0.681	0.630	0.583	0.540	0.540
Present value					549	538	528	519	509	499	490	481	9685

Sum of present values: enterprise value					13798								
Net debt					1328								
Equity value					12470								
Number of shares outstanding					213								
Stock price					58.5								
Current stock price					60.2								
Implied upside						−3%							
NWC	566	599	631	659	699	740	785	832	882	935	991	1050	1071
Invested capital	3982	4068	4206	4301	4424	4554	4692	4838	4993	5158	5332	5517	5538
ROIC	14%	16%	15%	16%	17%	17%	18%	18%	19%	19%	20%	20%	20%

Notes: FY2014–FY2017 relate to the historical financial performance of the company. 2018e–2026e are projections of expected (i.e. future) financial performance made by the analyst. WACC is the weighted average cost of capital, the rate at which the company's CFs are discounted. Terminal value (or continuing value) growth is the assumed growth rate after the explicit forecast period. EBIT is earnings before interest and taxes, also known as operating profit. CAPEX is the capital expenditure made by the company. NWC is net working capital, i.e. short-term liquid assets minus short-term finance. NOPLAT is net operating profit less adjusted taxes. Gross CF is the cash flow before investment. FCF is the free cash flow to the company.

be a mere extrapolation of the short term—that is, they do not necessarily reflect change or the relevance of ESG. Multiples (relative) valuation faces this problem as well, even to a larger extent, as it implicitly makes the same assumptions while giving the analyst a false sense of being objective.

In a DCF valuation, one can make explicit assumptions and choose to be very clear on which point one disagrees with the market. In such a valuation of the same company as in Table 8.2, an analyst uses, for example, exactly the same assumptions with one crucial difference: as he has a stronger belief in the company's competitive position, his margin assumptions are 4 percentage points higher (an EBIT margin of 16 instead of 12 per cent), resulting in a 35 per cent higher fair value of the stock.

Although academic corporate finance and asset pricing models are very much concerned with risk and discount rates, they tend to take the FCF as a given and do not analyse the basis for it. Not all analysts undertake the fundamental analysis that is crucial to really understand a company's value. Furthermore, most typically do not analyse a company's preparedness for a more sustainable economy. Corporate finance is more relevant than asset pricing since it does recognize the frictions within companies. Koller, Goedhart, and Wessels (2015) propose a useful split into the value drivers:

- **sales**, which can be decomposed into volumes and price;
- **margins**, which can be analysed by type of costs and before or after depreciation, taxes, etc.; and
- **capital**, which can be split into the cost of capital (discount rate) and the uses of capital (capital expenditures (CAPEX), working capital).

Making these splits can yield very useful insights into how efficiently and successfully a company is run. Moreover, one can also analyse what is driving the value drivers. That is, what are the sources of competitive advantage that determine how fast a company grows and how profitably it can sell its goods and services (see Chapter 5). This is also where the link to sustainability comes in, as intangible assets on material ESG issues, such as intellectual capital or social capital, tend to be the underlying value drivers. Think of a mining company that has much lower costs than its peers because it is much better at managing local stakeholders (and hence experiences less delays and production losses) and has a better safety record (and more efficient production). Or think of a mining company that currently enjoys lower costs than its peers because it is ignoring lots of safety regulations and is paying its employees poorly without pension or social security arrangements. The latter cost advantage is likely to be temporary and entails a high risk of costly disruptions, which should be factored into its cost of capital. Section 8.2 illustrates the ways in which the value drivers provide a very good connection between sustainability and finance.

8.2 **Why does sustainability matter to equities?**

The link between sustainability and equity value is not directly obvious, as many assume a separation between the social and business domains. But in fact, business models are the missing link between ESG and finance. Financial analysts who want to understand the long-term value drivers for an equity valuation need to investigate the business model. And ESG analysts, who want to truly understand a company's position and incentives on ESG issues, also need to understand the business model. However, as the business model is often only casually studied by both groups of analysts, they tend to miss this crucial link. Figure 8.2 illustrates the link between ESG and finance.

Moreover, in most cases, corporate success in creating shareholder value also involves an increase in societal value. Companies are typically able to make money by offering products and services that are valuable to people. The line of causality to shareholder value starts from a company's social purpose of providing valuable products or services at prices people are able and willing to pay. Shareholder value is then a reflection or outcome of the company's success in satisfying its customers and other stakeholders (see Figure 8.3 based on

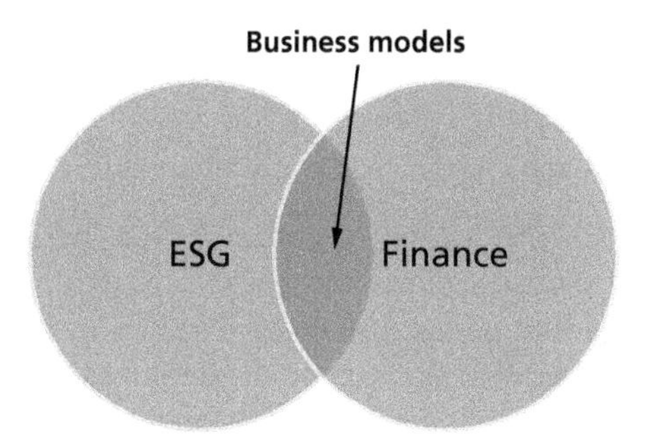

Figure 8.2 Business models as the link between ESG and finance

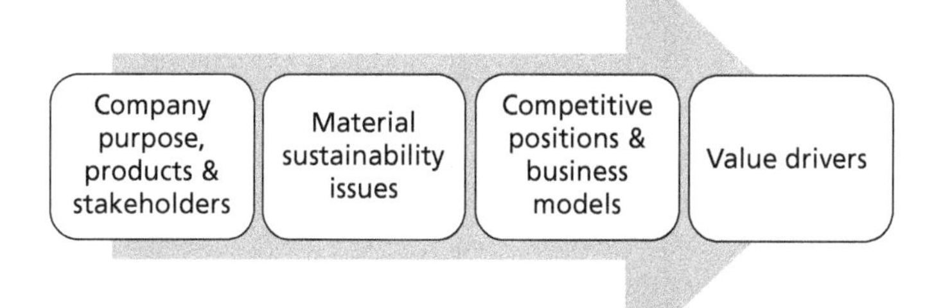

Figure 8.3 Why sustainability matters for shareholder value

Source: Schramade (2016a).

Schramade, 2016a and 2016b). In terms of the transition to be made and the Sustainable Development Goals (SDGs) to be achieved is a company, on the whole, part of the problem or part of the solution?

As this link between sustainability and equity value is not well recognized, the material issues (i.e. the issues relevant for the company's business model) tend not to be properly priced. Thus, ESG analysis offers opportunities for superior performance by benefiting from market inefficiencies. Moreover, it is a natural extension of fundamental equity analysis, which is concerned with better understanding a company's value drivers.

8.2.1 EVIDENCE THAT SUSTAINABILITY MATTERS TO EQUITY PRICING

Figure 8.3 illustrates how, logically, sustainability should matter to equity valuation, as discussed in Chapter 5. There is indeed a growing body of empirical academic evidence that supports this view. The empirical evidence should, however, be structured somewhat differently to Figure 8.3:

1. from (proxies for) sustainability performance to value drivers;
2. to stock performance at the company level;
3. to investor performance.

8.2.1.1 **From sustainability performance to value drivers...**

There is increasing evidence that strong sustainability performance is helpful for value driver performance. Ortiz-de-Mandojana and Bansal (2016) find that companies that adopt better sustainability practices have lower financial volatility, higher sales growth, and higher chances of survival when evaluated over a 15-year period. These findings are anecdotally confirmed in discussions with corporate executives. For example, Hindustan Unilever executives told us that the products that are most closely linked to their Sustainable Living Plan are also the ones that grow fastest.

Eccles and Serafeim (2013) find that the importance of the different sustainability issues likely varies systematically across companies and industries, a view which is confirmed in survey evidence by Amel-Zadeh and Serafeim (2018). This variation is visible in the materiality matrices reported by companies, which show large differences across industries in issues mentioned in materiality matrices.

Less tangible than the impact on sales growth and margins is the impact of sustainability on a company's cost of capital. But here too, an impact is found. For a large sample of US companies, El Ghoul and colleagues (2011) find that companies with better sustainability scores have cheaper equity financing. Their findings suggest that investment in improving responsible employee relations, environmental policies, and product strategies contributes substantially to reducing companies' cost of equity. They also find that operating in two 'sin' industries, namely, tobacco and nuclear power, increases companies' cost of equity.

Similarly, Cheng, Ioannou, and Serafeim (2014) find that companies with stronger sustainability performance have better access to finance. They find that both better stakeholder engagement and transparency around sustainability performance are important in reducing capital constraints. Moreover, they show that both the social and environmental dimensions drive the relationship.

Strong sustainability performance is also associated with higher levels of trust, which is crucial to economic activity, and higher resilience. Lins, Servaes, and Tamayo (2017) find that during the 2008–9 global financial crisis, companies with high social capital (proxied by high sustainability ratings) had stock returns that were 4 to 7 percentage points higher than companies with low social capital. They also experienced higher profitability, growth, and sales per employee. Lins, Servaes, and Tamayo (2017) argue that this suggests that the trust between the company and both its stakeholders and investors, built through investments in social capital, pays off when the overall level of trust in corporations and markets suffers a negative shock.

8.2.1.2 ... To stock performance at the company level

The positive relationship between sustainability and value drivers does not necessarily lead to a positive relationship with stock performance, as the value drivers themselves are (by definition) major drivers of valuation and stock performance. Moreover, other drivers of stock performance may obscure the relationship. Nevertheless, Khan, Serafeim, and Yoon (2016) find that companies that perform well on material ESG issues as identified by the Sustainability Accounting Standards Board (SASB) also outperform in the stock market with a positive risk-adjusted return (alpha) of 2 to 4 per cent (see Chapter 7 on alpha). Moreover, they find that companies that perform well on immaterial ESG issues underperform the stock market. This is consistent with the idea that strong management of material ESG issues brings a real competitive advantage, whereas strong management of immaterial resources is a waste of resources indicative of weak priority setting by management. In fact, many see strong ESG performance as a sign of management quality.

In addition to actual sustainability performance, disclosure of material issues matters as well. Grewal, Hauptmann, and Serafeim (2017) find that companies voluntarily disclosing more sustainability information, identified as material by the SASB, have stock prices reflecting more company-specific information and thereby lower synchronicity with market returns. This indicates that sustainability information matters at the company level. The result is stronger for companies with higher exposure to sustainability issues, more institutional and socially responsible investment fund ownership, and more coverage from analysts with less company-specific experience and lower portfolio complexity. The latter suggests that sustainability disclosure adds to analysts' understanding of the company's business and value drivers.

ESG performance is often proxied by sustainability ratings, which have serious shortcomings (see Section 7.2 in Chapter 7) and tend to be rather static. The levels of ratings are therefore unlikely to impact stock returns, but changes in ratings are more promising. Indeed, the European Centre for Corporate Engagement (ECCE, 2016) finds that companies with improving sustainability ratings outperform the stock market, whereas companies with already high ratings do not outperform it. The reason is that high scores tend to be quite stable and are no longer news. However, this is slightly different in emerging markets, as follow-up research by the ECCE (2017) finds. In those markets, both companies with improving ratings and companies with higher ratings outperform in the stock market. The researchers attribute this finding to lower efficiency in emerging markets and the often more recent interest in sustainability issues in those markets, which is consistent with the adaptive markets hypothesis (AMH) (see Chapter 3). Note that the results of Khan, Serafeim, and Yoon (2016) are also based on changes in ESG performance (momentum) rather than on levels of ESG performance.

8.2.1.3 Investor performance

Yet another step and question is whether and to what extent the stronger stock price performance of more sustainable companies also translates into better performance by sustainability minded investors. To what extent are they able to pick up the (underpriced) sustainability performance of companies? In a meta-study on the link between sustainability and investment performance, Friede, Busch, and Bassen (2015) find that the relationship between ESG and corporate financial performance (i.e. company performance on the value drivers and stock performance at the company level) is well established, but that the relationship between ESG and investment performance is much weaker. In fact, at first the relationship even seems to be negative. A widely cited study by Hong and Kasperczyk (2009) finds underperformance by socially responsible investing (SRI) funds due to their avoidance of so-called sin stocks such as tobacco, alcohol and gambling. However, more recent evidence shows that the favourable risk–return characteristics of those sin stocks can be replicated with other stocks, without the negative (sin) characteristics (Blitz and Fabozzi, 2017).

Even more importantly, the weak performance of many SRI funds found in older studies can be explained by ethical funds. Derwall, Koedijk, and Ter Horst (2011) find that ethical funds underperform the market, while ESG integrated funds do not. The reason is that ethical investors tend to have lower demand on financial returns and they give up performance by extreme reductions in their investment universe. In fact, retail investors expect ethical

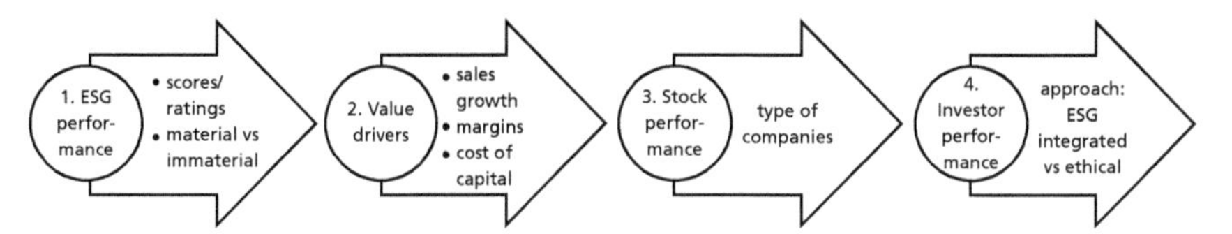

Figure 8.4 Indirect link between ESG and investor performance

funds to give up performance and find them less credible if they do not (Riedl and Smeets, 2017).

The problem with a lot of the older literature is that the relationships have mainly been studied by trying to directly make the link between ESG performance and investor performance. Figure 8.4 gives a more realistic picture, highlighting the intermediate steps and interaction variables from ESG performance to investor performance.

The starting point is that markets are not very efficient (as argued in Chapter 7), because they tend to ignore ESG information. If investors analysed such ESG information, they would get better at valuing companies, improving stock performance (and investment performance depending on the approach). An overview paper by Clark and Viehs (2014) finds a positive relation between ESG factors, corporate financial performance, and investment performance. The authors argue that the relationship is partly obscured by authors typically studying individual factors in isolation, that is, studying only E, S, or G, or only the cost of capital. We would add that the relationship is also partly obscured by attempts to measure it directly rather than in steps, as the relationship is stronger in each of the steps in Figure 8.4 than directly from the first to the last. Going directly from ESG performance to investor performance means losing important information, which economists would call an incomplete model. This is due to causalities depending on various factors along the chain, with, for example, the relevance of individual ESG issues likely depending on the type of company (as shown by Khan, Serafeim, and Yoon (2016)) and the translation of stock performance into investor performance depending on the nature of the investor (Derwall, Koedijk, and Ter Horst, 2011). The remainder of this section looks into such relations per type of issue.

More generally, investor performance also depends on how SRI funds exploit the ESG information. If many funds are exploiting the same information, there will be little opportunities left for adding value, in line with the AMH of Chapter 7.

8.2.2 EVIDENCE THAT E (ENVIRONMENTAL) MATTERS

The link between environmental issues and financial performance has been studied by several authors and has mainly been focused on companies' carbon and waste footprints. Such footprints do not equal carbon risks or climate risks. Schramade (2017b) gives the example of an aluminium company (i.e. high carbon footprint) that benefits from a higher carbon price (positive carbon exposure). Although an energy-intensive process, aluminium production does provide light-weighting solutions to the aerospace and car industries, thereby reducing the emissions of those industries and their customers. Moreover, aluminium producers can reduce their own emissions by sourcing clean energy.

Environmental footprints have a significant impact on financial performance. Derwall and colleagues (2005) find that eco-efficient companies (companies that produce relatively little waste) deliver significantly higher stock returns. Disclosure on these issues matters as well. For an admittedly short time frame (2005–9), Liesen and colleagues (2017) find that investors achieved abnormal risk-adjusted returns of up to 13 per cent annually by exploiting inefficiently priced positive effects of (complete) greenhouse gas (GHG) emissions disclosure and good corporate climate change performance in terms of GHG efficiency. These results imply that, during the period analysed, financial markets were inefficient in pricing publicly available information on carbon disclosure and performance.

Mandatory and standardized information on carbon performance would consequently not only increase market efficiency, but also result in better allocation of capital within the real economy. Andersson, Bolton, and Samama (2016) find that one can quite easily construct portfolios with very low climate risk at no extra cost (see Box 8.2 later in this chapter). This also suggests that climate risk as such is not yet priced, as not many investors are currently paying attention to it. This is consistent with the AMH, explained in Chapters 3 and 7. Nevertheless, this may change when more companies start to publish climate-related financial risks, following the recommendations of the Task Force on Climate-related Financial Disclosures (TCFD, 2017).

8.2.3 EVIDENCE THAT S (SOCIAL) MATTERS

There is less evidence that social issues matter than there is for environmental issues. The reason is that such data tends to be more problematic. Still, Edmans (2011; 2012) finds that companies with higher employee satisfaction levels tend to have better stock returns, higher valuations, and more positive earnings surprises. In subsequent research, however, Edmans, Li, and Zhang (2017) find that employee satisfaction is associated with positive abnormal returns in countries with high labour market flexibility, such as the United States and the United Kingdom, but not in countries with low labour market flexibility, such as Germany.

The S appears to correlate with the G. Using over 100,000 employee surveys, Huang and colleagues (2015) find significantly higher satisfaction and approval in employees of companies with active founders. Employees of founder-run companies were found to maintain significantly higher satisfaction and approval ratings during the recent financial crisis.

In addition, there is small sample evidence of the materiality of social issues, for example in the sense that several mining companies lost billions of dollars each on projects where local stakeholders were poorly managed (see the examples of Barrick and Anglo American in Chapter 5).

8.2.4 EVIDENCE THAT G (GOVERNANCE) MATTERS

Governance is particularly well documented. The classic survey article by Shleifer and Vishny (1997) already documents a history of research finding a positive relationship between governance and company value, while Gompers, Ishii, and Metrick (2003) find that companies with strong shareholder rights have higher company value, higher sales growth, higher profitability, and lower CAPEX.

Governance is a complex issue, which is highly context dependent, as various factors may have positive or negative effects, depending on the presence of other factors. A typical example is family ownership. Villalonga and Amit (2006) find that family ownership creates value only when the founder serves as the CEO of the family company or as its chairman with a hired CEO. Dual share classes, pyramids, and voting agreements reduce the founder premium. Moreover, when descendants serve as CEOs, company value is usually destroyed.

Moreover, there seems to be a correlation between G on the one hand and E and S on the other, with G being the driving force behind E and S. Shrivastava and Addas (2014) find that high-quality corporate governance can engender strong performance on E and S as well. Likewise, weak governance can result in weak E and S. For example, at Volkswagen, shareholder infighting (F) and the local government pushing for employment (S) resulted in poor incentives and dieselgate, as F and S were effectively maximized at the expense of E.

Corporate governance also plays a role at the country level, since it needs to be enforced by the legal system and country culture in which the company operates. La Porta and colleagues (1997) show that countries with poorer investor protection have smaller and narrower capital markets. Overall valuations are higher in countries with better investor protection (La Porta et al. 2002), as investors are more likely to get their money back and corporate investments are more likely to yield a good return.

8.2.5 EVIDENCE THAT ENGAGEMENT MATTERS

In addition to incorporating ESG information, Chapter 7 highlights effective engagement as a condition for LTVC by investors. In fact, Dimson, Karakaş, and Li (2015) find that successful engagements are followed by positive abnormal returns, improved accounting performance, better governance, and increased institutional ownership. Moreover, unsuccessful ones do not result in negative returns. Furthermore, long-term investors intervene more intensely than short-term investors (McCahery, Sautner, and Starks, 2016). The rise of institutional investors, which now own about 75 per cent of equity holdings (see Chapter 4), and their more active stance have increased engagement. On the effectiveness of interventions, Grewal, Serafeim, and Yoon (2016) find that filing shareholder proposals is effective in improving the performance of the company on the focal ESG issue, even without majority support.

They also find that proposals on immaterial issues are associated with subsequent declines in company value, while proposals on material issues are associated with subsequent increases in company value. Companies seem to focus on immaterial issues when there are agency problems, low awareness of the materiality of ESG issues, or attempts to divert attention from poor performance on material issues.

8.3 Integrating sustainability into equity investing

The most fundamental reason for investors to undertake ESG integration would be to better perform the function of the financial sector, namely to allocate resources to the best societal uses. In reality, investors mainly seem to be motivated by client demand at the level of the financial institution. It is different at the individual investor level (i.e. fund managers within asset managers). In a survey of mainstream investment professionals, Amel-Zadeh and Serafeim (2018) find that the primary reason for survey respondents to consider ESG information in investment decisions is because they find it financially material to investment performance.

The extent to which investors actually undertake ESG integration is debatable. The headlines are positive, with more and more money flowing to SRI-labelled funds (e.g. Eurosif, 2016). Van Duuren, Plantinga, and Scholtens (2016) find that many conventional managers integrate responsible investing in their investment process. They find that ESG information in particular is being used for red flagging and to manage risk. Moreover, they show that ESG investing is highly similar to fundamental investing.

But Cappucci (2017) suggests that 'the existence of a written document is not a reliable indicator of a company's commitment to or performance on sustainable long term goals'. Krosinsky (2014) argues that SRI needs to become mainstream in the sense that 'we need a form of sustainable investing, which is positive, future oriented and opportunity directed, mindful of social and environmental considerations, to become the new paradigm for all investors'. Mooij (2017) finds that asset owners move slowly and are not satisfied with the quality of ESG integration at their asset managers.

According to the CFA Institute (2015), the following three are the most important reasons why ESG issues receive insufficient consideration in investment cases:

- It is difficult to express sustainability effects in monetary terms and to integrate them into quant models;
- ESG-related disclosure by companies may be limited, unverified, and non-standardized;
- ESG issues tend to influence financial performance in the long term, whereas many investors have relatively short-term horizons.

So, the diffusion of ESG integration still seems to have a long way to go. Bansal (2003) finds that organizational responses to emerging issues (such as how to deal with sustainability in investing) are determined not just by top management making decisions and setting organizational values, but also by individual concerns at lower levels, with individuals championing specific issues and solutions. Ailman and colleagues (2017) see a generational component to it, with millennials being more interested, especially millennial women.

8.3.1 HOW: METHODS FOR CONSIDERING ESG ISSUES

The CFA Institute (2015) distinguishes six methods for considering ESG issues:

1. **Exclusionary/negative screening**: A method of deliberately not investing in companies that do not meet certain pre-set criteria.
2. **Best in class**: An approach to sustainable investing that focuses on investing in companies that perform better on ESG issues than their peers do.
3. **Active ownership**: Engaging with companies to improve their ESG performance.
4. **Thematic investing**: Focusing on those parts of the universe that benefit from and provide solutions for certain ESG trends.
5. **Impact investing**: An approach to investing that deliberately aims for both financial and societal value creation, as well as the measurement of the latter.
6. **ESG integration**: The explicit integration of E, S, and G issues into the valuation and selection of securities.

In a survey of mainstream investment professionals, Amel-Zadeh and Serafeim (2018) find that negative screening is the most used method of these six methods. At the same time, however, investment professionals perceive negative screening to be the least useful method. They see more merit in positive screening and in full ESG integration into stock valuation.

Table 8.3 Suitability of methods per type of investing

Suitability of the approach	Fundamental equities	Quant equities	Passive equities	Explanation
Exclusionary screening	High	Medium–high	Medium–high	Can be done on scores
Best in class	High	Medium	Medium–low	Can be done on scores, to a certain degree
Thematic investing	High	Medium	Low	Fundamental analysis is needed
Active ownership	High	Low	Low	Fundamental analysis is needed, which can be bought externally with loss of quality
Impact investing	High	Very low	Very low	Fundamental analysis is needed
ESG integration	High	Very low	Not at all	Fundamental analysis is needed

Still, they consider ESG information more in terms of risk than in terms of a company's competitive positioning. Limited comparability due to the lack of reporting standards is the primary hurdle to the use of ESG information.

Table 8.3 provides an overview of how suitable the six methods are to the three types of equities investing:

- Fundamental equities.
- Quant equities.
- Passive equities.

Fundamental equities is by far the most suitable to all six approaches, since it allows for a thorough analysis of a company's business model and transition preparedness. Passive investing is least suitable, as it relies on indices. Chapter 7 shows that ESG-adjusted indices, which rely on external ESG ratings, have their own limitations. Quant passive is better, as it does not need indices but can directly use ratings or other relevant data. As data gets better, quant and passive equities will be better able to incorporate ESG factors.

8.3.1.1 Integrating sustainability into fundamental equity investing

Many investors struggle to integrate ESG analysis into their fundamental analysis. Often, the 'integration' is limited to using ESG scores to reduce the investment universe. This is not really ESG integration, in spite of its label. Eurosif (2012) defines ESG integration as follows:

> This type (of strategy) covers explicit consideration of ESG factors alongside financial factors in the mainstream analysis of investments. The integration process focuses on the potential impact of ESG issues on company financials (positive and negative), which in turn may affect the investment decision.

Unfortunately, many ESG approaches do not meet this definition, as they fail to connect ESG issues to company financials. This is surprising as fundamental analysis is naturally suited for ESG integration. Introducing the value driver adjustment (VDA) approach, Schramade (2016a; 2016b) proposes a three-step approach to integrating ESG into fundamental equity investing, with a fourth step added by Vanderlugt (2018):

1. identify and focus on the most material issues;
2. analyse the impact of these material factors on the individual company;
3. quantify competitive advantages to adjust for value driver assumptions;
4. have an active dialogue with the investee company.

8.3.1.1.1 **Step 1: Identify and focus on the most material issues** Since material ESG factors, by definition, can have a substantial impact on business models and value drivers, analysts should take them into account in their valuation models. One needs a disciplined approach to identify material ESG factors in the first place. Ideally, one undertakes a materiality analysis of the industry (or has such analyses at one's disposal for all industries), plotting the likelihood of impact of an ESG issue against its likely size.

So, for example, for a mining company one could identify the management of local stakeholders, environmental management, and operational health and safety as material issues. For a pharmaceutical company, the likely material issues are innovation management, human capital management, and product quality and safety. Then for a particular mining or pharmaceutical company, the importance of an issue can be more or less important than for the industry overall. For example, operational health and safety tends to be even more important for highly manual types of mining (such as in gold or platinum) than in highly mechanized types of mining such as typically found in iron ore mining.

8.3.1.1.2 **Step 2: Analyse the impact of these material factors on the individual company** After establishing the material ESG factors, the analyst draws up an assessment of the company's performance on these factors. Such analysis is not only undertaken on an absolute basis, but also relative to peers, which is critical when establishing whether a company enjoys a competitive advantage (or disadvantage) in managing a given ESG issue. For example, Novozymes' competitive edge in human capital and innovation management means that it is able to attract the best talent in enzymes. At the other end of the spectrum, Anglo American's and Barrick's weak management of local stakeholder relations resulted in serious local opposition to projects, operational mistakes, and long delays in project ramp-ups (see Chapter 5).

8.3.1.1.3 **Step 3: Quantify competitive advantages to adjust for value driver assumptions** In the next step, the equity analyst makes deliberate, and often significant, adjustments to value drivers that are based on ESG-driven competitive advantages or disadvantages. These changes in value driver assumptions result in changes to the target price and recommendations for the company's stock. To give a sense of the magnitude of this, if the analyst raises profit margins for all periods from 20 to 23 per cent (that is, a 15 per cent increase) to reflect the company's proficiency in managing an ESG issue, the target price will likely also go up by 15 per cent, which may be the difference between a HOLD and a BUY recommendation. In the case of Novozymes, the impact was much bigger as its competitive edge in innovation and talent resulted in superior products that replaced traditional chemicals at double the margins and double the growth rate of the traditional chemicals industry.

8.3.1.1.4 **Step 4: Have an active dialogue with the investee company** In the final step, the analyst or portfolio manager uses the knowledge generated in the first three steps to ask the investee company meaningful questions on the management of material ESG issues. For example, one might ask a strong performer on human capital what the source of its strength is, how that strength is maintained, what kind of internal key performance indicators (KPIs) the company uses, what kind of benefits accrue from that strength in terms of value drivers, and so on. For a weak performer, the questions would be similar, but slightly differently framed, and it would also be asked why the company seems to be underperforming, how it aims to close the gap, and so on.

Vanderlugt (2018) argues that having an active dialogue with the investee companies is important because the company can benefit from feedback, its disclosure can improve, and it allows the investor to gain a more complete understanding of a company's management and board quality. This means proactively addressing the management of ESG issues and its value creation impact with the company concerned. This helps driving improved disclosure as the company comes to understand the investor's perspective and identifies blind spots. It is an iterative process that involves all actors in the investment decision-making process: portfolio managers, financial analysts, and ESG specialists. Box 8.1 provides an example of how the VDA approach can be applied.

While the VDA approach is very practical, it is quite a move to take these steps. The approach involves changing behaviour and is quite labour intensive. Schramade (2016a; 2016b) claims that few equity analysts at asset managers take the first two steps, and even fewer take the third step. Analysts tend to be hesitant in attempting to quantify the value of these ESG advantages, wrongly

BOX 8.1 KUKA VDA EXAMPLE

For KUKA, a German robotics maker, the four steps were as follows:

1. **Identification of material issues**: For the industry, the analyst identified the following issues as material: innovation management; product stewardship; high-growth market strategy; capital management; and human capital management.
2. **Performance on material issues**: The analyst assessed KUKA's key strengths to be in innovation management, human capital, and capital management, while the others are too close to call.
3. **Make VDAs**: The analyst estimated KUKA's growth advantage from innovation management at 2 per cent and its margin advantage at 1 per cent, while also benefiting from a 1 per cent lower cost of capital thanks to strong capital management. The net result of these effects is an increase in target price of 48 per cent from €67 to €99.
4. **Active dialogue**: The analyst had a good call with the company, but soon afterwards the company was taken over.

Value driver	Sales growth	Margins	Cost of capital	Target price
Benchmark (performance excluding ESG advantage)	5–6%	5–6%	10%	€67
Impact from ESG factors	Innovation and high-growth markets: +200bps	Innovation: +100bps	Capital management: −100bps	€32
Total	7–8%	6–7%	9%	€99

Note: bps = basis point.
Source: Adapted from Schramade (2016b).

arguing that such estimates are too subjective. The combined insights from ESG analysis and traditional fundamental analysis allow one to make better-informed decisions. Schramade (2017a; 2017b) argues that the impact can be substantial and reports target price impacts ranging from -23 to +71 per cent for a sample of 127 investment cases.

VDAs can be made on any ESG issue, but some are more frequent than others. Innovation, corporate governance, environmental management, and supply chain management are frequently used. The way VDAs are made also differs: while VDAs on innovation tend to be made to sales growth and margins, those on corporate governance are mostly concerned with adjusting the cost of capital.

The VDA approach is geared towards fundamental investment processes in which valuation plays an important role, but the approach can be generalized (see, for example, Zeidan and Spitzeck, 2015). In the end, the target price is only an intermediate step in reaching an investment decision.

8.3.1.2 Integrating sustainability into quant equity investing

Quant investing is an approach to investing that selects securities using (often advanced) quantitative analysis. It follows a set of predefined rules, based on patterns that have been identified as historically profitable by exploiting market inefficiencies. By leaving it to such rules or algorithms, the quant strategies are said to take a more disciplined and less biased approach than human investors. This is often achieved using 'factor exposures', such as growth, value, size, or momentum factors. In practice, it means that portfolios are constructed with algorithms that pick stocks which have more favourable factor exposures, say higher growth, smaller size, higher momentum, or cheaper valuation, all else being equal.

As indicated in Table 8.3, quant equity investing is suitable for exclusionary screening, best in class, and thematic investing, but not very suitable to active ownership, impact investing, and ESG integration. A major problem with quant investing is that it is not very forward looking. It cannot deal very well with regime changes, such as the transition to a more sustainable economy (see Chapter 12) or simpler regime changes such as more investors becoming interested in ESG. After all, its basis lies in historical patterns, which are exploited. It cannot deal with situations that have not happened yet, such as rising carbon prices or the demise of the fossil fuel industry.

In exclusionary screening, quant strategies could, for example, achieve a reduction of carbon footprint by including less or no energy companies. Best-in-class quant ESG approaches use ESG scores as a quasi-factor in that they select companies with higher ESG scores, all else being equal. Some approaches, called smart beta ESG, aim to combine the benefits of passive investing (i.e. lower cost) with the benefits of active investing (capturing investment factors or market inefficiencies). They are effectively in-between passive and quant investing. Melas, Nagy, and Kulkarni (2016) finds that ESG scores have positive correlations with size, quality, and low volatility. They also find that applying ESG criteria to passive strategies generally improved risk-adjusted performance over the period 2007 to 2016 and tilted the portfolio towards higher-quality and lower-volatility securities.

Ultimately, quant approaches to ESG remain dependent on the availability of quant data and ratings, which have serious limitations versus fundamental research, as argued. And the historic, backward-looking nature of the data makes quant approaches unsuitable for transition thinking. Nevertheless, quant is very useful, as it can uncover relationships that are not otherwise visible or prove relationships that are suspected. Moreover, there is promise in (non-linear) machine learning applications. But patience is warranted as results so far have mainly been achieved on short-term data.

Most promisingly, there are also hybrid approaches ('quantamental'), in which fundamental investors take into account factor exposures when making their otherwise fundamentally based investment decisions. In fact, quant and fundamental together can be very powerful, reinforce and guide each other, just like chess player and chess computer together are stronger than either one separately. Figure 7.3 in Chapter 7 illustrates the state of ESG, suggesting two ways to go to the (optimal) upper right area:

1. Dive deeper into companies by means of fundamental analysis. This is time-consuming and costly, but essential for SF 2.0 and meaningful engagement.
2. Data scraping using quant approaches.

8.3.1.3 Integrating sustainability into passive equity investing

So far, the only sustainability approach that seems credible and suitable for passive investing is exclusionary screening. In passive ESG equity investing, sustainability hits the investment process in the first (screening) and last (monitoring, voting) phases of the investment process, but not in the second (analysis) and third (portfolio construction) phases.

As explained in Chapter 7, there are serious disadvantages to passive investing. First, selectiveness is very limited in passive strategies. It is not possible to invest only in the subset of companies that are able and willing to transform into sustainable business models. Secondly, the larger the number of stocks owned, the harder it becomes to have sufficient knowledge about, and really engage with, multiple companies in the benchmark portfolio.

Nevertheless, passive ESG equity investing is clearly superior over mainstream passive equity investing. Selectiveness may be low, but unlike mainstream passive it is not zero. It is possible to build passive investments on sustainability-adjusted indices. Such indices are becoming more sophisticated and are now typically based on ESG ratings to account for the sustainability of operations. Box 8.2 provides an example of constructing a low-carbon index.

BOX 8.2 CONSTRUCTING A LOW-CARBON INDEX

Andersson, Bolton, and Samama (2016) have developed a dynamic investment strategy that allows long-term passive investors to hedge climate risk without sacrificing financial returns. This investment strategy is based on selecting low-carbon companies within each sector (a low-carbon index with 50 per cent less carbon footprint than its benchmark), while minimizing the tracking error with respect to a benchmark index. One can thus quite easily construct portfolios with very low climate risk, at no extra cost, with this best-in-class method.

By investing in such a decarbonized index, investors in effect are holding a 'free option on carbon'. As long as climate change mitigation actions are pending, the low-carbon index obtains the same return as the benchmark index, but once carbon emissions are priced, or expected to be priced, the low-carbon index should start to outperform the benchmark.

To account for product exposures, sustainability-adjusted indices may exclude the really bad industries like coal and tobacco. Next, some adjusted indices include sales exposures to 'green' industries to positively account for the sustainability of products. That is promising, but investors are still exposed to the vast majority of listed companies. Furthermore, the little selection that is being done is based on ratings, which have serious limitations (see Section 7.2 in Chapter 7).

On engagement too, passive ESG equity investing is an improvement over mainstream passive equity investing, at least as far as voting on the companies in the portfolio is concerned. However, as there are thousands of companies, it is impossible to properly analyse them and cast an informed vote, let alone engage with them (see the discussion in Section 7.3 in Chapter 7). So, voting is typically done by following the recommendations of proxy voting advisors. Alternatively, voting can be based on thematic work by ESG specialists, where dozens of companies are sent a letter on a single issue that may not even be a material ESG issue for that particular company. In some cases, voting is based on the work of fundamental investors within the company that happen to hold the same stock. But there is no engagement with the other, say 3,000, stocks.

In sum, passive ESG equity investing is a rather crude measure, but it does steer capital away from the worst investments (SF 1.0). Over time, ESG indices may improve as competition among them intensifies.

8.3.2 HOW SELL-SIDE RESEARCH ANALYSTS (SOMETIMES) INTEGRATE SUSTAINABILITY INTO EQUITY INVESTING

In reaching their own investment conclusions, institutional investors (the 'buy side') tend to use the research published by research analysts of banks and brokerage companies (the 'sell side'). Those sell-side analysts have the advantage of typically following only ten or so stocks, which should allow them to build deep insights on them. So, they are uniquely positioned to educate their clients, that is, institutional investors, on material ESG issues. They could provide company-specific data, industry-specific frameworks, and long-term stock recommendations, as well as pressing companies for better disclosure. In practice, however, that rarely happens. Instead, sell-side analysts tend to focus on reporting mainly on what is currently happening and making forecasts on the next few quarters. Occasionally, they will do a deep dive into the company's businesses, often implicitly addressing ESG issues as well. But a structural approach to ESG is typically lacking.

Schramade (2015) provides a 'wish list' of what the sell side could do on ESG after sketching what is already there. This existing ESG research from the sell side comes in two types: thematic reports and the mapping of industry issues. In the latter category, brokers like Morgan Stanley and UBS have

ESG teams that try to compare ESG across the industries covered by their colleagues. But the influence they have with those colleagues varies a lot, so that there may be very interesting ESG research on, say, mining companies, but nothing on oil and gas companies. Examples of thematic research include reports by Kepler Cheuvreux and HSBC, which focus on specific ESG themes, such as climate change, and (partially) translate these themes to the company level.

One of the major challenges of ESG integration on the equity buy side is getting better and comparable data. There is enormous potential for the sell side to help on this. And it would be good to see peer group analyses of sustainability performance: How do companies within a certain peer group (say European chemicals or US machinery) perform on a number of key metrics for that particular industry? To what extent do they report KPIs and targets on this?

Moreover, an assessment of management quality is usually missing. This is a potentially controversial issue as it may cost the company corporate clients (which is another reason to keep research separated from mergers and acquisitions, equity issues, and other business for corporates). Of course, analysts do talk about their intuition, but they cannot publish on this for lack of objectivity. But they can publish on objective metrics. Some have done exactly that. Examples are reports on management quality by French broker ODDO (see Box 8.3) and Deutsche Bank's report on the mining industry called 'back the team'.

In sum, there is a lot the sell side can do to boost ESG integration, but resources are limited. The people involved tend to be good and highly motivated, but the teams are small and struggle to show that they are valued by the buy side. The buy side should reward them and be clear on what they want from them. It should ask them for specific analyses—not just talk to their ESG specialists, but have buy-side sector specialists ask sell-side sector specialists for material ESG analysis.

8.4 Impact investing

Impact investing is a type of investment that aims to generate both positive societal and positive financial returns. It thus fits naturally with SF 3.0 as it explicitly aims at achieving more than a financial return, taking a step beyond ESG integration, as Table 8.1 illustrates. The Global Impact Investing Network identifies four characteristics for impact investing:

1. **Intentionality**: It should be the explicit goal of the investor to generate a positive social or environmental impact.
2. **Investment with return expectations**: It is not a charity, but should yield a return on capital.

BOX 8.3 ODDO'S SCORING MODEL FOR MANAGEMENT QUALITY

The French brokerage firm ODDO wrote a long and thorough report on management quality (ODDO, 2014), which outlined the scoring model of management in Table 8.4, based on discussion of management theory. One may agree or disagree with the exact classification and weightings given, but it is certainly a useful checklist for assessing management quality.

Table 8.4 ODDO's scoring model for management quality

Category (% weight)	Criterion#	Criterion name	Score given	Maximum score
CEO (30%)	1	Internal succession planning		10
	2	Reliability		5
	3	Competence		5
	4	Anti-star		5
	5	Vision and leadership		5
Executive committee (25%)	6	Size of the executive committee		3
	7	Executive committee's composition and functioning		5
	8	Reorganization/restructuring management		6
	9	Integration of acquisitions		6
	10	Stake in capital		5
Organization and middle management (25%)	11	Matrices and management levels		3
	12	Organic growth and market-share gains		8
	13	Innovation capacity		5
	14	Learning organization		2
	15	Lean management		2
	16	Entrepreneurship culture		5
Human resources (20%)	17	Dysfunctions and social risks		5
	18	HR productivity		5
	19	Appeal and recruitment		3
	20	Training and career planning		4
	21	Employee shareholders		3
Total (100%)				100

Source: ODDO (2014).

3. **Range of return expectations and asset classes**: Impact investments can generate returns above or below the market in asset classes such as private equity, public equity, and fixed income.
4. **Impact measurement**: The investor is committed to measuring and reporting on the social and environmental performance and progress of underlying investments.

8.4.1 ACADEMIC RESEARCH ON IMPACT INVESTING

So far, very little research has been done on impact investing, and all of this has focused on private equity impact funds, which are a much less recent phenomenon than listed equity impact funds. In an analysis of over 5,000 private equity impact funds, Barber, Morse, and Yasuda (2015) find that demand for such funds exceeds the supply. Jackson (2013) argues that while the impact investing industry has made a lot of progress in developing impact metrics and data, its evaluation practices still tend to focus on counting inputs and outputs and on telling stories.

8.4.2 IMPACT INVESTING AND FINANCIAL PERFORMANCE

As impact investing in listed equity is a very recent phenomenon, there is no data yet on the relation between financial performance and impact performance. However, there are good reasons to suspect that listed equity impact investing should give at least market-rate financial returns. First, as Schramade (2017b) points out, impact stocks have the tailwind of the SDGs, which should help their value drivers: companies that provide solutions to the SDGs should, all else being equal, have higher growth rates, higher margins, and lower risk, whereas companies that are obstacles to the SDGs should have lower growth, lower margins, and higher risk going forward.

Schramade (2018) finds that in a universe of 15,000 stocks, the 2,300 stocks with positive impact potential already have historically stronger value drivers: on average, they have higher growth rates, higher cash flow return on capital invested, and a lower cost of capital—even when corrected for sector affiliation. Going forward, this relation is unlikely to weaken. As externalities are increasingly being internalized, the relationship between impact (societal) returns and financial returns will only get closer. This is illustrated in Figure 8.5, which provides a rough sketch of the current relation between financial and impact performance, with the arrows indicating the likely change for industries which have a mismatch between financial and impact returns, such as tobacco (negative impact, and a current positive return likely to deteriorate) and solar (positive impact, and a current negative return likely to get better).

8.4.3 CHALLENGES OF IMPACT INVESTING

Impact investing faces several challenges, such as poor data, lack of scale, barriers to change, perception problems, and complex investment chains (see Section 7.1 in Chapter 7). The big and obvious challenge in impact investing is data, as companies are not used to reporting on impact—not even those that are very advanced in ESG. Companies are only getting started on this journey

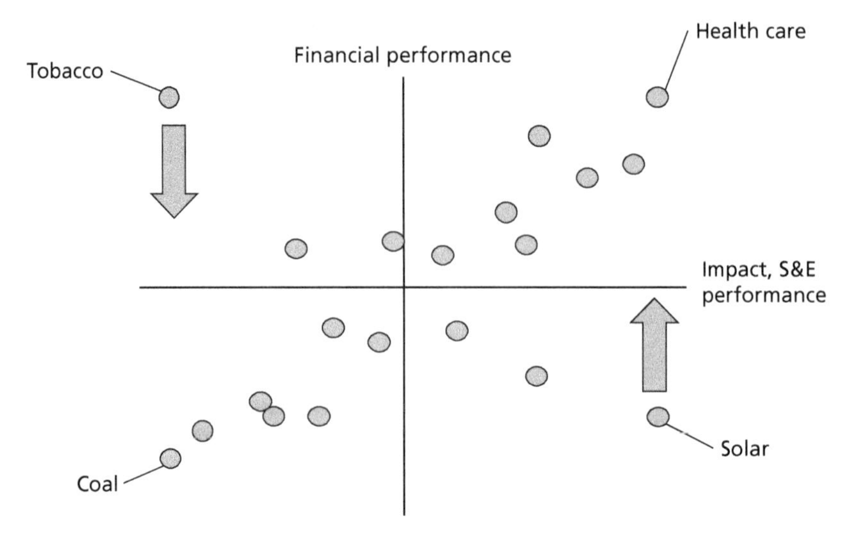

Figure 8.5 Internalization to align financial and societal performance

Note: S&E performance = social and environmental performance

and are often not even aware of what they can do. For example, a leading nutrition company reports very well on ESG but provides no information on the nutritional value of its products, nor on the number of people and animals that it helps feed. Thus, the quest for data and KPIs is just getting started.

Another issue is scale, whereby most impact investing activity takes place in relatively small private equity projects, that is, where the big ones are a few million euros and the small ones are a few thousand euros. It is hard for asset owners, such as large pension funds, to invest in such projects as they are looking to invest hundreds of millions at a time and billions in total. This is a gap that will likely be filled by intermediaries that aggregate projects.

Furthermore, Schramade (2017a) argues that impact investing is held back by other, more subtle challenges. First, impact investing is all about change: bringing about a transition to a more sustainable economy and society. Yet institutions, including the financial sector, are aimed at maintaining and preserving the current system. Existing organizational structures, incentives, and decision-making processes cannot really manage substantial change (see Chapter 12).

Secondly, there is a perception problem. Impact investing (apart from private equity) is still seen as new and unfamiliar. There is no single, common definition and many prejudices have already been built up. One such assumption is that impact investing is inevitably about small investments with low returns. Another prejudice is that restrictive and unnecessary ethical requirements make the investing universe very small, which often results in relatively low returns. In practice, this is not a problem.

Thirdly, Schramade (2017a) refers to the complexity of investment value chains, as discussed in Chapter 7. Many parties are involved before an investment can be made. These include asset managers, regulators, ratings agencies, pension funds, and consultants. Coordination among and within these parties is complicated and funds are often reduced to a few key figures, with important nuances being lost in the communication process. That is not conducive to visionary choices and change.

8.4.4 MAKING IMPACT INVESTING TANGIBLE

Given the lack of data and established methods, it is hard to make impact investing measurable and tangible. However, it can be done with a thorough fundamental approach. Managing impact means figuring out which effect is material and then trying to prevent the negative and increase the positive. The Impact Management Project, a private network of 700 practitioners building consensus on the practice of impact management, distinguishes five dimensions that help in assessing impact of a company or project:

- **What** outcome(s) does an effect relate to and how important is the outcome to the people (or the planet) experiencing it?
- **How much** of the effect occurs in a given time period?
- **Who** experiences an effect and how underserved are they in relation to the outcome?
- How does the effect compare and make a **contribution** to what is likely to occur anyway?
- Which **risk** factors are significant and how likely will the outcome be different from the expectation?

Figure 8.6 shows the impact dimensions and how they can be measured. Another step is to make the link to the global strategy for sustainable development, embodied in the SDGs. Schramade (2017b) describes how the SDGs can be a yardstick for screening on impact. His 'tagging' approach assigns pluses or minuses to portfolio holdings to convey the assessment of their exposures to each of the relevant SDGs. Besides revealing an investor's or company's exposure to the SDGs, this approach provides an indication of investment opportunities, both with respect to each SDG and across different sectors. However, one can falsify the impact of a company by considering impact criteria, such as how material, intentional, and transformational the company is (Schramade, 2018). Table 8.5 shows how these criteria can be filled in for Novozymes.

Such impact criteria can be scored to enable comparisons across companies. Ideally, the company reports on impact KPIs, and some indeed do. But most do not and even the best can improve their reporting on impact—opening up a valuable engagement role for investors. Table 8.6 shows how Novozymes

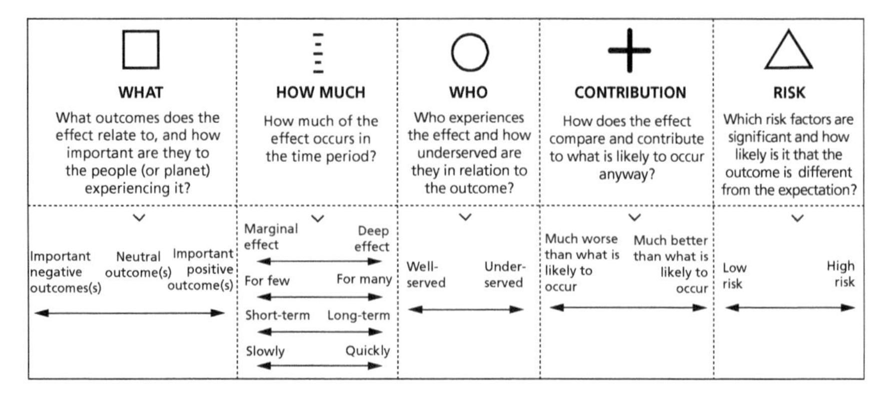

Figure 8.6 The impact dimensions of the Impact Management Project

Source: Impact Management Project.

Table 8.5 Impact criteria for Novozymes

Impact criterion	Company assessment
Material: Relevance to value drivers sales, profits, CAPEX, and risk	Superior performance and energy savings at clients help Novozymes grow twice as fast as the chemicals industry at twice the profitability.
Intentional: Deliberate choice, strategy, and purpose	Corporate strategy and business model are built towards providing more environmentally friendly solutions. Novozymes was involved in setting the SDGs.
	Works with partners to develop and drive adoption of proven biological innovations that improve feed efficiency and animal health. Novozymes is one of few companies that reports on its impact, with serious targets and reference to the SDGs.
Transformational: Does the company drive major change for the better by means of its business model, technology, scale, or standards?	Enzymes have the potential to replace nearly all chemical processes, which would mean a much lower environmental footprint (CO_2 emissions and waste).

Source: NN Investment Partners.

reports on impact KPIs to varying degrees. At an even more advanced level of data, the impact of several companies can be measured and quantified in a consistent way so as to compare which companies offer the most impact per euro invested.

8.5 **Conclusions**

Sustainability matters more to equity investors than most of them realize. As residual claimholders, equity investors are more heavily exposed than other investors. They bear most of the risk when companies fail and they also reap

Table 8.6 Mapping impact KPIs for Novozymes

	Emissions saved, SDG 7	Innovation, SDG 9	Health & well-being, SDG 3
Ideal impact KPI	Emissions saved	Value of innovations to society	Improvement in human health
Actual KPIs reported	Emissions saved	Number of transformative innovations; number of active patent families; R&D/sales; number of R&D employees; pipeline	Number of people reached with biological solutions
Number	69 million tons	Eight new products in 2016; 13% R&D/sales; 1,400 R&D employees; 1,123 active patent families	Reached approximately 5 billion consumers with more than one of their solutions on a weekly basis—100 million more than in 2015
Target	Save 100 million tons in 2020	Deliver ten transformative innovations from 2015 to 2020	Six billion people reached with biological solutions by 2020
Engagement on KPIs	N/A	Get more granularity	Get detail on quality—focus

Note: R&D = research and development.
Source: NN Investment Partners.

most benefits when companies succeed. Therefore, they have strong incentives to help companies achieve the conditions for LTVC described in Chapter 5.

However, most equity investors fail to properly take material sustainability issues into account. Even if they are interested, they typically lack the frameworks and incentives to really integrate sustainability into their investment decisions. This chapter shows how investors can achieve ESG integration (SF 2.0). Fundamental equity investing is identified as being most suitable and promising (as opposed to quant and passive investing) for ESG integration and other approaches to sustainability. In contrast, quant and passive are held back by lack of data and tend to waver between SF 1.0 and 2.0. However, these approaches should ultimately be complementary as all three of them find new ways of identifying valuable ESG information.

Finally, this chapter discusses impact investing, which is essentially an extreme form of sustainability integration into equity investing, that is, SF 3.0.

Key concepts used in this chapter

Absolute valuation is a valuation of an asset without reference to the valuation of other assets.

Accruals are adjustments for revenues earned and expenses incurred that are not yet recorded in the accounts.

Active ownership is an approach to investing that aims to improve companies' ESG performance by means of engaging with these companies.

Best in class is an approach to sustainable investing that centres on investing in companies that perform better on ESG issues than their peers.

Business model is the way a company makes a return on investment.

Buy side refers to analysts at asset managers.

Discounted cash flow, also known as DCF or NPV (Net Present Value), is a method that values an asset or project by calculating CFs and discounting them at a risk-adjusted discount rate.

Engagement refers to the investor dialogue with companies to ascertain and improve their ESG quality.

ESG refers to environmental, social, and governance factors.

ESG integration is the explicit integration of E, S, and G issues into the valuation and selection of securities.

ESG ratings are ratings that try to assess the quality of a company's management of E, S, and G.

Exchange traded funds are vehicles for passive investing.

Ethical investing is a type of investing in which investments are first screened on ethical grounds.

Exclusionary screening, also known as negative screening, is a method of deliberately not investing in companies that do not meet certain pre-set criteria.

Fair value is an assessment of the value of an asset according to a (relative or absolute) valuation method, which may deviate from the asset's current price.

Fundamental analysis is an approach to investing based on obtaining a good understanding of a company's business model and valuation.

Impact investing is an approach to investing that deliberately aims for both societal and financial value creation as well as the measurement of societal value creation.

Management quality is the degree to which a company's management succeeds in managing the company for LTVC.

Materiality is the relevance of a certain issue to value creation.

Multiples valuation is a type of relative valuation in which an asset's value is determined as a multiple of a financial statement metric such as profitability or book value.

Negative screening, also known as exclusionary screening, is a method of deliberately not investing in companies that do not meet certain pre-set criteria.

Net present value, also known as NPV or DCF (Discounted Cash Flow), is a method that values an asset or project by calculating CFs and discounting them at a risk-adjusted discount rate.

Passive investing is an approach to investing that buys widely diversified portfolios, often made up of entire market indices, and limits the amount of buying and selling so as to steadily build wealth over time.

Positive screening is an investment method that selects potential investments on the basis of desirable characteristics.

Quant investing is an investment approach that selects securities using advanced quantitative analysis.

Relative valuation is a valuation of an asset with reference to the valuation of other assets.

Reporting quality refers to the quality, reliability, and usefulness of reported financial and non-financial information.

Scenario analysis is the process of estimating the expected value of a security by analysing alternative possible future events and the associated outcomes.

Sell side refers to the analysts working at investment banking/brokerage companies who write research and investment recommendations to be used by buy-side analysts at asset managers.

Strategy is the art of designing a plan to achieve a long-term aim.

Thematic investing is a type of investing that centres on identifying the ideas and trends that are likely to reshape the economy. In an ESG context that means focusing on those parts of the universe that benefit from and provide solutions for certain ESG trends.

Transition preparedness analysis is an analysis aimed at assessing to what extent a company is prepared for the transition to a more sustainable economy.

Upside is the percentage price difference between an asset's fair value and its current market price.

Valuation is the process of arriving at a value estimate.

Value drivers are the main components of valuation and its formula, namely sales growth, profit margins, cost of capital, and investment.

Value driver adjustments are the adjustments made to value driver assumptions in a valuation model, based on an assessment of the company's material ESG issues.

Weighted average cost of capital is the minimum required return on a company's investments given its risk profile.

SUGGESTED READING

CFA Institute (2015), 'Environmental, social, and governance issues in investing: a guide for investment professionals', CFA Institute, Charlottesville, VA, http://www.sustainalytics.com/sites/default/files/cfa-esgissuesinvesting2015.pdf, accessed 3 July 2018.

Derwall, J., K. Koedijk, and J. ter Horst (2011), 'A tale of values-driven and profit-seeking social investors', *Journal of Banking and Finance*, 35(8): 2137–47.

Dimson, E., O. Karakaş, and X. Li (2015), 'Active ownership', *Review of Financial Studies*, 28(12): 3225–68.

Edmans, A. (2011), 'Does the stock market fully value intangibles? Employee satisfaction and equity prices', *Journal of Financial Economics*, 101(3): 621–40.

Friede, G., T. Busch, and A. Bassen (2015), 'ESG and financial performance: aggregated evidence from more than 2000 empirical studies', *Journal of Sustainable Finance & Investment*, 5(4): 210–33.

Schramade, W. (2016), 'Bridging sustainability and finance: the value driver adjustment approach', *Journal of Applied Corporate Finance*, 28(2): 17–28.

REFERENCES

Ailman, C., M. Edkins, K. Mitchem, T. Eliopoulos, and J. Guillot (2017), 'The next wave of ESG integration: lessons from institutional investors', *Journal of Applied Corporate Finance*, 29(2): 32–43.

Amel-Zadeh, A. and G. Serafeim (2018), 'Why and how investors use ESG information: evidence from a global survey', *Financial Analysts Journal*, forthcoming.

Andersson, M., P. Bolton, and F. Samama (2016), 'Hedging climate risk', *Financial Analysts Journal*, 72(3): 13–32.

Bansal, P. (2003), 'From issues to actions: the importance of individual concerns and organizational values in responding to natural environmental issues', *Organization Science*, 14(5): 510–27.

Barber, B. M., A. Morse, and A. Yasuda (2015), 'Impact investing', Working Paper, https://ssrn.com/abstract=2705556, accessed 3 July 2018.

Berk, J. and P. DeMarzo (2014), *Corporate Finance*, 4th edn, Pearson Education, Boston, MA.

Black, F. and M. Scholes (1973), 'The pricing of options and corporate liabilities', *Journal of Political Economy*, 81(3): 637–54.

Blitz, D. and F. Fabozzi (2017), 'Sin stocks revisited: resolving the sin stock anomaly', *Journal of Portfolio Management*, 44(1): 105–11.

Cappucci, M. (2017), 'The ESG integration paradox', Working Paper, https://ssrn.com/abstract=2983227, accessed 3 July 2018.

CFA Institute (2015), 'Environmental, social, and governance issues in investing: a guide for investment professionals', CFA Institute, Charlottesville, VA, http://www.sustainalytics.com/sites/default/files/cfa-esgissuesinvesting2015.pdf, accessed 3 July 2018.

Cheng, B., I. Ioannou, and G. Serafeim, G. (2014), 'Corporate social responsibility and access to finance', *Strategic Management Journal*, 35(1): 1–23.

Clark, G. and M. Viehs (2014), 'The implications of corporate social responsibility for investors: an overview and evaluation of the existing CSR literature', European Centre for Corporate Engagement Working Paper.

Derwall, J., K. Koedijk, and J. ter Horst (2011), 'A tale of values-driven and profit-seeking social investors', *Journal of Banking and Finance*, 35(8): 2137–47.

Derwall, J., N. Guenster, R. Bauer, and K. Koedijk (2005), 'The eco-efficiency premium puzzle', *Financial Analysts Journal*, 61(2): 51–63.

Dimson, E., O. Karakaş, and X. Li (2015), 'Active ownership', *Review of Financial Studies*, 28(12): 3225–68.
ECCE (European Centre for Corporate Engagement) (2016), 'The materiality of ESG factors for equity investment decisions: academic evidence', Maastricht, https://yoursri.com/media-new/download/ecce_project_the_materiality_of_esg_factors_for_equity_investment_decisi.pdf, accessed 3 July 2018.
ECCE (European Centre for Corporate Engagement) (2017), 'The materiality of ESG factors for emerging markets equity investment decisions: academic evidence', Maastricht.
Eccles, R. and G. Serafeim (2013), 'The performance frontier', *Harvard Business Review*, 91(5): 50–60.
Edmans, A. (2011), 'Does the stock market fully value intangibles? Employee satisfaction and equity prices', *Journal of Financial Economics*, 101(3): 621–40.
Edmans, A. (2012), 'The link between job satisfaction and firm value, with implications for corporate social responsibility', *Academy of Management Perspectives*, 26(4): 1–19.
Edmans, A., L. Li, and C. Zhang (2017), 'Employee satisfaction, labor market flexibility, and stock returns around the world', ECGI Working Paper No. 433/2014, https://ssrn.com/abstract=2461003, accessed 3 July 2018.
El Ghoul, S., O. Guedhami, C. Kwok, and D. Mishra (2011), 'Does corporate social responsibility affect the cost of capital?', *Journal of Banking and Finance*, 35(9): 2388–406.
Eurosif (2012), 'European SRI study', Brussels, http://www.eurosif.org/wp-content/uploads/2014/05/eurosif-sri-study_low-res-v1.1.pdf, accessed 3 July 2018.
Eurosif (2016), 'European SRI study', Brussels, http://www.eurosif.org/wp-content/uploads/2016/11/SRI-study-2016-HR.pdf, accessed 3 July 2018.
Friede, G., T. Busch, and A. Bassen (2015), 'ESG and financial performance: aggregated evidence from more than 2000 empirical studies', *Journal of Sustainable Finance & Investment*, 5(4): 210–33.
Gompers, P., J. Ishii, and A. Metrick (2003), 'Corporate governance and equity prices', *Quarterly Journal of Economics*, 118(1): 107–56.
Grewal, J., C. Hauptmann, and G. Serafeim (2017), 'Stock price synchronicity and material sustainability information', Harvard Business School Working Paper No. 17-098.
Grewal, J., G. Serafeim, and A. Yoon (2016), 'Shareholder activism on sustainability issues', Harvard Business School Working Paper No. 17-003.
Hong, H. and M. Kacperczyk (2009), 'The price of sin: the effects of social norms on markets', *Journal of Financial Economics*, 93(1): 15–36.
Huang, M., P. Li, F. Meschke, and J. Guthrie (2015), 'Family firms, employee satisfaction, and corporate performance', *Journal of Corporate Finance*, 34(C): 108–27.
Jackson, E. (2013), 'Interrogating the theory of change: evaluating impact investing where it matters most', *Journal of Sustainable Finance & Investment*, 3(2): 95–110.
Khan, M., G. Serafeim, and A. Yoon (2016), 'Corporate sustainability: first evidence on materiality', *Accounting Review*, 91(6): 1697–724.
Koller, T., M. Goedhart, and D. Wessels (2015), *Valuation: Measuring and Managing the Value of Companies*, 6th edn, John Wiley & Sons, New York.
Krosinsky, C. (2014), 'The long and necessary death of socially responsible investing', *Journal of Sustainable Finance & Investment*, 4(3): 297–8.
La Porta, R., F. Lopez-de-Silanes, A. Shleifer, and R. Vishny (1997), 'Legal determinants of external finance', *Journal of Finance*, 52(3): 1131–50.
La Porta, R., F. Lopez-de-Silanes, A. Shleifer, and R. Vishny (2002), 'Investor protection and corporate valuation', *Journal of Finance*, 57(3): 1147–70.

Liesen, A., F. Figge, A. Hoepner, and D. Patten (2017), 'Climate change and asset prices: are corporate carbon disclosure and performance priced appropriately?', *Journal of Business Finance and Accounting*, 44(1–2): 35–62.

Lins, K., H. Servaes, and A. Tamayo (2017), 'Social capital, trust, and firm performance: the value of corporate social responsibility during the financial crisis', *Journal of Finance*, 72(4): 1785–824.

McCahery, J., Z. Sautner, and L. Starks (2016), 'Behind the scenes: the corporate governance preferences of institutional investors', *Journal of Finance*, 71(6): 2905–32.

Melas, D., Z. Nagy and P. Kulkarni (2016), 'Factor investing and ESG integration', MSCI Research Insight, New York, https://yoursri.com/media-new/download/research_insight_factor_investing_and_esg_integration.pdf, accessed 3 July 2018.

Mooij, S. (2017), 'Asset owners and the diffusion of responsible investment: what explains the low rate of adoption?', Working Paper, Oxford University, https://www.researchgate.net/publication/318815429_Asset_Owners_and_the_Diffusion_of_Responsible_Investment_What_Explains_the_Low_Rate_of_Adoption, accessed 3 July 2018.

ODDO (2014), 'The quality of management', Frankfurt.

Ortiz-de-Mandojana, N. and P. Bansal (2016), 'The long-term benefits of organizational resilience through sustainable business practices', *Strategic Management Journal*, 37(8): 1615–31.

Riedl, A. and P. Smeets (2017), 'Why do investors hold socially responsible mutual funds?', *Journal of Finance*, 72(6): 2505–50.

Schramade, W. (2015), 'A wish list: how the sell-side can boost ESG integration', LinkedIn Pulse.

Schramade, W. (2016a), 'Bridging sustainability and finance: the value driver adjustment approach', *Journal of Applied Corporate Finance*, 28(2): 17–28.

Schramade, W. (2016b), 'Integrating ESG into valuation models and investment decisions: the value-driver adjustment approach', *Journal of Sustainable Finance & Investment*, 6(2): 95–111.

Schramade, W. (2017a), 'The challenges of impact investing', NN Investment Partners, The Hague, https://www.nnip.com/News-Display-on/The-challenges-of-impact-investing.htm, accessed 3 July 2018.

Schramade, W. (2017b), 'Investing in the UN Sustainable Development Goals: opportunities for companies and investors', *Journal of Applied Corporate Finance*, 29(2): 87–99.

Schramade, W. (2018), 'Bigger and better than expected: the listed equity impact universe', NN Investment Partners, The Hague.

SIFMA (Securities Industry and Financial Markets Association) (2017), 'The SIFMA fact book 2017', New York, https://www.sifma.org/wp-content/uploads/2016/10/US-Fact-Book-2017-SIFMA.pdf, accessed 3 July 2018.

Shleifer, A. and R. Vishny (1997), 'A survey of corporate governance', *Journal of Finance*, 52(2): 737–83.

Shrivastava, P. and A. Addas (2014), 'The impact of corporate governance on sustainability performance', *Journal of Sustainable Finance & Investment*, 4(1): 21–37.

TCFD (Task Force on Climate-related Financial Disclosures) (2017), 'Recommendations of the Task Force on Climate-related Financial Disclosures: final report (Bloomberg Report)', Financial Stability Board, Basel.

Vanderlugt, J. (2018), 'ESG integration', NN Investment Partners, The Hague.
Van Duuren, E., A. Plantinga, and B. Scholtens (2016), 'ESG integration and the investment management process: fundamental investing reinvented', *Journal of Business Ethics*, 138(3): 525–33.
Villalonga, B. and R. Amit (2006), 'How do family ownership, control and management affect firm value?', *Journal of Financial Economics*, 80(2): 385–417.
Zeidan, R. and H. Spitzeck (2015), 'The sustainability delta: considering sustainability opportunities in firm valuation', *Sustainable Development*, 23(6): 329–42.

APPENDIX: CASE STUDY: HOW TO UNDERTAKE ESG INTEGRATION

This case study allows you to undertake your own ESG integration analysis. The assignment is as follows:

- Choose a company and look up its most recent annual report and sustainability report.
- Then try to answer the questions on the ten subjects listed.

If concepts are not clear, please research them. And keep in mind: What is important (i.e. material) for the company?

8.1A **Business model**

See Chapter 5 for a description of these concepts:

- How would you describe the company's business model?
- What is the company's customer value proposition?
- How strongly do you rate the company's competitive position? What is the source of its competitive edge? What key intangibles are involved?
- What trends affect the company's business model and competitive position?

8.2A **Value driver: Part 1**

On sales growth:

- What has historical sales growth been?
- How important are volume and pricing as components of growth?
- How has this been different across divisions?
- What are the underlying drivers of growth? Can you distinguish long-term and short-term drivers?
- What do think is a realistic growth rate for this company?

On margins:

- How profitable has the company been in the past as measured by gross profit, EBIT, earnings before interest, taxes, depreciation, and amortization, and net income? Which of these metrics is most meaningful for this particular company?
- What are the main costs of the company?
- How flexible or fixed is the company's cost base?

- What are the main drivers of the company's cost base
- What do you think are realistic margins going forward?

On capital and return on capital:

- How much invested capital does the company have? And how does that relate to its sales?
- How much investment does the company need for its growth?
- How high has the company's return on capital been in the past?
- What do you think is the company's cost of capital?
- How much debt is there in the company's capital structure?

On CF (investment):

- To what extent have the company's profits been converted to FCF? Or: How much OCF does the company generate and what does it do with it?
- What explains that conversion rate?
- Do you expect it to change?
- What does the company do with its FCF?
- Explain the difference between OCF and FCF
- If FCF is negative, do you expect an inflection point to positive FCF?

8.3A **Sustainability**

- What is the company's purpose/raison d'être? In what way does the company create value for society? How does it get paid for that value creation?
- Who are the company's main stakeholders? Please fill out this stakeholder impact tool:

Material issue	Stakeholder 1	Stakeholder 2		Stakeholder n
Short-term goals				
Long-term goals				
How the company helps those goals				
How the company hurts those goals				

- Does the company generate serious externalities? Are they positive or negative? How do you assess the chances these externalities will be internalized?
- Given the nature of the company's operations, what kind of ethical dilemmas do you think the company faces? Do you see or expect to see a shift in what is regarded as morally acceptable?
- What are the most material ESG factors? That is, what issues are most critical to the success of the company's business model? Please fill out this table with regard to each of these most material ESG factors: (i) how the company performs on it; (ii) whether the company derives a competitive (dis)advantage from it; and (iii) how they might affect the value drivers:

Material issue	Performance	Competitive edge?	Impact on value drivers?
Issue 1			
Issue 2			
Issue 3			
Issue 4			

- What long-term trends do you see that might affect the company's performance?
- How do you rate the company on top-down versus bottom-up sustainability in the table, that is, in what cell would you put the company? With: 5 = very well positioned; 4 = above average; 3 = average; 2 = below average; 1 = very weak. Please explain:

		Top-down sustainability (exposure to trends)				
		1	2	3	4	5
Bottom-up sustainability (management of material issues)	5					
	4					
	3					
	2					
	1					

8.4A **Impact**

- Which of the SDGs (if any) does the company help achieve? Which negative SDG exposures (if any) does the company have?
- How does the company's impact score on the three impact criteria in the table? Please fill in the table:

Impact criterion	Company assessment
Material: How relevant is the impact to the company's value drivers, i.e. sales, profits, investment, and cost of capital?	
Intentional: To what extent is the company's impact a deliberate choice, part of its strategy and purpose?	
Transformational: Does the company drive major change for the better by means of its business model, technology, scale, or standards?	

- To what extent can the company's impact be measured? Does the company report on its impact? How can its reporting be improved?

8.5A Management quality and corporate culture

- What kind of ROIC has the company achieved (with and without goodwill)? How does this compare to its industry?
- Has the company been burdened by mistakes that were made by previous management?
- Please consider ODDO's matrix of management quality (Table 8.4 in Box 8.3). Which of the criteria could you assess? How?

8.6A Reporting quality

- How do you assess the company's financial reporting, considering the use of accruals/use of special items/gap between profits and OCF?
- How do you assess the company's non-financial reporting, considering the issues listed in this table?

Principle	Proxies	Company score
Strategic focus and future orientation	• Sustainability issues are discussed in the strategy discussion, management discussion, or letter to shareholders • Externalities are mentioned • Steps to tackle/address externalities are mentioned • One/some/all of the six capitals are mentioned • Trends are mentioned	
Connectivity of information	• There is a description of the business model (ideally graphically), outlining inputs, activities, output, and outcomes	
Stakeholder relationships	• Stakeholders are named • Stakeholder relations are explained	
Materiality	• Materiality is discussed • Process of determining materiality is explained • Materiality matrix is shown • Number of material factors mentioned • A relation between material factors and value drivers is made (also connectivity)	
Conciseness	• Annual report length	
Reliability and completeness	• Is there any assurance?	
Consistency and comparability	• Clear non-financial targets/KPIs are shown • Targets' measurement is clear, by means of ratios or benchmarks	

8.7A **Strategy**

- How would you describe the strategy of the company?
- To what extent does that strategy take into account the company's most material ESG issues?
- Is the strategy consistent with the company's purpose and management's incentives?

8.8A **Value drivers: Part 2**

Given all of the information in Sections 8.1A–8.7A:

- What sales growth do you forecast for the next ten years?
- What margins do you forecast for the next ten years?
- What capital spending do you forecast for the next ten years?
- What cost of capital do you use to discount the FCFs?

8.9A **Valuation**

Again, given all of the information in Sections 8.1A–8.8A:

- Using these assumptions, what fair value share price do you obtain from your model? How does that relate to the current share price?
- What happens to your fair value share price if you change your growth assumptions by 1 per cent upwards and downwards respectively?
- What happens to your fair value share price if you change your margin assumptions by 1 per cent upwards and downwards respectively?
- What happens to your fair value share price if you change your cost of capital assumptions by 1 per cent upwards and downwards respectively?
- What value drivers does the current share price imply?

8.10A **Investment conclusions**

In sum, how attractive do you find the company in terms of:

- business model;
- value drivers;
- sustainability;
- reporting quality;
- management quality and culture;
- strategy;
- valuation.

9 Bonds—investing without voting power

Overview

At first sight, sustainability seems less relevant for bonds than for equity, as bondholders do not have voting power and barely share in the opportunities or 'upside' like equities do. There are fewer examples of environmental, social, and governance (ESG) integration in bonds than in equities. Nevertheless, sustainability does matter in bonds. This chapter provides evidence that, for both corporate and sovereign bonds, E, S, and G matter for default or credit risk. We present evidence that ESG ratings and credit ratings are correlated.

Bond markets (here defined as corporate and sovereign bonds) are bigger than equity markets, with institutional investors typically holding more bonds than equity. In the case of insurers and pension funds, the main reason for these large bond holdings is to hedge the interest rate risk on their long-term liabilities. ESG factors are becoming integrated into corporate bonds. As in equities, studying the company's business model is very important to ESG integration in bonds. Perhaps even more so than in equities, there is substantial underestimated sustainability risk in bonds. There are also issues that make ESG integration harder in bonds than in equities, such as the lack of voting power and illiquid markets.

It appears that ESG factors for corporate and sovereign bonds largely overlap. Country sustainability ratings for sovereign bonds are recently emerging. Governance dominates in these ratings (just as in credit ratings), but environmental and social factors are also included. The Scandinavian countries receive the highest ratings, reflecting their leading position on environmental and social policies.

There is innovation in the form of green bonds and social bonds, which cater for sustainable finance (SF) 3.0. The challenge is to 'certify' the use of the proceeds for green or social projects and to overcome bureaucratic procedures.

Learning objectives

After reading this chapter, you should be able to:

- explain the state of play on ESG integration, potentially improving both financial and societal returns;

- understand how ESG integration in bonds can bring about a deeper understanding of issuers;
- explain that bond investors are more focused on downside protection and lack voting power;
- explain that bond investors have more capital to move and can choose from a wide range of issuers and projects;
- identity the green bond market as an interesting and fast-growing innovation.

9.1 **Basics of bonds**

> I used to think if there was reincarnation, I wanted to come back as the president or the pope or a .400 baseball hitter. But now I want to come back as the bond market. You can intimidate everybody.
>
> James Carville, lead strategist for President Clinton

While equity markets may get more attention, bond markets are actually bigger. At the end of 2016, the value of outstanding bonds globally was estimated at $92 trillion (i.e. about 120 per cent of global GDP) versus $70 trillion for outstanding listed equity (SIFMA, 2017). Bonds come in many guises and can be complex, but they have a lot in common as well. Bonds are certificates of debt issued by a government or corporation that promise payment of the borrowed amount, plus interest, by a specified future date.

9.1.1 BOND PAYMENTS

A bond certificate indicates the amounts and dates of all payments to be made. Payments are made until the final repayment date, known as the maturity date of the bond. The time until the maturity date is known as the term. Bond maturities or terms range from very short term (months) to decades or even perpetuity. There are still some bonds outstanding that were issued centuries ago. Two types of payments are made on a bond:

1. The **promised interest payments**, which are called **coupons**. The bond certificate specifies that the coupons are paid periodically, for example once or twice per year.
2. The **principal or face value** of the bond. This is the amount to be paid at maturity. The face value is typically denominated in standard increments such as €1,000.

For example, a bond with a face value of €1,000 bond and a 3 per cent coupon (payable annually) will pay coupon payments every 12 months of: €1,000 $\times$ 0.03 = €30. Some bonds do not pay coupon payments. Such bonds are known as zero-coupon bonds and can still offer the same return as coupon-paying bonds, by offering the same principal at a lower price.

9.1.2 TYPES OF BONDS

Whereas bonds are public debt, bank loans are a type of private debt and are discussed in Chapter 10. Figure 9.1 classifies bonds by the identity of the issuer, with the main distinction being between government and corporate bonds, as the latter carry more serious default risk.

There are several types of government bonds. Supranationals are issued by international supranational or multilateral agencies, such as the World Bank or the European Investment Bank. Sovereign bonds are issued by national governments (i.e. countries). Finally, municipal bonds are issued by state and local governments.

The main distinctions within corporate bonds are those between financial sector issuers and non-financial sector issuers; and between secured and unsecured bonds. Financial sector accounts form a very large part of the corporate bond market and are discussed separately in Chapters 10 and 11, on banking and insurance respectively.

Secured bonds, also labelled structured products, mean that specific assets are pledged as collateral that bondholders have a direct claim to in the event of bankruptcy. Examples are mortgage bonds, which are bonds secured by a pool of mortgages on real property, and asset-backed bonds (or asset-backed securities), which can be secured by any kind of asset. Such bonds were at the heart of the 2008–9 global financial crisis. Unsecured bonds have lower seniority or priority. In the event of bankruptcy, bondholders have a claim

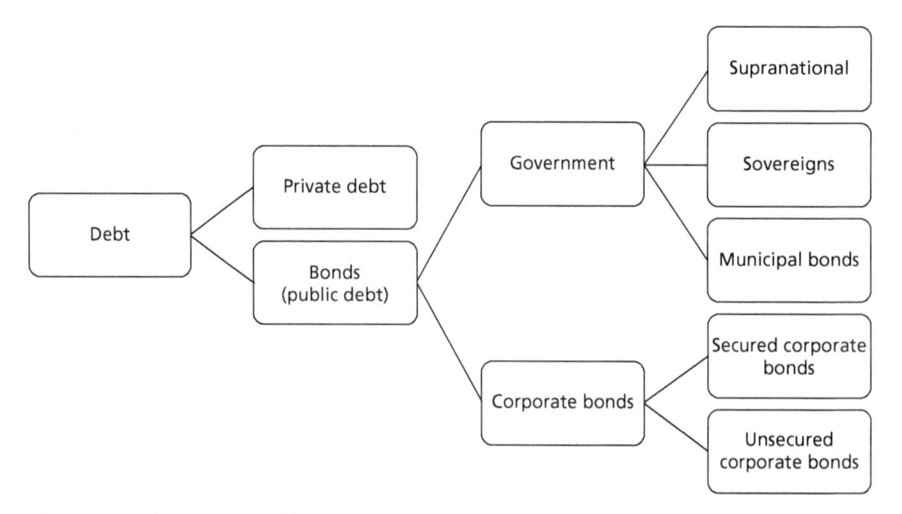

Figure 9.1 Classification of bonds

only to the assets of the company that are not already pledged as collateral on other debt. Among the unsecured bondholders there is further distinction in priority between senior bondholders, which are repaid first, and subordinated (or junior) bondholders, which are subsequently repaid.

Bonds can also differ in their provisions, which are specifications to the bond contract. For example, they may have repayment provisions that allow the issuer to redeem part of the issue early if that is attractive; or call provisions that allow the issuer to buy back the bond completely. The bond may also have a sinking fund, meaning that the issuer gradually builds a reserve to redeem the issue. Some bonds are convertible into equity (and hence a hybrid between bonds and equity) at a certain predefined strike price of the associated equity. In effect, a convertible bond is a regular bond plus a warrant (i.e. a call option issued by the company itself).

9.1.3 BOND VALUATION AND ITS DRIVERS

In comparison to equity, the pricing of bonds seems straightforward. In principle, bond prices result from discounting a clear pattern of promised CFs. The price or value of a coupon bond P equals the present value of all its coupons plus the present value of the face value of the bond with maturity N. The formula is as follows:

$$P = \frac{CPN}{(1 + YTM_1)} + \frac{CPN}{(1 + YTM_2)^2} + \ldots + \frac{CPN + FV}{(1 + YTM_N)^N} \qquad (9.1)$$

where YTM_N is the yield to maturity of a zero-coupon bond (a bond without coupons) that matures at the same time as the N-th coupon payment; CPN is the coupon payment; and FV is the bond's face value (see a textbook like Berk and DeMarzo (2014) for a more elaborate discussion).

The rates (yields) at which these CFs need to be discounted do vary, as interest rates fluctuate over time. This yield y or YTM on a bond is the discount rate that sets the present value of its payments equal to its current market price. More formally:

$$P = CPN * \frac{1}{YTM}\left(1 - \frac{1}{(1 + YTM)^N}\right) + \frac{FV}{(1 + YTM)^N} \qquad (9.2)$$

where YTM is the yield to maturity of this particular bond and reflects the yield received if all coupons received are reinvested at a constant interest rate. Put another way, the yield is the *IRR* (internal rate of return) of a bond. Market forces keep this relation intact: as interest rates and bond yields rise, bond prices fall, and vice versa. This means that bonds trade at times at a premium (at a price greater than face value), at times at a discount (at a price lower than face value), and very occasionally at par (at a price equal to face value).

As stated, interest rates fluctuate and bond prices move along with them. Equation 9.2 shows that if *YTM* increases by 1 per cent the effect is larger for a long than for a short bond. This can easily be seen by comparing Equation 9.2 with $N = 1$ to that with $N = 2$. So longer-term bonds are more exposed to interest rate fluctuations. It is possible to derive an exposure measure to interest rate/yield fluctuations, which is called duration. The duration of a bond is the sensitivity of a bond's price to changes in interest rates. The duration is higher for bonds of longer maturity, since more of their CFs are further away in the future and thus more affected by discount rates. Interest rates not only differ over time, they also differ across maturities. This variation is referred to as the term structure of interest rates (also called yield curve): the array of prices or yields on bonds with different terms to maturity. As bonds with a higher duration are more exposed to interest rate risk they carry a higher risk premium. The yield curve is therefore typically upward sloping.

9.1.3.1 Drivers of yields on government and agency bonds

National government bonds, also known as sovereign bonds, have been issued for centuries and their prices have tended to be driven by (expectations regarding) the fortunes of the states involved and their reliability in paying back their debt. In fact, Ferguson (2001) argues that Britain beat France in the struggle for colonial empire in the 1700s because it managed to finance its wars at low interest rates, thanks to reliability in repaying debt and an efficient bureaucracy. France's cost of funding was consistently higher due to its poor reputation in repaying debt.

Nowadays, countries have formal credit ratings, set by credit rating agencies (as explained in Section 9.1.4). In an empirical study of the determinants of sovereign credit ratings, Cantor and Pecker (1996) find that credit ratings and sovereign borrowing costs can be explained by per capita income, GDP growth, inflation, external debt, the level of economic development, and default history. Sovereign bonds by the same issuer (or by an issuer with the same rating) may still have different prices, driven by issues of maturity and liquidity. Moreover, different dynamics may occur during crises, with a prominent role for contagion (Beirne and Fratzscher, 2013).

9.1.3.2 Drivers of yields on corporate bonds

Corporate bonds differ from sovereigns in some important respects. The most important difference is that corporate bonds tend to carry more serious default and liquidity risks. Liquidity risk refers to lower trading frequencies and higher transaction costs due to lower competition among bond traders and smaller sizes of corporate bonds, which make it harder to trade such bonds. Given that corporates are (much) smaller entities than governments and cannot tax people, they are also much more likely to default.

Such default risk or credit risk means that the bond's expected return, which is equal to the firm's cost of capital, is less than the YTM on the promised payments (Equation 10.1 in Chapter 10 gives the mathematical relationship between the promised or contracted rate and the expected rate). The reason is that the expected payments are lower than the promised payments, if there is a risk of default. So, a higher YTM on bond X than on bond Z does not necessarily imply that the expected return on X is higher than on Z. The credit spread is the difference between yields of corporate bonds and Treasury yields and reflects the default and liquidity risks. The higher the default (and liquidity) risk, the larger the spread will be. This spread can be calculated for all maturities and be expressed in the so-called corporate yield curve.

There is a large strand of literature concerned with modelling corporate bond prices, and several drivers of yields have been identified, some of them a long time ago. Fisher (1959) finds that default risk is the prime determinant of yield spreads on corporate bonds and that liquidity or marketability is the second most important determinant. Cohan (1962) finds the following additional (and related) drivers: rating (essentially an assessment of default risk), type of bond, and maturity. Of course, these factors are to some extent related to each other. For example, larger firms tend to have more stable CFs, lower default risk, larger issues, and higher ratings. More recent research finds that, at issue, yields are also affected by the reputation of the underwriting bank (Fang, 2005) and underwriter competition (Gande, Puri, and Saunders, 1999). Section 9.3 shows that there is also evidence that yields are affected by sustainability factors, especially governance.

9.1.4 CREDIT RATINGS

Bond ratings are assessments of the possible risk of default, prepared by independent private companies that specialize in such ratings. Credit ratings are calculated for efficiency reasons: it is inefficient for every investor to privately investigate the default risk of every bond. Instead, a limited number of credit ratings agencies assess the creditworthiness of bonds and certify the issuers. They make this information available to investors, who can decide whether to undertake additional work on it. The best-known credit rating agencies are Moody's, Standard & Poor's (S&P), and Fitch.

Credit ratings are typically classified as investment grade (the top four ratings categories, with low default risk) or junk/high yield/speculative (the bottom five categories, with high likelihood of default). The mandate of institutional investors often allows only investment in investment-grade bonds. This increases the demand for investment-grade bonds, resulting in higher bond prices and lower yields. A major governance issue is that credit ratings are paid by the issuer and not by the investor, which creates a conflict of interest.

9.1.5 CORPORATE BONDS AND AGENCY COSTS

A company that has bonds outstanding also has equity. In fact, owning the equity of a company is like having the right to buy the company by paying the face value of debt to the bondholders—the more debt there is, the riskier that right becomes (Merton, 1974). Equity holders have all the upside and limited downside risk, while bondholders have limited upside and all downside risk. While both parties benefit from higher profits and growth, equity holders benefit from volatility (risk), while bondholders suffer from volatility or uncertainty. This may give rise to a conflict of interest between equity holders and bondholders.

The presence of debt may, for example, cause an underinvestment problem. In this situation equity holders have no incentive to invest new capital, not even in positive net present value (NPV) projects: as the company is highly levered, equity holders know the pay-offs go to bondholders anyway. Myers (1977) has stated the debt overhang problem formally: if management is aligned with equity holders, it will only attract new capital for projects that have returns which are high enough to pay back not just bondholders but leave a residual return for shareholders as well.

The situation is different when there is already capital in the company (e.g. through retained earnings) and an overinvestment problem might occur: equity holders might prefer risky investments in negative NPV all-or-nothing projects where their expected pay-off is higher but that of the bondholders is lower. Galai and Masulis (1976) outline several such situations of risk-shifting that increase the value of equity at the expense of bondholders.

There are ways of limiting agency conflicts, for example by including covenants that protect the interest of bondholders and limit the decisions of management, say when a certain threshold profitability or threshold debt-to-equity ratio is crossed. But there are also costs related to such arrangements, which are called monitoring costs (more on this in Chapter 10). Shareholders will want to limit those monitoring costs, as they ultimately bear most of them as residual claimants. In case of default, bondholders bear them. Shareholders can disclose information to facilitate the work of control. For that information to be credible, its accuracy has to be verified by independent outside auditors. This results in bonding costs: the costs of providing information, contracting auditors, and self-imposed restrictions such as covenants. Smith and Warner (1979) list a number of bond covenants: restrictions on investment policies, restrictions on dividend payments, restrictions on subsequent financing, and the modification of the patterns of pay-off to the bondholders, for example convertibles or callability provisions. Such provisions provide an option to the bondholders (in the case of convertibles) or to the issuing firm (call provision).

In contrast to bank lending (see Chapter 10), bondholders rely on delegated monitoring and have little control over the issuer. Debt holders typically have no voting power, except when the company goes bankrupt. As the original equity is then wiped out, the debt is turned into equity. Such control transfers do not happen very frequently and they may not be very swift. Bolton and Scharfstein (1996) analyse the optimal number of creditors a company borrows from. They find that debt structures which lead to inefficient renegotiation are beneficial in that they deter default, but they are also costly if default is beyond a manager's control.

9.2 **Why does sustainability matter to bonds?**

Chapter 8 highlights why and how sustainability matters to equity investing. It matters for similar reasons for bond valuation: sustainability issues include value-relevant issues that are not yet properly priced (inefficiencies). As in equities, sustainability analysis is a natural extension of fundamental fixed income analysis, providing the link between value drivers and material ESG issues. Though compared to equity, the focus in fixed income valuation is much more on risk than opportunities, except perhaps in high yield. The reason is that bondholders are mainly exposed to downside risk and benefit much less from upside potential than shareholders do.

Nevertheless, Hanson and colleagues (2017) argue that some fixed-income investors are equally if not more concerned than equity investors about ESG exposures since they can have pronounced effects on performance by generating tail risks that may materialize in both going-concern and default scenarios. For example, as the dieselgate scandal hit Volkswagen in September 2015, its CDS spread rose from 75.5 basis points (bp) on 17 September to 299.5bp on 28 September (the CDS spread is the credit default swap spread, which measures the default risk on a bond). This can also happen with sovereigns. After Russia seized the Crimea from Ukraine in 2014, the Russian five- and ten-year CDS spread rose from a 200–300bp range to spike over 600bp. Ukraine's CDS spread spiked at over 5,000bp. Figure 9.2 visualizes the materiality of ESG issues to bonds. The underlying factors differ slightly when comparing sovereigns and corporates (Table 9.1).

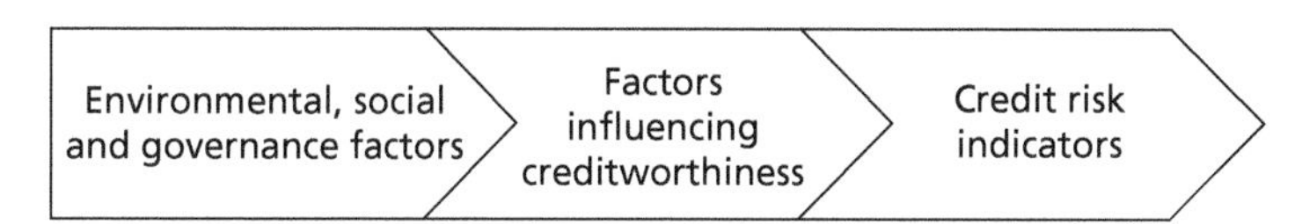

Figure 9.2 From ESG to credit risk

Source: Adapted from PRI (2013a; 2013b).

Table 9.1 Sovereign and corporate bonds: Underlying factors

Factor	Corporate and sovereign	Mostly sovereign	Mostly corporate
Traditional factors			
Factors influencing creditworthiness	Cash reserves	Economic strength Economic growth prospects Balance of trade Fiscal performance External (and domestic) debt Budget deficit Foreign liquidity Monetary flexibility Implicit liabilities from social security*	Profitability Employee productivity Competitive advantage Cost of capital Leverage Intangibles*
Credit risk indicators	Credit ratings CDS spreads Bond yields and prices Volatility		Default probability Breach of covenants
ESG factors			
Environmental	Climate change Biodiversity Energy resources & management Biocapacity & ecosystem quality Air/water/physical pollution Renewable & non-renewable natural resources	Natural disasters Land system change*	Product stewardship* Redemption of used products*
Social	Human rights Education & human capital Health & safety Innovation management*	Political freedoms Demographic change Employment levels Social exclusion & poverty Trust in society/institutions Crime Food security Implicit or explicit promises made by the political establishment*	Product responsibility Diversity Employee relations & access to skilled labour Community/stakeholder relations Consumer relations
Governance	Financial policy Accounting standards	Institutional strength Corruption Regime stability Political rights & civil liberties Rule of law Regulatory effectiveness & quality	Shareholder rights Incentives structure Audit practices Board expertise Independent directors Transparency/disclosure & accountability Business integrity

Note: Issues with an* have been added by the authors.

Source: Adapted by the authors based on PRI fixed income working groups (2013a; 2013b).

All of the issues mentioned in Table 9.1 merit a paragraph by themselves, but that is beyond the scope of this chapter. For illustration purposes, we elaborate on one issue. The implicit liabilities from social security refer to the current and future payments to citizens, such as retirement incomes or subsidies on health insurance, which have been promised by politicians but may not be sustainably affordable. Examples are the very high and unfunded pension obligations in countries such as Japan and Italy, and to a lesser extent the United States, France, and Germany.

It is striking that many issues are relevant for both corporate and sovereign bonds, especially on the environmental side. The environmental side is also better developed than the social side, in terms of both data and impact investing. The green bond market has, for example, taken off while the social bond market is very small (see Section 9.4). Because of the data and nature of the issues, it is much harder in social issues than in environmental ones to decide which companies are part of the solution and which part of the problem.

9.2.1 SOVEREIGN BOND PRICING AND SUSTAINABILITY

Many of the (governance) issues mentioned in Section 9.1 as drivers of sovereign bond yields, such as the fortunes and reliability of states, can actually be considered ESG issues. Principles for Responsible Investment (PRI, 2013b) cites the recent sovereign crisis as a reminder that the debt of the highest-rated countries can be volatile, which is important given the size of the sovereign bond market and its stabilizing role in the portfolios of insurers and pension funds.

Sustainalytics (2017) finds a correlation between country ESG scores and credit ratings (Figure 9.3) and a correlation between mean country ESG momentum (i.e. incremental change on ESG performance) and GDP growth for the 2010–16 period (Figure 9.4). Both these findings support the idea that ESG issues are linked to determinants of economic development.

Table 9.1 lists a number of environmental risks that are relevant for sovereign bond pricing. PRI (2013b) identifies risks to economic growth from water scarcity, loss of biodiversity, and climate change. However, there is little empirical evidence for the value relevance of these issues. For example, environmental factors showed weak correlations with sovereign bond performance in studies carried out by AXA and others.

Social issues that should matter for sovereign bonds include trust, standards of health and education, and respect for labour rights. For example, Wälti (2012) finds that trust in the European Central Bank at the country level is negatively correlated with sovereign bond yields and financial market turbulence. Next, a highly educated, IT-literate population paired with a repressive political system can increase the risk of political regime change (PRI, 2013b).

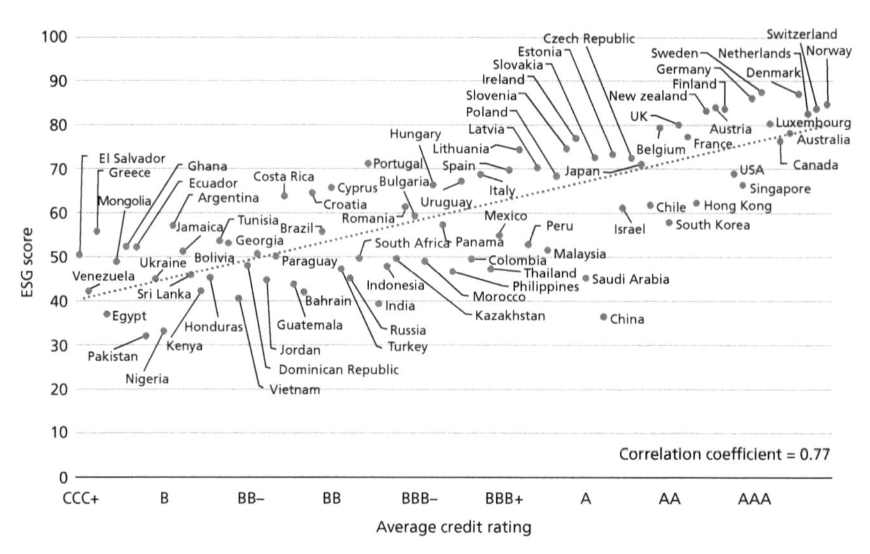

Figure 9.3 Correlation of country ESG scores and credit ratings

Source: Sustainalytics (2017).

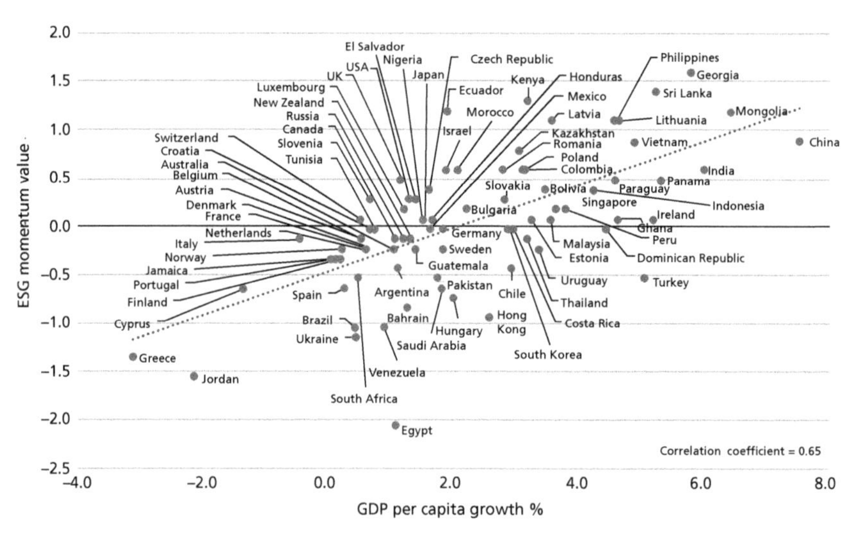

Figure 9.4 Correlation of mean country ESG momentum and GDP growth (2010–16)

Source: Sustainalytics (2017).

As mentioned in Section 9.1.3, differences in governance have determined credit for centuries, where unreliable debtors, such as 17th-century Spain, 18th-century France, and more recently Argentina, either failed to attract new funding or did so at much higher prices. Governance has several components, such as financial policy, strength of institutions, corruption, regime stability,

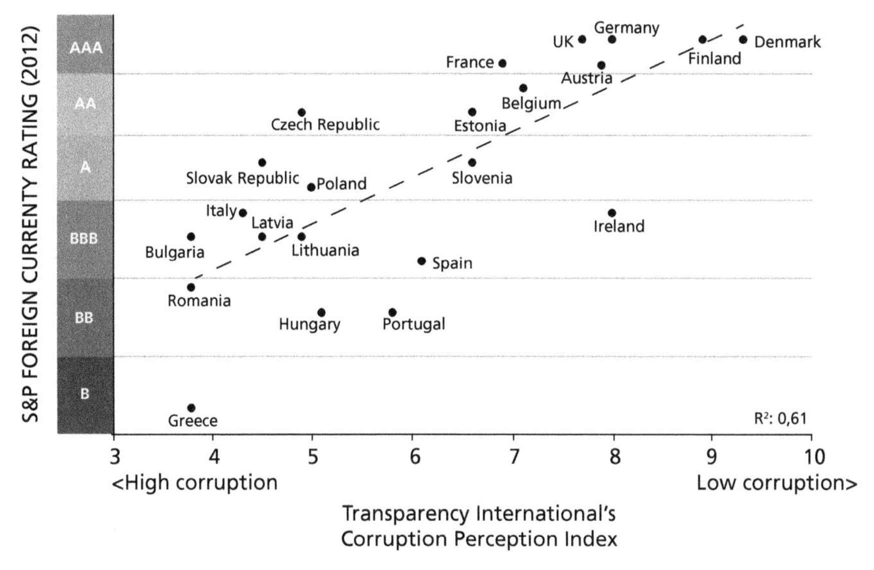

Figure 9.5 Control of corruption versus foreign credit rating

Source: PRI (2013b).

political rights and civil liberties, rule of law, and regulatory effectiveness and quality.

Butler and Fauver (2006) find that the quality of a country's legal and political institutions plays a vital role in determining country credit ratings. In particular, corruption has a negative impact on sovereign bond performance (Ciocchini, Durbin, and Ng, 2003). PRI (2013b) argues that 'corruption, a key indicator of governance failings, proved to be one of the most important factors of the euro-zone debt crisis. Tax avoidance and false financial statements on a massive scale undermine nations' credit strength and mislead investors.' Figure 9.5 illustrates the strong negative relationship between corruption and credit rating.

9.2.2 CORPORATE BOND PRICING AND SUSTAINABILITY

In line with the evidence presented in Chapter 8 on the value relevance of ESG for equities, strong ESG performance has been found to result in better price performance and lower spreads (Polbennikov et al. 2016) and higher credit ratings (Attig et al. 2013). Analysing the relationship between ESG ratings and corporate bond spread and performance, Polbennikov and colleagues (2016) find that corporate bonds with high composite ESG ratings have slightly lower spreads and have modestly outperformed their lower rated peers. Attig and colleagues (2013) find that credit rating agencies tend to award relatively high ratings to firms with good social performance. They also find that the individual components of ESG that relate to primary stakeholder management (i.e. community relations, diversity, employee relations, environmental performance, and product characteristics) matter most in explaining firms' creditworthiness.

Looking at the individual components of ESG, the relevance of environmental issues to bond yields has recently received more academic attention. It appears that stronger environmental performance means a lower cost of debt. For a dataset of over 2,200 US corporate bonds, Bauer and Hahn (2010) document a significantly negative relationship between good environmental management and a company's loan spread. The authors claim that a corporation's environmental management practices can have an effect of up to 64bp on the spread.

In a study of the chemicals and pulp and paper industries, Schneider (2011) finds an economically significant relationship between a firm's environmental performance and its bond yields. Poor environmental performers face future environmental liabilities related to compliance and clean-up costs due to increasingly strict environmental laws and regulations. These liabilities are large enough to drive polluting firms into bankruptcy and can leave bondholders' claims subordinate to environmental liabilities. He also finds evidence that the relationship between environmental performance and bond yields fades as bond quality increases, which is consistent with the non-linear pay-off structure of bonds.

Wilkins (2017) reports that S&P finds climate risk increasingly important for corporate credit ratings, affecting 717 ratings cases over a two-year period, with the biggest impacts seen in oil refining and utilities. In addition, the sector composition of the corporate bond market suggests very high exposure to carbon risk, as it is geared to energy, utilities, and banks that tend to finance the former and whose risk is multiplied by their high leverage.

The value relevance of social issues to corporate bonds is least studied among ESG issues. The available evidence mostly relates to employee relations, just as on the equities side. Kane, Velury, and Ruf (2005) find that companies with good employee relations are better placed to bear financial distress, as they are more likely to win concessions from their workforce in difficult periods. Using a similar dataset on employee relations, Bauer, Derwall, and Hann (2009) find that firms with stronger employee relations have a statistically and economically significant lower cost of debt financing, with the quality of employee relations explaining 22 to 42 per cent of the spread over US Treasuries paid by 568 US companies. The study finds that companies where employees quit, perform poorly, or take action against the company see reduced or more volatile CFs, posing a source of risk to bondholders.

The relevance of corporate governance for corporate bond yields is well documented. Bhojraj and Sengupta (2003) record lower cost of debt for companies with stronger governance, either in the form of more institutional ownership or in the form of more outside directors on their boards. Similar evidence has been found for specific governance mechanisms. For example, Klock, Mansi, and Maxwell (2005) and Ashbaugh-Skaife, Collins, and LaFond (2006) find that companies with more anti-takeover mechanisms have a higher cost of debt.

9.3 Integrating sustainability into bond investing

As discussed in Chapter 8, investors appear to undertake ESG integration for two main reasons: to meet client demands and because they consider it financially material to investment performance (Amel-Zadeh and Serafeim, 2018). Nevertheless, the penetration rate of ESG integration in bond investing is lower than in equities.

9.3.1 ESG INTEGRATION INTO GOVERNMENT BONDS

Figure 9.6 shows that ESG analysis happens less frequently in government bonds ('Fixed income—SSA' in the figure) than in other type of fixed income: between 50–75 per cent of principles for responsible investment (PRI) signatory asset managers. Moreover, this is an overstatement as the figure lists the percentage of asset managers that undertake some form of ESG analysis (i.e. not necessarily in all their funds) among those asset managers that are signatories and hence more interested in ESG (i.e. a favourable subset).

It is still quite hard to find examples of ESG integration in sovereign bonds. Notable exceptions are the RobecoSAM country sustainability ranking and the oekom country rating. The former evaluates 65 countries (of which 43 are emerging market economies) on 17 ESG indicators, whereby each indicator is assigned a predefined weight and countries can score between 1 and 10. Table 9.2 outlines the structure, including the weightings given, of the country sustainability ranking. Governance dominates with a 60 per cent weight, followed by social with 25 per cent and environmental with 15 per cent. This implies an overlap with credit ratings, which also consider governance issues.

RobecoSAM (2015) finds a clearly negative correlation between their country sustainability rankings and country CDS spreads. They claim that their rankings pick up problems earlier than credit ratings do. Interestingly, the country sustainability ratings are quite dynamic, being updated and published twice per year. The Nordic countries typically lead the pack, followed (end of 2017) by the likes of Switzerland, Canada, Australia, New Zealand, and the Netherlands (see Figure 9.7). These countries are known for their inclusive societies and are leading in terms of social and environmental policies.

75–100%	50–75%	0–50%
• Listed equity • Fixed income corporate • Private equity • Inclusive finance • Farmland • Forestry • Infrastructure	• Property • Fixed income securitized • Fixed income – SSA	• Hedge funds • Commodities

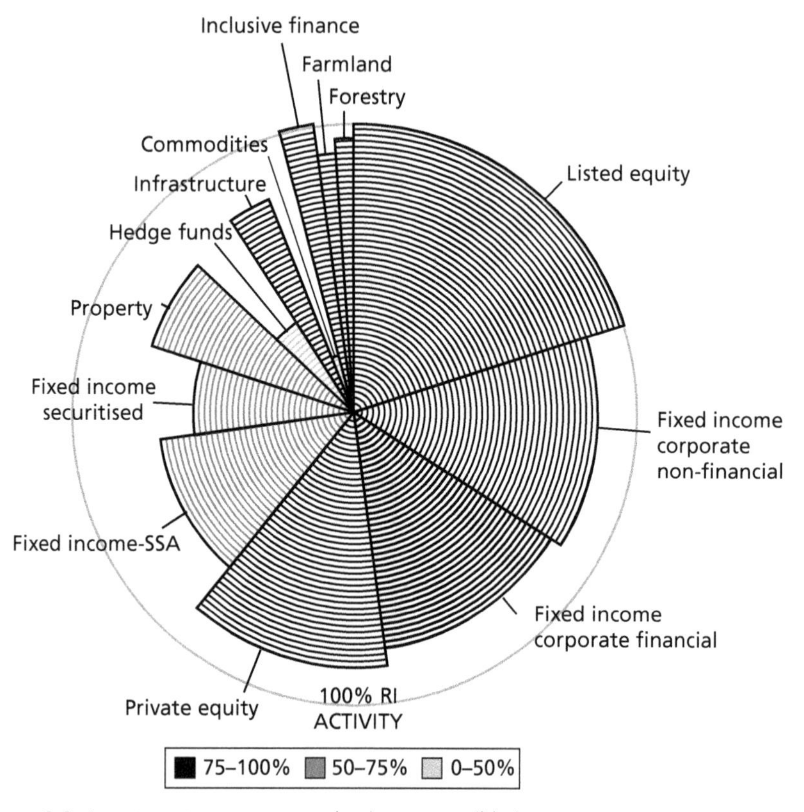

Figure 9.6 Investment managers conducting responsible investment

Note: This figure represents the proportion of reporting PRI investment managers conducting some level of responsible investment by asset class, in %, in 2016.

Source: PRI (2017).

Table 9.2 The RobecoSAM country sustainability framework

Sub-indicator level		Indicator level	Dimension level	Country sustainability score
Emissions	Biodiversity	Environmental status (10%)		
Energy use	Energy sources	Energy (2.5%)	Environmental (15%)	
Exposure to environmental risks	Risk mitigation	Environmental risk (2.5%)		
Human welfare	Work and equality	Social indicators (10%)		
Education	Life expectancy	Human development (10%)	Social (25%)	
Confidence in government	Local job market	Social unrest (5%)		
Rights and liberties	Inequality	Liberty and inequality (10%)		
Human capital and innovation	Physical capital	Competitiveness (10%)		
Internal risks and inefficiencies	External conflicts	Political risks (10%)		Country sustainability score (100%)
Management of public goods	Policy responses	Effectiveness (2.5%)		
Protection of property rights	Judicial system	Rule of law (2.5%)		
Democratic participation	Civil society	Accountability (2.5%)	Governance (60%)	
Corruption level	Transparency/policies	Corruption (2.5%)		
Terrorism and political crimes	Government stability	Stability (2.5%)		
Competition/liberalization	Business regulations	Regulatory quality (2.5%)		
Demographic profile	Age-related policies	Aging (10%)		
Monetary policy independence	Other institutions	Institutions (5%)		

Note: The first two columns give the sub-indicators. For each indicator, relative scores ranging from 1 to 10 are calculated, based on various data series for each country. Each indicator is also assigned a predefined weight. Each dimension weight is the sum of the relevant indicator weights. The country score is the weighted sum of standardized indicator scores.

Source: RobecoSAM (2015).

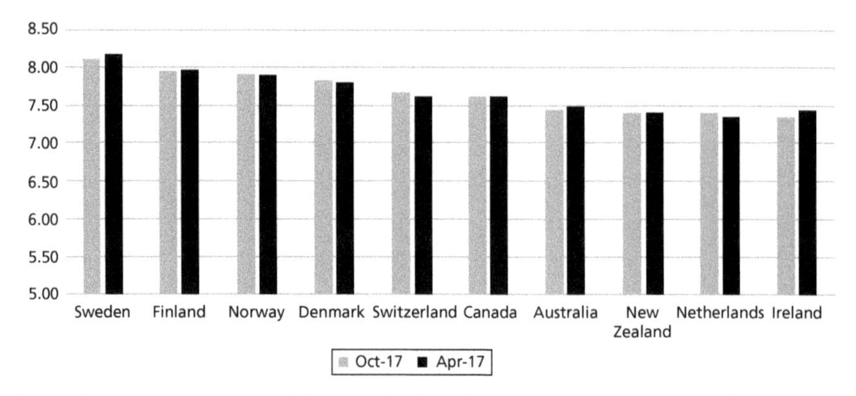

Figure 9.7 Top ten country ESG scores in the RobecoSAM country sustainability ranking

Source: RobecoSAM (2017).

While ESG factors assess the performance on environmental, social, and governance dimensions, the ultimate goal is achieving the United Nations (UN) Sustainable Development Goals (SDGs) by 2030. The Dutch Central Bureau for Statistics (2018) has, for example, started to measure and report on the performance of the Netherlands with respect to achieving the 17 SDGs.

Another matter is how such a sustainability ranking is integrated in an investment process. At Robeco, the rankings and changes in ranking are used in a rules-based way to adjust portfolio weights in a sovereign bond portfolio, which is in effect a quant approach. But of course, one could use the sustainability scores in a fundamental approach as well, to adjust for those factors that are not well captured by the ranking. In fact, the CFA Institute (2017) cites Robeco's emerging debt team in using the change in rankings to adjust its Brazilian sovereign bonds exposure.

However, it is not clear what mechanism Robeco uses exactly. Ideally, in a fundamental ESG-integrated approach to sovereign bonds investing, the ESG assessment should show up in an analyst recommendation, preferably via its valuation and rating. This would make the PRI-inspired arrow of Figure 9.2 operational and use the factors mentioned in Table 9.1. However, we are not aware of an investment team that does this systematically. Yet it may be a useful method, in particular for larger investors, which need to become less dependent on credit ratings (as suggested after the global financial crisis). For them, independently studying how ESG affects credit risk is important to undertake this analysis properly.

9.3.2 ESG INTEGRATION INTO CORPORATE BONDS

Figure 9.6 indicates that ESG integration in corporate bonds is more practised than in sovereign bonds, but less than in equities. PRI (2013a) argues that

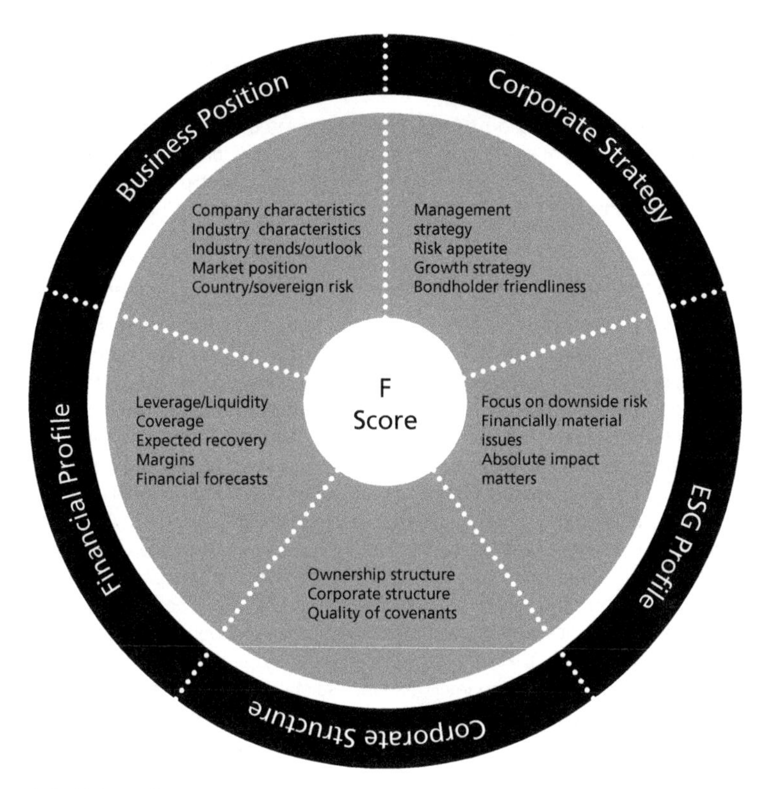

Figure 9.8 Robeco F-score

Source: Robeco.

corporate bond investors are ramping up efforts, but that full integration is still some way off. In practice, such efforts are usually limited to ESG specialists raising red flags on specific bonds, mostly on governance issues, which remain the focus. Nevertheless, environmental issues are becoming increasingly important for corporate bonds.

As of 2018, there are only a few known examples of funds with ESG integration approaches in corporate bonds. An example is the approach taken by the Robeco credits team, which gives bonds so-called F-scores (see Figure 9.8). These are based on five indicators that can take a value of –1, 0, or 1, and the F-score can be between –3 and +3. One of the five factors is an assessment of ESG quality, which can change the needle on a score from, say, 0 to 2 or from 1 to −1. The attractiveness of a bond is rated on the pricing of the bond versus other bonds with the same rating, where positive F-scores deserve a premium and negative ones a discount.

To give more insight in ESG integration into corporate bonds, Box 9.1 provides an interview with a corporate bonds fund manager.

BOX 9.1 INTERVIEW WITH A CORPORATE BONDS FUND MANAGER

Mariska Douwens is a portfolio manager with MN, a large pension asset manager in the Netherlands with €125bn assets under management. She is part of the Euro IG Credits team which manages a > €10 billion credits (corporate bonds) portfolio. We asked her about the differences she sees in ESG integration and engagement between equities and corporate bonds.

What differences do you see between corporate bonds and equities?

Douwens: 'There are quite a few differences, and some of them make engagement harder from the corporate bond side, both for the bondholder and for the corporations. Most importantly, bondholders are *not* owners of the company and do not share in the company's value creation, unlike shareholders. It is all about downside risk and preserving capital instead of undertaking risky projects with higher upside opportunities. This results in conflicts of interest between shareholders and bondholders, which are often not well understood by ESG specialists. Another important difference is that bonds and their holders are much more heterogeneous than equities, coming in different maturities and seniorities. All of these have relatively small markets, which makes the trading much more expensive than in equities, which often has just one share class. As a result, bondholders take much more of a buy and hold approach, or buy and maintain approach, i.e. reinvest the proceeds of bonds whose principal is repaid. Equities investors are much more active and opportunistic. Information is fed into prices much faster, thanks to centralised exchanges and high liquidity. The fact that bonds trade in an OTC (over the counter) market, also makes it hard for companies to identify their bondholders after issuance. In the pre-issue phase it is much easier to engage, as you will have companies visiting. Overall, engagement is simply not yet as institutionalised in fixed income as it is in equities.'

What differences do you see between corporate and sovereign bonds?

'Sovereigns and emerging market debt are very different than corporate bonds due to the political angle which can create more volatility', Douwens explains. 'This does not only concern emerging markets: just think of Trump's victory, Brexit and the vote for Cataluña's bid for independence which reinvigorate fears for a Euro break-up. With countries, you need to look at IMF indicators, tax morale, governance etc. Next, dialogue with governments is tough. Just imagine, CalPers reduced their engagement with the US government since Trump was elected. It is much easier to have a dialogue with corporates.'

What is your own approach to ESG?

Douwens: 'Our process is driven by materiality. Companies with low scores and ratings require further analysis and may lead us to adjust our credit assessment. Framing is important: don't get distracted by labels or what ESG data providers pick and value in their assessment, as they are also still in a learning phase and need to be educated and fed by people in the field. It doesn't really matter if something is called sustainability: we look at everything that may affect credit quality. It's very fundamental, all about investment beliefs and your fiduciary duty to know and explain your investments. Ideally you start from 0, and forget the benchmark, but that is hard. However, you can customise a benchmark to better reflect core beliefs regarding specific risks and their return characteristics. For instance, our universe is much more concentrated than for equities, with some 480 issuers and 1,900 bonds to pick from.'

How do you get the most out of your engagement?

'First of all, bondholder engagement is still in its infancy and developing. It requires quite some resources, also from the corporations involved. Therefore, you have to prioritise and keep the focus on materiality. Also, the carrot works better than the stick: corporations prefer the positive angle of seeing opportunities. We tell them that more and regular disclosure is a way to stand out from the crowd and improve visibility of their business model, now and in the future—thus reducing agency costs.'

To what extent do you think ESG is priced?

'Partly', Douwens thinks. 'You can see the impact of ESG on the price of credit quality, which itself varies over time and is not solely driven by fundamentals. Technicals can also be an important return driver, as we have seen with the central bank's asset purchases. And you see it most clearly in the tails. It is a very inefficient market with lagging price adjustments, not always reflecting real underlying trades. Furthermore, insurers have a preference for longer maturities to better align their long duration liabilities, which may mean they have to pay a higher price for this specific segment.'

To what extent do you cooperate on ESG?

Douwens: 'At MN, there is joint work on a company's ESG issues, primarily between people from Credits and our Responsible Investment & Governance (RI&G) team. The latter is also in charge of our shareholder engagement activities; and the equities teams are typically in the lead on existing relations/topics. But it is an informal and ad hoc process: If I see an issue, I approach our RI&G team and feed them with detailed company information.' She sees limited external cooperation between other credit investors on bondholder engagement, not least because these investors cannot be easily identified as a bondholder. 'Although they recognise the relevance of ESG factors, investors are still looking for ways how to integrate it into their investment process. The challenge is how to best educate analysts on (the importance of) ESG issues and—in return—how to encourage analysts to educate ESG team members and ESG data providers on practical matters. There is still a lot to learn from each other in order to take ESG to the next level for corporate bonds!'

Is there anything you would like to see changed or any advice you would like to give?

There are a few things she recommends companies do: 'First of all, why isn't management compensation tied to bond metrics like CDS spreads as well? That would give more alignment with other stakeholders than say earnings per share or stock returns, which are very equity focused metrics. Second, corporates could try to more proactively and effectively engage with bondholders, simply by having their investor relations team and treasury desk work together more closely and inform each other of their contacts and feedback.'

9.3.3 ESG INTEGRATION INTO CREDIT RATINGS

ESG integration into credit ratings is still in its infancy. The ratings agencies do talk about this and show signs of interest, but no substantial action has been taken as yet. For example, Moody's (2015) announced they would integrate

ESG issues into their ratings, but qualified these efforts by saying that: 'We reflect ESG considerations in our holistic assessment of credit risk for rated entities, and note that such considerations are already implicitly scored factors in some of our ratings methodologies.' The report goes on to say that 'even for issuers or sectors where ESG risks have material implications, the credit impact may be mitigated by other considerations... Additionally, the impact of ESG risks is not always clear-cut in terms of materiality, scale and timing.' Such comments are fair, but they also seem like a justification to avoid implementing ESG factors very thoroughly.

Wilkins (2017), who is S&P's managing director of environmental and climate risk research, states that S&P considers ESG risks and opportunities in its assessment of a company's business risk, specifically its competitive position, financial risk (through CF and leverage assessment), and management and governance. S&P also launched its Green Evaluation Tool in April 2017, which scores green bonds in transparency, governance, and use of proceeds. Then again, as the author is an S&P employee, he has incentives to exaggerate S&P's level of ESG integration.

9.4 Green bonds and social bonds

As with impact in equities, green bonds and social bonds take ESG integration a step further, to SF 2.5 or 3.0.

9.4.1 GREEN BONDS

Green bonds are a recent but fast-growing phenomenon. The first green bond was launched by the European Investment Bank in July 2007, and it took six years for the green bond market to pass $10 billion in cumulative issues. The market then accelerated fast, passing $200 billion in February 2017. At first, the market was dominated by supranationals, but from 2012 onwards agencies, sovereigns, corporates, municipalities, financial institutions, and so on also entered this market. In addition, related products were launched, such as green bonds funds and green bond indices. Standards followed suit, such as the Climate Bond Standards (November 2010) and the Green Bond Principles (January 2014). Figure 9.9 shows the market value of the annual issuance of green bonds.

Green bonds are bonds that finance green projects, that is, provide environmental or climate change benefits, but are otherwise the same as other bonds. The vast majority (82 per cent) of green bonds issued are investment-grade bonds and the energy sector is the main sector involved, accounting for 43 per

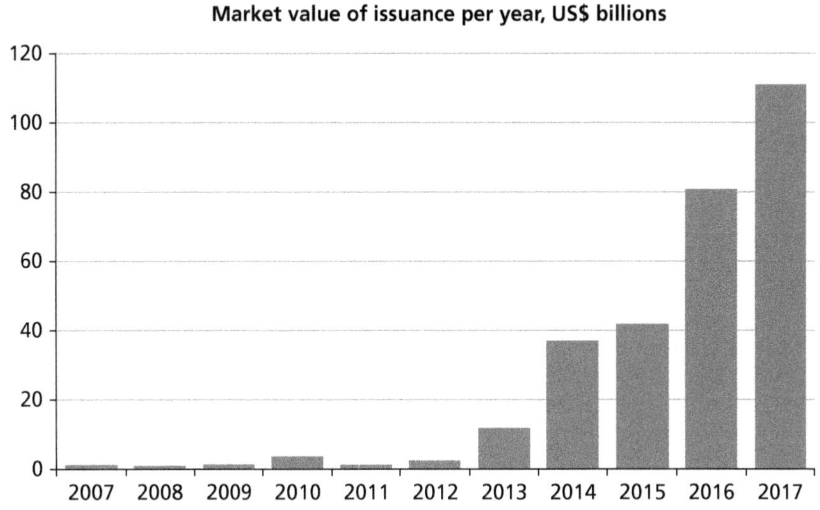

Market value of issuance per year, US$ billions

120
100
80
60
40
20
0
2007 2008 2009 2010 2011 2012 2013 2014 2015 2016 2017

Figure 9.9 Green bond issues, 2007–17

Source: Green Bond Initiative.

cent of outstanding green bonds (Zerbib, 2017). Green bonds thus have the potential to contribute to the financing needs in new energy supply and energy efficiency, which is estimated at around $6 trillion per year (Calderón and Stern, 2014). At the same time, those institutional investors that pursue sustainable investing policies can buy these investment-grade bonds. International Capital Markets Association (ICMA, 2017a) gives four criteria for green bonds:

1. **Use of proceeds:** Proceeds are exclusively for green projects, which should be appropriately described in the legal documentation of the bond.
2. **Process for project evaluation and selection:** The issuer should clearly communicate to investors what the environmental objectives are, the process by which the issuer determines how the project fits within the eligible green projects categories (see Box 9.2), and the related eligibility criteria.
3. **Management of proceeds:** The net proceeds of the green bond should be credited to a subaccount, and subsequently be tracked and verified.
4. **Reporting:** There should be mandatory reporting on the use of the proceeds.

But what is green? There are several competing definitions. For example, the Chinese guidelines published by the National Development and Reform Commission seem much less strict that those of the Green Bond Principles, which requires 95 per cent of proceeds to be used for green projects. The High-Level Expert Group on Sustainable Finance (2018) recommends an EU sustainability taxonomy be established and European sustainability standards for some financial assets, starting with green bonds, be developed. This

BOX 9.2 GREEN BOND INITIATIVES OF THE IFC

The IFC is involved in several green bond initiatives. This box reports on two of them.

IFC forest bonds

In October 2016, the IFC issued a forest bond to support a Wildlife Works project in east Kenya. It protects a migration corridor for endangered elephants and benefits thousands of nearby rural farmers. The project has been approved under the UN's Reducing Emissions from Deforestation and forest Degradation (REDD+) programme. Its CFs are generated from the REDD+ carbon credits it creates. In addition, the sale of the credits provided revenues for wildlife conservation, jobs for women, and other benefits for local communities.

The $152 million bond has a five-year maturity and pays a coupon of 1.55 per cent. Investors can choose to have the coupon paid in cash, or in carbon credits, or a combination of the two. Mining giant BHP Billiton ensures that the bond can sell a minimum quantity of carbon credits every year until the bond matures.

Deforestation and forest degradation account for about 20 per cent of global GHG emissions. The issuers estimate that the bond will facilitate the sequestration of 11.8 million tons of carbon dioxide over its life. The World Bank estimates that between $75 billion and $300 billion will have to be invested over the next decade to reduce deforestation by 50 per cent.

Source: Environmental Finance (2017).

Amundi–IFC emerging markets green bonds

Green bonds have become an effective way to channel capital towards energy transition and the global market for green bonds has grown rapidly. But huge gaps persist in emerging markets where financing needs related to energy transition are tremendous.

Amundi, a leading French asset manager, and IFC, the private financing arm of the World Bank, have joined forces in a public–private partnership setting up a $2 billion Green Cornerstone Bond Fund. The expertise of Amundi (the private part) is combined with protection by IFC (the public part). The IFC will take a junior tranche of $125 million in the $2 billion bond issue.

The green bonds are issued by emerging market financial institutions. Technical assistance is provided to the issuers to analyse green assets (to identify use of proceeds; good governance on these projects is important to prevent green washing) and to provide impact reporting for the bond issuer and in aggregate for the Fund. The Green Cornerstone Bond Fund means that money from developed markets is channelled towards banks in developing markets that are working on aligning their economies with a low-carbon economy.

Source: IFC

highlights the central role of the green bond market in the transition to a more sustainable economy.

Although green bonds are meant exclusively for financing green projects (criterion 1 in the ICMA list), they are not ring-fenced. That is, the bond's payments are not necessarily tied to the green project (unless the project constitutes all of the issuer's assets). So, the bond carries the same risk as other bonds by the same issuer with the same conditions. This suggests there should be no price differential with otherwise comparable bonds. In fact, Morgan

Stanley (2017) analysed 121 green-labelled bonds across most sectors and found that investors can buy most green bonds at similar yield spread levels to conventional issues, adjusting for sector, curve, and currency. Thus, investors do not have to sacrifice spread. For investors, it means that valuation is likely less of a driver than commitment to climate change or the desire to diversify the investor base. NN Investment Partners (2018) finds similar results, with initially lower yields for green bonds disappearing as the market grows.

By contrast, Zerbib (2017) finds evidence that the average green bond premium is significantly negative at 8bp. The green bond premium is defined as the difference in yield between two matching bonds (one green and one conventional) after controlling for the difference in liquidity (which is important as the bond market is illiquid). Zerbib (2017) argues that the negative premium indicates that there is a shortage of green bonds relative to the investment demand and calls for operational and fiscal measures to increase the pipeline of green bonds issued. It should be noted that a negative premium of 8bp is relatively small.

Box 9.2 discusses several green bond initiatives of the World Bank's International Finance Corporation (IFC), which is an international non-profit organization, while Box 9.3 presents an interview with a green bonds fund manager.

BOX 9.3 INTERVIEW WITH A GREEN BONDS FUND MANAGER

Bram Bos manages the green bonds fund at NN Investment Partners, a Dutch asset management company that is part of NN Group, the Netherlands' largest listed insurance company. In an interview he talks about the peculiarities of green bonds.

How do we know that a green bond really is a green bond?

Bos: 'Several standards have been developed to define green bonds, such as the Green Bond Principles and the Climate Bond Initiative. These have brought some much needed clarity. Nevertheless, investors will always need to check for themselves if a bond meets the Green bond criteria or not.'

Why are green bonds attractive to investors?

'Green bonds allow investors to have a direct and measurable positive impact on the environment. And they allow institutional investors to show their stakeholders what the impact of their green investments is.' He adds: 'Moreover, unlike private debt, green bonds offer liquidity, which is something that large investors appreciate a lot since the financial crisis.'

Why has the green bond market grown so fast over the past few years?

Bos: 'The publication of the Green Bond Principles in 2014 brought a lot of much needed clarity. The 2015 Paris agreement gave another boost. Despite Donald Trump, the growth of the green bond market is set to continue.'

9.4.2 CHALLENGES

The green bond market is growing fast but it faces some serious challenges. For example, there is no clear agreement on what constitutes a green bond. There are several standards and numerous interpretations of those standards. As discussed, there are plans for developing official European sustainability standards for green bonds. Green bonds also need better investor communication. Many investors do not know how green bonds work and what the costs are. Demystifying those issues could help to broaden the investor base.

Green bonds can, for example, be used for green infrastructure projects (Caldecott, 2010), as large investments are needed for new energy infrastructures. Some countries (e.g. Indonesia, Poland, and France) have started to issue green bonds. These green bond issues for environmentally friendly projects can in some cases provide investors with a dilemma: How seriously should they take these countries' environmental ambitions? Indonesia, for example, relies on coal for more than half of its electricity production and is the fifth-largest emitter of greenhouse gases (GHGs) in the world, while Poland generates 80 per cent of its energy from coal (*Financial Times*, 2018).

Green bonds are not suitable for complex transactions. Waste management company Renewi (the former Shanks) used, for example, bank finance for its merger with Van Gansewinkel rather than the green bond market. Companies also face reputational risk by issuing a green bond, as it may not be recognized as such. In 2015, Unilever issued a £250 million green bond that was excluded from the Bloomberg Barclays MSCI Green Bond Index.

9.4.3 SOCIAL BONDS

Social bonds are bonds that are meant to provide clear social benefits. So far, the market for social bonds is less developed than the green bonds market.

Social Bond Principles (ICMA, 2017b) define a social bond as 'any type of bond instrument where the proceeds will be exclusively applied to finance or re-finance in part or in full new and/or existing eligible social projects and which are aligned with the four core components of the Social Bond Principles'. As with green bonds, that means the bonds are earmarked, but not ring-fenced, for social projects, and hence bear the same risk as otherwise similar bonds from the same issuer.

The Social Bond Principles have the same four core components as the Green Bond Principles:

1. use of proceeds;
2. process of project evaluation and selection;
3. management of proceeds;
4. reporting.

As with green bonds, there is no clear agreement on what exactly is a social bond. However, the Social Bond Principles do give an indication of what eligible social projects look like. Social project categories include, but are not limited to: affordable basic infrastructure; access to essential services; affordable housing; employment generation; food security; socioeconomic advancement; and empowerment. But of course, one could argue over what fits in these categories.

For further guidance, the Social Bond Principles also state that examples of target populations include: those living below the poverty line; excluded/marginalized communities; vulnerable groups; migrants or displaced persons; the undereducated; the underserved; and the unemployed. Whatever the project may be, the principle is very clear: it should provide clear social benefits. Social bonds have been criticized for being complex, expensive, and bureaucratic. It has been difficult to create accurate measures of social results.

Social bonds are often confused with social impact bonds (SIBs), which are not really bonds. Rather, a SIB is a payment by results contract where an organization, typically one with a social purpose, agrees to deliver a certain outcome. If this outcome is achieved, investors are paid back their initial investment plus an additional return on that investment. The United Kingdom is leading the way in SIBs. The Peterborough SIB was the world's first in 2012. It invests £5 million in reducing reoffending in prisoners leaving Peterborough prison.

9.5 Conclusions

At first sight, sustainability seems less relevant for bonds than for equity, since bondholders do not have voting power and barely share in the opportunities of companies or 'upside' as equities do. Moreover, there seem to be even less examples of ESG integration in bonds than in equities. However, sustainability does matter in bonds. For both corporate and sovereign bonds, there is evidence that E, S, and G matter.

Bond markets are bigger than equity markets, with institutional investors typically holding more bonds than equity. So if they move capital, the impact in bonds is potentially bigger than in equity. Institutional investors, which care about long-term value creation (see Chapters 4, 7, and 8), are thus in a position to advance ESG integration in bond investing.

As in equities, studying the company's business model is very important in ESG integration in corporate bonds. This chapter finds that even more than in equities there is a lot of underestimated sustainability risk in bonds. There are also issues that make ESG integration harder in bonds than in equities, such as the lack of voting power and illiquid markets. Sustainability ratings are also emerging for sovereign bonds. Indicators include inter alia carbon emissions, energy use, environmental risk, social welfare, work and equality, and aging policies.

There is exciting innovation in the form of green bonds and social bonds to cater for SF 3.0. The challenge is to 'certify' the use of the proceeds for green or social purposes and to overcome bureaucratic procedures.

Key concepts used in this chapter

Asset-backed securities are debt securities collateralized by a pool of assets.

Agency costs reflect the difference between the value of the firm in an ideal contracting situation and its value in the real (and suboptimal) contracting situation.

Bond is a form of public debt.

CDS spread is the credit default swap spread, which measures the default risk on a bond.

Coupon is the interest paid on a bond.

Covenants are promises by management of the borrowing company to adhere to certain limits in the company's operations.

Credit rating is a rating of the creditworthiness of a company or country given by a credit rating agency; a high rating reflects a low default risk (and vice versa).

Default risk or credit risk is the risk of an issuer not making a coupon payment or principal repayment; see also *credit rating*.

Duration is the sensitivity of a bond's price to changes in interest rates.

Face value, also known as the principal, is the amount that needs to be repaid at the end of the bond's life.

Green bonds are bonds that finance green projects (i.e. provide environmental or climate change benefits), but are otherwise the same as other bonds.

High-yield bonds, also known as junk bonds, are high coupon-paying bonds with a lower credit rating than investment-grade corporate bonds.

Investment-grade bonds are bonds with a high credit rating and relatively low risk of default.

Junk bonds, also known as high-yield bonds, are high coupon-paying bonds with a lower credit rating than investment-grade corporate bonds.

Maturity is the time until the final repayment date of the bond.

Principal, also known as the face value, is the amount that needs to be repaid at the end of the bond's life.

Seniority is the order of repayment on various securities of the same issuer in the event of a sale or bankruptcy of the issuer.

Social bonds are bonds that finance social projects (i.e. provide clear social benefits), but are otherwise the same as other bonds.

Tax shield is a reduction in taxable income achieved through claiming allowable deductions from corporate or income tax such as interest payments.

Term structure is the array of prices or yields on bonds at different terms or maturities.

Yield is the return on a bond.

Yield to- maturity is the discount rate that sets the present value of the bond's payments equal to the bond's current market price.

SUGGESTED READING

Ashbaugh-Skaife, H., D. Collins, and R. LaFond (2006), 'The effects of corporate governance on firms' credit ratings', *Journal of Accounting and Economics*, 42(1–2): 203–43.

Hanson, D., T. Lyons, J. Bender, B. Bertocci, and B. Lamy (2017), 'Analysts' roundtable on integrating ESG into investment decision-making', *Journal of Applied Corporate Finance*, 29(2), 44–55.

Polbennikov, S., A. Desclée, L. Dynkin, and A. Maitra (2016), 'ESG ratings and performance of corporate bonds', *Journal of Fixed Income*, 26(1): 21–41.

RobecoSAM (2015), 'Measuring country intangibles: RobecoSAM's country sustainability ranking', Rotterdam, http://www.robecosam.com/images/Country-Sustainability-Paper-en.pdf, accessed 4 July 2018.

Zerbib, O. (2017), 'The green bond premium', Working Paper, https://ssrn.com/abstract=2889690.

REFERENCES

Amel-Zadeh, A. and G. Serafeim (2018), 'Why and how investors use ESG information: evidence from a global survey', *Financial Analysts Journal*, forthcoming

Ashbaugh-Skaife, H., D. Collins, and R. LaFond (2006), 'The effects of corporate governance on firms' credit ratings', *Journal of Accounting and Economics*, 42(1–2): 203–43.

Attig, N., S. El Ghoul, O. Guedhami, and J. Suh (2013), 'Corporate social responsibility and credit ratings', *Journal of Business Ethics*, 117(4): 679–94.

Bauer, R. and D. Hann (2010), 'Corporate environmental management and credit risk', ECCE Working Paper, Maastricht University, https://ssrn.com/abstract=1660470, accessed 4 July 2018.

Bauer, R., J. Derwall, and D. Hann (2009), 'Employee relations and credit risk', ECCE Working Paper, Maastricht University, https://ssrn.com/abstract=1483112, accessed 4 July 2018.

Beirne, J. and M. Fratzscher (2013), 'The pricing of sovereign risk and contagion during the European sovereign debt crisis', *Journal of International Money and Finance*, 34(C): 60–82.

Berk, J. and P. DeMarzo (2014), *Corporate Finance*, 4th edn, Pearson Education, Boston, MA.

Bhojraj, S. and P. Sengupta (2003), 'Effect of corporate governance on bond ratings and yields: the role of institutional investors and outside directors', *Journal of Business*, 76(3): 455–75.

Bolton, P. and D. Scharfstein (1996), 'Optimal debt structure and the number of creditors', *Journal of Political Economy*, 104(1): 1–25.

Butler, A. and L. Fauver (2006), 'Institutional environment and sovereign credit ratings', *Financial Management*, 35(3): 53–79.

Caldecott, B. (2010), 'Green infrastructure bonds: accessing the scale of low cost capital required to tackle climate change', Climate Change Capital, London.

Calderón, F. and N. Stern (2014), 'Better growth, better climate: the new climate economy report', New Climate Economy, Washington DC, https://www.unilever.com/Images/better-growth-better-climate-new-climate-economy-global-report-september-2014_tcm244-425167_en.pdf, accessed 4 July 2018.

Cantor, R. and F. Pecker (1996), 'Determinants and impact of sovereign credit ratings', *Federal Reserve Bank of New York Economic Policy Review*, October: 37–54.

Central Bureau for Statistics (2018), 'Duurzame ontwikkelingsdoelen: de stand voor Nederland [Sustainable Development Goals: performance of the Netherlands]', The Hague.

CFA Institute (2017), 'ESG in equity analysis and credit analysis. An overview', Charlottesville, VA.

Ciocchini, F., E. Durbin, and D. Ng (2003), 'Does corruption increase emerging market bond spreads?', *Journal of Economics and Business*, 55(5): 503–28.

Cohan, A. B. (1962), 'Yields on new underwritten corporate bonds, 1935–58', *Journal of Finance*, 17(4): 585–605.

Environmental Finance (2017), 'Sustainable forestry: IFC forests bond', Washington DC, https://www.cbd.int/financial/2017docs/ifc-forestbond2017.pdf, accessed 4 July 2018.

Fang, L. (2005), 'Investment bank reputation and the price and quality of underwriting services', *Journal of Finance*, 60(6): 2729–61.

Ferguson, N. (2001), *The Cash Nexus: Money and Power in the Modern World, 1700–2000*, Allen Lane/Penguin Press, London.

Financial Times (2018), 'Indonesia set to join green bond club', London, 22 February.

Fisher, L. (1959), 'Determinants of risk premiums on corporate bonds', *Journal of Political Economy*, 67(3): 217–37.

Galai, D. and R. Masulis (1976), 'The option pricing model and the risk factor of stock', *Journal of Financial Economics*, 3(1–2): 53–81.

Gande, A., M. Puri, and A. Saunders (1999), 'Bank entry, competition, and the market for corporate securities underwriting', *Journal of Financial Economics*, 54(2): 165–95.

Hanson, D., T. Lyons, J. Bender, B. Bertocci, and B. Lamy (2017), 'Analysts' roundtable on integrating ESG into investment decision-making', *Journal of Applied Corporate Finance*, 29(2): 44–55.

High-Level Expert Group on Sustainable Finance (2018), 'Financing a sustainable European economy', Final Report, European Union, Brussels.

ICMA (International Capital Markets Association) (2017a), 'Green bond principles', ICMA Paris.

ICMA (International Capital Markets Association) (2017b), 'Social bond principles', ICMA Paris.

Kane, G., U. Velury, and B. Ruf (2005), 'Employee relations and the likelihood of occurrence of corporate financial distress', *Journal of Business Finance and Accounting*, 32(5–6), 1083–105.

Klock, M., S. Mansi, and W. Maxwell (2005), 'Does corporate governance matter to bondholders?', *Journal of Financial and Quantitative Analysis*, 40(4): 693–719.

Merton, R. C. (1974), 'On the pricing of corporate debt: the risk structure of interest rates', *Journal of Finance*, 29(2): 449–70.

Moody's (2015), 'Moody's: incorporating environmental, social and governance risks into credit analysis', New York, 8 September.

Morgan Stanley (2017), 'Behind the green bond boom', *Morgan Stanley Research*, New York, 11 October.

Myers, S. (1977), 'Determinants of corporate borrowing', *Journal of Financial Economics*, 5(2): 147–75.

NN Investment Partners (2018), 'Unravelling the green bond premium', The Hague, https://www.nnip.com/Default-Display-on-2/Unravelling-the-Green-Bond-Premium.htm, accessed 4 July 2018.

Polbennikov, S., A. Desclée, L. Dynkin, and A. Maitra (2016), 'ESG ratings and performance of corporate bonds', *Journal of Fixed Income*, 26(1): 21–41.

PRI (Principles for Responsible Investment) (2013a), 'Corporate bonds: spotlight on ESG risks', London, https://www.unpri.org/fixed-income/corporate-bonds-spotlight-on-esg-risks/41.article, accessed 4 July 2018.

PRI (Principles for Responsible Investment) (2013b), 'Sovereign bonds: spotlight on ESG risks', London, https://www.unpri.org/fixed-income/sovereign-bonds-spotlight-on-esg-risks/40.article, accessed 4 July 2018.

PRI (Principles for Responsible Investment) (2017), 'Shifting perceptions: ESG, credit risk and ratings', London.

RobecoSAM (2015), 'Measuring country intangibles: RobecoSAM's country sustainability ranking', Rotterdam, http://www.robecosam.com/images/Country-Sustainability-Paper-en.pdf, accessed 4 July 2018.

RobecoSAM (2017), 'Country sustainability ranking update', Rotterdam, November.

Schneider, T. (2011), 'Is environmental performance a determinant of bond pricing? Evidence from the US pulp and paper and chemical industries', *Contemporary Accounting Research*, 28(5): 1537–61.

SIFMA (Securities Industry and Financial Markets Association) (2017), 'The SIFMA fact book 2017', New York, https://www.sifma.org/wp-content/uploads/2016/10/US-Fact-Book-2017-SIFMA.pdf, accessed 3 July 2018.

Smith, C. and J. Warner (1979), 'On financial contracting: an analysis of bond covenants', *Journal of Financial Economics*, 7(2): 117–61.

Sustainalytics (2017), 'Game of bonds: reassessing sovereign credit ratings', ESG Spotlight No. 16, Amsterdam.

Wälti, S. (2012), 'Trust no more? The impact of the crisis on citizens' trust in central banks', *Journal of International Money and Finance*, 31(3): 593–605.

Wilkins, M. (2017), 'Climate increasingly important for ratings, says S&P', *Environmental Finance*, 24 November.

Zerbib, O. (2017), 'The green bond premium', Working Paper, https://ssrn.com/abstract=2889690, accessed 4 July 2018.

10 Banking—new forms of lending

Overview

The *traditional business of banking* is the provision of long-term loans that are funded by short-term deposits. Banks have developed technologies to screen and monitor borrowers in order to reduce asymmetric information between the lender and the borrower. This monitoring function enables banks to assess social and environmental risks as part of the credit risk management process. Banks can also analyse sector-wide sustainability trends and discover best practices.

This chapter identifies two main approaches towards integrating sustainability into lending: *risk based* and *value based*. The risk-based approach examines whether environmental, social, and governance (ESG) factors matter for credit risk in ways that have not been incorporated in current credit risk assessment and screening methodologies. In the value-based approach, stakeholders, such as depositors or client-investors, may care about ESG factors for non-monetary reasons.

In the risk-based approach, banks use social and environmental factors (in additional to traditional credit risk factors) to determine the risk premium. There is ample evidence that social-environmental performance and financial performance reinforce each other. Better scores on social and environmental factors thus allow banks to offer lower interest rates to companies.

The *nudging* theory of change suggests applying a base lending rate for projects with low or no ESG risks, and a risk premium for projects with ESG concerns. An interesting example in retail banking is low interest rate mortgages for energy efficient houses.

In values-based banking, also called impact lending, banks primarily lend to projects with a positive social or environmental impact, such as health care, social inclusion, renewable energy, and sustainable agriculture. Impact lending involves lending to companies that are changing from a linear to a sustainable business model. This also creates uncertainty: Which technology or business concept is going to win? Lending to companies with a circular business model poses new opportunities and challenges.

It should be noted that many sustainable alternatives are offered by start-ups that face credit constraints (due to limited collateral, size, or track record). These start-ups may look for venture capital or crowd-funding, which are beyond the scope of this book.

Finally, *microfinance* is a banking service (lending, payments, and savings) for low-income individuals or micro-enterprises, which otherwise have no access to financial services. Microfinance institutions, which emerged in low-income countries such as Bangladesh and Bolivia, are now found throughout the developing world. They contribute to reducing poverty and improving living conditions.

Learning objectives

After you have studied this chapter, you should be able to:

- explain the role of banks in screening and monitoring (potential) borrowers;
- explain the relevance of sustainability for banking;
- understand how ESG risks can be incorporated in the credit risk assessment;
- list the barriers and incentives to sustainable lending;
- understand the various forms of impact lending and microfinance.

10.1 Basics of banking

Banks perform the important societal function of financing the economy and thus enable business to develop. This is particularly relevant for small and medium-sized enterprises (SMEs), which are largely dependent on bank financing. The traditional business of banks is lending to companies as well as households. Before a bank grants a loan, it screens the creditworthiness of a potential borrower. After the loan is granted, a bank monitors whether the borrower takes excessive risks. The lending business generates income for banks. As loans are funded with deposits, the difference (or spread) between the lending and borrowing rate determines a bank's profitability.

Banks also make profits through various fee-earning activities, like capital-market transactions for companies and governments, such as underwriting and trading securities, and derivatives transactions. Banks use modern risk-management models to measure and control the risks arising from these transactions. These risk-management models are built on the monitoring technology that banks use in their lending business.

10.1.1 LENDING BUSINESS

Banks take deposits from the public and grant loans on their own account. These loans are typically held to maturity (the 'originate and hold' model).

Balance sheet		Profit & loss account
Loans (L)	Equity (E)	Interest income ($L \cdot r_C$) (+)
	Deposits (D)	Fee-based income (F) (+)
		Interest paid ($D \cdot r_D$) (–)
		Loan losses ($Loss$) (–)
		Expenses (Exp) (–)
Total assets	Total liabilities	Profit (π) (+/–)

Figure 10.1 Simplified balance sheet and P&L account of a bank

Banks are thus engaged in the transformation of liquid deposits into illiquid loans. The intermediation function of banks can be explained using a simple balance sheet and profit and loss (P&L) account (see Figure 10.1). On the liability side, banks fund themselves with many small deposits D from the public. The effective deposit rate r_D includes both the explicit interest paid and the cost of free services (e.g. free access to ATMs).

Banks provide loans L. The expected loan rate r_L is different from the contracted rate on loans, as some borrowers default on their loan. Assuming a risk-neutral bank, the difference between the contracted loan rate r_C and the expected loan rate r_L is given by:

$$E(1 + r_C) = (1 + r_C) \cdot (1 - p) + (1 + r_C) \cdot p \cdot \gamma = 1 + r_L \qquad (10.1)$$

where p is the *probability of default* and γ the *recovery rate* (the fraction of the principal and interest recovered in case of default). The recovery rate is based on the loss that would arise in the event of default. The *loss given default* is calculated as $(1 - \gamma)$. Thus, if the recovery rate is 80 per cent, the loss given default is 20 per cent. Equation 10.1 can be illustrated with a simple example. Assume a contracted loan rate of 6 per cent, a probability of default of 5 per cent, and a recovery rate of 80 per cent. The expected loan rate is 4.94 per cent, calculated as (1.06 * 0.95) + (1.06 * 0.05 * 0.8) = 1.0494.

The bank's profit π is the interest margin and fees F (see Section 10.1.2) net of expenses Exp and is given by:

$$\pi = L \cdot r_L - D \cdot r_D + F - Exp \qquad (10.2)$$

An important determinant of bank profitability is the risk premium RP, that is, the difference between the contracted loan rate and the deposit rate $(r_C - r_D)$. The *risk premium* or *credit spread* covers the expected loan losses—$Loss = L \cdot (1 + r_C) \cdot p \cdot (1 - \gamma)$ (which is a function of the probability of default p and the loss given default $(1 - \gamma)$)—the cost of the loan business Exp, and the reward for risk-taking on the loans π. Section 10.4 explains how ESG factors and risks can be incorporated in the risk premium.

10.1.2 FEE-BASED BUSINESS

Banks also make profits from fee-earning activities F. These off-balance sheet activities are related to the traditional loan business and include securitization of assets, credit lines, and guarantees, such as letters of credit. Off-balance sheet activities also encompass derivative transactions, such as forwards, options, and swaps. Nowadays, large banks are the key players in the derivatives markets.

Asset securitization involves the sale of income-generating financial assets (such as mortgages, car loans, trade receivables, credit card receivables, and leases) by a bank, the originator of the financial assets, to a *special purpose vehicle* (SPV). The SPV finances the purchase of these financial assets by the issue of commercial paper, which is secured by those assets. Banks can thus liquefy their illiquid loans. The resulting 'originate and distribute' model separates the functions of granting loans and funding loans. When loans on their balance sheet are securitized, banks can provide new loans.

Finally, banks are increasingly involved in fee-earning capital-market and asset management activities. *Investment banking* relates to services like underwriting securities, advising on mergers and acquisitions (M&As), and managing assets. Banks thus play a key role in both initial public offerings and seasoned public offerings of bonds and equities. In their M&A advice (including fairness opinions discussed in Chapter 3) and prospectuses for securities offerings, banks should incorporate not only financial information but also information on social and environmental factors.

10.1.3 MONITORING ROLE

Asymmetric information lies at the core of banking. A borrower has private information on the CF of an investment project that is unobservable to outside lenders. Banks therefore monitor (potential) clients. *Monitoring* is defined here in a broad sense (Freixas and Rochet, 2008) as:

- screening projects ex ante (adverse selection);
- preventing opportunistic behaviour of the borrower during the project (moral hazard);
- auditing a borrower who fails to meet his or her contractual obligation (costly state verification).

Banks have a comparative advantage in monitoring (potential) borrowers if the following conditions are met (Diamond, 1984). First, a bank can develop economies of scale in monitoring by financing many investment projects. Secondly, the capacity of individual lenders is small compared to the size of many investment projects so that each project needs several lenders who would then need to monitor the borrowers. Finally, the costs of delegating this monitoring to a bank are small.

There is an important difference in incentives to acquire information between equity and bond investors (see Chapters 8 and 9) and banks. Market investors face a *free-rider problem*: when an investor acquires information about an investment project and behaves accordingly, he reveals this information to all investors, thereby dissuading other investors from devoting resources towards acquiring information. So investors do not have strong incentives to properly acquire information, as they cannot keep the benefits of this information. Specialist intermediaries, such as investment analysts at investment banks and credit rating agencies, produce equity valuations and credit risk information for market participants.

Banks, however, may keep the information they acquire, often by having long-run relationships with companies, and use it in a profitable way. Since banks can make investments without revealing their decisions immediately in public markets, they have a good incentive to undertake research on investment projects. Furthermore, banks with close ties to companies may be more effective than atomistic markets at exerting pressure on companies to repay their loans. Often, companies obtain a variety of financial services from their bank and also maintain checking accounts with it, thereby increasing the bank's information about the borrower. For example, the bank can learn about the company's sales by monitoring the cash flowing through its checking account or by factoring the company's accounts receivables. Companies may profit from these long-term relationships in the form of access to credit at lower prices. In their information role, banks analyse sector trends culminating in sector studies. Banks use these sector studies both to advise clients and to assess credit risk.

What determines the choice between market lending through bonds and bank lending? When the uncertainty about the company's CFs is relatively small (i.e. the asymmetric information between the firm and the lenders is limited), the company can borrow on the market (Freixas and Rochet, 2008). As the uncertainty increases, banks come into play as they have more possibilities than credit rating agencies to ask for information and to intervene when necessary. When the uncertainty becomes too great, a company cannot obtain finance.

In addition, the fixed cost for capital-market entry is too high for small companies. The resulting equilibrium is that large, well-capitalized companies with a track record of published annual reports finance themselves directly on the market, while smaller, new companies have to turn to banks.

10.1.4 TYPES OF LENDING

There are several types of loans, which can be segmented in various ways. The main categories of bank lending are distinguished by type of borrower:

- corporates: SME loans, corporate loans, financial sector loans (e.g. interbank), syndicated loans, mortgages, credit lines;

- governments (and governmental agencies): loans, mortgages, credit lines;
- social enterprises: loans, mortgages, credit lines;
- households: mortgages, consumer credit, microfinance, overdraft facilities.

An important feature is whether loans are secured by collateral or not. Examples of secured loans are mortgages (both on residential and commercial real estate), inventory loans, and car loans. The collateral reduces credit risk. Nevertheless, the value of the collateral can also fluctuate. Unsecured loans are, for example, credit cards, personal loans, and SME or corporate loans without collateral. These loans typically carry a higher interest rate because of the higher credit risk.

Finally, bank loans have different maturities: from short-term personal loans to long-term mortgages (with variable or fixed interest rates). The maturity is typically well below 10 years, although mortgages have a maturity of up to 25 or 30 years. To manage the interest rate risk on such long-term mortgages, banks provide fixed interest rates up to ten years, after which the rate has to be renegotiated between the bank and the borrower. Banks offer longer-term fixed rates, but often with a higher interest margin to discourage potential borrowers. The latter turn to insurance companies and pensions funds, which are more willing to provide mortgages at longer fixed interest rates because of their long-term liabilities and discourage short-term fixed rate mortgages in a similar way.

10.2 **Sustainability of banks**

The corporate governance of banks themselves matters. Recent studies show that social capital improves the viability of stakeholder-oriented banks (Ostergaard, Schindele, and Vale, 2016). Banks with the strongest shareholder-oriented governance performed worse during the crisis. Moreover, those institutions that had most of their funding in interbank markets as well as a high leverage have been the most vulnerable (Kotz and Schmidt, 2017).

In a comparative study, the Global Alliance for Banking on Values (GABV, 2016) contrasts the activities and performance of *values-based banks* (VBBs)—defined as banks that aim to deliver economic, social, and environmental impact as part of their mission statement—with those of *global systemically important banks* (G-SIBs). Table 10.1 shows that VBBs are more involved with the real economy, with 77 per cent of loans to assets (compared to 42 per cent for global banks) and 82 per cent of deposits to assets (compared to 52 per cent for global banks). VBBs are also safer. They have lower leverage—that is, more equity as share of total assets: 8.1 per cent for VBBs compared to 7.3 per cent for global banks. As discussed in Chapter 1, the average return on equity (ROE) for the group of VBBs is slightly lower, at 8.3 per cent compared to 8.7 per cent for the global banks, over the 2006–15 period, but the variance is

Table 10.1 Financial comparison of values-based and global banks, 2015

	2015	
	VBBs	Global banks
Real economy		
Loans/assets	76.8%	41.6%
Deposits/assets	81.7%	52.2%
Capital strength		
Equity/assets	8.1%	7.3%
Tier 1 ratio	12.8%	14.0%
Risk-weighted assets/total assets	61.6%	44.2%
	Ten years (2006–15)	
	VBBs	Global banks
Financial returns and volatility		
ROA	0.65%	0.53%
Standard deviation ROA	0.26%	0.35%
ROE	8.3%	8.7%
Standard deviation ROE	4.9%	7.7%

Note: The table analyses values-based banks (VBBs) and global systemically important banks (G-SIBs).
Source: GABV (2016).

lower for the VBBs at a standard deviation of 4.9 per cent compared to 7.7 per cent for the global banks. Given lower leverage, this implies a higher return on assets (ROA) for the VBBs. The lower variance for both ROE and ROA makes VBBs more stable.

10.2.1 STRUCTURAL REFORMS

In the aftermath of the great financial crisis, governments across the world have adopted structural reforms to restrict risk-taking in the core banking system financed with insured deposits. In particular, proprietary trading in financial markets (as opposed to the real economy) has been restricted. *Proprietary trading* occurs when financial firms trade equities, bonds, currencies, commodities, their derivatives, or other financial instruments for their own direct gain instead of earning commission income by trading on behalf of their clients.

In the United States, the Volcker Rule prohibits proprietary trading by deposit-taking banks. The underlying intention of the rule is to safeguard the core of the commercial banking system. It is also an attempt to make this important core of 'traditional' banking easier to understand and to prohibit it from engaging in more complex activities that are prone to conflicts of interest with the core objective of commercial banking (taking deposits and making loans). The Volcker Rule is subject to exemptions for market-making, hedging, and trading in US government securities.

In Europe, the Liikanen Report takes a slightly different approach. Proprietary trading and other significant trading activities (on behalf of clients) should be assigned to a separate legal entity if these activities amount to a significant share of a bank's business (for example, 10 per cent of its business). This ensures that trading activities beyond the threshold are carried out on a stand-alone basis and separate from the deposit bank. As a consequence, deposits, and the explicit and implicit guarantee they carry, no longer directly support risky trading activities. The long-standing universal banking model—combining commercial and investment banking activities—in Europe remains untouched, as the separated activities are still carried out in the same banking group. Hence, banks' ability to provide a wide range of financial services to their customers is maintained (Liikanen Report, 2012).

10.2.2 MATERIAL ESG RISKS IN BANKING

Following best practices of companies, banks have started to present a materiality matrix that outlines those sustainability issues that a bank and its stakeholders consider most material (see Chapter 5). An early adopter is the Swedish bank, Handelsbanken, which has a strong stakeholder orientation and has performed well during the global financial crisis. In its 2016 sustainability report, Handelsbanken has defined, in dialogue with its stakeholders, six material sustainability topics:

1. **The bank and its customers**: Satisfied customers; high availability; responsible lending; responsible sales and advisory services; integrity and confidentiality.
2. **The bank's role in the community**: Local presence; the bank as taxpayer; the bank should not be a burden on society; financial stability and profitability.
3. **The bank's indirect impact**: Responsible credits and investments with regard to human rights, working conditions, environmental concerns, and anti-corruption.
4. **The bank as an employer**: Responsible employer; working conditions and union rights; employee commitment; leadership and development; work environment and health; gender equality and diversity.
5. **The bank's business culture**: High ethical standards; salaries and remuneration (no performance- or volume-related bonuses); anti-corruption and bribery; counteracting money laundering and financing of terrorism.
6. **The bank as an investment**: Creating shareholder value, which can only be achieved by simultaneously creating long-term value for its customers and society as a whole.

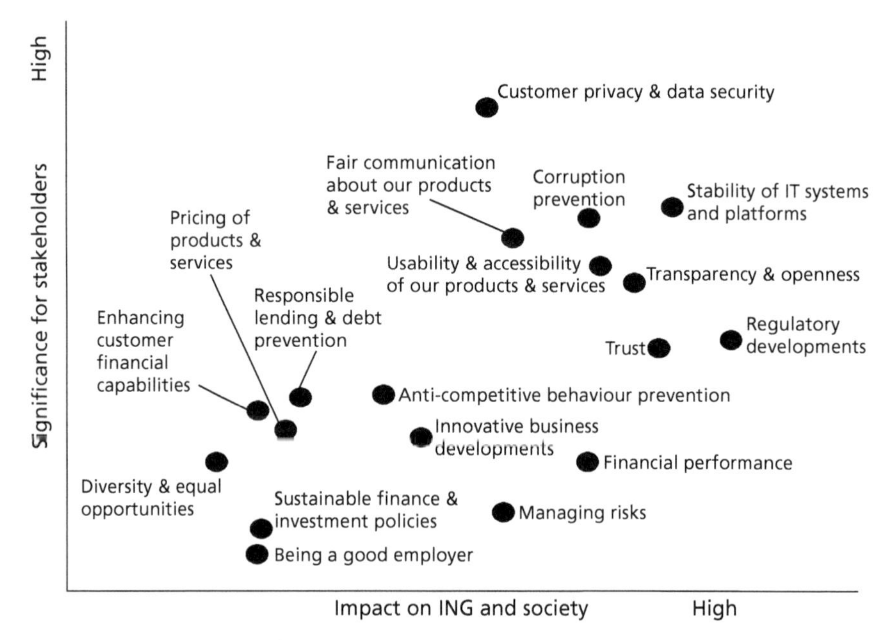

Figure 10.2 ING's materiality matrix, 2016

Source: ING 2016 Annual Report.

Handelsbanken considers its overall goal of profitability as a prerequisite to take a long-term approach, which is supported by its track record of strong earnings with low variance. Figure 10.2 gives the materiality matrix of one of the global banks, ING. While there is much overlap between Handelsbanken and ING regarding material issues (consumer satisfaction, responsible lending, anti-corruption, diversity, and equality), there are also some differences. ING, for example, highlights customer privacy and data security as a very significant issue for its stakeholders. In addition, regulatory developments are found to have a strong impact on ING. As discussed in Chapter 5, such materiality matrices tend to differ between banks.

10.3 **Why does sustainability matter to lending?**

In their monitoring role, there is an opportunity for banks to collect more information on firms, including ESG factors and risks. Banks can thus analyse sector-wide sustainability trends and discover best practices. Banks can in turn transfer these best practices in sustainability back to firms in their advisory role. In that way, banks can help firms with their transition to sustainable business models. Banks will, of course, also use the information to calibrate the risk premium (see Section 10.4).

In the approval of a loan proposal, a bank's credit committee considers the viability of the company (or individual). Can the company generate sufficient CFs to cover the periodic interest payments and ultimately the principal at the due dates? Chapters 5, 8, and 9 explain that sustainability matters to the value of companies and their securities, but also that relevant social and environmental factors are not yet properly incorporated. It is therefore important for banks, when granting loans, to consider the full impact of sustainability on a company's business model, because that affects the company's credit risk (as highlighted in Chapter 9). What are the transition challenges for the company's sector? How far is the company, in the transition of its business model, also in comparison with its sector peers? The move to a circular economy, for example, not only transforms the business model but also the financing proposition (see Section 10.5).

Sustainability also has an impact on collateral values. The energy efficiency of real estate is, for example, a key determinant of its future value. Similarly, traditional cars with combustion engines operating on fossil fuel may lose their value, while hybrid or electric cars may maintain theirs. But there are also environmental questions about electric cars. A major concern is the mining and disposal of rare raw materials, such as lithium, for the batteries. The example of electric cars illustrates that there are sometimes sustainability dilemmas: what is good for the reduction of carbon emissions can be bad for the land system. More generally, Chapter 9 provides evidence that a stronger environmental, social, or governance factor means a lower cost of debt.

Bank credit is an important source of finance for the private sector in Asia and Europe. Figure 10.3 illustrates that 157 per cent of GDP in China and

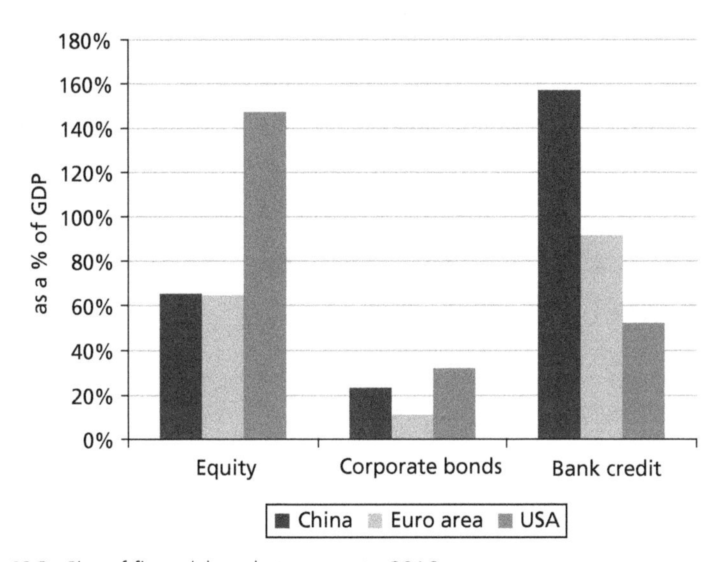

Figure 10.3 Size of financial market segments, 2016

Note: Given as % of GDP.

Source: Authors' calculations based on Bank for International Settlements for corporate bonds and bank credit to the private non-financial sector and World Bank for equity.

Table 10.2 Integration of sustainability into lending

SF typology	Bank loans	Approach
SF 1.0	Exclusion	Risk based
SF 2.0	ESG integration	
SF 3.0	Impact lending; microfinance	Value based

Source: Expansion of Table 1.4 in Chapter 1.

91 per cent in the Euro area is provided through bank credit, and only 65 per cent through equity. By contrast, equity is the most important form of financing for the private sector in the United States at 147 per cent. Moreover, close to 60 per cent of bank credit is provided in the form of mortgages on residential and commercial real estate (Jordà, Schularick, and Taylor, 2016). Real estate is thus very important for banks.

10.3.1 INTEGRATING SUSTAINABILITY INTO LENDING

There are two broad approaches towards integrating sustainability into lending: risk based and value based (Jeucken, 2004). Table 10.2 illustrates that sustainable finance (SF) 1.0 and 2.0 are risk based, with a focus on how to incorporate ESG factors in the credit risk assessment. SF 1.0 puts unsustainable companies on an exclusion list to avoid reputation risk. SF 2.0 is more advanced and includes social and environmental factors and risks in the calculation of the risk premium. Banks use new information on ESG factors to calculate the credit risk of companies operating on linear business models. Section 10.5 discusses SF 3.0, which is value based with a focus on lending to companies and projects that are transforming to sustainable business models.

10.4 **Risk-based approach towards sustainable lending**

In the *risk-based approach*, various social and environmental factors and risks are included in the credit risk analysis. These risks can affect both the probability of default p and the loss given default $(1-\gamma)$ in Equation 10.1. A wide range of economic, environmental, and social sustainability criteria is provided in Table 10.3. Contaminated sites and toxic waste, for example, are ranked as economic instead of environmental, because they have a major impact on the economic profit. They are also likely to lead to high loss given default, given the large costs of cleaning-up and potential liability risks. Other

Table 10.3 Sustainability criteria integrated into credit risk management

Economic sustainability criteria	Environmental sustainability criteria	Social sustainability criteria
Net debt service	Costs of environmental measures	Wage policy
Sustained growth	Emissions	Health policy
Quality of growth	Environmentally friendly construction	Social security of the employees
Sector development	Consideration of nature and landscape	Workers' participation
Integration of environmental aspect in economic decision-making	Soil erosion	Conservation of workplaces
Robustness against crises	Sealing of soil	Flexible working conditions and working hours
Personal resources	Sewage emission	
Community relations	Sewage quality	
Risk of accidents	Air emission	
Job creation	Noise emission	
Adequate firm size	Resource protection	
Eco-efficiency	Material use	
Information and communication	Ratio of renewable resources	
Material productivity	Use of non-renewable energy sources	
Spatial relation	Use of renewable energy	
Commuter mobility	Use of water (amount)	
Fleet		
Energy efficiency		
Technical update of power plants and machines		
Amount of waste		
Waste management		
Toxic waste		
Contaminated sites		
Technology management		
Material substitution		
Longevity		
Recycling capacity		
Redemption of used products		
Miniaturization of products		
Ecological product design		
Contracting		

Source: Weber, Scholz, and Michalik (2010).

criteria, such as soil erosion or emissions, are environmental. Finally, wage and health policies are examples of social sustainability criteria. Integrating these sustainability criteria in the credit risk management procedures, Weber, Scholz, and Michalik (2010) find that the ability of a credit rating system to predict defaults and non-defaults correctly improves by nearly 5 per cent.

These sustainability criteria should not only be incorporated in the credit risk assessment phase, but should also be used to determine the cost price of the loan: the credit spread or risk premium. A higher interest rate pushes companies to invest more in socially and environmentally friendly business models (see Section 10.4.5 on incentives for sustainable lending). Banks can thus help change the perspective of companies and foster sustainable development. The engagement of banks on sustainability topics and dialogue with their clients in the respective industries is important.

In a similar vein, Zeidan, Boechat, and Fleury (2015) developed a more refined Sustainability Credit Score System. They explicitly recognize that sustainable development is about the future. In addition to business as usual, they examine the sustainable business stage (mid-term, around 2020) resulting from adopting new sustainable practices by companies, and the future sustainable business stage (long term, around 2050) marked by the foreseen role of the industry in achieving sustainable development. From these development stages of a company, Zeidan, Boechat, and Fleury (2015) deduce risks and opportunities, which are the source of their credit score system. The Sustainability Credit Score System follows several steps:

1. Analysing the company's industry: economic outlook, product life-cycle analysis, value chain, legislation and public policy, industry self-regulation, and innovation.
2. Developing paths for the average company: business as usual, sustainable business, and future sustainable business.
3. Defining variables related to individual companies, in each of six sustainability dimensions: economic growth, environmental protection, social progress, socio-economic development, eco-efficiency, and socio-environmental development.
4. Unveiling the materiality issues pertaining to the average company, plus vulnerabilities and opportunities regarding the sustainability of the industry.
5. Combining the information on steps 1–4 to obtain questions for the composition of the score system.
6. Defining the weights for the six sustainability dimensions.

The result is a credit score system that rates companies and is composed of six matrices for the six sustainability dimensions. For each dimension, five questions are formulated. A final questionnaire of 30 questions is developed. The relative scores on the answers are then weighted (step 6). The final output is a sustainability credit score that ranges from 0 to 1 and is used as tool to assess the sustainability of a company in a selected industry (Zeidan, Boechat, and Fleury, 2015). This detailed approach allows banks to assess the sustainability risks and opportunities of their (potential) borrowers in a forward-looking way. The sustainability credit scores can be used as criteria to improve a bank's lending policies. As these credit score models have only recently been introduced, there is still no hard evidence that incorporating sustainability into credit score systems leads to less defaults.

Box 10.1 provides an example where ING links the interest rate on a loan facility for health technology company Philips to its sustainability performance and rating. If the rating goes up, the interest rate goes down and vice versa. Philips is thus incentivized to improve its sustainability, while ING reduces the risk of its loan.

For the risk-based approach, a challenge is to focus on material factors and risks, which differ across companies. The social and environmental risks can be incorporated in an online scoring system or in a tailored approach (as discussed earlier in this section). In line with new reporting methods, banks should request companies to submit their business plan based on integrated reporting (see Chapter 6). In that way, social and natural capitals are included in the analysis together with financial capital.

Banks are increasingly adopting sustainability policy frameworks stating their policies on social and environmental issues. These general policy

BOX 10.1 ING PROVIDES SUSTAINABLE LOAN TO PHILIPS

In April 2017, the health-care technology company Philips agreed an innovative €1bn loan facility with a consortium of banks that features an interest rate linked to the technology firm's year-on-year sustainability performance. The nature of the revolving credit facility means if Philips' sustainability performance improves, the interest rate it has to pay goes down, and vice versa. The five-year loan facility, which matures in April 2022, will be used for 'general corporate purposes'. The loan differs from previous green loans and bonds, where the pricing was linked to specific green covenants, or the use of proceeds was limited to green purposes.

As part of the consortium of 16 banks offering the loan, ING Bank has conducted the credit risk assessment and acts as the sustainability coordinator for the syndicated loan. Philips' current sustainability performance has been assessed and benchmarked by Sustainalytics, an independent provider of environmental, social, and corporate governance research and ratings.

ING indicates that the loan agreement with Philips was an additional way for the bank to support and reward clients seeking to become more sustainable. The loan facility follows Philips' 'Healthy People, Sustainable Planet' programme, through which it is aiming to become 'carbon-neutral' throughout its global operations and source all of its electricity needs from renewable sources by 2020 (SDG 12) and to improve the lives of 3 billion people a year by 2025 by making the world healthier and more sustainable through innovation (SDG 3).

Source: ING and Philips.

frameworks can be augmented with specific sector policies for socially or environmentally sensitive sectors to which particular banks are more heavily exposed. Leading agricultural banks, such as the Australian Westpac and the Dutch Rabobank, have, for example, developed sector-specific policies for agribusiness (see Box 10.2).

BOX 10.2 LENDING POLICIES FOR AGRIBUSINESS

While agribusiness plays a fundamental role worldwide in feeding the global population, reducing poverty, and supporting livelihoods, the sector has a range of environmental and social impacts.

Deforestation is a big environmental concern in Australia and Southeast Asia. Without clear policies to regenerate degraded forests and protect existing forest tracts on a massive scale, Australia stands to lose a large proportion of its remaining endemic biodiversity (Bradshaw, 2012). Westpac, one of the four big Australian banks, has prioritized the establishment of internal mechanisms such that by 2020 all corporate banking customers whose operations include significant production or processing of palm oil, timber products, or soy in markets at high risk of tropical deforestation can verify that these operations are consistent with zero net deforestation.

Climate change, raw material scarcity, environmental contamination, and an exploding world population are problems that will strongly influence each other in the coming decades. As a global food and agri bank, Rabobank looks for sustainable solutions in the food and agri chain and has formulated the following five guiding principles for its food and agribusiness:

1. **Safe and sufficient food production**: Experts forecast that to meet the food needs of the growing world population, worldwide food production will have to double between now and 2050. The first priority in the food and agri chain is to meet the world's food needs at a reasonable price, with products that are not a threat to human and animal health.
2. **Responsible use of natural resources**: Ensuring the continuity of food production will require attention to factors such as soil degradation and erosion and soil and surface water pollution. The water available to the food and agri chain must be conserved, overfishing must be prevented, and valuable nature areas must be protected.
3. **Promotion of smart choices on the part of citizens and customers**: Food and agribusinesses can better inform consumers of the origins of products to enable them to make better choices. As the demand for sustainable products rises, the use of sustainable production methods will increase.
4. **Responsible animal husbandry and stock management**: The way animals are treated by actors in the livestock chain (livestock farmers, dealers, fish farmers, animal transporters) must be appropriate to a society with high legal and ethical standards.
5. **Promoting social welfare**: The food and agri chains can only truly be called sustainable when they safeguard the social welfare and living environment of the people working within this environment. This means eliminating corruption, discrimination, human rights violations, forced labour, harmful child labour practices, and poor working conditions.

Source: Westpac Group (2014); Rabobank (2017).

10.4.1 COMPETITION IN SUSTAINABLE LENDING

While banks should incorporate ESG factors in their risk management to improve their risk profile and track record on responsible lending, they can also (mis)use ESG factors to undercut competitors. By ignoring standards on banning child labour or land degradation, less responsible banks could continue to provide project finance, often in developing countries, where more responsible banks would refuse finance because of social and environmental concerns.

Social and environmental risks in project finance can be divided into three types (Weber, 2017b). First, projects have an impact on the environment and society, known as their inside-out relation. Although this is typical for many business activities, big projects, such as hydro dams or mining projects, have greater impacts than smaller business activities. Secondly, projects may be affected by environmental or societal risks: the outside in. The income of a project may suffer from environmental risks, such as extreme weather events, workers' strikes, and non-governmental organization (NGO)- or government-initiated blockades or delays of permits because of the reputation of a project sponsor. Thirdly, project financiers are exposed to reputation risk. Project-related controversies published in the news or on websites may affect not only project sponsors but also project financiers.

To avoid negative competition on ESG standards, leading international banks developed the Equator Principles in 2010. These Equator Principles aim to be a global benchmark, providing a framework for due diligence to support responsible risk decision-making on social and environmental issues in financing projects.

The most recent Equator Principles (2013) are as follows:

1. **Review and Categorization**: When a client proposes a project for financing, the bank categorizes, as part of its internal environmental and social review and due diligence, the project based on the magnitude of its potential environmental and social risks and impacts.
2. **Environmental and Social Assessment**: When the project has (potential) adverse social and environmental risks, the bank requires the client to conduct an assessment to address the relevant social and environmental risks and impacts on the proposed project to the bank's satisfaction.
3. **Applicable Environmental and Social Standards**: The assessment process should address compliance with relevant host country laws, regulations, and permits for environmental and social issues. In countries without a proper regulatory and institutional framework, the performance standards on environmental and social sustainability of the International Financial Corporation are applicable.
4. **Environmental and Social Management System**: For projects with (potential) adverse risks, the bank requires the client to develop or maintain an environmental and social management system.

5. **Stakeholder Engagement:** For projects with (potential) adverse risks, the bank requires the client to demonstrate effective stakeholder engagement as an ongoing process in a structured and culturally appropriate manner with affected communities and, where relevant, other stakeholders.
6. **Grievance Mechanism:** For projects with adverse risks, the bank requires the client to establish a grievance mechanism designed to receive and facilitate resolution of concerns and grievances about the project's environmental and social performance.
7. **Independent Review:** For projects with adverse risks, an independent environmental and social consultant carries out an independent review and assesses compliance with Equator Principles.
8. **Covenants:** For all projects, the client covenants in the financing documentation to comply with all relevant host country environmental and social laws, regulations, and permits in all material respects. Where a client is not in compliance with its environmental and social covenants, the bank works with the client on remedial actions to bring the project back into compliance. If the client fails to re-establish compliance within an agreed grace period, the bank reserves the right to exercise remedies, as considered appropriate.

The Equator Principles are a good starting point and have been adopted by 91 international banks, covering over 70 per cent of project finance (see Table 4.3 in Chapter 4). But there are also limitations. There is no mechanism to monitor adherence to the principles by member banks, as explained in Table 4.3. Weber (2017a) finds that though the participating banks follow the reporting guidelines, only about 5 per cent disclose all the information required by the guidelines. Weber recommends that further mechanisms, such as standardization and assurance, are needed to guarantee transparent reporting of environmental and social project risks. Moreover, the Equator Principles assess climate impact on the basis of scope 1 and 2 greenhouse gas (GHG) emissions, while the Bloomberg principles recommend disclosure of scope 1, scope 2, and, if appropriate, scope 3 GHG emissions and the related risks.

10.4.2 REGULATORY APPROACH TO SUSTAINABLE LENDING

A more direct, albeit not widespread, approach is regulatory guidance. Brazil is a frontrunner in this field. In an effort to preserve the rainforest, the Brazilian central bank has issued a number of resolutions on socio-environmental risk to strengthen the efficiency and soundness of the financial system, including on forestry and low-carbon agriculture. Following a voluntary Green Protocol from the banking sector and considerable dialogue, the Brazilian central bank introduced requirements for all banks to establish socio-environmental risk systems based on the principles of relevance and proportionality and to integrate socio-environmental risks in its risk assessment alongside the more traditional credit, market, and operational risks. The underlying assumption of the Brazilian regulatory requirements is that integrating environmental and social factors into risk management is a way of strengthening the resilience of the financial system (UNEP Inquiry, 2015).

10.4.3 EVIDENCE ON SUSTAINABLE LENDING

On the empirical side, Chava (2014) reports that many large banks have started to incorporate climate change concerns in their lending decisions, with some explicitly stating a target for reducing GHG emissions in their lending. Bank debt is an important source of debt financing, even for large public companies (see Figure 10.3). If a significant number of lenders adopt environmentally sensitive lending policies, this could have an impact on the cost of borrowers' debt capital. Chava (2014) finds that lenders charge a significantly higher interest rate on bank loans to companies with environmental concerns compared to companies without such concerns. Banks are concerned about both environmental issues that are already regulated, such as hazardous waste and substantial emissions of toxic chemicals, and environmental concerns that are not yet regulated, such as GHGs or other climate change aspects. At the same time, Chava (2014) finds that lenders charge lower interest rates on bank loans to companies that derive significant revenue from environmentally beneficial products.

In another study, Goss and Roberts (2011) examine the link between corporate social responsibility (CSR) and bank debt. Are banks exploiting their specialized role as delegated monitors of the company? Using a sample of 3,996 loans to US companies, Goss and Roberts (2011) find that companies with social responsibility concerns pay between 7 and 18 basis points more than companies that are more responsible. Lenders are more sensitive to CSR concerns in the absence of security. Low-quality borrowers that engage in discretionary CSR spending face higher loan spreads and shorter maturities, as bank lenders are afraid of wasteful CSR expenditures. The latter is consistent with the overinvestment hypothesis.

In a study on the Canadian banking system, Weber (2012) reports that Canadian banks integrate environmental risks into credit risk management strategies and procedures to avoid financial risks. However, the six large commercial banks in particular manage sustainability and the environment in isolation rather than as a part of the general business strategy. By contrast, the smaller credit union, Vancity, emphasizes the opportunity to have a positive impact on the environment through all its products and services. Consequently, a significant part of its lending portfolio is invested in projects with a social impact (see Section 10.5 on values-based banking).

10.4.4 BARRIERS TO SUSTAINABLE LENDING

There are barriers to integrate sustainability into lending decisions. Banks need to train their account managers to understand social and environmental risks and also to include these risks in the due diligence of clients and the calculation of the risk premium. That is a major task, because banks have many account managers, which are typically trained to grant loans whenever possible. While the sustainability frameworks, as described in Section 10.4, are implemented top down, banks can monitor and compare adoption across business units.

Another barrier is the status quo of existing clients. If they are not prepared to adapt their business model it may become difficult to impose change on them. Clients may not appreciate a higher risk premium due to unsustainable business practices. Account managers may be reluctant to fully impose such a higher risk premium on clients with whom they have a long-standing relationship. A typical approach taken is to phase in new requirements in the form of a higher risk premium for, or a ban on, unsustainable activities (see Box 10.3).

Finally, the maturity of bank loans is typically well below ten years, while social and environmental risks are more long term (but may materialize much sooner than expected). Myopic bankers may thus ignore these risks in their short- to medium-term credit decisions. But the underlying collateral, such as real estate, can have longer maturities and lose their value. Also companies may become unviable in the short to medium term when they do not adapt their business models in time (see Chapter 5).

10.4.5 INCENTIVES FOR SUSTAINABLE LENDING

Banks can choose to charge a higher rate (risk premium) for loans with ESG risks or a lower rate (discount) for loans without ESG risks. The *nudging*

BOX 10.3 BANNING NEW OR EXISTING CLIENTS

In November 2017, BNP Paribas decided to cease its financing related to tobacco companies, because of the negative impact on the health of its customers. This decision concerned all professional players whose principal activity is linked or dedicated to tobacco. BNP Paribas announced it would respect existing contracts, but would not engage in any new financing of tobacco companies. Tobacco loans will thus be phased out over time, as existing loan contracts mature.

However, there have also been cases of banning existing clients. A case in point is the controversial Dakota Access Pipeline, which affects the indigenous population. A number of banks have pulled out the $2.5bn credit line provided by 17 banks funding the controversial pipeline, following environmental and human rights concerns from the public and big investors that it would contaminate drinking water and damage sacred burial sites of the Standing Rock Sioux tribe. In early 2017, several banks, including ING, BNP Paribas, and some Scandinavian banks, sold their loan to the oil pipeline.

Sources: BNP Paribas (2017); *Financial Times* (2017).

BOX 10.4 ENERGY-EFFICIENT MORTGAGES

The EU has set itself an overall 20 per cent energy savings target by 2020 and is considering increasing this to a 30 per cent target by 2030. In the EU, buildings are responsible for 40 per cent of total energy consumption and 36 per cent of carbon emissions. About 35 per cent of the EU's buildings are over 50 years old and 75–90 per cent of the building stock is predicted to remain standing in 2050, making energy efficient renovation a top priority for Europe. By improving the energy efficiency of buildings alone, the EU's total energy consumption could be reduced by 5–6 per cent and carbon emissions by 5 per cent. Improving the energy efficiency of the current housing stock will play a crucial role in reducing energy consumption and carbon emissions.

The scale of the investment needed to meet the 2020 target is estimated at around €100 billion per year, with it considered necessary beyond that to invest €100 billion per year until 2050 in EU building stock in order to deliver Europe's commitments on climate change. The EU has increased the amount of public funds available for energy efficiency, but the European Commission suggests there is a need to boost private energy efficiency investments.

The European Mortgage Federation (2017) launched a project to deliver a pan-European private financing initiative to support households in making energy efficient improvements to their homes, which is independent from public money and tax relief. The idea is to incentivize homeowners to move their properties out of the 'brown' zone (e.g. energy rating E–G) and into the 'green' zone (e.g. energy rating A–D) by way of preferential interest rates or additional funds at the time of origination of the mortgage. This private market initiative leads to a win-win situation for the mortgage provider and the household.

Similarly, it can be expected that the interest rate on new houses in the green zone will become the standard, with higher rates on energy inefficient houses. The underlying rationale is that energy efficient houses will maintain their collateral value in the medium to long term, while energy inefficient houses will decline in value. The same applies to commercial real estate, where energy inefficient offices and shopping centres are quickly losing their value and thereby their access to finance.

theory of change (Thaler and Sunstein, 2008) suggests applying a base lending rate for projects with low or no ESG risks and a risk premium (or credit spread) for projects with ESG concerns. The default option is then a low interest rate for ESG-compliant projects. Box 10.4 reports on an initiative to create a standardized 'energy-efficient mortgage', which can impact consumer behaviour. The heating and cooling of real estate is a major source of GHG emissions (see Figure 2.9 in Chapter 2). Moreover, up to 60 per cent of bank lending is related to mortgages, as reported in Section 10.3.

In a similar way, the *capital adequacy framework* can be employed to nudge banks towards lending to low ESG risk projects (Schoenmaker and Van Tilburg, 2016). There is evidence that regulated banks reduce lending in response to tighter capital requirements (Aiyar, Calomiris, and Wieladek, 2014). Green projects are not necessarily safer, as there is inherent uncertainty about technology (which renewable technologies will become cheaper and win) and climate change (what will happen to global warming and subsequent carbon taxes). Faced with this uncertainty, there is no reason to lower capital risk weights for green exposures. To differentiate between green and brown exposures, the risk weights for brown assets can be increased. That is justified because brown assets might become stranded (see Chapter 2). With an effective wedge between risk weights, banks can be nudged towards green lending. The new Bloomberg recommendations for climate-related financial disclosures (TCFD, 2017) can be used to determine the carbon intensity of companies and subsequent capital surcharge.

But the use of the capital framework for sustainability policies is controversial. Carney (2015) argues that attempts to accelerate the financing of a low-carbon economy by adjusting the capital regime for banks and insurers are flawed. History shows the danger of attempting to use such changes in prudential rules—designed to protect financial stability—for other ends. Carney (2015) continues:

> Financial policymakers will not drive the transition to a low-carbon economy. It is not for a central banker to advocate for one policy response over another. That is for governments to decide.

As governments are ultimately responsible for the capital framework, they can decide to change the risk weights in pillar 1 of the Basel III capital framework (see Box 2.4). In addition, supervisors could apply a pillar 2 capital add-on for a concentration of brown exposures, provided that there is sufficient evidence.

China has implemented a more direct approach towards sustainable lending (Weber, 2017a). The Green Credit Policy, implemented in 2006, is overseen by three agencies, the Ministry of Environmental Protection, the Peoples' Bank of China, and the China Banking Regulatory Commission. The Green Credit Policy demands that banks restrict loans to polluting industries and offer adjusted interest rates depending on the environmental performance of the borrowers' industries. Pollution control facilities as well as borrowers involved in environmental protection and infrastructure, renewable energy, circular economics, and environmentally friendly agriculture qualify for loans with reduced interest rates. The Green Credit Policy even asks lenders to limit loans to polluting industries, and to withdraw loans that have been already provided should environmental controversies or instances of non-compliance occur. Furthermore, interest rates for polluting industries have to be higher than for non-polluting borrowers.

The regulations are compulsory for all Chinese banks, regardless of whether they are government owned, joint-stock banks, or credit unions. This coordinated approach mitigates free-riding and competition effects to a minimum. Moreover, the Chinese government has a lot of control on the interest rate differential, so it can easily influence that simultaneously. Finally, from 2009 to 2013, China recovered quite well from the financial crisis, giving the policy a potential confounding effect.

Weber (2017a) finds that the environmental and social performance of Chinese banks increased significantly between 2009 and 2013. Furthermore, he determines a two-way causality between financial performance and sustainability performance of Chinese banks. These findings suggest that corporate sustainability performance and financial performance are not trade-offs but correlate positively.

10.5 Values-based banking

In *values-based banking*, banks lend to companies that transition to the sustainable economy. VBBs are mission driven: it is part of their mission to let their money work for projects with a positive societal impact. Linking to the United Nations Sustainable Development Goals (SDGs), VBBs provide lending services to individuals and companies that deliver value to, or have a positive impact on, society in the areas of:

- **Economic resilience** through microfinance for individuals and microenterprises and economic inclusion.
- **Social empowerment** through education, health care, social inclusion, and special needs housing.
- **Environmental regeneration** through renewable energy, energy efficiency or retrofits, green-oriented housing and buildings, sustainable agriculture, and water efficiency and access.

The GABV (2017 and 2018) has developed a *scorecard* to measure the societal impact, which is central in the mission of VBBs. Financial viability of prospective lending projects is an important condition, but not a goal in itself (see SF 3.0 in Chapter 1). While the risk-based approach is two-dimensional, the values-based approach is three-dimensional, looking at return, risk, and impact (see Figure 10.4). Project proposals are submitted to a bank's credit committee, which judges the viability of projects in an integrated way, considering both impact and risk.

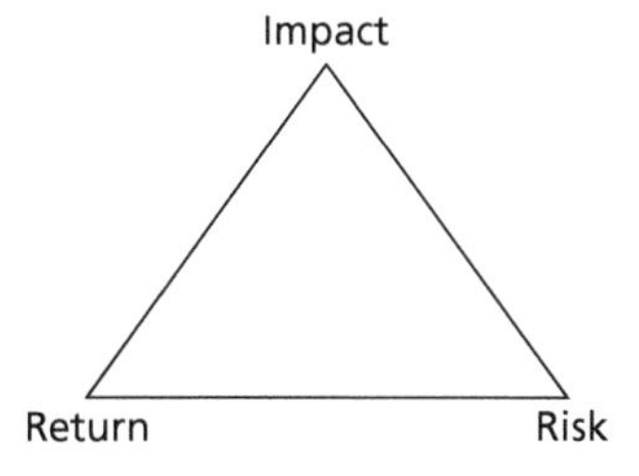

Figure 10.4 Dimensions of values-based banking

Table 10.4 Scorecard for values-based banking

Quantitative factors	Weight	Minimum	Benchmark
Financial viability			
Return on average assets (3-year average)	10%	0%	Peer market
Equity/total assets	10%	3%	8%
Low-quality assets	5%	0%	Peer market
Real economy focus			
Real economy exposures/total assets	15%	30%	65%
Real economy revenues/total revenues	10%	50%	75%
Client funding/total assets	10%	30%	75%
Triple bottom line focus			
Triple bottom line exposures/total exposures	40%	10%	55%

Qualitative factors	Consistent analysis of factors
1) Leadership	Values-based mission, strategy, and culture; gender diversity
2) Organizational structure	Values-based commitment of owners and partner organizations
3) Products and services	Impact of products and services; gender diversity clients
4) Management systems	Risk and lending processes; capital allocation; ALM
5) Human resources	Recruitment; training; culture; compensation equality
6) Performance reporting	Publicly available information on ESG activities and impacts

Note: The scorecard methodology consists of a quantitative and qualitative part. ALM = asset and liability management.
Source: Adapted from GABV (2017 and 2018).

The scorecard methodology in Table 10.4 consists of a quantitative and a qualitative part. The quantitative part has three segments: (i) financial viability; (ii) real economy focus (see Section 10.2); and (iii) triple bottom line focus. The real economy focus and the triple bottom line focus are key elements that differentiate values-based banking from other banking models. The weight of the factors is in the second column of Table 10.4, where the triple bottom line impact deliberately receives the largest weight at 40 per cent. For each factor, the relative score between the minimum (score 0) to the benchmark (score 100) is calculated. The benchmark for the triple bottom line is a net score, whereby positive impact projects contribute positively, neutral impact projects have no contribution, and negative impact projects contribute negatively. The quantitative factors yield a base score ranging from 0 to 100.

The qualitative part captures a bank's core culture and capabilities in the six core areas of: (i) leadership; (ii) organizational structure; (iii) products and services; (iv) management systems; (v) human resources; and (vi) performance reporting. The GABV is developing a methodology for a consistent analysis of the qualitative factors. The qualitative assessment allows for an increase/decrease of 20 in the base score, with the calibrated score capped at 100.

Values-based banking, also called impact lending, works on the principle of inclusion. Projects that meet the (minimum) criteria on societal impact form the universe of environmental and social projects that are eligible for lending. Examples of such non-financial criteria are bio-based farming in agriculture, humane care and use of animals in health care research, and a high energy-efficiency label for real estate.

Impact lending is about lending to companies that are changing, or have changed, their business model from the linear to the sustainable economy. This process of change also creates uncertainty. Which technology is going to win, for example, wind or solar energy? Are electric cars the cars of the future (justifying the high stock valuation of Tesla at the time of writing in early 2018) or is it a bubble? Because of this inherent uncertainty, there is a need for scenario thinking in the assessment of credit risk.

An example of uncertainty is the transition towards circular business models:

- demand for circular products needs to develop;
- entire supply chain needs to adapt;
- it takes longer time to break even.

10.5.1 FINANCING CIRCULAR BUSINESS MODELS

The *linear production and consumption system* is based on extraction of raw materials (take), processing into products (make), consumption (use), and disposal (waste). The financing of the linear production process is relatively straightforward, because the bank can use the buildings, machine equipment, raw materials, semi-finished and finished products as collateral for the required loans. These loans can subsequently be repaid when products are sold to consumers (sales model).

By contrast, the *circular production system* is restorative or regenerative by intention and design. The use of raw materials is minimized and their reuse is maximized at the end of the lifetime of a product. To optimize the reuse of raw materials, ownership often stays with the producer as the party in the value chain that can make the most productive use of these materials. Chapter 5 highlights the product-as-a-service model, whereby the producer offers the products to end users for the required utilization period, including repair and maintenance. After this period, the producer can refurbish or remanufacture the product.

But the product-as-a-service model raises also legal and financial questions. A builder would, for example, remain the legal owner of the bricks of a new house or office building, as he could reuse them when the house is demolished at the end of its lifetime. On the legal side, the bricks are a rigid part of the house and cannot be separated, which prohibits separate legal ownership of the bricks by the builder. On the financing side, the bricks generate future CFs in the form of periodic lease payments instead of a current CF at the time of sale.

In practice, therefore, circular business models design products in a more circular way extending the lifetime (use of materials in the product cycle) and reuse (use in multiple product cycles). In our example, a house can be constructed and built in such a way that the raw materials can be more easily recaptured at the end of its lifetime. Rau and Oberhuber (2016) introduce the concept of a materials passport, so that the specifications and value of materials can be traced. A materials passport specifies the bricks, glass, beams, wiring, and so on used in a building. It also requires a transformation of the production process to ensure that raw materials can be put together and subsequently decomposed in an energy- and cost-efficient way.

Oliver Wyman (2017) estimates that 65 per cent of Dutch circular businesses struggle to obtain financing. Banks need to develop risk mitigation mechanisms to make them bankable. In the start-up phase, the owner-entrepreneur, family members, or venture capitalists provide equity financing to circular business. As circular start-ups become SMEs, they normally begin to access banking lending. As is the case in other innovation markets with a large technology component, bank funding for the *circular economy* is more complex. The cost of assessing creditworthiness through established procedures is out of proportion with the relatively small size and significant risk of the loans.

Given the likely growth of circular business models, banks should see this effort as a strategic investment that can generate growth and attractive economics. Examples could include obtaining guarantees or insurance for CFs and supply-chain risks or reviewing collateral eligibility criteria to include circular technology.

Just as the circular economy requires a redesign of manufacturing and services systems, it also requires a redesign of the financing model (Ewen et al. 2017). Circular products have a longer lifespan and a higher residual value. This requires a larger investment with a longer payback period, while bank loans cover typically five to seven years. The additional CFs from the longer lifespan and higher residual value should be taken into account by the bank. Moreover, a larger investment is needed to ensure the circularity of the product, component, or raw materials through ownership or cooperation in the supply chain, which leads to a lease or service model (see Chapter 5). The remaining ownership of the product creates a concentration risk for the producer or intermediary in the supply chain. Car leasing companies had, for example, to write down on diesel cars in their car fleet, when several cities (notably in Germany and the Netherlands) started to ban diesel cars from city centres, which reduced their second-hand value (see Section 2.3 on stranded assets).

Circular products also have advantages as they reduce reliance on scarce raw materials in the production process. Finally, the move from a sales to a service model produces more stable CFs. Several strategies can be adopted to facilitate the financing of circular business (Ewen et al. 2017):

1. reducing technological risk;
2. cooperation in supply chain;

3. phasing of finance (just in time);
4. isolation of least risky part of business for financing;
5. pre-financing by client;
6. move from historical financials to future CFs in credit evaluation.

Furthermore, the product design can be adapted. The option to easily uninstall removable office walls or light armaments makes it possible to use these products as collateral (with a haircut for the risk on the collateral). At the more basic level, the underlying raw materials can be used as collateral, which is facilitated by the materials passport (see Chapter 5). In sum, new integrated thinking is needed for the financing of circular business models.

10.5.2 MICROFINANCE

Microfinance is a banking service that is provided to unemployed or low-income individuals or groups who otherwise have no other access to financial services. The pioneering business models grew out of experiments in low-income countries such as Bolivia and Bangladesh—rather than from adaptations of standard banking models in richer countries (Armendáriz and Morduch, 2010). Box 10.5 describes the roots of microfinance.

BOX 10.5 THE ROOTS OF MICROFINANCE

The roots of microfinance go back to Muhammad Yunus and the founding of Bangladesh's Grameen Bank. In the mid-1970s, Bangladesh was starting to build a new nation after independence from Pakistan had been won after a fierce war and widespread flooding had caused a famine that killed tens of thousands. In 1973–4, government surveys found over 80 per cent of the population were living in poverty.

Muhammad Yunus, a trained economist, started a series of experiments lending to poor households in a nearby village, Jobra. Even the little money he could lend from his own pocket was enough for villagers to run simple business activities like rice husking and bamboo weaving. Yunus found that borrowers were not only profiting greatly by access to the loans but that they were also repaying reliably, even though the villagers could offer no collateral. Realizing that he could only go so far with his own resources, Yunus convinced the central bank of Bangladesh to help him set up a special branch that catered to the poor of Jobra. That soon spawned another trial project, this time in Tangail in north-central Bangladesh. Assured that the successes were not region-specific flukes, Grameen went nationwide.

One innovation that allowed Grameen to grow was group lending, a mechanism that essentially allows the poor borrowers to act as guarantors for each other. With group lending in place, the bank could quickly grow village by village as funding permitted. And funding—supplied in the early years by the International Fund for Agriculture and Development, the Ford Foundation, and the governments of Bangladesh, Sweden, Norway, and the Netherlands—permitted rapid growth indeed.

The 2006 Nobel Peace Prize was awarded to the microfinance pioneers Muhammad Yunus and Grameen Bank.

Source: Armendáriz and Morduch (2010).

Table 10.5 Missions of the ten largest microfinance institutions

Institution	Outreach (as % of country's population)	Country	Legal status	Main mission	Other mission(s)
Grameen Bank	4.4%	Bangladesh	Regulated bank	Poverty reduction	Focus on women
ASA	3.3%	Bangladesh	NGO	Income generation	Integrate women
Vietnam Bank for Social Policies	5.4%	Vietnam	State-owned regulated bank	Poverty reduction	Low interest rates
BRAC*	2.9%	Bangladesh	NGO	Poverty reduction	Literacy & disease
BRI	1.4%	Indonesia	Regulated bank	Wide financial services to small entrepreneurs	Best corporate governance & profits for stakeholders
Spandana	0.1%	India	Regulated financial institution	Leading financial service provider	Marketable & equitable solutions for benefit of stakeholders
SHARE	0.1%	India	Regulated financial institution	Poverty reduction	Focus on women
Caja Popular Mexicana	0.6%	Mexico	Regulated cooperative	Cooperative for improving members' quality of life	Offer competitive financial products to its members
Compartamos	0.6%	Mexico	Regulated bank	Create development opportunities	Develop 'trust relationships'
Banco Caja Social of Columbia	1.3%	Colombia	Regulated bank	Leading in 'popular banking'	To develop social objectives among community members

Note: * Formerly the Bangladesh Rural Advancement Committee.
Source: Armendáriz and Szafarz (2011).

While it started with 'microcredit' referring to small loans, 'microfinance' currently comprises efforts to collect savings from low-income households, to provide insurance and to also help in distributing and marketing clients' output. In this banking chapter, we focus on lending and savings (deposits). Chapter 11 covers microinsurance. The primary focus of microfinance is on poverty reduction and social change. Table 10.5 shows the missions of the ten largest microfinance institutions worldwide. The majority of these institutions are regulated and privately operating banks, with poverty reduction, income generation, or improving quality of life as their main missions. Other missions include focus on women and low interest rates. The first five banks from Table 10.5 have an outreach of 2 to 5 per cent of the country's population. To illustrate the working of microfinance, Box 10.6 details the operations of one of the oldest microfinance institutions: Bank Rakyat Indonesia (BRI).

One of the main challenges of microfinance is providing small loans at an affordable cost in the absence of marketable assets as collateral. In a seminal

BOX 10.6 BANK RAKYAT INDONESIA

In the world of microfinance, BRI is a giant with total assets of $70 billion. BRI is a majority government-owned bank with a main role of supporting national economic development in the vast archipelago. To achieve this, BRI has been focusing on micro-, small-, and medium-sized enterprises. Micro loans—below $10,000—make up a third of its loan book, the largest segment. Local farmers, for example, can, through these micro loans, increase their investments in fertilizer and seed and thus expand their planted area.

As more people across the globe go online to manage their finances, banks have been quick to offer smartphone apps for paying on the move. But in rural Indonesia 'mobile banking' has a very different meaning: it involves putting a loan officer, a bank teller, and a security guard into a van or a boat and sending them to remote areas to facilitate the provision of banking services to the as yet unreachable and unserviceable segments of the population. In 2016, BRI launched its own satellite to connect its mobile vans and boats as part of its network of over 10,000 banking offices. While BRI has 56 million customers, only 36 per cent of the population aged 15 and above possess a bank account in Indonesia.

BRI operates on sound financial principles. Tier 1 capital is over 20 per cent of risk-weighted assets. ROE has been above 20 per cent over the last five years, with non-performing loans not exceeding 2 per cent. This makes BRI a creditworthy bank that makes riskier, high-margin micro loans. These have interest rates as high as 22 per cent, completely funded by deposits paying below 5 per cent.

Sources: BRI 2016 Annual Report; *Financial Times* (2015).

book, Armendáriz and Morduch (2010) analyse the economics of microfinance. Microfinance is seen as a way to break the vicious circle by reducing transactions costs and overcoming information problems. Banks typically face relatively high transactions costs when working in poor communities as handling many small transactions is far more expensive than servicing one large transaction for a richer borrower.

Moreover, banks have incomplete information about poor borrowers (adverse selection), while poor borrowers have no collateral to offer as security to banks (moral hazard). The social capital of communities is typically applied to ensure repayment, for example, through group lending (see Box 10.5). Feigenberg, Field, and Pande (2010) indicate that group lending is successful in achieving low rates of default without collateral not only because it harnesses existing social capital, as has been emphasized in the literature, but also because it builds new social capital among participants. Armendáriz and Morduch (2010) report that the average interest rate, after adjusting for inflation, is 25 per cent for NGOs. But far higher rates, from 35 to 100 per cent, are also found.

A key element of microfinance programmes has been the provision of small loans—microcredit—to poor women via neighbourhood groups. This approach thus claimed it had the potential to promote women's empowerment and alleviate poverty by including women in finance and business, as well as socially and politically, making it an attractive intervention all over the developing world. Garikipati and colleagues (2017) argue that the claims of empowerment have become controversial over time. Several recent systematic reviews have confirmed that results are mixed and effectiveness on a range of indicators of income and well-being is, at best, modest. The debate has broadened from the role of microfinance in empowering women to the question of whether and how negative discrimination might operate in the sector itself. There is evidence of discrimination in business lending worldwide and poverty and discrimination tend to go hand in hand. By targeting women, the microfinance sector has discriminated in favour of women in the initial stage of credit approval, but women face harsher credit rationing, which means that they are granted smaller loans than men.

Table 10.6 analyses the global outreach of microfinance institutions. Over 1,000 distinct microfinance institutions serve about 117 million borrowers and nearly 100 million depositors worldwide, in particular in Africa, South and East Asia and Latin America. The average loan and deposit size varies very widely across regions, partly in line with GDP per capita. The smallest loans are found in South Asia (about $280), while Eastern Europe and Latin America support the largest loans of $2,000 to $3,000. The average loan is about $800 and the average deposit $600.

10.5.2.1 Measuring impact

Despite the apparent success and popularity of microfinance, no clear evidence exists that microfinance programmes have positive impacts (Armendáriz and Morduch, 2010). A proper research design filters out village factors, observable and unobservable factors, and macroeconomic changes. Moreover, the results from the treatment group should be checked against a control group.

Table 10.6 Global outreach of microfinance institutions, 2015

Region	Number microfinance institutions	Number borrowers ('000)	Gross loans ($m)	Average loan ($)	Number depositors ('000)	Deposits ($m)	Average deposit ($)
Africa	193	5,778	8,490	1,469	17,928	9,212	514
East Asia and Pacific	136	16,258	15,064	927	16,118	7,687	477
Eastern Europe and Central Asia	136	3,083	9,900	3,211	5,091	7,664	1,505
Latin America and Caribbean	345	22,495	38,843	1,727	23,709	27,293	1,151
Middle East and North Africa	27	2,148	1,353	630	465	251	540
South Asia	196	66,929	18,794	281	35,109	6,886	196
Grand Total	1,033	116,691	92,444	792	98,420	58,993	599

Source: MIX Market (2015).

In a systematic review of over 2,600 studies, Duvendack and colleagues (2011) show that almost all impact evaluations of microfinance suffer from weak methodologies and inadequate data, thus the reliability of impact estimates are adversely affected. In studies based on randomized control trials, they do not find convincing improvement of well-being. Moreover, they find no robust evidence of positive impacts on women's status, or girls' enrolment in education, which is partly due to these topics not being addressed in valid studies.

Developing a measurement method, Zeller and colleagues (2006) pose the simple research question: To what extent does a project reach the poorest households in its intervention area? They construct a relative poverty index, which enables the measurement of the impact of microfinance. In an empirical study of microfinance in Bangladesh (where microfinance started), Mazumder and Lu (2015) find that microfinance appears to have reasonably increased recipients' access to basic rights and improved quality of life, as indicated by reduced food insecurity, improved nutrition, food, and health, improved clothing, housing, sanitation, and drinking water, and better health-care access and education facilities. The changes were stronger for private microfinance institutions than for government-related institutions.

10.6 **Conclusions**

Banks play a crucial role in the financing of business, both of SMEs and larger companies. In the credit evaluation process, potential borrowers have to provide banks with detailed private information on their business model. This chapter suggests that the credit assessment should also include social and environmental risks and factors. Banks can use this information to improve the risk assessment. Lower ESG risks can thus lead to lower borrowing costs, which provides an incentive for companies to transition to sustainable business models.

Banks can transform information on individual clients to sector-wide sustainability trends. They are thus instrumental in the diffusion of best business practices in sustainability. Furthermore, financial supervisors can employ the capital adequacy framework to penalize brown exposures with higher capital charges, which are warranted by the higher risks. All these credit risk-based methods are part of the risk-based approach to sustainable bank lending (SF 2.0).

Moving to values-based banking, banks only lend to companies or projects with a positive social or environmental impact (SF 3.0). Financial viability is an important condition, but no longer the goal. The goal is financing the transition to a sustainable economy. This requires an in-depth assessment of the sustainability of a company's business model in the screening phase.

Finally, microfinance is a banking service that is provided to unemployed or low-income individuals or groups who otherwise have no other access to financial services. This reinforces the important social function of banking: providing finance to business and households in society.

Key concepts used in this chapter

Capital adequacy framework defines the amount of capital a bank (or other financial institution) has to hold as required by its financial regulator; this is usually expressed as a capital adequacy ratio of equity that must be held as a percentage of risk-weighted assets or as a leverage ratio of equity as a percentage of total assets.

Circular economy is an industrial system that is restorative or regenerative by intention and design.

Commercial banking or *traditional banking* is the provision of long-term loans to firms and individuals that are funded by short-term deposits.

Free-rider problem is a market failure that occurs when people take advantage of being able to use a common resource (for example, information collected about an investment project) without paying for it.

Impact lending see *values-based banking*.

Investment banking relates to the delivery of bank services such as underwriting securities, advising on M&As, and managing assets.

Linear production and consumption system is based on extraction of raw materials (take), processing into products (make), consumption (use), and disposal (waste).

Loss given default is the loss on a bank loan in the case of the default of the borrower; it is (1—the recovery rate).

Microfinance is a banking service (lending, payments, and savings) for low-income individuals or micro-enterprises, which otherwise have no access to financial services.

Monitoring involves the screening of borrowers (adverse selection) and the controlling of the borrower during the project (moral hazard) to reduce asymmetric information between a bank and its borrowers.

Nudging theory is a concept in behavioural economics, which proposes positive reinforcement and indirect suggestions to try to achieve non-forced compliance to influence the motives, incentives, and decision-making of groups and individuals.

Probability of default is the probability that a borrower (company or household) defaults on its loan.

Proprietary trading occurs when financial firms trade equities, bonds, currencies, commodities, their derivatives, or other financial instruments for their own direct gain instead of earning commission income by trading on behalf of their clients.

Recovery rate is the amount a bank can recover on a loan when the borrower defaults; see also *loss given default.*

Risk-based approach to sustainable lending includes various social and environmental factors and risks in the (credit) risk analysis.

Risk premium or *credit risk spread* is the difference between the contracted loan rate and the risk free rate; the risk premium depends on the probability of default and the loss given default.

Scorecard can be used to measure the societal impact (in the form of economic resilience, social empowerment, and environmental regeneration) of a project for which a loan is requested.

Sustainable focused banks or *values-based banks* are banks that aim to deliver economic, social, and environmental impact as part of their mission statement.
Traditional banking see *commercial banking.*

Values-based banking or *impact lending* concerns the provisions of loans to individuals and companies that deliver value to, or have a positive impact on, society and the environment; values-based banking is mission driven.

SUGGESTED READING

Armendáriz, B. and J. Morduch (2010), *The Economics of Microfinance*, 2nd edn, MIT Press, Cambridge, MA.

Freixas, X. and J. C. Rochet (2008), *Microeconomics of Banking*, 2nd edn, MIT Press, Cambridge, MA.

Goss, A. and G. Roberts (2011), 'The impact of corporate social responsibility on the cost of bank loans', *Journal of Banking & Finance*, 35(7): 1794–810.

Jeucken, M. (2004), *Sustainability in Finance: Banking on the Planet*, Eburon Academic Publishers, Delft.

Weber, O. and B. Feltmate (2016), *Sustainable Banking: Managing the Social and Environmental Impact of Financial Institutions*, University of Toronto Press, Toronto.

REFERENCES

Aiyar, S., C. Calomiris, and T. Wieladek (2014), 'Does macro-prudential regulation leak? Evidence from a UK policy experiment', *Journal of Money, Credit and Banking*, 46(s1): 181–214.

Armendáriz, B. and J. Morduch (2010), *The Economics of Microfinance*, 2nd edn, MIT Press, Cambridge, MA.

Armendáriz, B. and A. Szafarz (2011), 'On mission drift in microfinance institutions', in: B. Armendáriz and M. Labie (eds.), *The Handbook of Microfinance*, World Scientific Publishing, London and Singapore, 341–66.

BNP Paribas (2017), 'BNP Paribas announces new measures regarding the financing of tobacco companies', BNP press release, 24 November.

Bradshaw, C. (2012), 'Little left to lose: deforestation and forest degradation in Australia since European colonization', *Journal of Plant Ecology*, 5(1): 109–20.

Carney, M. (2015), 'Breaking the tragedy of the horizon: climate change and financial stability', Speech at Lloyd's of London, 29 September.

Chava, S. (2014), 'Environmental externalities and cost of capital', *Management Science*, 60(9): 2223–47.

Diamond, D. W. (1984), 'Financial intermediation and delegated monitoring', *Review of Economic Studies*, 51(3): 393–414.

Duvendack, M., R. Palmer-Jones, J. Copestake, L. Hooper, Y. Loke, and N. Rao (2011), 'What is the evidence of the impact of microfinance on the well-being of poor people?', EPPI-Centre, Social Science Research Unit, Institute of Education, University of London.

Equator Principles (2013), 'Equator Principles III', Equator Principles Association, London.

European Mortgage Federation (2017), 'Energy efficient mortgages action plan', Brussels.

Ewen, D., L. Ossenblok, H. Toxopeus, G. Braam, and K. Maas (2017), *Route Circulair: Een roadmap voor een circulair bedrijfsmodel*, Uitgeverij Koninklijke Van Gorcum, Assen.

Feigenberg, B., E. Field, and R. Pande (2010), 'Building social capital through microfinance', NBER Working Paper No. 16018.

Financial Times (2015), 'Bank Rakyat: max micro?', 20 December.

Financial Times (2017), 'Dakota pipe lenders under pressure to withdraw', 8 May.

Freixas, X. and J. C. Rochet (2008), *Microeconomics of Banking*, 2nd edition, MIT Press, Cambridge, MA.

GABV (Global Alliance for Banking on Values) (2016), 'Real economy – real returns: a continuing business case for sustainability-focused banking', Research Report, Zeist, http://www.gabv.org/news/real-economy-real-returns-continuing-business-case-sustainability-focused-banking, accessed 5 July 2018.

GABV (Global Alliance for Banking on Values) (2017), 'Values-based banking scorecard: an overview', Zeist.

GABV (Global Alliance for Banking on Values) (2018), 'Values-based banking (VBB) scorecard: instructions', Zeist.

Garikipati, S., S. Johnson, I. Guérin, and A. Szafarz (2017), 'Microfinance and gender: issues, challenges and the road ahead', *Journal of Development Studies*, 53(5): 641–8.

Goss, A. and G. Roberts (2011), 'The impact of corporate social responsibility on the cost of bank loans', *Journal of Banking & Finance*, 35(7): 1794–810.

Jeucken, M. (2004), *Sustainability in Finance: Banking on the Planet*, Eburon Academic Publishers, Delft.

Jordà, Ò., M. Schularick, and A. Taylor (2016), 'The great mortgaging: housing finance, crises, and business cycles', *Economic Policy*, 31(85): 107–52.

Kotz, H. and R. Schmidt (2017), 'Corporate governance of banks: a German alternative to the "standard model"', SAFE White Paper No. 45, House of Finance, Frankfurt.

Liikanen Report (2012), 'Final report', High-level Expert Group on reforming the structure of the EU banking sector, Brussels, http://ec.europa.eu/internal_market/bank/docs/high-level_expert_group/report_en.pdf, accessed 5 July 2018.

Mazumder, M. and W. Lu (2015), 'What impact does microfinance have on rural livelihood? A comparison of governmental and non-governmental microfinance programs in Bangladesh', *World Development*, 68: 336–54.

MIX Market (2015), Global outreach and financial performance benchmark report: 2015, MIX, Washington DC, https://www.themix.org/sites/default/files/publications/global_benchmark_report_fy2015_0.pdf, accessed 5 July 2018.

Oliver Wyman (2017), 'Supporting the circular economy transition: the role of the financial sector in the Netherlands', Amsterdam, http://www.oliverwyman.com/content/dam/oliver-wyman/v2/publications/2017/sep/CircularEconomy_print.pdf, accessed 5 July 2018.

Ostergaard, C., I. Schindele, and B. Vale (2016), 'Social capital and the viability of stakeholder-oriented firms: evidence from savings banks', *Review of Finance*, 20(5): 1673–718.

Rabobank (2017), 'Food & Agribusiness Principles', Utrecht.

Rau, T. and S. Oberhuber (2016), *Material Matters*, Bertram and De Leeuw Uitgevers, Haarlem.

Schoenmaker, D. and R. van Tilburg (2016), 'What role for financial supervisors in addressing environmental risks?', *Comparative Economic Studies*, 58(3): 317–34.

TCFD (Task Force on Climate-related Financial Disclosures) (2017), 'Recommendations of the Task Force on Climate-related Financial Disclosures: final report (Bloomberg Report)', Financial Stability Board, Basel.

Thaler, R. and C. Sunstein (2008), *Nudge: Improving Decisions about Health, Wealth, and Happiness*, Yale University Press, New Haven, CT.

UNEP Inquiry (2015), 'The coming financial climate: the Inquiry's 4th progress report', UNEP Inquiry into the Design of a Sustainable Financial System, London.

Weber, O. (2012), 'Environmental credit risk management in banks and financial service institutions', *Business Strategy and the Environment*, 21(4): 248–63.

Weber, O. (2017a), 'Corporate sustainability and financial performance of Chinese banks', *Sustainability Accounting, Management and Policy Journal*, 8(3): 358–85.

Weber, O. (2017b), 'Equator principles reporting: factors influencing the quality of reports', *International Journal of Corporate Strategy and Social Responsibility*, 1(2): 141–60.

Weber, O., R. Scholz, and G. Michalik (2010), 'Incorporating sustainability criteria into credit risk management', *Business Strategy and the Environment*, 19(1): 39–50.

Westpac Group (2014), 'Financing Agribusiness', Sydney.

Zeidan, R, C. Boechat, and A. Fleury (2015), 'Developing a sustainability credit score system', *Journal of Business Ethics*, 127(2): 283–96.

Zeller, M., M. Sharma, C. Henry, and C. Lapenu (2006), 'An operational method for assessing the poverty outreach performance of development policies and projects: results of case studies in Africa, Asia, and Latin America', *World Development*, 34(3): 446–64.

11 Insurance—managing long-term risk

Overview

The insurance industry has been important in reducing the impact of both major and minor tragedies in society. The function of *insurance* is to protect individuals and firms from the financial consequences of adverse events. By combining the risks of various clients in a pool, insurance companies can spread the risks over this (large) group of clients.

This chapter discusses how the insurance industry manages and models catastrophe risk resulting from natural hazards. Global warming caused by climate change intensifies several natural hazards, such as floods, storm surges, hurricanes, and droughts, leading to catastrophes. Climate change is a slow-moving process with long lead times and uncertainty about the underlying trend. As catastrophes are a risk to organizations and society, the insurance industry plays a key role in managing these risks and absorbing financial losses from catastrophes.

As single insurers cannot absorb the losses of these low-probability but high-impact events on their own, re-insurance plays an important role in diversifying risk. In response to major catastrophes, leading re-insurers have developed catastrophe models to quantify catastrophe risk, which are often the best predictors of what is on the horizon. This chapter analyses the key components of these models, which translate an estimate of the extent and intensity of catastrophes ultimately into financial losses.

While the insurance industry typically expresses total damages in monetary terms (financial losses and the income losses of victims), this chapter also presents a lifeyears index (years that dead, injured, and otherwise affected persons have lost as a result of the disaster and financial losses divided by annual income). The lifeyears index offers a better basis for measuring the way disasters affect people.

Next to physical risks, the insurance industry is also exposed to liability risks. These liability risks include environmental contamination (pollution) and liabilities imposed by lawsuits. Large liability claims and settlements are problematic not only for the affected companies but also their insurers, insofar as the claims are covered by insurance policies.

Finally, microinsurance has the potential to protect low-income individuals or micro-enterprises, which otherwise have no access to financial services, against specific risks with low-priced targeted products. These risks include both health risks (illness, injury, or death) and property risks (damage or loss). Microinsurance could reduce the vulnerability of low-income income individuals to unexpected shocks. It could thus play, just like microfinance and microcredit in Chapter 10, a role in reducing poverty. Digital technology (e.g. the increased use of mobile phones for premium payment and claim settlement) can radically expand the distribution of microinsurance.

Learning objectives

After you have studied this chapter, you should be able to:

- explain the nature of the insurance business;
- identify the physical risk of catastrophes;
- appreciate the liability risk for environmental hazards;
- understand the basics of catastrophe modelling;
- explain the function of microinsurance.

11.1 **Basics of Insurance**

The function of *insurance* is to protect individuals and firms against the financial impact of adverse events. Insurance companies are able to provide this financial protection through the pooling of individual risks. By combining the risks of various clients in a pool, insurance companies can spread the financial impact of risks over this (large) group of clients. There are different types of insurance. *Life insurance* protects against the financial consequences of premature death, disability, and retirement. While it is difficult to predict the death of an individual, death rates for large populations are fairly stable and therefore easier to predict. Other types of insurance are grouped under the name of *non-life insurance*, which protects against the financial consequences of risks such as natural catastrophes, accidents, fire, and liability. Non-life insurance is sometimes also called property and casualty or property and liability insurance.

11.1.1 INSURANCE BUSINESS

The risk dynamics of non-life insurance are more diverse than those of life insurance. Relatively small accidents (like car accidents) are fairly predictable and can easily be pooled by an insurance company. But larger accidents or catastrophes follow a different pattern: they are low-probability but high-impact events. A good example is Hurricane Katrina in New Orleans in 2005 with an insured loss of $81 billion (see Table 11.1). The risk of such a catastrophe is too big for one insurance company and is therefore divided among different insurance and re-insurance companies. The insurance industry is thus very important in reducing the impact of major (and minor) tragedies in society and has developed a high level of expertise in modelling and managing long-term risk, such as weather-related catastrophe risk due to climate change (see Section 11.3).

The intermediation function of insurers can be illustrated using a simple balance sheet and profit and loss account (see Figure 11.1). Insurers collect premiums P from clients and make payouts on claims C by these clients (i.e. policyholders) when the risk materializes. On the asset side, insurers invest the collected premiums in assets A, which earn a return r_A. On the liability side, insurers make technical provisions TP to cover expected future claims. In addition, insurers maintain a capital buffer E to cover unexpected claims.

For their business, insurers evaluate the risk of prospective clients. If a client is accepted, the insurers have to decide how much coverage a client should receive and how much he should pay for it. The function of an underwriter is to acquire—or to 'write'—business that will bring the insurance company profits. The insurance business is viable only when the collected premiums exceed the payout on claims. The *claim ratio* measures the adjusted claims as a ratio to premiums earned, that is, C/P. A claim ratio of less than 100 per cent means that premiums earned are sufficient to cover claims.

The insurance company also has to cover its expenses Exp. The biggest expenses are commissions paid to insurance agents for the acquisition of business. The insurer must also gather information about potential clients to assess the underwriting risk and avoid adverse selection (see Section 11.1.4). A common economic measure to assess the profitability of non-life insurers is the combined ratio CR, which expresses claims and expenses relative to premiums earned:

$$CR = {}^{C}\!/_{P} + {}^{Exp}\!/_{P} = \frac{C + Exp}{P} \tag{11.1}$$

Balance sheet		Profit & loss account
Assets (A)	Equity (E)	Premium income (P) (+)
	Technical provisions (TP)	Investment income ($A \cdot r_A$) (+/–)
		Policyholders claims (C) (–)
		Expenses (Exp) (–)
Total assets	Total liabilities	Profit (π) (+/–)

Figure 11.1 Simplified balance sheet and P&L account of an insurer

The combined ratio provides an incomplete view of a non-life insurer's profitability. Premiums are invested before payouts are made. Investment returns r_A are therefore an important source of income for insurers. The profitability π, as a percentage of premium earned, is equal to the results on claims and expenses $(100-CR)$ and the investment returns:

$$\pi = 100 - CR + {}^{A \cdot r_A}\!/_{P} = 100 + \frac{A \cdot r_A - C - Exp}{P} \tag{11.2}$$

Equation 11.2 illustrates that the successful management of an insurance company depends on making adequate investment returns and properly calculating underwriting risks while restricting acquisition and administrative expenses. This equation can be illustrated with a simple example. Assume a claim ratio of 65 per cent of earned premiums, an expense ratio of 36 per cent, and allocated investment income of 8 per cent. The profit is 7 per cent of earned premiums (100 + 8 − 65 − 36 = 7).

11.1.2 DIFFERING PROBABILITY DISTRIBUTIONS

The stochastic properties of large claims are very different from those of small claims. Small claims have a distribution with light tails (e.g. the normal distribution). In a large portfolio, the expected claim size approaches the average claim size according to the law of large numbers. In contrast, large claims are characterized by distributions with heavy tails. Insurance portfolios with heavy-tailed claim sizes are dangerous. Figure 11.2 shows the log-normal distribution, an example of a heavy-tailed distribution. In the tail on the right are events x with a low probability $P(x)$ but a large impact on the overall claim amount. The distribution needs to be drawn from a relatively small number of observations (the excesses over high thresholds). Weitzman (2009) stresses the structural uncertainty in the analysis of low-probability, high-impact catastrophes (see Section 11.3).

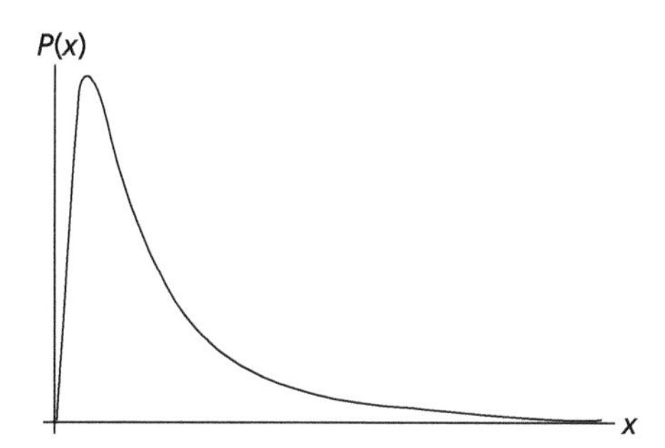

Figure 11.2 Heavy-tailed distribution

Source: Authors.

Table 11.1 Catastrophes: The 25 most costly insurance losses, 1970–2017

Insured loss (in $ billion)	Victims	Date (year)	Event	Country
82.4	1,836	2005	Hurricane Katrina: storm surge, floods	USA, Mexico
38.1	18,451	2011	Earthquake (Mw 9.0) triggers tsunami	Japan
32.0	136	2017	Hurricane Maria	USA, Puerto Rico, Caribbean
30.8	237	2012	Hurricane Sandy: storm surge	USA (New York)
30.0	126	2017	Hurricane Irma	USA, Puerto Rico, Caribbean
30.0	89	2017	Hurricane Harvey	USA
27.9	65	1992	Hurricane Andrew: floods	USA, Bahamas
26.0	2,982	2001	Terror attack on WTC, Pentagon	USA
25.3	61	1994	Northridge earthquake (Mw 6.7)	USA
23.1	193	2008	Hurricane Ike: floods, damage to oil rigs	USA, Caribbean
19.1	185	2011	Earthquake (Mw 6.1), aftershocks	New Zealand
16.8	119	2004	Hurricane Ivan: damage to oil rigs	USA, Caribbean
16.3	815	2011	Heavy monsoon rains: extreme flooding	Thailand
15.8	53	2005	Hurricane Wilma: torrential rains, floods	USA, Mexico
13.5	34	2005	Hurricane Rita: floods, damage to oil rigs	USA, Mexico
11.7	123	2012	Drought in the Corn Belt	USA
10.2	36	2004	Hurricane Charley	USA, Caribbean
10.2	51	1991	Typhoon Mireille	Japan
9.0	78	1989	Hurricane Hugo	USA, Caribbean
9.0	562	2010	Earthquake (Mw 8.8) triggers tsunami	Chile
8.8	95	1990	Winter storm Daria	France, UK, Benelux
8.7	–	2010	Earthquake (Mw 7.0); over 300 aftershocks	New Zealand
8.5	110	1999	Winter storm Lothar	Switzerland, UK, France
8.0	321	2011	Major tornado outbreak: 349 tornadoes	USA (Alabama et al.)
7.7	22	2017	Wildland fire 'Tubbs Fires'	USA (California)

Notes: Mw = moment magnitude scale. The losses include property and business interruption, but exclude liability and life-insurance losses. The losses are indexed to 2017. Victims refer to those dead and missing.

Source: Swiss Re (2018).

11.1.2.1 Catastrophes

Large losses are caused not only by nature (natural catastrophes: earthquakes and weather-related catastrophes) but also by man (man-made disasters). Table 11.1 provides an overview of the largest catastrophes over the last 50 years. Hurricane Katrina in New Orleans caused an insured loss of $82 billion, while the total loss (*insured* and *uninsured*) mounted to $140 billion. The tsunami, triggered by an earthquake, damaged the nuclear plant at Fukushima (Japan) and caused an insured loss of $38 billion (with total loss of $230 billion). In 2017, three hurricanes, Maria, Irma, and Harvey, caused devastating insured losses (including destroyed homes) at a combined $92 billion in the Caribbean and the United States. Hurricane Sandy flooded the southern part of New York causing $31 billion of insured losses. Lloyd's (2014) estimates that the 20 cm sea-level rise at New York since the 1950s increased Sandy's surge losses by 30 per cent. The terrorist attack on the Twin Towers and the Pentagon in 2001 led to an insured loss of $26 billion. Europe has experienced several winter storms, such as Daria in 1990 and Lothar in 1999, causing an insured loss of more than $8 billion each. California had the costliest fire event, Tubbs, after prolonged dry conditions in 2017. The highest insured losses have been suffered in the USA, Europe, and Japan due to higher insurance density in developed countries.

Developing countries generally have a lower insurance density, so only a small proportion of victims benefit from insurance cover (see Section 11.4 on microinsurance). An example was the tsunami in the Indian Ocean in 2004, with a death toll of 220,000 in Indonesia and Thailand. Yet this extreme event is not included in Table 11.1 as only insured losses are counted. Box 11.1

BOX 11.1 ALTERNATIVE WAYS TO MEASURE THE IMPACT OF NATURAL DISASTERS

To assess the importance of disasters and the need to prepare for them, we need a way to measure disaster impacts. The adverse impacts of natural hazards are typically measured by the number of victims M and the financial losses that they cause. The standard calculation of total damages is as follows:

$$Total\ damages = Losses + M * n * Annual\ income \quad (11.3)$$

whereby n represents the years lost, which is the life expectancy minus the age of death. The annual income (or wage) per capita varies across countries and values the damages of mortality M at a higher dollar amount in high-income countries than in low-income countries.

Noy (2016) proposes an alternative measure of disaster impact, which builds on the conceptual underpinnings of the calculations of disability adjusted life years lost due to the burden of diseases and injuries used by the World Health Organization. The proposed lifeyears index combines the impact on human lives and a quantification of the importance of destruction of infrastructure, capital, and housing into an overall assessment.

The lifeyears index converts all measures of impact into 'lifeyears' units (Noy, 2016). The basic premise is that the value of human life should be considered as equal everywhere, while the value of monetary damages is not. Indeed, a dollar lost in high-income countries (with an average GDP per capita of $41,000) exerts less of an adverse impact on society than a dollar lost in low-income countries (with an average GDP per capita of $610). The lifeyears index is calculated as:

$$Lifeyears = {}^{Losses}/_{Annual\ income} + M * n + N^{affected} * t \quad (11.4)$$

whereby $N^{affected}$ represents the number of people who were injured (and hospitalized) or otherwise affected by the disaster (e.g. houses destroyed, livelihoods adversely impacted, temporarily or permanently displaced). t measures the years it takes for an affected person to return to normality.

Noy (2016) argues that this people-centric measure offers a better basis for measuring the way disasters affect people and for international policies to allocate resources for disaster risk reduction.

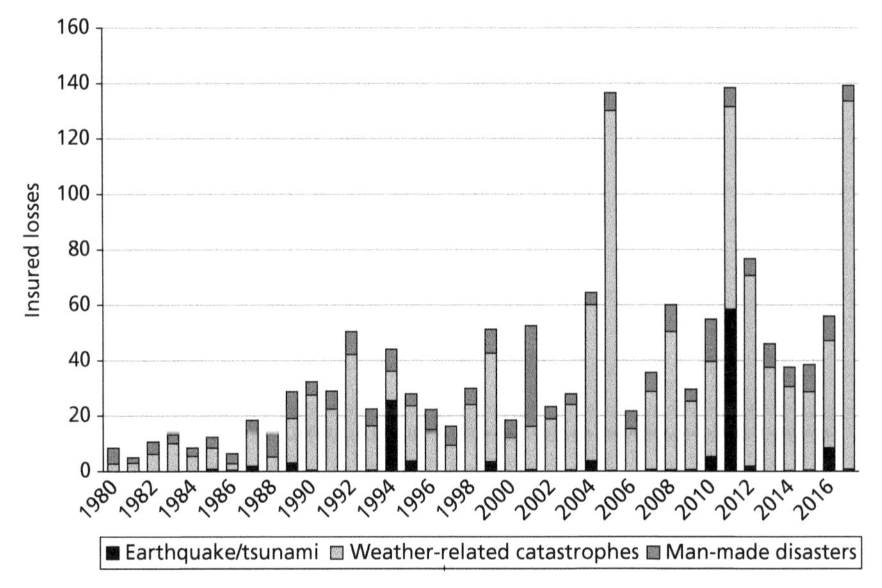

Figure 11.3 Insured catastrophe losses, 1980–2017 (in $ billions)

Note: The large losses in 2005 relate to the Hurricanes Katrina, Rita, and Wilma; in 2011 to the Japan and New Zealand earthquakes; in 2012 to Hurricane Sandy; and in 2017 to Hurricanes Harvey, Irma, and Maria (see Table 11.1).

Source: Swiss Re (2018).

discusses alternative measures to assess the impact of natural disasters on people, as this goes beyond insured losses and the number of victims.

Figure 11.3 highlights that insured catastrophe losses (i.e. the claim amounts C for the insurance industry) strongly vary over time. Moreover, weather-related catastrophes form the majority of insured catastrophe losses and show an upward trend. The ten-year average for insured losses is $58 billion, while the ten-year average for economic losses (i.e. uninsured and insured losses) is over $200 billion as of 2017 (Swiss Re, 2018). So, less than one third of total economic losses are insured. These economic losses include inter alia property damage, business contingency, and agriculture (impaired food production).

11.1.3 RE-INSURANCE

Individual insurers cannot bear these large financial losses on their own—their equity would be wiped out when an extreme event occurs. The risks (and premiums) of catastrophe insurance are therefore shared among insurers (Rejda, 2005). A common mechanism for sharing insurance risk is *re-insurance*,

Table 11.2 Largest re-insurance companies, 2015

Name	Country	Gross re-insurance premium (in $ billions)
Swiss Re	Switzerland	$19.6
Munich Re	Germany	$19.3
Lloyd's	United Kingdom	$12.7
Hannover Rueck	Germany	$10.2
Berkshire Hathaway	United States	$7.0

Note: The re-insurance premium covers only non-life insurance and is expressed in US$ billions.
Source: AM Best.

that is, shifting part or all of the insurance originally written by one insurer to another insurer. The insurer that originally writes the business is called the ceding company. The insurer that accepts part or all of the insurance risk from the ceding company is the re-insurer. Table 11.2 lists the largest re-insurers worldwide.

The insurance risk of extreme events is thus sliced in different layers and divided between different insurers. Re-insurance can be designed in different ways. One format is proportional re-insurance. The insurer cedes a proportion of the premiums and the risks to a re-insurer. The remainder of the premiums and risks is retained by the ceding insurer (the retention amount). Another format, in particular used for catastrophe insurance, is excess-of-loss re-insurance. Losses in excess of a certain limit (i.e. the retention limit) are paid by the re-insurer up to an agreed maximum limit. Excess-of-loss contracts allow for tailor-made slicing of the insurance risk. The terrorist attacks on 11 September 2001 show the importance of re-insurance. Re-insurers paid out at least half of the insured losses (Rejda, 2005). As they are heavily exposed, re-insurers have a strong incentive to model catastrophe risk (see Section 11.3).

In case of large catastrophes, traditional insurance and re-insurance may not suffice. The financial losses due to, for instance, a large flood can supersede the absorption capacity of individual insurers and re-insurers. Therefore, many countries have a government programme that covers part of the risk. An example is the US National Flood Insurance Program that covers losses through river and coastal flooding.

An alternative to traditional re-insurance and government insurance is issuing catastrophe bonds (also known as cat bond). Cat bonds are corporate bonds that permit the issuer of the bond to skip or defer scheduled payments if a catastrophic loss beyond a certain threshold occurs. The bonds pay relatively high interest rates and help (institutional) investors to diversify their portfolio, because natural disasters occur randomly and are not correlated with the stock market or other common factors (Rejda, 2005).

11.1.4 ASYMMETRIC INFORMATION

Under the assumption of full information, complete insurance is possible at actuarially fair premium rates. But complete coverage is not always available in insurance markets due to asymmetric information (Loubergé, 2000). First, insurance is subject to *adverse selection*. The ex ante information asymmetry arises because the insured generally knows more about his risk profile than the insurer. The risk type of the insured cannot be determined ex ante by the insurer; the insurer can only charge the same premium rate based on aggregate risk. The high-risk types are the ones who are most eager to buy insurance, producing an undesirable outcome for the insurer.

To solve this problem, Rothschild and Stiglitz (1976) propose a two-tier contract structure with self-section. This forces the low-risk types to distinguish themselves from the high-risk types in order to gain insurance at an actuarially fair premium. The low-risk types get partial insurance in the form of a 'deductible' (i.e. own risk for the client) or 'co-insurance' (fractional compensation). The high-risk types prefer the contract with full coverage at a higher premium.

Secondly, insurance is subject to *moral hazard* when the contract outcome is partly influenced by the behaviour of the insured yet the insurer cannot observe, without costs, to which extent reported losses can be attributed to the behaviour of the insured. Complete coverage may not be attainable under moral hazard. This is due to the trade-off between the goal of efficient risk-sharing, which is met by allocating the risk to the insurer, and the goal of efficient incentives, which requires leaving the consequences of decisions about care with the decision-maker, that is, the insured.

More broadly, Shiller (2012) reviews missing insurance markets. Extending insurance to larger segments of the population is not exclusively a challenge for the poorest regions in the world (see Section 11.4), but also for advanced countries. Examples are home equity insurance (which insures people against a drop in the market value of their homes), earthquake insurance in California (only about 10 per cent of residential houses are insured for earthquakes in this high-risk area), and livelihood insurance (private sector insurance for loss of wage due to unemployment or reduced wage). In these examples, insurers would need to manage the underlying macro-economic risk.

11.1.5 INSURANCE COMPANIES AS ASSET MANAGERS

On the asset side, (re-)insurance companies, just like pension funds, are long-term institutional investors. Chapters 7 to 9 discuss their role in asset management. Some insurers are leading sustainable investors. Chapters 3 and 4 discuss their role in corporate governance, steering corporates to sustainable business practices.

11.2 Why does sustainability matter to insurance?

Following best practices of companies, insurance companies have started to present a materiality matrix that outlines those sustainability issues that an insurer and its stakeholders consider most material (see Chapter 5). We provide an example of a leading insurance company and a leading re-insurance company.

AXA is a leading French insurance company. For AXA, creating long-term value means anticipating risks that could threaten its development and that of its customers, while capitalizing on the new opportunities offered by the changing world. AXA's materiality matrix (see Figure 11.4) is based on external and internal (AXA) stakeholders and aims to identify the top emerging risks with the highest impact on the society at large in the next five to ten years. Together with integrated reporting, the creation of the materiality matrix enables AXA to promote integrated thinking and decision-making based on information that is broader, more interconnected, and more forward looking than traditional business-as-usual analysis.

Figure 11.4 shows that AXA has identified several sustainability risks and opportunities. On the environmental front, climate change, natural resources management, and pollution are listed. On the social side, terrorism, demographic changes, health (pandemics, chronic diseases), and access to the social

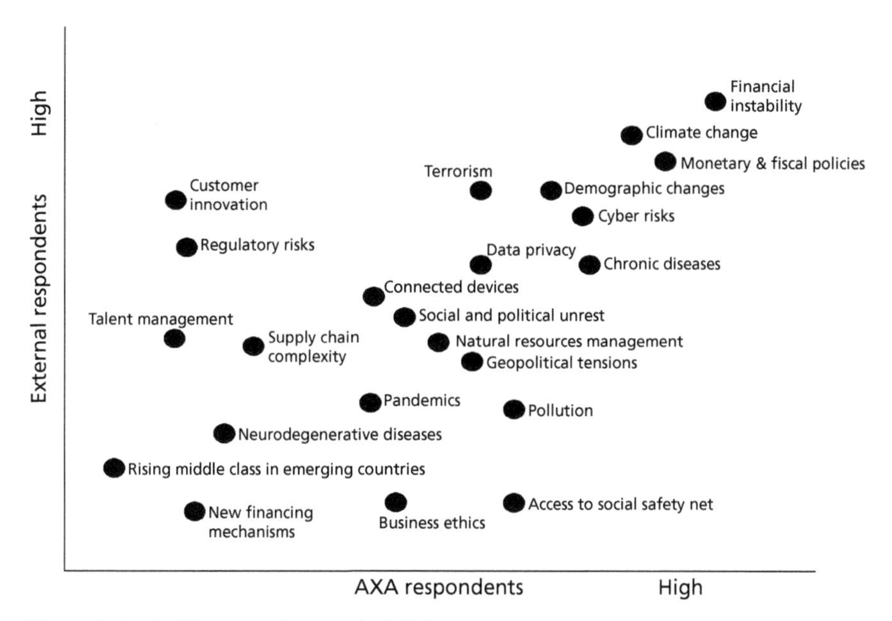

Figure 11.4 AXA's materiality matrix, 2016

Source: AXA.

safety net are included. Similar to ING (see Section 10.2), data privacy and cyber risk are identified as major risks for AXA and its stakeholders.

Box 11.2 contains the materiality matrix for the largest re-insurer, Swiss Re. As Swiss Re provides cover for weather-related catastrophe risk, managing climate change risk is at the top of its list. Interestingly, Swiss Re also advances renewable energy solutions to mitigate climate change, for example, by using its capacity and technical expertise to provide effective risk covers for complex

BOX 11.2 MATERIALITY MATRIX OF SWISS RE

As an ultimate risk-taker in society, Swiss Re has an interest in maintaining active and ongoing dialogue with key stakeholders. Swiss Re shares its risk expertise, thus helping stakeholders—and society at large—to form effective responses. In turn, Swiss Re benefits from the dialogue as it is able to sharpen its understanding of key risks, including ESG issues, and to set priorities. Based on the insights gained through this process, Swiss Re considers the following ESG issues as the most material in the context of its own business:

- Climate change:
  - managing climate and natural disaster risk;
  - advancing sustainable energy solutions.
- Funding longer lives.
- Partnering for food security.
- Supporting financial resilience.
- Managing sustainability risks.
- Empowering its people.
- Ensuring good governance and compliance.

Climate change

Climate change has been Swiss Re's most important material issue for many years. For a re-insurer like Swiss Re, it constitutes a key material topic because it will lead to an increase in the frequency and severity of natural catastrophes such as floods, storms, excessive rainfall, and drought. In combination with growing asset concentrations in exposed areas and more widespread insurance protection, this will cause a steady rise in losses. The main challenge is the uncertainty surrounding climate change that makes it difficult for them to price this risk. Of the key material topics listed, two are directly connected to climate change (managing climate and natural disaster risk and advancing sustainable energy solutions).

Since detecting the long-term threat posed by climate change in the 1990s, Swiss Re has been an acknowledged thought leader on the topic. To tackle the issue, the company pursues a comprehensive strategy with four pillars:

1. Advancing its knowledge and understanding of climate change risks, quantifying and integrating them into its risk management and underwriting frameworks.
2. Developing products and services to mitigate or adapt to climate risk.
3. Raising awareness about climate change risks through dialogue with clients, employees, and the public, and advocating a worldwide policy framework for climate change.
4. Tackling its own carbon footprint and ensuring transparent, annual emissions reporting.

Source: Swiss Re.

offshore wind farm projects. Swiss Re also creates solutions to improve food security by giving farmers protection against natural perils. Through its commitment to the Grow Africa Partnership, Swiss Re offers, for example, protection against weather risks to 1.4 million smallholder farmers in Africa.

11.2.1 EVIDENCE THAT E (ENVIRONMENTAL) MATTERS

A major risk for insurers is the physical risk posed by weather-related catastrophes. Lloyd's (2014) has investigated the impact of climate change on the frequency of extreme weather events. The frequency of heatwaves has increased in Europe, Asia, and Australia and more regions show an increase in the number of heavy rainfall events than a decrease. There has been an increase in the intensity of the strongest tropical cyclones in the North Atlantic Basin (as evidenced by the three strong cyclones in 2017). The sensitivity of hurricane losses is influenced by a number of factors related to climate change, such as sea-level rise and sea surface temperature. There is a relationship between sea surface temperatures and hurricane strength, which suggests a gradual increasing trend.

Table 11.1 and Figure 11.3 confirm the upward trend of weather-related losses due to climate change and land-system change. Section 11.3 discusses climate change and catastrophe risk modelling in more detail.

Another environmental hazard for insurance is pollution. Pollution insurance provides cover for liability to third parties arising from contamination of air, water, or land due to the sudden and accidental release of hazardous materials from the insured site. The policy usually covers the costs of clean-up and may include coverage for releases from underground storage tanks (see Section 11.2.3 for more general liability risks). Historical events have shown that over time liability claims can increase dramatically; for example, apparent low-probability risks can transform into large and unforeseen liabilities for insurers. Total net asbestos losses are, for example, estimated at $85 billion in the United States (Prudential Regulation Authority, 2015).

Shapira and Zingales (2017) analyse the case of DuPont, one of the most respectable US companies, which caused environmental damage that ended up costing the company around a billion dollars. By using internal company documents disclosed in trials, they rule out the possibilities that this bad outcome was due to ignorance or an unexpected realization. The documents rather suggest that the harmful pollution was a rational decision: under reasonable probabilities of detection, polluting was ex ante optimal from the company's perspective, albeit a very harmful decision from a societal perspective (raising important governance issues). Shapira and Zingales (2017) then examine why different mechanisms of control, such as legal liability, regulation, and reputation, all fail to deter socially harmful behaviour. One common reason for the failures of deterrence mechanisms is that a company controls most of the information and its release.

11.2.2 EVIDENCE THAT S (SOCIAL) MATTERS

As people live longer, health and vitality is becoming more important. Due to an ageing population, health-care costs have outgrown education costs in government budgets. Governments are keen to offload part of the rising health-care costs to the private insurance sector. Private insurers then also have an incentive to contain health-care costs, both at health-care providers, such as hospitals and pharmaceutical companies, and health-care takers (i.e. insured clients).

A case in point is the Vitality programme of AIA, a leading Asian insurance group. AIA Vitality is a science-backed wellness programme that helps its clients make a positive change to their health. AIA Vitality provides the knowledge, tools, and motivation (including rewards) to promote healthy living. Not only does AIA Vitality encourage clients to get healthier, engaged clients have lower health-care costs too.

Another important area in the social domain is the provision of social security insurance, such as supplementary income insurance in case of unemployment or disability. As governments are reducing the social welfare state, there is more demand for private solutions. Also developing countries require insurance solutions, which microinsurance can provide (see Section 11.4).

Next, terrorism has been on the rise since the early 2000s. The infamous terror attack on the World Trade Center (WTC) in New York on 9/11 resulted in up to 3,000 victims and $25 billion in insured losses (see Table 11.1). The ideological and religious divide between and within societies is a root cause of terrorism.

The evolution of technology, and related law, may change the nature of risk, resulting in behavioural changes in society. A prime example is the development of driverless cars, which poses challenges for 'personal' liability law. The new technology and rules will impact risk management practices and human behaviour. Another example is new laws on the data privacy of clients in response to increased use of client data by large tech companies such as Apple and Google, as well as other companies. A final area with an increasing impact is cyber security.

11.2.3 EVIDENCE THAT G (GOVERNANCE) MATTERS

Liability insurance protects the insured from the risks of liabilities imposed by lawsuits and similar claims. Large liability claims and settlements can be problematic not only for the affected companies but also their insurers, insofar as the claims are covered by insurance policies.

A major example is the liability risk of big tobacco companies, which have been sued on conspiracy to deceive the American public about nicotine addiction and the health effects of cigarettes. Tobacco companies paid hundreds of millions to settle smoking lawsuits. The big oil companies might face similar liability risks on the climate effects of fossil fuels. Moreover, the oil companies face the risk of stranded assets, as discussed in Chapter 2. These risks raise important corporate governance issues.

Although strongly opposed by the board, ExxonMobil shareholders passed, with 62 per cent majority, a resolution calling for an annual assessment of the impact of technological change and climate policy on the company's operations (*Financial Times*, 2017). Disclosures will help shareholders assess the long-term resilience of Exxon's operations in a world where governments deliver on their pledges to tackle global warming. Its new disclosure policies could mean Exxon will have to discuss more radical changes. Among the issues that the company has said it will assess in its new disclosures are the sensitivity of energy demand to policy changes and 'positioning for a low-carbon future'. Several oil companies, particularly in Europe, have seen an opportunity in climate policy, arguing that more should be done to shift power generation away from coal and towards natural gas, which emits less carbon dioxide for an equivalent amount of electricity.

There are also governance issues at country level. Billette de Villemeur and Leroux (2016) propose the creation of a carbon liabilities market to address climate change. Each period countries would be made liable for their share of responsibility in current climate damage. These carbon liabilities can be traded on a market like financial debt. When purchasing extra liability, a country commits to repaying the corresponding climate debt, as future harm occurs. In turn, a seller of liability will be exempt from the associated debt payments. Trade will occur at a price between what the seller is willing to pay and what the buyer is willing to accept to endorse the liability. The trading is based on decentralized beliefs about the severity of the climate problem. From an informational standpoint, implementation relies only on realized harm and on the well-documented emission history of countries. A country's climate policy (or lack of it) may also have an impact on its sovereign bond rating, as discussed in Chapter 9.

11.2.4 SUSTAINABLE ASSESSMENT IN PRACTICE

RobecoSAM analyses sustainability trends across industries and makes corporate sustainability assessments. For the insurance sector, RobecoSAM (2017) finds that the industry is integrating sustainability considerations into its core business. Most notably, leading insurers are increasingly considering long-term sustainability trends and factors in their risk assessments and claims management processes. At the same time, the industry faces both significant threats as well as opportunities as it embraces digitalization.

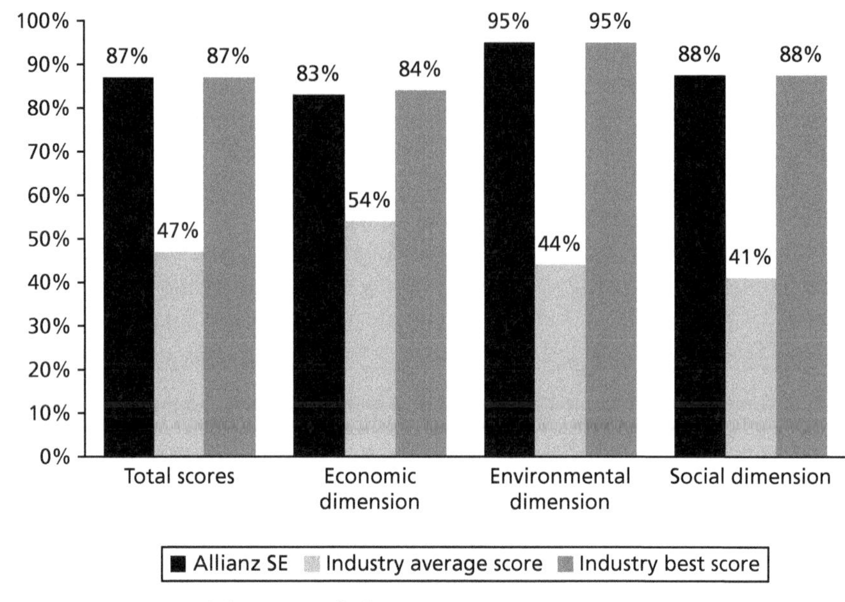

Figure 11.5 Sustainability scores of Allianz, 2017

Source: RobecoSAM (2017).

RobecoSAM (2017) has identified Allianz as a sustainability leader. Allianz's sustainability strategy focuses on three areas: low-carbon economy, social inclusion, and business integration. Allianz has developed instruments to integrate environmental, social, and governance (ESG) concerns into its underwriting, investment, and asset management activities. Furthermore, it offers a broad range of products, such as microinsurance products or green life insurance. Through a social inclusion programme, Allianz is expanding its low-cost financial services, widening access through financial literacy initiatives, and enabling more people to access insurance through a digital strategy. In this way, Allianz is not only addressing a growing social need, but also facilitating sustainable local development and thus increasing its potential customer and employee base. Figure 11.5 summarizes the sustainability scores of Allianz across the different dimensions.

11.3 **Managing long-term catastrophe risk**

In its broadest sense, a *catastrophe* is something that exceeds the capacity of those affected to cope with, or absorb, its effects. In the context of natural hazards, the driver is an extreme event causing widespread and usually sudden damage or suffering (Mitchell-Wallace et al. 2017). Global warming caused by climate change is intensifying several natural hazards, such as floods, storm surges, hurricanes, and droughts. Climate change is a slow-moving process with long lead times and uncertainty about the development of the underlying trend (i.e. the atmospheric concentration of greenhouse gases (GHGs) and its effect on global warming). As catastrophes are a risk to organizations and society, risk management in the form of mitigation (actions taken to curb carbon emissions) and adaptation (actions taken to help communities and ecosystems cope with the changing climate condition) is important. The insurance industry plays a key role in managing these risks and absorbing losses from catastrophes. In response to major catastrophes, insurers and re-insurers have developed catastrophe models, which are often the best predictors of what is on the horizon (see Muir-Wood (2016) for an accessible overview on disaster risk and catastrophe modelling).

11.3.1 CATASTROPHE MODELLING

Insurers and re-insurers use sophisticated catastrophe models to assess the economic losses from catastrophes. A catastrophe model consists of five components (Mitchell-Wallace et al. 2017):

1. The **hazard** component estimates the extent and intensity of the catastrophe (i.e. the natural phenomenon with the potential to cause damage or loss). It is expressed in a hazard metric, such as peak gust wind speeds across a storm track.
2. The **vulnerability** component assesses the relative damage to assets (such as property and their contents and infrastructure) that are likely to be damaged by the hazard. Most vulnerability models are arranged as series of damage functions, which connect the hazard intensity with the estimated damage as a ratio of total value.
3. The **exposure** component is used in two distinct ways in catastrophe models. First, exposure data for the specific objects being modelled are entered into the model. Secondly, a representative industry exposure for the region is also used for the model. The result is exposure values, which may be split between building values, contents values, and business interruption values.
4. The **financial loss** component translates the physical damage into total monetary loss (also called ground-up loss), that is, before the application of any insurance or re-insurance financial structures. It takes the damage to a building and its contents and estimates which party is responsible for paying. The results of that determination are then interpreted by the model user and applied to business decisions.

5. The **platform** component provides the software that implements and integrates the four model components of hazard, vulnerability, exposure, and loss. The platform usually also provides a structured way of inputting, validating, analysing, visualizing, and storing the different data components and running result reports.

Catastrophe models are designed to quantify catastrophe risk (see Woo (2011) for more on calculating catastrophe risk). The exceedance probability is the probability that a loss will exceed a certain amount in a year. The fundamental output from catastrophe models is a probability distribution of loss at the appropriate aggregation level. The distribution of the maximum loss in a year is called the occurrence exceedance probability distribution. The distribution of the sum of losses in a year is termed the aggregate exceedance probability distribution (Mitchell-Wallace et al. 2017). Loss data, the output of the models, can then be queried to arrive at common metrics, such as:

- The **average annual loss** is the average loss of all modelled events, weighted by their probability of annual occurrence. It is sometimes called the annual mean loss or pure premium. The average annual loss corresponds to the area underneath the aggregate exceedance probability curve, or to the average expected losses that do not exceed the norm.
- The **standard deviation** around the average loss measures the variation of each set of damage outcomes estimated in the vulnerability module. This is important because damage estimates with a high standard deviation are more volatile. The annual average loss (mean) and the standard deviation (variance) are inputs which help form the technical price. However, this misses the uncertainty associated with the hazard generation process (i.e. the primary uncertainty).
- The **exceedance frequency** is the annual frequency of events expected to give greater losses than a reference amount. Since this is a frequency and not a probability, the exceedance frequency can be larger than 1. The return period of a particular size event is the reciprocal of its exceedance frequency.
- The **return period loss** describes the expected time interval over which such an amount might be exceeded. For example, a 0.5 per cent probability of exceeding a loss amount in a year corresponds to a probability of exceeding that loss once every 200 years, or 'a 200-year return period loss'.
- The **value at risk (VaR)** is the loss value at a specific quantile of the relevant loss distribution. For example, a 99.5 per cent VaR based on the aggregate loss distribution would be the value at the 0.5 per cent level (1 in a 200-year return period).

Table 11.3 illustrates the metrics for a fictive portfolio with three events. It should be noted that these metrics express the likelihood or probability of events ex ante (e.g. a 200-year return period loss of $20,000). The occurrence

Table 11.3 Event loss table for a simple portfolio

Loss	Event frequency	Exceedance frequency	Return period
$20,000	0.5%	0.5%	200 years
$10,000	0.5%	1.0%	100 years
$2,000	0.5%	1.5%	67 years

Note: The table represents the metrics for a portfolio with three events, each of which with a frequency of 0.5 per cent.

of events ex post may happen more or less often (e.g. the actual time interval between occurrences of loss exceedance of $20,000 is not exactly 200 years; it is thus possible to have two 200-year return period losses of $20,000 in a 10-year time interval).

As catastrophes are very rare events, we are interested in the right tail of the distribution (see Figure 11.2). In the tail on the right are events with a low probability but a large impact on the overall claim amount. Extreme value statistics can be used to model these large claims. The distribution needs to be drawn from a relatively small number of observations (the excesses over high thresholds). Embrechts, Klüppelberg, and Mikosch (1997) provide an overview of modelling extreme events.

Historical insurance claim patterns are of limited use, as the underlying trends or cycles within the data are changing (Mitchell-Wallace et al. 2017). While climate change projections are made at a 50-year horizon and beyond, there are also other trends relevant for this horizon. Important long-term trends relevant for catastrophe models include, among others:

- the economy becoming digital (e.g. impact on flood warnings);
- wealth creation in eastern China and Southeast Asia and possibly other areas (e.g. money becoming available for building flood defences);
- demographics (e.g. ageing and population growth);
- urbanization (e.g. impact on type and location of exposures);
- changes in building standards (e.g. wind-loading codes);
- changes in infrastructure (e.g. flood defences).

11.3.2 CLIMATE CHANGE AND NATURAL HAZARDS

Climate change (i.e. global warming) is a major cause of several intensifying natural hazards. Through its continuous exchanges with the atmosphere, the ocean plays a major role in the world's climate. Our planet mainly receives energy from solar radiation. While the Earth captures part of this energy, the remainder is reflected beyond the atmosphere and thus leaves the planet. The rapid increase in GHG emissions into the atmosphere causes an accumulation of heat within the climate system. The ocean absorbs over 90 per cent of excess heat (energy) accumulated in the climate system and gets warmer. The ocean plays thus a crucial regulation role in the Earth's energy balance. However, the quantity of heat accumulated in the ocean also causes rising sea levels, increasing temperatures, and changing weather patterns, such as more intense tropical cyclones (Von Schuckmann and Le Traon, 2011).

This book refers to the dominant scientific view and evidence on climate change from the United Nations Intergovernmental Panel on Climate Change (IPCC) (see Box 2.2, in Chapter 2, on climate scepticism). The IPCC's 'Special Report on Managing the Risks of Extreme Events and Disasters to Advance Climate Change Adaptation' lists the following anticipated climate risks and assigns confidence levels:[1]

1. **Temperature change** (heatwaves): A global increase in warm temperature extremes and a global decrease in cold extremes are 'virtually certain', with longer, more frequent, and stronger heatwaves 'very likely' for most land areas.
2. **Sea-level rise**: Rising coastal high water levels are 'very likely'. There is high confidence that locations currently experiencing adverse impacts, such as coastal erosion and floods, will continue to do so in the future due to increasing sea levels.
3. **Drought**: Medium confidence levels are assigned to the intensification of droughts, due to lack of observational data and the complexity of droughts. This applies to regions including southern Europe and the Mediterranean region, central Europe, central North America, Central America and Mexico, northeast Brazil, and southern Africa. Elsewhere there is low confidence on projected drought changes.
4. **Wind** (tropical cyclones): While it is 'likely' that overall global frequency of tropical cyclones will either decrease or remain essentially unchanged, it is 'more likely than not' that the frequency of the most intense storms will increase substantially in some ocean basins. For tropical cyclones an increase in the average maximum wind speed is 'likely', although increases may not occur in all ocean basins.
5. **Heavy rainfall**: It is 'likely' that the frequency of heavy rainfall (precipitation) will increase over many areas of the globe. This is particularly the case in the high latitudes (distance north or south of the equator) and tropical regions, and in winter in the northern mid-latitudes. Heavy rainfall associated with tropical cyclones is 'likely' to increase with continued warming.
6. **Flood**: Projected rainfall and temperature changes imply possible changes in floods, although overall there is 'low confidence' in projections of

[1] Summarized by ClimateWise and Cambridge Institute for Sustainability Leadership (2012).

changes in riverine floods, due to limited evidence and because the causes of regional changes are complex. There is 'medium confidence' that projected increases in heavy rainfall will contribute to increases in local flooding in some regions.

7. **Landslides**: There is 'high confidence' that changes in heatwaves, glacial retreat, and permafrost degradation will affect high mountain phenomena such as slope instabilities, movements of mass, and glacial lake outburst floods. There is also 'high confidence' that changes in heavy rainfall will affect landslides in some regions.

This overview highlights that there are several anticipated climate risks, surrounded by less or more uncertainty. The following terms indicate the assessed likelihood:

- virtually certain: 99–100 per cent probability;
- very likely: 90–100 per cent probability;
- likely: 66–90 per cent probability;
- about as likely as not: 33–66 per cent probability;
- unlikely: 0–33 per cent probability;
- very unlikely: 0–10 per cent probability;
- exceptionally unlikely: 0–1 per cent probability.

On global temperature increase and sea-level rise, Figure 11.6 gives the different pathways projected by the IPCC (2014). The black line reflects the most stringent carbon emission reduction scenario that aims to keep increases in global temperature to 2°C. The grey line reflects the highest emission scenario (carbon emissions rising from the current 40 gigatons (Gt) per year to 100 Gt per year). The lines present the mean of the distribution and the shaded area the 5 to 95 per cent confidence interval. The sea-level rise in the stringent scenario, for example, has a wide range from 28 to 60 cm, with a mean at 44 cm in 2100. Climate change has an impact on the frequency, severity, and geography of natural hazards. Insurers therefore frequently update their catastrophe models to evaluate and manage catastrophe risks. The underlying climate risks show structural uncertainty.

Weitzman (2009) analyses the implications of structural uncertainty for the economics of low-probability, high-impact catastrophes. Even when updated by Bayesian learning, uncertain structural parameters induce a critical 'tail fattening' of posterior-predictive distributions. Such fattened tails have strong implications for situations such as climate change where a catastrophe is theoretically possible, because prior knowledge cannot place sufficiently narrow bounds on overall damages. Weitzman (2009) shows that the economic consequences of fat-tailed structural uncertainty (along with uncertainty about high-temperature damages) can readily outweigh the effects of discounting in climate change policy analysis.

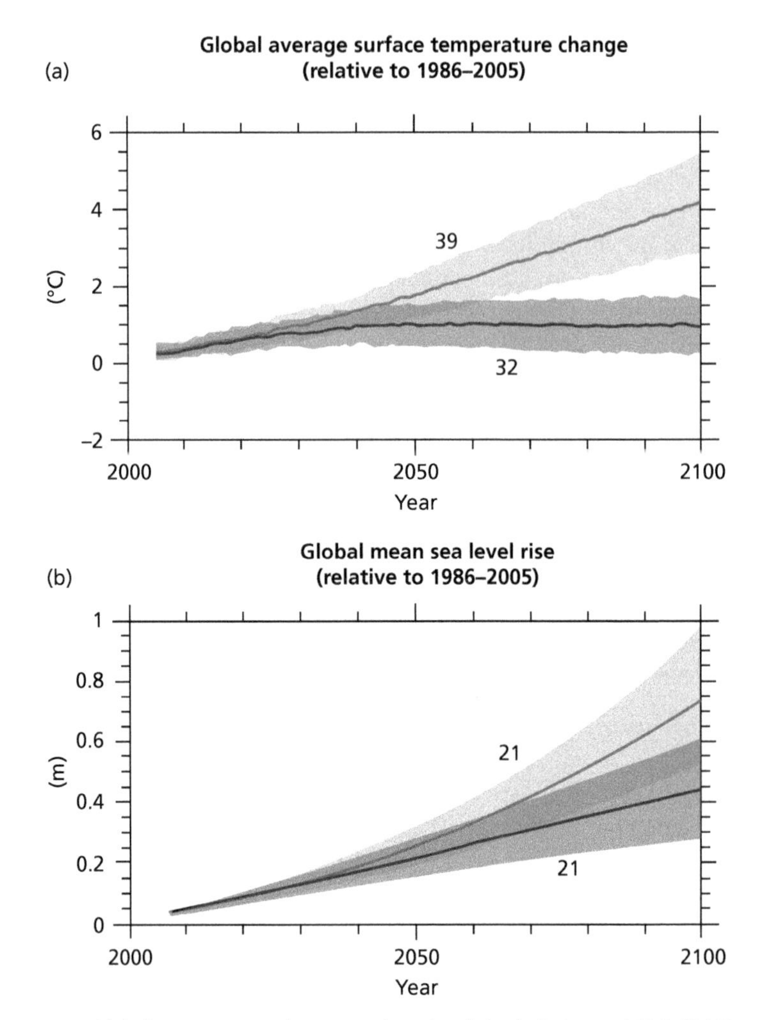

Figure 11.6 Global temperature change and sea-level rise (relative to 1986–2005)

Note: The black line (bottom line) reflects representative concentration pathway (RCP) 2.6: the most stringent carbon emission reduction scenario that aims to keep increases in global temperature to 2°C; the grey line (top line) reflects RCP 8.5: the highest emission scenario. The shaded area gives the 5 to 95 per cent confidence interval, reflecting the uncertainty of the pathways.

Source: IPCC (2014).

11.3.2.1 Example of sea-level rise

We can illustrate the non-linearity and long-term nature of climate risk with the example of sea-level rise, caused by thermal expansion due to warming of the ocean (since water expands as it warms) and increased melting of land-based ice, such as ice sheets and glaciers. The rising sea level has a major

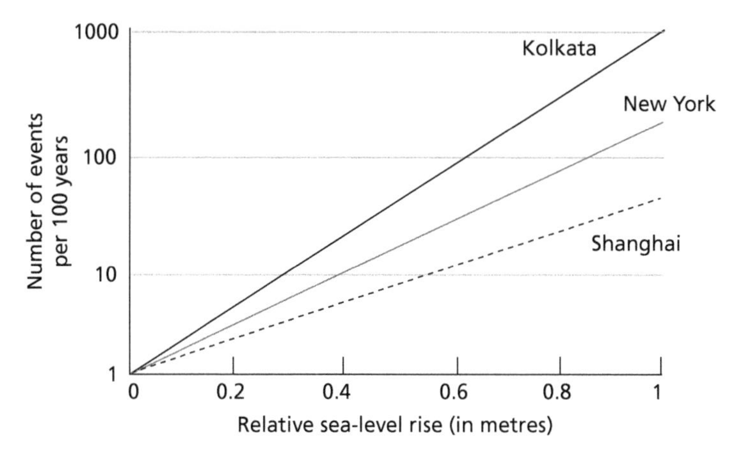

Figure 11.7 Increase of frequency of present 100-year events with rising sea levels

Source: Adapted from Nicholls et al. (2015).

impact on coastal areas with a long lead time. Flood risks grow with sea-level rise as it raises the likelihood of extreme sea levels. Nicholls and colleagues (2015) show the increase in the frequency of current 100-year events in New York, Shanghai, and Kolkata, as sea levels rise. A 1 metre rise in the relative sea-level rise, for example, increases the frequency of current 100-year flood events by about 40 times in Shanghai, about 200 times in New York, and about 1,000 times in Kolkata (see Figure 11.7).

On islands the impact is even more dramatic. In New Zealand, for example, sea level is projected to rise by about 30 centimetres between 2015 and 2065 (mid-point of the four IPCC scenarios for global mean sea-level rise with an additional rise of 10 per cent projected for New Zealand). For a 30 cm sea-level rise, the frequency of current 100-year flood events is expected to increase to every four years at the port of Auckland, every year at the ports of Wellington and Christchurch, and every two years at Dunedin. Table 11.4 shows the expected increases in frequency. Both Figure 11.7 and Table 11.4 indicate that flooding risk is expected to increase at an exponential rate.

There are knock-on effects on the housing stock and communities in coastal areas at risk. With increasing flooding risk, property insurance may retreat from coastal areas and/or premiums may become prohibitive (Storey and Noy, 2017). As insurance retreats from particular locations, house prices in those areas are likely to decline and infrastructure investments may be more difficult to justify. Insurance is often a requirement for residential mortgages and failing to maintain insurance can trigger ‘technical’ default. The possibility of default is exacerbated by maturity mismatches between residential insurance (annual renewal) and mortgages (often a decade or more). As a consequence, in the future, bankers may lend to owners of coastal property less

Table 11.4 Increase of frequency of present 100-year floods in New Zealand

Sea-level rise	Auckland	Wellington	Christchurch	Dunedin
0 cm	Every 100 years	Every 100 years	Every 100 years	Every 100 years
10 cm	Every 35 years	Every 20 years	Every 22 years	Every 29 years
20 cm	Every 12 years	Every 4 years	Every 5 years	Every 9 years
30 cm	Every 4 years	Once a year	Once a year	Every 2 years
40 cm	Every 2 years	Every 2 months	Every 3 months	Every 9 months
50 cm	Every 6 months	Twice a month	Twice a month	Every 3 months
60 cm	Every 2 months	3 times a week	Twice a week	Once a month
70 cm	Every month	Every tide	Every day	Once a week
80 cm	Every week	Every tide	Every tide	4 times a week
90 cm	Twice a week	Every tide	Every tide	Every tide
100 cm	Every day	Every tide	Every tide	Every tide

Source: Parliamentary Commissioner for the Environment (2015).

often, require more equity as collateral, or offer shorter mortgage terms. Unless defences are significantly upgraded, coastal areas may thus be abandoned well before the risks materialize, impacting the local community.

Translating flooding risk to financial losses, Hallegate and colleagues (2013) make the following estimates concerning the future of coastal flooding in the 136 largest coastal cities (in 2005) over the next 50 years or so:

- Damage could rise from $6 billion to $52 billion per year solely due to increase in population, and in property and its value.
- With additional climate change and subsidence, global losses could approach $1 trillion or more per year if flood defences are not upgraded.
- Even if protection levels are maintained (i.e. flood probability is kept the same thanks to upgraded defences), annual losses will grow to $60–63 billion per year in 2050 as individual floods become more severe due to flood depths increasing with relative sea-level rise. To maintain present levels of flood risk (average losses per year), protection will need to be upgraded to reduce flood probabilities to below present values.
- Even with upgraded protection, the magnitude of losses when flood events do occur would increase for the reasons stated in this list, making it critical to also prepare for larger disasters than we experience today.

11.3.3 MITIGATION AND ADAPTATION MEASURES

Natural disasters have adverse consequences. A combination of effective mitigation strategies and appropriate coping measures—decreasing both vulnerability and exposure—can reduce their detrimental impact (Noy, Kusuma, and Nguyen, 2017). Insurance is the most common financial risk transfer tool, but other informal and formal risk-sharing arrangements also exist (e.g. mutual (informal) insurance, micro- and macro-contingent loans, catastrophic bonds, and contingent sovereign credit). A prudent combination of financial risk transfer tools and relevant disaster risk reduction measures, such as an early warning system, risk education and communication, and defensive infrastructure, can minimize disruptions and losses to societies when catastrophic hazards occur (Muir-Wood, 2016).

Moreover, insurance can strengthen incentives for other risk-mitigating behaviours. However, insurance covers only about 10 per cent of disaster losses in developing countries and about 40 per cent in developed countries (Noy, Kusuma, and Nguyen, 2017). Different types of disaster insurance products are found globally. Some examples are flood (re-)insurance in the United States and the United Kingdom, microinsurance for crop losses in Bangladesh and India, earthquake insurance in New Zealand and Turkey, tropical cyclone sovereign insurance for the Caribbean and Pacific island countries, drought sovereign insurance in Sub-Saharan Africa, and agricultural insurance in Europe.

Weather events such as droughts and floods have adverse consequences for the overall economy and particularly for agriculture. Many middle- and low-income countries are especially reliant on the agricultural sector as an important sector of their economies and typically also as a main export sector. As such, these countries are more affected by adverse weather events that damage agricultural production. Box 11.3 suggests how a global climate risk pool can help the most vulnerable countries at the macro level.

Moving to sea-level rise, Nicholls and colleagues (2015) argue that climate mitigation can stabilize the rate of sea-level rise, which makes adaptation more feasible. However, even if the global temperature is stabilized, the sea level will continue to rise for many centuries as the deep ocean slowly warms and the large ice sheets reach a new equilibrium: this has been termed the 'commitment to sea-level rise' (see also the mitigation scenario with the black line in Panels A and B of Figure 11.6). This suggests that in coastal areas mitigation and adaptation must be considered together as the committed sea-level rise necessitates an adaptation response. This perspective changes the mitigation discussion towards avoiding high-end changes in climate over longer time spans than are typically considered.

As a final word of caution, Noy, Kusuma, and Nguyen (2017) stress that insurance only transfers the financial component of risk. It most certainly does not save lives directly and may only indirectly improve people's well-being after catastrophic events. It should therefore only follow important risk reduction measures and mitigation strategies that should be prioritized.

BOX 11.3 A GLOBAL CLIMATE RISK POOL

Global warming leads to more and more-intense disasters, such as storms, flooding, and droughts. The low- and middle-income countries around the equator are especially vulnerable to these extreme weather events, which can damage a large part of their production capacity. The temporary loss of tax revenues and increase in expenditures to restore agriculture and reconstruct factories and infrastructure might put vulnerable countries into a downward fiscal and macro-economic spiral (Schoenmaker and Zachmann, 2015).

While protecting each country against the most extreme possible events is neither possible nor cost-efficient, a global climate risk pool, with contributions from all countries, could help the most affected countries recover from the initial macro-economic shock (and smooth the way towards a broader deal). As extreme events, such as storm surges, will increase because of climate change, the pool can only insure events that significantly exceed the trend line. Figure 11.8 provides a stylized example of annual storm surge. The pool would, for example, cover the higher point for country A at 11.3 metres, but not the lower point of 10.2 metres in 2063.

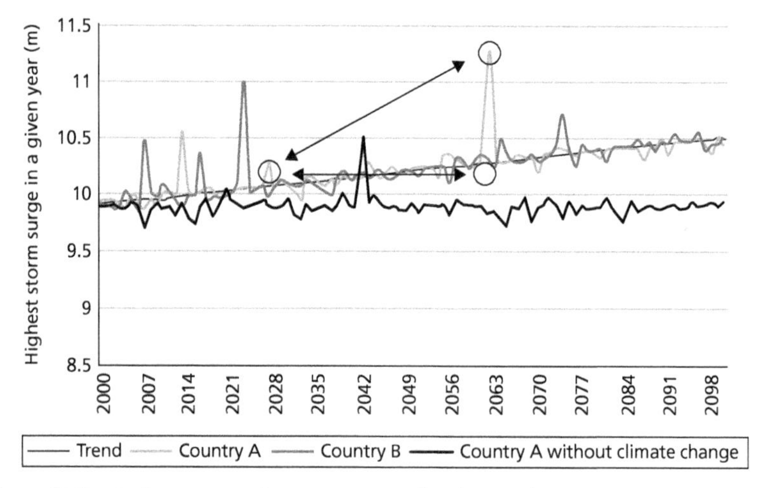

Figure 11.8 Maximum annual storm surge, stylized example

Source: Schoenmaker and Zachmann (2015).

11.4 **Microinsurance**

Microinsurance is the financial protection of low-income people and micro-enterprises against specific risks using low-priced targeted products. These risks include—like regular insurance—both health risks (illness, injury, or death) and property risks (damage or loss). A wide variety of microinsurance products exist to address these risks, including crop insurance, livestock/cattle insurance, insurance for theft or fire, health insurance, life insurance, disability insurance, and insurance for natural disasters. Microinsurance has a positive impact on the use of health care and decreases catastrophe expenditures (Apostolakis, Van Dijk, and Drakos, 2015).

In general, the poverty trap can also be attributed to the poor's vulnerability to cope with unexpected shocks. Microinsurance mitigates this vulnerability by replacing the uncertainty of the future outcome with the obligation of making small, regular payments for receiving an important level of assurance in exchange. Microinsurance could thus play, just like microfinance and microcredit (see Chapter 10), a role in reducing poverty and spurring growth. The risk-pooling (ex ante) and shock-absorbing (ex post) mechanisms of insurance reduce the poor's vulnerability to shocks, smoothing income and consumption (Apostolakis, Van Dijk, and Drakos, 2015).

Arena (2008) investigates whether insurance market activity contributes to economic growth, both as a financial intermediary and provider of risk transfer and indemnification, by allowing different risks to be managed more efficiently and by mobilizing domestic savings. In an empirical test covering 55 countries between 1976 and 2004, Arena (2008) finds that both life and non-life insurance have a positive and significant causal effect on economic growth. For life insurance, high-income countries drive the results, while for non-life insurance, both high-income and developing countries drive the results.

The share of emerging market premiums of the global total has been increasing since the financial crisis in 2008, when high-income economies were in recession and the global insurance sector growth stagnated. Emerging markets now account for about 20 per cent of global life and non-life premiums, up from 5 per cent in 2000 (Swiss Re, 2017). Nevertheless, insurance coverage remains inaccessible or unaffordable to many people in emerging markets.

11.4.1 SUPPLIERS OF MICROINSURANCE

A particular challenge for the distribution of microinsurance is reaching the poor. According to Apostolakis, Van Dijk, and Drakos (2015), the main models for supplying microinsurance are:

- commercial insurers;
- community-based organizations, mutuals, and cooperatives;
- microfinance institutions.

Commercial insurers balance profitability and social impact (see Section 11.2 on Allianz). They often lack the potential to reach the poorest segment of the population. Churchill (2007) stresses that insurers need to become more familiar with the preferences and behaviour of poor persons, and educate the market about insurance to create low-income consumers.

Community-based schemes have the advantage of better knowledge of the local market and potentially have large outreach, but lack professionalism and managerial skills and are vulnerable to common risk shocks (Apostolakis, Van Dijk, and Drakos, 2015). Many emerging markets lack a viable health insurance sector, partly due to a lack of health-care infrastructure, but also due to barriers such as affordability and high distribution costs. A mutual health insurance programme has been particularly successful in Rwanda, where 84 per cent of the defined population had enrolled in a community-based health insurance scheme by April 2017 (Swiss Re, 2017). Rwanda reduced its maternal mortality rate by 79 per cent from 1990 to 2015, becoming the first African country to meet this Millennium Development Goal. Its health insurance programme was cited as a big part of the reason for this success.

The professional skills and diversification capacity of the commercial supplier and the local outreach of the mutual schemes can be combined. The partner–agent model can upgrade mutual programmes or downscale commercial programmes (Apostolakis, Van Dijk, and Drakos, 2015). In the partner–agent model, two institutions are involved in the provision of insurance where the partner, typically an established commercial insurer, is responsible for product manufacturing and the local mutual insurer provides the product distribution. The only microinsurance programmes (for catastrophe risk) that have managed to be maintained are ones that have a very large component of government subsidies. In India, for example, the biggest global microinsurance crop programme is subsidized so that most farmers pay only about 10 per cent of the premium.

Microfinance institutions have a unique position in providing microinsurance, as they have extensive networks and are already offering financial services to poor clients (see Chapter 10). In some cases, microfinance institutions link with formal insurance companies and act as agents. They also form joint ventures with formal insurers (Apostolakis, Van Dijk, and Drakos, 2015).

Finally, Box 11.4 shows that digital technology can radically change the production and distribution of microinsurance. Nevertheless, there also factors that impede microinsurance, such as low understanding of its working conditions and its potential benefits due to illiteracy. Furthermore, the low rate of claims and difficulties in the claim process are responsible for low renewals.

11.4.2 MEASURING IMPACT

The financial and social impact of microinsurance programmes are measured separately. Reviewing the empirical evidence, Apostolakis, Van Dijk, and Drakos (2015) report that size and organizational structure are important

BOX 11.4 DIGITALLY ENABLED INSURANCE

Digital technology can make insurance more accessible and affordable, especially for younger people (Swiss Re, 2017). Mobile technology, which is spreading rapidly, can be combined in innovative ways with other technology tools. Geospatial technologies can be used to track behaviour such as driving, risk accumulation, weather, and so on.

Parametric insurance products relying on weather stations for data can pay claims in an automated manner using mobile money methods. Swiss Re (2017) reports that by 2016 such systems had helped, for example, more than 1 million farmers in Kenya, Tanzania, and Rwanda buy risk protection via the crop and livestock index insurance offerings developed by the Agriculture and Climate Risk Enterprise, the largest index insurance programme in Africa in which the farmers pay a market premium.

It should be noted that index insurance is subject to basis risk, which is the difference between an index and the specific losses of the farmer. The insurance payout will thus differ from the farmer's expectation (and needs). When the basis risk is significant (e.g. the index measurement location and production field are far apart), the cover against losses is very imprecise and the insurance product becomes more like a lottery ticket.

factors in the efficiency of microinsurance programmes. For-profit microinsurance organizations seem to be more efficient than non-profit. Large and for-profit microinsurance providers are more capable of efficiently allocating the available resources and producing a more cost-efficient insurance output, achieving better allocation and cost efficiency.

Microinsurance institutions are facing difficulties attaining sustainability and profitability goals. Factors such as fraud, adverse selection, and moral hazard impede the financial performance of such programmes. In particular, the sustainability of early microinsurance programmes is often at stake. These programmes have limited data availability and no good actuarial tables and have therefore to use the trial-and-error method in setting the premiums.

On social impact, participation in microinsurance programmes is related to improved access to health-care services, and to improvement of health care and health protection. In particular, several studies find greater use of hospitals by the insured households and a substantially higher number of visits to the doctor (Apostolakis, Van Dijk, and Drakos, 2015). Participation is also related to financial protection and reducing the poor's vulnerability to poverty by reducing catastrophic expenditure. So, microinsurance delivers not only improved access to health care, but also a positive economic impact by reducing the probability of catastrophic expenditures.

Countries can also be heavily impacted through catastrophes eroding the tax base (as production capacity is destroyed) and increasing expenditures to restore infrastructure. Insurance at the country level can thus help countries and their people to recover faster after a catastrophe. Box 11.3 discusses the idea of a global climate risk pool.

11.5 Conclusions

Insurers play a crucial role in managing long-term catastrophe risk. Climate change is intensifying the natural hazards, such as floods and hurricanes, leading to more frequent and larger catastrophes. By pooling risks, insurance can help absorb the financial losses from these catastrophes. To manage their long-term exposure, insurers are active in both mitigation (curbing emissions) and adaption (dealing with natural hazards).

The long-term impact of climate change is uncertain. Advanced catastrophe models aim to capture long-term trends in the development of natural hazards, which often span a 50-year horizon. The projected sea-level rise from 2015 to 2065 can, for example, increase the flooding of coastal areas, such as the port of Auckland, from once every 100 years to once every four years.

The insurance industry also plays a major role in managing liability risks from climate effects and other environmental hazards. Big tobacco companies have been sued, and are still being sued, and have to pay out large sums of money in settlement agreements. Fossil fuel companies may face similar claims in the future with regard to climate change.

Microinsurance has the potential to protect low-income individuals or micro-enterprises, which otherwise have no access to financial services, against the financial impact of specific risks using low-priced targeted products. These risks include both health risks (illness, injury, or death) and property risks (damage or loss). Microinsurance could reduce the vulnerability of poor people to unexpected shocks.

Key concepts used in this chapter

Catastrophe is an event that exceeds the capacity of those affected to cope with, or absorb, its effects. In the context of natural hazards, the driver is an extreme event causing widespread and usually sudden damage or suffering.

Catastrophe model is a sophisticated model to assess the economic losses from catastrophes.

Claim or insurance claim is a formal request to an insurance company for coverage or compensation for a covered loss or policy event. The insurance company validates the claim and, once approved, issues payment to the insured.

Combined ratio expresses an insurer's claims and expenses relative to premiums earned.

Economic losses are the losses caused by catastrophes and include inter alia property damage, business contingency, and agriculture (impaired food production). The economic losses can be split into insured and uninsured losses.

Exceedance frequency is the annual frequency of events expected to give greater losses than a reference amount.

Insurance protects individuals and firms from the financial consequences of adverse events through the pooling of risks. Life insurance protects against premature death, disability, and retirement. Non-life insurance protects against risks such as accidents, illness, theft, and fire.

Insured losses are those economic losses from a catastrophe that are covered by insurance.

Liability insurance protects the insured from the financial risks of liabilities imposed by lawsuits and similar claims.

Lifeyears index is a people-centric measure to assess disaster impacts. It combines missed life years of victims and injured people, with losses divided by annual income.

Microinsurance is an insurance service for low-income individuals or micro-enterprises, which otherwise have no access to financial services.

Monitoring involves the screening of potential insured individuals and firms (adverse selection) and the controlling of the insured during the cover period (moral hazard) to reduce asymmetric information between an insurer and its insured.

Natural hazards are naturally occurring physical phenomena caused either by rapid or slow onset events, which can be geophysical (earthquakes, landslides, tsunamis, and volcanic activity), hydrological (avalanches, storm surges, and floods), climatological (extreme temperatures, drought, and wildfires), meteorological (cyclones, tornadoes, and storms), or biological (disease epidemics and insect/animal plagues).

Re-insurance occurs when multiple insurance companies share risk by purchasing insurance policies from other insurers (re-insurers) to limit the total loss the original insurer would experience in case of disaster.

Uninsured losses are those economic losses from a catastrophe that are not covered by insurance.

SUGGESTED READING

Apostolakis, G., G. van Dijk, and P. Drakos, (2015) 'Microinsurance performance: a systematic narrative literature review', *Corporate Governance*, 15(1): 146–70.

Carney, M. (2015), 'Breaking the tragedy of the horizon: climate change and financial stability', Speech at Lloyd's of London, 29 September.

Mitchell-Wallace, K., M. Jones, J. Hillier, and M. Foote (2017), *Natural Catastrophe Risk Management and Modelling*, John Wiley & Sons, Hoboken, NJ.

Muir-Wood, R. (2016), *The Cure for Catastrophe: How We Can Stop Manufacturing Natural Disasters*, Oneworld Publications, London.

Woo, G. (2011), *Calculating Catastrophe*, Imperial College Press, London.

REFERENCES

Apostolakis, G., G. van Dijk, and P. Drakos, (2015) 'Microinsurance performance: a systematic narrative literature review', *Corporate Governance*, 15(1): 146–70.

Arena, M. (2008), 'Does insurance market activity promote economic growth? A cross-country study for industrialized and developing countries', *Journal of Risk and Insurance*, 75(4): 921–46.

Billette de Villemeur, E. and J. Leroux (2016), 'A liability approach to climate policy: a thought experiment', MPRA Paper No. 75497, University Library of Munich.

Churchill, C. (2007), 'Insuring the low-income market: challenges and solutions for commercial insurers', *Geneva Papers on Risk and Insurance*, 32(3): 401–12.

ClimateWise and Cambridge Institute for Sustainability Leadership (2012), 'Why should insurers consider climate risk?', Cambridge, http://financehub.cisl.cam.ac.uk/sites/financehub.cisl.cam.ac.uk/files/public/sumissions/SREX%20Summary%20for%20Insurers%20-%20Dec%202012.pdf, accessed 5 July 2018.

Embrechts, P., C. Klüppelberg, and T. Mikosch (1997), *Modelling Extremal Events for Insurance and Finance*, Springer, Heidelberg.

Financial Times (2017), 'ExxonMobil bows to shareholder pressure on climate reporting', 12 December.

Hallegatte, S., C. Green, R. Nicholls, and J. Corfee-Morlot (2013), 'Future flood losses in major coastal cities', *Nature Climate Change*, 3(9): 802–6.

IPCC (Intergovernmental Panel on Climate Change), 'Climate change 2014: synthesis report', Geneva, http://www.ipcc.ch/pdf/assessment-report/ar5/syr/SYR_AR5_FINAL_full_wcover.pdf, accessed 5 July 2018.

Lloyd's (2014), 'Catastrophe modelling and climate change', London.

Loubergé, H. (2000), 'Developments in risk and insurance economics: the past 25 years', in: G. Dionne (ed.), *Handbook of Insurance*, Kluwer, Dordrecht, 3–33.

Mitchell-Wallace, K., M. Jones, J. Hillier, and M. Foote (2017), *Natural Catastrophe Risk Management and Modelling*, John Wiley & Sons, Hoboken, NJ.

Muir-Wood, R. (2016), *The Cure for Catastrophe: How We Can Stop Manufacturing Natural Disasters*, Oneworld Publications, London.

Nicholls, R., T. Reeder, S. Brown, and I. Haigh (2015), 'The risks of sea-level rise for coastal areas', in: D. King, D. Schrag, Z. Dadi, Q. Ye, and A. Ghosh (eds.), *Climate Change: A Risk Assessment*, Centre for Science and Policy, University of Cambridge, Cambridge, 94–8.

Noy, I. (2016), 'A global comprehensive measure of the impact of natural hazards and disasters', *Global Policy*, 7(1): 56–65.

Noy, I., A. Kusuma, and C. Nguyen (2017), 'Insuring disasters: a survey of the economics of insurance programs for earthquakes and droughts', SEF Working Paper No. 11/2017, Victoria Business School, Wellington.

Parliamentary Commissioner for the Environment (2015), 'Preparing New Zealand for rising seas: certainty and uncertainty', Wellington, http://www.pce.parliament.nz/publications/preparing-new-zealand-for-rising-seas-certainty-and-uncertainty, accessed 6 July 2018.

Prudential Regulation Authority (2015), 'The impact of climate change on the UK insurance sector', London, https://www.bankofengland.co.uk/-/media/boe/files/prudential-regulation/publication/impact-of-climate-change-on-the-uk-insurance-sector.pdf, accessed 6 July 2018.

Rejda, G. E. (2005), *Principles of Risk Management and Insurance*, 9th edn, Addison Wesley, Boston, MA.

RobecoSAM (2017), 'Industry group leader report: Allianz SE', Zurich.

Rothschild, M. and J. Stiglitz (1976), 'Equilibrium in competitive insurance markets: an essay on the economics of imperfect information', *Quarterly Journal of Economics*, 90(4): 629–49.

Schoenmaker, D. and G. Zachmann (2015), 'Can a global climate risk pool help the most vulnerable countries?', Policy Brief 2015/04, Bruegel, Brussels.

Shapira, R. and L. Zingales (2017), 'Is pollution value-maximizing? The Dupont case', CEPR Discussion Paper No. 12323.

Shiller, R. (2012), *Finance and the Good Society*, Princeton University Press, Princeton, NJ.

Storey, B. and I. Noy (2017), 'Insuring property under climate change', *Policy Quarterly*, 13(4): 68–79.

Swiss Re (2017), 'Insurance: adding value to development in emerging markets', Sigma, 4, http://institute.swissre.com/research/overview/sigma/4_2017.html, accessed 6 July 2018.

Swiss Re (2018), 'Natural catastrophes and man-made disasters in 2017', Sigma, 1, http://www.swissre.com/library/publication-sigma/sigma_1_2018_en.html, accessed 6 July 2018.

Von Schuckmann, K. and P.-Y. Le Traon (2011), 'How well can we derive Global Ocean Indicators from Argo data?', *Ocean Science*, 7(6): 783–91.

Weitzman, M. (2009), 'On modeling and interpreting the economics of catastrophic climate change', *Review of Economics and Statistics*, 91(1): 1–19.

Woo, G. (2011), *Calculating Catastrophe*, Imperial College Press, London.

Part IV

How to get there?

12 Transition management and integrated thinking

Overview

This book is about the why, how, and what of sustainable finance (SF), which integrates financial, social, and environmental dimensions. Yet the financial risk–return thinking of traditional finance is still the dominant culture in the financial industry. This final chapter therefore discusses transition management: how to transition from an old to a new regime.

Transition is about transformational change rather than incremental change. It is seen as an iterative process of the build-up of a new regime and breakdown of an old regime over a period of time, with disruptions along the way. There are attempts to incorporate sustainability (e.g. through environmental, social, and governance (ESG) ratings) into the current methods and practices of investing and lending. Transition management starts with rethinking current persistent methods and structuring the underlying shortcomings. The next step is developing a new vision for the long term, which is then backcasted to new approaches for the medium term and concrete experiments in the short term.

What could be a new visionary perspective of finance? The building blocks are twofold. First, the relationship between the financial institution and the company is important. Companies are not only causing social and environmental externalities (negative impact), but can also contribute to achieving the Sustainable Development Goals (SDGs) (positive impact). There is a need to include these social and environmental dimensions in investment and lending. Secondly, there is a widely felt need to reorient finance from the short term to the long term (see Chapter 3). In this chapter, a new *vision for the financial sector* is to invest in, lend to, and engage with corporates that aim for long-term value creation (LTVC)—consistent with achieving the SDGs by 2030.

This new perspective requires integrated thinking, which integrates financial, social, and environmental dimensions. As people determine the success of a transition (in interplay with the system), individuals matter. While there are some change agents who start to look for alternatives, most people prefer the status quo. So, there is a need to reboot the current culture—or software of the financial system—and develop a new culture. To make the transformation lasting, it is crucial it impacts the intrinsic motivation of the people in the financial industry, including its leaders. Responsible management education can contribute to that. Just providing incentives will not do.

Learning points

After you have studied this chapter, you should be able to:

- understand the dynamics of transition management;
- explain a new vision and approaches in the financial sector;
- understand the need for an interdisciplinary approach;
- apply the concept of integrated thinking.

12.1 Transition governance

The transition of the financial sector is part of a wider transition to a sustainable and inclusive economy (Grin, Rotmans, and Schot, 2010; see also Chapter 1). The current regime of traditional finance is based on the neoclassical paradigm of shareholder value maximization and confines itself to the financial risk–return space. A newly emerging regime of SF envisions LTVC as the objective for companies and builds on the concept of integrated value, which combines financial, social, and environmental values. This changing perspective is not an incremental change, but a non-linear, shockwise transformational change.

Figure 12.1 depicts the dynamics of societal transitions as iterative processes of build-up and breakdown over a period of decades (Loorbach, Frantzeskaki,

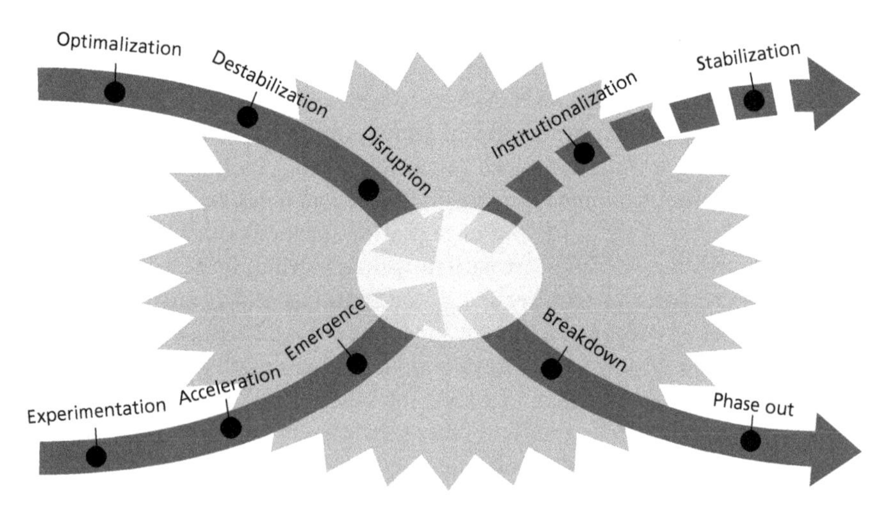

Figure 12.1 The x-curve of transition dynamics

Source: Loorbach, Frantzeskaki, and Avelino (2017).

and Avelino, 2017). In a changing societal context, incumbent regimes develop path-dependently through optimization, while change agents start to experiment with alternative ideas, technologies, and practices. Over time pressures build on regimes to transform, leading to destabilization as alternatives begin to accelerate and emerge. The actual transition is then chaotic and disruptive and new combinations of emerging alternatives and transformative regime elements grow into a new regime. In this process elements of an old regime that do not transform are broken down and phased out.

Looking at the transition dynamics of the financial sector, there are both attempts to reform within the old regime and experiments to find a new regime. The application of ESG ratings (e.g. negative screening or best-in-class strategies; see Chapter 8) to investment and lending portfolios can, for example, be seen as incremental changes to optimize the investment and lending process from a societal perspective. These changes take place within the current regime, which is based on market benchmarking. The maximization of the financial return, subject to risk, is still the guiding objective, with, sometimes, a moral dimension (e.g. no investment in fur or tobacco). These incremental changes are not durable and provide opportunities for alternatives.

Methods to holistically and fundamentally analyse and engage with companies with regard to their contribution to sustainable development are emerging. These methods shape the investment and lending process in a new regime of SF. These are transformative changes replacing old methods and habits. A new guiding principle is the optimization of integrated value, which combines financial, social, and environmental values, in the long run (see Chapters 3 and 5). These emerging methods are still in the experimental phase and not yet widely or forcefully applied. Engagement, for example, has had until now marginal effects, seldom leading to the ultimate consequence of investors leaving a company if engagement is not successful (e.g. fossil fuel utilities suddenly faced problems with investments and financing, but not because of earlier engagement).

Transition governance looks at how actors can influence transition processes (Loorbach, Frantzeskaki, and Avelino, 2017). Several actors in both the current regime and in niches can explore initiatives for fundamental transition. But effective transition agency requires selective participation (front-runners and radical outsiders), because it is important to steer clear of unsustainability lock-in and to mobilize and empower disruptive innovations and transformative capacity from the system towards desirable sustainability transitions. Actors' outside-in perspective is important to understand the desired transition. Agency, and interaction in networks, influences the pace and direction of transitions. Transition governance is a multi-actor process in which systemic solutions, disruptive innovations, and (reflexive) institutions are formed by experimenting and learning.

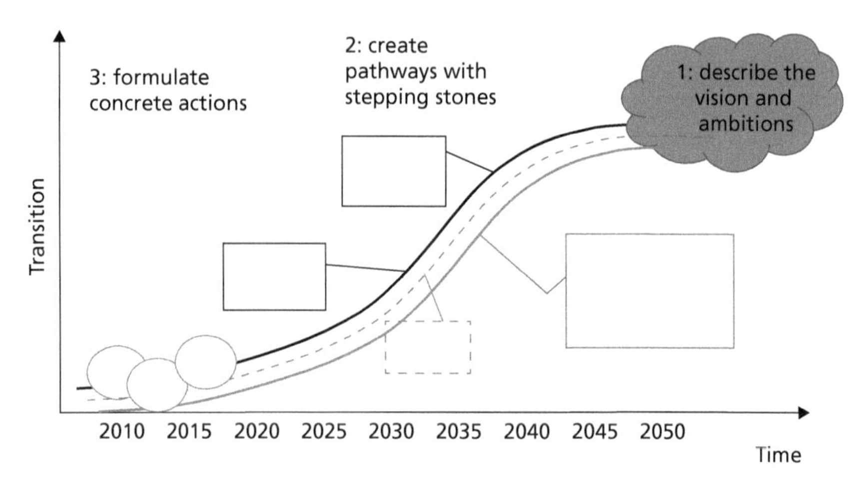

Figure 12.2 Backcasting: From long-term thinking to short-term action

Source: Adapted from Loorbach (2010).

12.1.1 NEW VISION AND APPROACHES

Transition governance has several dimensions. It starts with formulating a new vision at the strategic level. That is the desired direction of the transition. The move from long-term thinking to short-term action is called *backcasting* (see Figure 12.2). The vision is then translated via a transition agenda and pathways with stepping stones at the tactical level. The next step is the formulation of concrete actions and experiments. The final step is monitoring the new approaches and experiments.

12.1.1.1 Vision

There is an emerging consensus that LTVC consistent with achieving the SDGs by 2030 is a relevant perspective for all players (governments, corporates, households, and financial institutions) in the system. Figure 12.3 indicates that corporates play a key role in LTVC. They provide products and services that can contribute to the SDGs. Companies' production processes are also relevant for sustainable development (e.g. using renewable energy, minimizing use of virgin materials or fresh water). That is increasingly recognized. The front-runners in the World Business Council for Sustainable Development (see Chapter 4) have adopted the SDGs as a leading framework for the future. The renewed corporate governance codes in the United Kingdom and the Netherlands have laid down LTVC as guiding objective for corporates.

So, what is a visionary perspective of SF in this new setting? Using its allocation role, the financial sector can direct the transition in the corporate

Panel A: Financial value creation in traditional finance

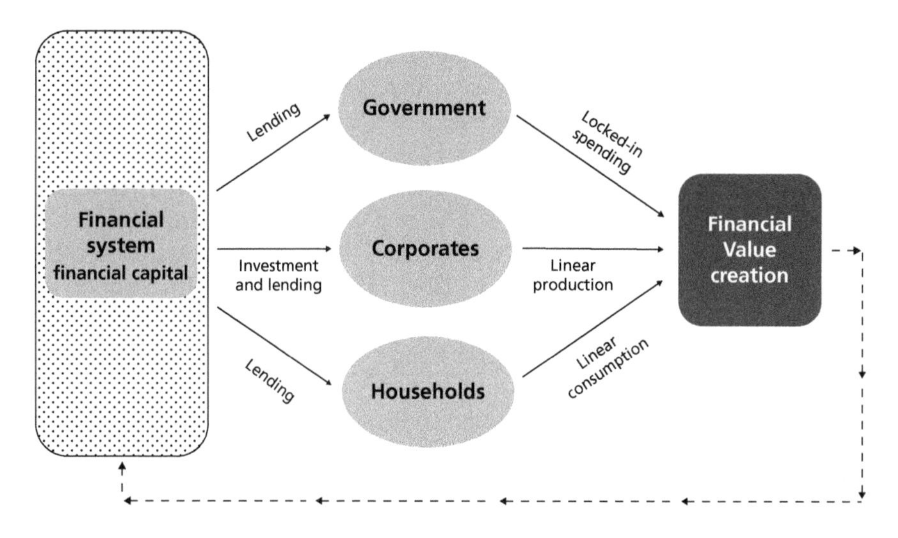

Panel B: Long-term value creation in sustainable finance

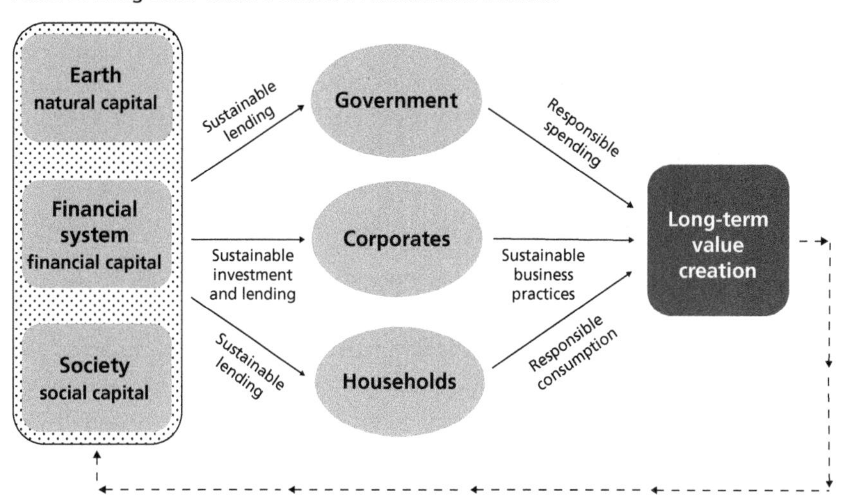

Figure 12.3 Value creation: From an old to a new vision

Note: See Chapter 1 for explanation.

sector by investing in and lending to companies that contribute positively to the SDGs and by divesting and ceasing lending to companies that have a negative impact. In this way, the financial sector can accelerate the transition to LTVC. Thus, a new *vision for the financial sector* is to invest in, lend to, and engage with corporates that aim for LTVC.

A guiding principle or norm for investment and lending moves from financial return maximization subject to risk (incumbent regime) to optimization of integrated value combining the financial, social, and environmental dimensions subject to integrated risk (new regime). The social and environmental dimensions ultimately incorporate the contribution to the SDGs. The evidence presented throughout the book (in particular Chapters 5 to 11) indicates that there is a business case for full ESG integration into investment, lending, and insurance, which is a first step towards achieving the SDGs. Companies that perform well on material ESG issues also outperform in the stock market (e.g. Clark, Feiner, and Viehs, 2015; Khan, Serafeim, and Yoon, 2016). This is consistent with the idea that strong management of material ESG issues brings a real competitive advantage, including in the transition to a sustainable and inclusive economy.

A new vision for the financial system contrasts with a piecemeal or project-based approach. The financial sector is then, for example, called upon to invest in new infrastructures for the energy transition. Such a project-based approach would be too narrow as a perspective for the financial system. Moreover, when the orientation of the financial system remains financially focused, financial institutions may keep asking for public subsidies (or tax incentives) before investing in new sustainable projects as they ignore the social and environmental potential. A rebooting of the financial system from managing on financial value to managing on integrated value offers a broader perspective. The financial system can then be fully exploited to achieve LTVC and truly perform its social function of steering financial capital to the most productive ends.

12.1.1.2 Transition agenda and pathways

The next step at the tactical level is setting the agenda and building coalitions to develop new approaches based on a new vision. Focus Capital on Long-Term Global (FCLTGlobal) and the United Nations (UN) Principles for Responsible Investment (PRI) are examples of such coalitions at the international level (see Chapter 4). Also at the national level, similar coalitions are emerging, such as the Purposeful Company in the United Kingdom (Purposeful Company, 2017) and SHIFT TO Long-term investing in the Netherlands (e.g. Van Dam and Dijkstra, 2018).

Two common themes can be identified across these coalitions. The first is moving away from portfolio investing towards investing in individual companies. The link between the investor and the company is rediscovered (e.g. purpose of company and engagement). The second theme is the orientation on the long term, which is even in the name of some of these coalitions. The coalitions are worried that long investment chains lead to short-term performance measurement, while the beneficiaries or asset owners want to invest for the long term.

New approaches and pathways to long-term investing are explored. Examples are the total value approach (see Chapter 2) and various forms of fundamental investing with concentrated portfolios (see Chapters 7 and 8). Also the investment mandate, which sets the parameters for the investment relationship between asset owners and asset managers, is addressed. Well-designed mandates explicitly integrate provisions that reflect long-term objectives (FCLTGlobal, 2017). Chapter 7 provides a summary of best practices on long-term investing.

There are also coalitions on the official side. To initiate the transition to SF, the UN Environment Programme set up an Inquiry into the Design of a Sustainable Financial System, which operated from 2014 to 2018. During this period, the Inquiry team acted as an initiator, promoting best practices and linking players at the national and international level (see, for example, the UN Environment Inquiry's Roadmap, 2017). During its presidency of the Group of Twenty, China introduced a Green Finance Study Group in 2015. More recently, the European Commission set up a High-Level Expert Group on Sustainable Finance (2018), which delivered its final report in early 2018.

In terms of transition governance, the members in the private and official coalitions are connectors between the activities and projects of front-runners. New networks emerge and best practices are spread through the investment management industry.

12.1.1.3 Concrete actions

The third stage is experimenting with new approaches. As of the time of writing in early 2018, financial institutions are tiptoeing into SF. First, an increasing number of financials are applying ESG ratings, via screening or best-in-class methods, to their investment and lending portfolio. These approaches are attempts to optimize sustainability within the current regime and only scratch the surface of SF (see Chapter 7). Secondly, some financials are starting to allocate small parts (e.g. 5 to 10 per cent) of their investment or lending portfolio to specific investment themes or companies that contribute to the SDGs. These are true experiments in the new regime. Thirdly, a few front-runners conduct fundamental analysis into and engage with investee or borrowing companies that pursue LTVC. These front-runners have a concentrated portfolio of shareholdings (Box 7.3 in Chapter 7 provides the example of Alecta), green bonds (Box 9.2 in Chapter 9 provides the example of Amundi), or impact loans (Section 10.5 in Chapter 10 on values-based banks).

Next, there are experiments with better information provision, which is important for fundamental investment analysis. Chapter 6 discusses the new concept of integrated reporting and provides examples of leading companies such as Adidas and Philips that are publishing integrated reports. Another example is the Bloomberg Task Force promoting a set of voluntary, consistent disclosure standards for companies to provide information to investors, lenders, and insurance underwriters about their climate-related financial risks (TCFD, 2017). This increases transparency on carbon exposures in the value chain.

The latest development is that sustainability data providers, discussed in Chapter 6, are starting to link the performance of companies directly to the SDGs. An example is the oekom Sustainability Solutions Assessment, which provides a comprehensive assessment of products and services aligned to the SDGs. It enables investors to identify the share of products and services with a positive or negative impact on social and environmental objectives.

Finally, there is better dialogue between investors and corporates on sustainability issues, which enhances engagement (e.g. Grewal, Serafeim, and Yoon, 2016). The front-runners integrate investment analysis and engagement (see Section 12.3). Some of the passive benchmark investors are also stepping up their engagement efforts with companies on LTVC. BlackRock is planning to double the size of its corporate governance team over the next three years (*Financial Times*, 2018). It is not yet clear which approach (engagement based on fundamental or on passive investment) will yield better results and whether they will complement each other. So, monitoring of the different experiments is valuable.

12.1.1.4 **Monitoring**

The final step is reflective and monitors and evaluates the new approaches and experiments. These insights can then be fed back into the vision, approaches, and experiments. As the early evidence with concentrated portfolios is favourable (Choi et al. 2017; Cremers and Pareek, 2016), institutional investors can take a deep dive into long-term investing with large parts of their portfolio, whereby investors analyse the business model of companies to detect material sustainable issues and engage with companies to further improve business performance. It should be noted that not only equities, but also corporate and sovereign bonds, can be invested in a sustainable way, as discussed in Chapter 9. The transition potential is thus the full amount of global assets under management at $163 trillion (see Chapter 4).

12.2 **Transition management**

A transition can be implemented in many different ways and needs to be adapted to the context in which it is used. Loorbach (Loorbach 2010; Loorbach and Oxenaar, 2018) provides a *transition management* framework, including transition management instruments for implementing strategies that help to

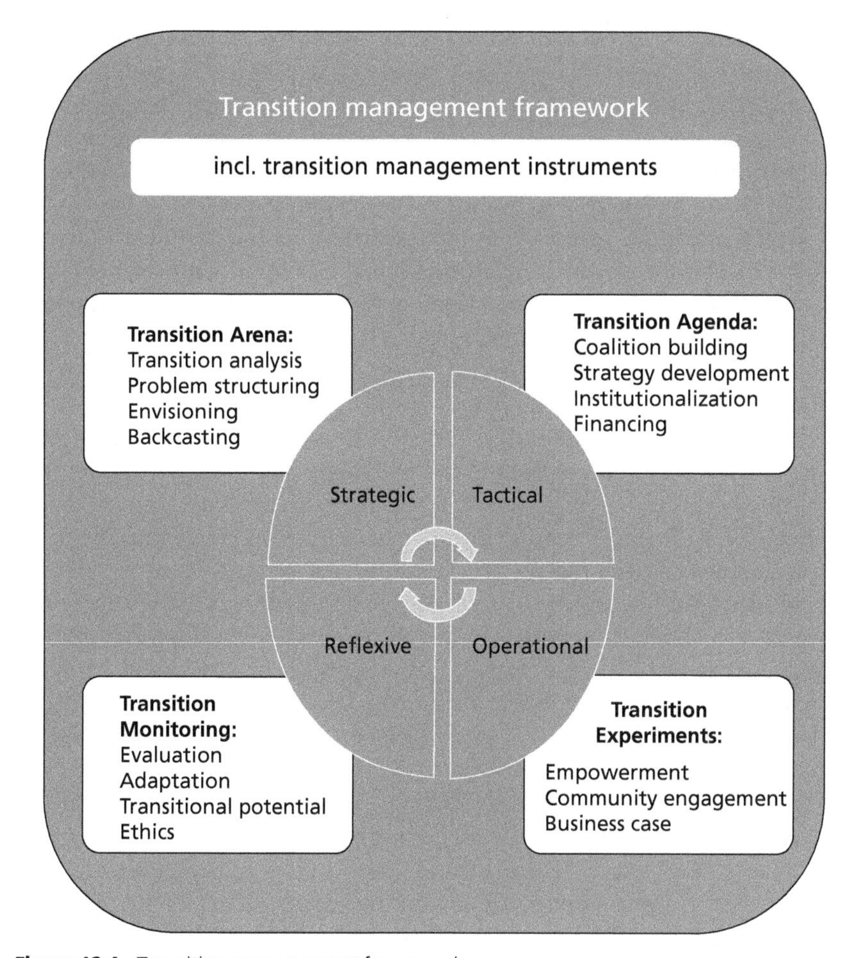

Figure 12.4 Transition management framework

Source: Loorbach (2010).

guide and accelerate transitions (see Figure 12.4). These instruments operate at the strategic, tactical, operational, and reflexive levels:

1. **Transition Arenas (strategic)**: These are instruments for selective participation involving transformative actors. These actors go through a facilitated process of problem structuring, envisioning, and backcasting. A sharp analysis and structuring of the problem is needed to prevent muddling through. Facilitation is based on the initial transition analysis and steers the process to achieve a shared discourse capturing the transitional challenge and desired direction. This includes creating visions of the future and long-term goal formulation, including collective goal setting and norm setting. The transition arena is an instrument to empower participants to use the

new discourse and shared agenda to bring transformation to their own organizations, networks, and daily contexts. An example is the Bloomberg Task Force, where investors and companies were brought together under the leadership of Michael Bloomberg. The Task Force has developed recommendations on climate-risk related financial disclosures by companies (TFCD, 2017). These disclosures enable investors to manage the climate risk (including the carbon footprint) of their investments. Other examples of transition arenas are the Natural Capital Coalition that brings together leading initiatives and organizations to harmonize approaches to natural capital, and Reporting 3.0 that connects business practitioners and develops and promotes systems based reporting (Thurm, Baue, and van der Lugt, 2018).

2. **Transition Scenarios and a Transition Agenda (tactical)**: With the representative actors now engaged in the transition, and the long-term visions having been developed, transition scenarios, pathways, and agendas can be created. In these processes, the government engages with representatives from organizations that are active in a transition and seeks to align and realign ambitions, goals, and actions. In the resulting transition agenda attention is also drawn to phase-out strategies and the required policy change. FCLTGlobal and the UN PRI (see Chapter 4) are examples of such coalitions at the international level. Activities at the tactical level are aimed at the mid- and long term, targeting changes in established structures, institutions, regulations, and financial infrastructures.
3. **Transition Experiments (operational)**: The actors in and around the coalitions are mobilized to start implementing first projects and experiment with alternative practices. For example, they could start experimenting with concentrated investment portfolios that generate positive impact. Activities at the operational level focus on experimenting with alternative ideas and practices and practising and showcasing new social relations. Ideally, they achieve encouraging results in the short run.
4. **Transition Monitoring (reflexive)**: The implementation of tools 1–3 is monitored and evaluated, which facilitates collective learning. The insights gained here are fed back into the transition arena, scenarios, agenda, and experiments. Activities at the reflexive level are aimed at learning about the present state of the system and the dynamics in the system, and possible future states and how to get there.

Is an actual transition happening in the financial system, with disruption of the current regime and emergence of a new regime (see Figure 12.1)? A still widespread belief in the current regime, based on investing in market benchmarks and fear of entering uncharted waters, is currently holding back a full transition. Section 12.3 discusses a need for leadership and changing the mindset of actors in the financial industry (i.e. investors and lenders).

12.3 **A change of mindset: Towards integrated thinking**

The challenge for the transition of the financial sector is to change the dominant culture embedded in financial risk–return thinking, as discussed in Chapter 7. It is about a change of mindset of the people in the financial industry. Moreover, people tend to think and work in separate silos. The market view of conventional portfolio investors is that restricting the investment universe to responsible investment must lead to lower returns. Paradoxically, sustainability teams often come to a similar conclusion from a very different starting point. They tend to think that responsible investing is less profit driven and therefore has a lower return (Riedl and Smeets, 2017). From different backgrounds and reasoning, the narrative is that responsible or ethical investing carries a lower return. Breaking through these silos and opening up to the views of other groups would greatly facilitate the transition process.

A key driver for sustainable development is integrated thinking. Integrated thinking requires, first and foremost, a mindset that is open and willing to integrate the social foundations and the planetary boundaries in one's own field of expertise, such as finance (see Chapter 1). This book promotes integrated thinking in finance by combining financial, social, and environmental returns. The narrative then changes. By focusing on material sustainable issues, investors may even realize a superior performance. Derwall, Koedijk, and Ter Horst (2011) find that ethical funds underperform the market (the old narrative), while ESG-integrated funds do not (the new narrative).

Another key driver is leadership. The tone at the top matters for the culture of an organization. When the CEO and his or her team in the board develop a new vision, send signals consistent with this vision, and act accordingly in decisions from investment to human resource management decisions, changes may be set in motion. Modern organizations develop such a vision through co-creation, with steering from the top and genuine input from employees. Reporting 3.0 identifies the role of 'positive mavericks' who question current sustainability strategies and demand more ambitious goals and actions from a system perspective (Thurm, Baue, and van der Lugt, 2018).

Integration of the financial, social, and environmental dimensions is also relevant for the structure of financial institutions. In the current regime, the sustainability teams responsible for engagement are a staff division operating separately from the financial decision-makers (i.e. portfolio investors and lenders). It is striking that this is a common feature across the financial industry (both asset managers and banks). Within the current regime, there is some experimenting whereby the investors or lenders (instead of the sustainability team) engage with companies, as they are the primary point of contact. However, that is still an attempt to optimize SF within the current regime, with separate teams for financial decision-making and sustainability.

In a new regime, integrated teams take the investment or lending decision and also engage with companies about their long-term strategy (De Jong et al. 2017). Engagement then becomes an integrated part of the investment and lending process and thus moves from a staff function to a line function in financial institutions. It also allows for forming interdisciplinary teams, which challenge traditional professional boundaries and provide new insights and working methods (e.g. Nancarrow et al. 2013).

Integrated thinking is also relevant in the wider financial eco-system. Auditors, for example, need to integrate the measurement of financial and manufactured capitals with that of human, social, intellectual, and natural capitals in the integrated report. That requires new skills, interdisciplinary teams, some experimenting, and ultimately new accounting standards.

12.3.1 PERSONAL CHANGE

As people determine the success of a transition (in interplay with the system), individuals matter. While there are some change agents who start to look for alternatives, most people prefer the status quo. So, there is a need to reboot the current culture—or software—of the financial system and develop a new culture. To make the transformation lasting, it is crucial to understand the intrinsic motivation of those working in the financial industry, including its leaders.

What are the current beliefs motivating people's behaviour? Koger and Winter (2010) argue that the dominant social paradigm is that humans rule the planet and that (linear) economic growth brings prosperity. This paradigm encourages people to continue with their non-sustainable behaviour. By contrast, the new environmental paradigm rejects the idea that nature exists solely for human use and argues instead to preserve the balance of nature. It acknowledges the limits to growth. The Club of Rome already voiced this new paradigm in the 1970s (see Chapter 1).

Another factor is the degree of materialism, defined as whether society should place more or less emphasis on money and material possessions (Yan, Ferraro, and Almandoz, 2018). In societies where materialism is valued less highly it is easier to move to integrated thinking, which combines financial, social, and environmental dimensions. Yan, Ferraro, and Almandoz (2018) find that to be the case in the Asian-Pacific and European regions, which is consistent with the prevailing stakeholder model in these regions (see Chapter 3). By contrast, in societies where materialism is valued highly the prevalence of financial logic remains high. This is found for the North American region, where the shareholder model is dominant. Moreover, education in finance and economics imprints in people a cognitive mindset that is conducive to self-interested and profit-maximizing behaviour (Yan, Ferraro, and Almandoz, 2018).

12.3.1.1 Instruments

While providing information can raise awareness about sustainability, it may in itself not be sufficient to move people towards sustainable action (Mees, 2017). The *nudging theory* of change (Thaler and Sunstein, 2008) suggests using positive reinforcement and indirect suggestions to influence the motives, incentives, and decision-making of groups and individuals. While this may help to steer behaviour in the right direction, the effect of external incentives is often temporary. Old behaviour may re-emerge when the incentives are discontinued.

Mees (2017) proposes responsible education to build people's capacity to overcome motivational challenges for sustainable action. *Responsible management education* aims to develop the capabilities of students to be future generators of sustainable value for business and society (PRME, 2018). While sustainability values may initially be seen as external to students, they come to more and more fully understand and internalize these values through the educational process. This results in self-determined motivation and action.

Responsible management education in SF is not only relevant for students (see Box 12.1), but also for professionals who are already working in the

BOX 12.1 SUSTAINABILITY IN FINANCE EDUCATION

As teachers and authors of this textbook, we have the vision that SF should not become a new subsection of finance, but that sustainability should become part of mainstream finance (an example of full ESG integration in education). In the 2016–17 academic year, we introduced a SF course in the MSc Finance & Investments Advanced at the Rotterdam School of Management. We made the following curriculum design choices:

- **Core course**: While a new course is typically offered as an elective, we insisted that this course was part of the core curriculum.
- **Timing**: The course was scheduled as the last one in the core curriculum (which is halfway through the overall programme). In this way, the 'ESG dimension' could be integrated with existing tools (e.g. discounted cash flow analysis) taught in the earlier core courses.
- **Experimenting**: We have used scenario analysis for a group assignment. Based on an analyst report of an investment bank with the CF forecasts for a leading company, students had to identify two or three material ESG factors and to develop scenarios (e.g. climate scenarios) without further guidance. The end goal was a new valuation of the company. We were presently surprised by the high quality of the student reports.
- **Follow-up**: In the remainder of the programme (e.g. living management cases with companies, master's theses, and company internships), sustainability was frequently chosen as topic or theme. In this way, the course was connected to other parts of the curriculum.

Before the course, the students were not aware of the link between finance and sustainability. As they had to apply this to real companies and as millennials, they quickly adopted the new thinking. We got positive feedback in the course evaluation as well as in the living management cases and internship reports. The students were surprised by the traditional finance thinking in several financial institutions during their internships.

financial industry (executive education). Finance students and finance professionals are then ready to take their stewardship role in society. Such education also helps to deal with the fear of fundamental change and rejection of old habits. An important feature is extending one's horizon in order to avoid a limited awareness of the consequences of one's behaviour. The outcome is intrinsic motivation, whereby someone dares to follow his or her inner compass. The new thinking first starts intuitively and later on leads to a new action perspective.

Transformative actors at new institutions (the challengers) or incumbent institutions can then start adopting the new models and approaches. The early adopters are able to attract human talent, as millennials tend to care about sustainability.

12.4 **Conclusions**

This chapter discusses the transition dynamics towards a new regime of SF, which integrates the financial, social, and environmental dimensions. Yet the financial risk–return thinking of traditional finance is still the dominant culture in the financial industry. Transition is about non-linear shockwise transformational change rather than incremental change. It is seen as an iterative process of the build-up of a new regime and breakdown of an old regime over a period of time, with disruptions along the way.

Transition management starts with rethinking current persistent methods and structuring the underlying shortcomings. The next step is developing a new vision for the long term, which is then backcasted to new approaches for the medium term and concrete experiments in the short term. In this chapter, a new *vision for the financial sector* is to invest in, lend to, and engage with corporates that aim for LTVC—consistent with achieving the SDGs by 2030.

This new perspective requires integrated thinking, which integrates financial, social, and environmental dimensions. As people determine the success of a transition (in interplay with the system), individuals matter. While there are some change agents who start to look for alternatives, most people prefer the status quo. So, there is a need to reboot the current culture of the financial system and develop a new culture. To make the transformation lasting, it is essential that those in the financial industry have a strong intrinsic motivation towards this. Responsible management education can contribute to this.

Key concepts used in this chapter

Backcasting is a planning method that starts with defining a desirable future and then works backwards to identify policies and programmes that will connect that specified future to the present.

Integrated thinking refers to taking into account the connectivity and interdependencies between the factors that affect an organization's ability to create value over time; it combines financial, social, and environmental dimensions.

Integrated value is obtained by combining financial, social, and environmental values in an integrated way (with regard for the interconnections).

Long-term value creation refers to the goal of companies that optimize financial, social, and environmental value in the long run.

Nudging theory is a concept in behavioural economics, which proposes positive reinforcement and indirect suggestions to try to achieve non-forced compliance to influence the motives, incentives, and decision-making of groups and individuals.

Responsible management education aims to develop the capabilities of students to be future generators of sustainable value for business and society.

Transition governance looks at how actors can influence transition processes. Transition governance is a multi-actor process in which systemic solutions, disruptive innovations, and (reflexive) institutions are formed by experimenting and learning.

Transition management refers to the management of transformational change from an old regime to a new regime through different stages.

Vision for the financial sector means to invest in, lend to, and engage with corporates that aim for LTVC (consistent with achieving the SDGs by 2030).

SUGGESTED READING

Grin, J., J. Rotmans, and J. Schot, in collaboration with F. Geels and D. Loorbach (2010), *Transitions to Sustainable Development: New Directions in the Study of Long Term Transformative Change*, Routledge, New York.

Loorbach, D., N. Frantzeskaki, and F. Avelino (2017), 'Sustainability transitions research: transforming science and practice for societal change', *Annual Review of Environment and Resources*, 42(1): 599–626.

Thurm, R., B. Baue and C. van der Lugt (2018), 'Blueprint 5: The Transformation Journey: A Step-By-Step Approach to Organizational Thriveability and System Value Creation', Reporting 3.0, Berlin.

REFERENCES

Choi, N., M. Fedenia, H. Skiba, and T. Sokolyk (2017), 'Portfolio concentration and performance of institutional investors worldwide', *Journal of Financial Economics*, 123(1): 189–208.

Clark G., A. Feiner, and M. Viehs (2015), 'From the stockholder to the stakeholder: How sustainability can drive financial outperformance', Working Paper, University of Oxford, https://ssrn.com/abstract=2508281, accessed 6 July 2018.

Cremers, M. and A. Pareek (2016), 'Patient capital outperformance: the investment skill of high active share managers who trade infrequently', *Journal of Financial Economics*, 122(2): 288–306.

De Jong, A., D. Schoenmaker, M. Gruenwald, and A. Pala (2017), 'Large shareholders in corporate governance', Research for the Monitoring Committee Corporate Governance, Rotterdam School of Management, Erasmus University, Rotterdam.

Derwall, J., K. Koedijk, and J. ter Horst (2011), 'A tale of values-driven and profit-seeking social investors', *Journal of Banking and Finance*, 35(8): 2137–47.

FCLTGlobal (Focus Capital on the Long-Term Global) (2017), 'Institutional investment mandates: anchors for long-term performance', Focus Capital on the Long-Term Global, Boston, MA, https://www.fcltglobal.org/docs/default-source/publications/institutional-investment-mandates—anchors-for-long-term-performance.pdf?sfvrsn=5ea8268c_2, accessed 6 July 2018.

Financial Times (2018), 'BlackRock chief Larry Fink issues companies with code of conduct', London,16 January.

Grewal, J., G. Serafeim, and A. Yoon (2016), 'Shareholder activism on sustainability issues', Harvard Business School Working Paper No. 17–003.

Grin, J., J. Rotmans, and J. Schot, in collaboration with F. Geels and D. Loorbach (2010), *Transitions to Sustainable Development: New Directions in the Study of Long Term Transformative Change*, Routledge, New York.

High-Level Expert Group on Sustainable Finance (2018), 'Financing a sustainable European economy', Final Report, European Union, Brussels.

Khan, M., G. Serafeim, and A. Yoon (2016), 'Corporate sustainability: first evidence on materiality', *Accounting Review*, 91(6): 1697–724.

Koger, S. and D. Winter (2010), *The Psychology of Environmental Problems*, 3rd edn, Psychology Press, New York.

Loorbach, D. (2010), 'Transition management for sustainable development: a prescriptive, complexity-based governance framework', *Governance: An International Journal of Policy, Administration, and Institutions*, 23(1): 161–83.

Loorbach, D. and S. Oxenaar (2018), 'Counting on nature: transitions to a natural positive economy by creating an enabling environment for natural capital approaches', Dutch Research Institute for Transitions (DRIFT), Rotterdam, https://drift.eur.nl/wp-content/uploads/2018/02/Counting-on-Nature.-Transitions-to-a-natural-capital-positive-economy.pdf, accessed 6 July 2018.

Loorbach, D., N. Frantzeskaki, and F. Avelino (2017), 'Sustainability transitions research: transforming science and practice for societal change', *Annual Review of Environment and Resources*, 42(1): 599–626.

Mees, R. (2017), 'Sustainable action: perspectives for individuals, institutions, and humanity', PhD thesis, Utrecht University.

Nancarrow, S., A. Booth, S. Ariss, T. Smith, P. Enderby, and A. Roots (2013), 'Ten principles of good interdisciplinary team work', *Human Resources for Health*, 11(19): 1–11.

PRME (Principles for Responsible Management Education) (2018), 'The six principles', New York, http://www.unprme.org/about-prme/the-six-principles.php, accessed 6 July 2018.

Purposeful Company (2017), 'The Purposeful Company: policy report', London, http://www.biginnovationcentre.com/media/uploads/pdf/TPC_Policy%20Report.pdf, accessed 6 July 2018.

Riedl, A. and P. Smeets (2017), 'Why do investors hold socially responsible mutual funds?', *Journal of Finance*, 72(6): 2505–50.

TCFD (Task Force on Climate-related Financial Disclosures) (2017), 'Recommendations of the Task Force on Climate-related Financial Disclosures: final report (Bloomberg Report)', Financial Stability Board, Basel.

Thaler, R. and C. Sunstein (2008), *Nudge: Improving Decisions about Health, Wealth, and Happiness*, Yale University Press, New Haven, CT.

Thurm, R., B. Baue and C. van der Lugt (2018), 'Blueprint 5: The Transformation Journey: A Step-By-Step Approach to Organizational Thriveability and System Value Creation', Reporting 3.0, Berlin.

UN Environment Inquiry into the Design of a Sustainable Financial System (2017), 'Roadmap for a sustainable financial system', Geneva, http://unepinquiry.org/wp-content/uploads/2017/04/Roadmap_for_a_Sustainable_Financial_System_Summary.pdf, accessed 6 July 2018.

Van Dam, J. and L. Dijkstra (2018), 'Long-term investing in public equity markets: what does success look like... and how to organize it?', The 300 Club, London, and SHIFT TO Long-term investing, Amsterdam.

Yan, S., F. Ferraro, and J. Almandoz (2018), 'The rise of socially responsible investment funds: the paradoxical role of the financial logic', *Administrative Science Quarterly*, forthcoming.

NAME INDEX

Note: Boxes are indicated by an italic *b* following the page number.

SUBJECT INDEX

Note: Tables, figures, and boxes are indicated by an italic *t*, *f*, and *b* following the page number.